PART 1

THE KASHMIR STORY

through the ages

Arjan Nath Chaku
Inder K Chaku

Vitasta
Let Knowledge Spread

Published by
Renu Kaul Verma
Vitasta Publishing Pvt Ltd
2/15 Ansari Road, Daryaganj
New Delhi - 110 002
info@vitastapublishing.com

ISBN 978-93-82711-74-2

First Edition 2016
Third Reprint 2024

MRP: ₹695

Cover and Layout: Vitasta Publishing Pvt Ltd
Printed at Vikas Computer and Printers, New Delhi

The book is dedicated to the cherished memories of

Sumit Chaku

who departed so young, leaving us shattered.

He will always remain in our hearts.

Contents

Acknowledgements

The making of the book *The Kashmir Story* started as an initiative of its writers Arjan Nath Chaku and Inder K Chaku and transformed into a dedicated project for our family. Every single member of the family has been emotionally involved in the progress of this work. Invaluable contributions came from everyone in the shape of interactions, discussions, critical analysis, furnishing of software material and more.

Dr Shiban Chaku's continued support and insightful, perceptive and frank commentary helped immensely in giving a direction and flow to the book.

Opender Chaku who worked tirelessly towards collecting informative material and his expert inputs in printing truly gave shape to the book.

Bimal Chaku who inspired and prompted the authors to pen the History of Kashmir.

Shanta Mirza's concern for the progress of the book became a source of inspiration.

S Sachin Chaku, Natasha Chaku/Kaul, Shivani Chaku/Garyali and Neha Chaku/Tankha also contributed in their own way.

Ms Sushma Zutshi, Guddi as we affectionately call her, for her enormous support in providing the reference material and valuable suggestions from time to time.

I acknowledge my editor Veena Batra with a deep sense of gratitude. Her enthusiasm coupled with meticulous scrutiny, scientific, rational and strictly professional approach is truly laudable.

I am also grateful to:

Ms Indira Laisram, who initially corrected about 18 chapters.

Dr P L Kaul for his passionate interest in the development of the book that really motivated us. His discussions regarding the Flora, Fauna and other subjects enriched the book.

Shri Bansi Kaul, whose discussions helped bring refinement in our thought process.

Shri B K Gaind for his help in shaping the chapters related to Crafts and Art of Kashmir.

Dr Animesh Arya, famous Chest and Allergy Specialist of India, who kept the ailing author Arjan Nath Chaku alive till the last chapter of the book was completed.

One
Lore and Legends

There is an interesting legend in the *Nilamatapurana* about Kashmir's name and its landscape. The Kashmir valley, ensconced in the Himalayas, was filled with water. This lake was known as Satisar. It was the time when six Manus out of the seven divine saints (saptrishi) were present. Since one of the sages, Kasyapa, drained Satisar, the place came to be known by his name—Kasheer.

There are other interpretations about the name Kasheer. Godfery Thomas Vigne writes,[1] "The word Kush is of very common occurrence in the east; we have Kush in Mesopotamia and Arabia; Ethiopia was also called Kush; and we have Kashmir pronounced Kasheer by the natives." However, Godfrey further states that,[2] "Thomas Maurice, in his *Indian Antiquities* identifies Kasyapa with the Seth of Moses, and thinks that he was doubtless a Brahmin who flourished in the earliest ages of the world and invented the Indian system of astronomy." At another place, he writes that during his visit to the Valley he was told,[3] "In Kashmir, on the contrary, Solomon is supposed, by the Musalmans, to have done wonders, and to have drained the Valley, through the instrumentality of one of his servants, a demon named Kashuf, who is the Kasyapa of Hindu history."

He further says,[4] "The word Kashmir is Kashuf-mir, the country of Kashuf." However, the legendary tales of *Nilamatapurana* give a vivid account as to how Lake Satisar was transformed into the Valley of Kashmir.

Lake Satisar

***Nilamatapurana* Shloka 45-46:**[5] "The goddess Sati, with the body in the form of a boat, becomes the earth and on that earth comes into being a lake of clear water, known as Satidesa, six Yojanas long and half of that in breadth, enrapturing, and the sporting-place of gods."

***Nilamatapurana* Shloka 80:** "Due to compassion, the Nagas brought up that child in the waters. As he was born in the water so he was called Jalodbhava (water-born)." The legend goes on to say that a water-demon named Jalodbhava killed many people who dwelt there.

***Nilamatapurana* Shloka 82-83:** "Having obtained the magical power, that Daitya-chief devoured human beings who lived in various countries near that lake—the inhabitants of Darvabhisara, Gandhara and Juhundara, the Sakas, the Khasas, the Tanganas, the Mandavas, the Madras and the inhabitants of Antargiri and Bahirgiri."

With the arrival of the seventh Manu, Vaivasvata, the Prajapati Kasyapa prayed to Gods for the destruction of this demon. The Gods led by Druhina, Upendra and Rudra killed the demon.

Nilanaga

Nilamatapurana also gives us a legend about Nilanag. It is said that Kasyapa Rishi was offered thirteen daughters by Daksa for marriage.[5]

Nilamatapurana Shloka 48: "O King! At the approach of this Vaivasvata Manvantara, Daksa gave his thirteen daughters to Kasyapa, the son of Marica." Out of the thirteen wives, Kasyapa Rishi's two wives, Kadru and Vinata, became jealous of each other. From Kadru he got a son who was named as Nilanag. From Vinata the two sons born were named Garuda and Aruna.

***Nilamatapurana* Shloka 53:** O! King, the Nags are the sons of Kadru, and Garuda and Aruna, the best among the birds, are the two sons of Vinata.

***Nilamatapurana* Shloka 54:** Kadru and Vinata, always jealous of each other were at daggers drawn.

Naga has two meanings; it means spring as well as serpent. Nilanag, for a long time, was considered a serpent who would transform into a human form. Nilanag is considered head of the Naga tribe.

Nilamatapurana **Shloka** 72: "O highly fortunate one, coronate Nila in the kingdom of those highly strong Nagas who shall dwell in the country of Sati." The spring Verinag was also known as Nilanag. People worshiped these springs. Nilanag is a magnificent spring, which is enclosed in a fine stone basin.

Sources of Kashmir History

Kashmir has the distinction of having recorded the first ever history written by poet and historian Pandit Kalhana, the author of *Rajatarangini* (River of Kings). M A Stein, the translator and the commentator of this monumental book *Rajatarangini* says,[6] "The interest and importance which Kalhana's works possess, lies in its characters as a historical record and in the mass of detailed information it furnishes regarding the conditions of ancient Kashmir."

It is difficult to say how many manuscripts Kalhana must have consulted before he wrote *Rajatarangini*. However, there are some chroniclers, the references of which we find in his work. Authors such as Padmamihira Pasupata, Helaraja, Chavillakara and Suvrata and Kshemendra were earlier poets before Kalhana. Their writings, except some of Kshemendra, are unavailable. Even two of Kshemendra's works, *Rajavali* and *Nrapavali*, are not found.

Nilamatapurana

Most historians are silent about the author of *Nilamatapurana*. According to *Baharistan-i-Shahi*, this most valuable ancient manuscript is said to have been written by poet Suvrata.[7] Hindus of Kashmir consider this manuscript as a legendary (Mahatmaya) scripture containing a mine of information about social, political and cultural history of that time. It also tells the names of sacred pilgrimages that helped in determining the topography of the valley. M A Stein observes,[8] "*Nilamata* is the canonical authority for Brahminical cult in Kashmir." *Nilamatapurana* gives us descriptions of a variety of subjects such as tribes, as well as, a great insight into their social, economic and cultural lives. It also tells us about mountains, rivers and geography of Kashmir that has enabled us to correctly comprehend Kalhana's narration of *Rajatarangini*. This valuable manuscript, written in Sanskrit, is considered a Purana and is also a genre of Jain and Buddhist scriptures. According to Ved Kumari Ghai, an eminent scholar of Jammu and Kashmir,[9] "The *Nilamata*, probably, existed originally as an independent Purana on the rites, ceremonies and Tirthas of Kasmira, but as it did not enjoy the status of a Mahapurana, it was considered necessary, in order to give an air of authenticity to the rites and ceremonies of Kashmir to incorporate some portions of *Nilamata* in the Brahma Purana."

According to Abu-al-Fazal,[10] "In ancient times a volume, which they call *Nilamata*, arose from its (Nila Naga) depths, which contained a detailed description of Kashmir and the history and particulars of its temples." It has 1453 Shlokas in Sanskrit poetry. Ved Kumari Ghai, who has translated these Shlokas into English, writes,[11] "The most relieving feature of the family-life of Kasmira as seen in the *Nilamata* is the position of women. Nowhere is she considered the living torch illuminating the way to hell or the devourer of the intellect of men."

When Buddhism spread in India, *Nilamatapurana* had directly prescribed the celebration of Buddha's birthday as a great festival of Kashmir. That moment is known as the "doctrine of the sage." *Nilamata* tells us that Shaivism, Vaishnavism and Buddhism happily co-existed during this period.

According to Ved Kumari Ghai,[12] "The textual study of the work shows that some alterations and additions have been made in it after the 9th or 10th century AD in order to incorporate into it the monistic Shaiva philosophy of Kasmira. Had the *Nilamata* been composed after the 9th century AD, would there have been a scope for such a change? The lower limit of the date thus may be 8th century AD and the upper one about 6th century AD, as Buddha began to be regarded as an incarnation of Vishnu from about 550 AD."

According to DC Sircar,[13] "We know that, of no less than twelve chronicles dealing with the ancient history of Kashmir, including the works of Nilamuni, Helaraja, Chavillakara, Padmamihira, Suvrata and Kshemendra (11th Century), which were available to Kalhana in the 12th Century, only a part of Nilamuni's chronicle has so far been discovered."

Rajatarangini

In the words of MA Stein, "This manuscript contains information on the heritage of Kashmir and its history which is of monumental importance." It consists of 7,826 verses and the book is divided into eight cantos.

It may be pointed out that during Asoka's time Sanskrit in the rest of India was written in Khasi and Brahmi script. Kashmir evolved its own script known as Sharda Script which differs from Devanagri. *Rajatarangini* gives us a vivid account of kings, their rule and misrule and an all-encompassing fabric of the existing political, administrative, economic and social life.

Truly, in the absence of initial sources, Kalhana must have had to depend on legends, and the first few cantos of *Rajatarangini*, clearly carry us to the legendry world. However, one can attribute authenticity to the Mauryan and Kushan periods. Kalhana gives dates from the Fourth Book, which starts from the ninth century.

In short, it can be safely said that Kalhana's *Rajatarangini* is the only indigenous work of continuous history. The original manuscript is written in Sanskrit in the Sharda script. However, many scholars tried to translate it in Devanagri script. The book has been translated into Persian and French languages too. According to B Barauh,[14] "The first attempt in bringing out the earliest edition of the *Rajatarangini* was to the laudable efforts of Moorcroft. During 1823, he visited Srinagar and obtained a copy of the Devanagri script of the *Rajatarangini*." He further writes, "In 1875, Buhler (George Buhler) undertook a tour of Kashmir in search of Sanskrit manuscripts and obtained a copy of the chronicle written in Sarada character. This copy of the text became the basis of Stein's monumental translation of the chronicle published in 1909."

This monumental and gigantic work so impressed King Zain-ul-Abidin, that he ordered Mullah Ahmed, a Persian scholar, to translate it into Persian.

Prof NK Gunrtoo has mentioned in the introductory note of the translation of Srivara's *Zaina Rajatarangini* which has been translated by Kashi Nath Dhar:[15] "Perhaps it would not be an exaggeration to point out that this is the only part of our vast country where we find an uninterrupted and written record of history right from the beginning of Kalyuga, in Sanskrit verse, usually known as *Rajatarangini*."

Jogesh Chandra Dutt, in his preface of the book *Translation of Rajatarangini of Jonaraja* says, "The narration left by Kalhana, who may be called the father of Indian history..."

E Sreedharan, the famous historian of India records,[16] "The *Rajatarangini* is the only Sanskrit work so far discovered which may be called history, and Kashmir the only region of India with a tradition of historical writing." He further states,[17] "Ancient Indian historiography conformed to a certain pattern in respect of theme, mode of treatment, and conclusions drawn."

India's first Prime Minister, Jawaharlal Nehru, in his foreword for the book[18] *Rajatarangini 'The Saga of the Kings of Kashmir'*, translated by Ranjit Sitaram Pandit, said, "And yet Kalhana's book is something far more than a record of king doings. It is a rich storehouse of information—political, social and, to some extent, economic." In the translator's note of the book *Rajatarangini,* Ranjit Sitaram Pandit says,[19] "Kalhana brings before our eyes a vivid picture of a bygone age through episodes which contain the different Rasa or sentiments of love and heroism, of pathos and marvel."

Rama Shankar Tripathi, the eminent historian, has mentioned,[20] "The only work in Sanskrit, which can be described as a near approach to history, as we understand it, is the *Rajatarangini* of Kalhana."

According to A K Warder, and Ramesh Chandra Majumdar, [21] "There is only one historical work, properly so called, written by Kalhana in the 12th century AD. This is *Rajatarangini*, which deals with the history of Kashmir from the earliest time up to the date of composition of that work. It assumes, however, a regular historical form only from the seventh century AD, the earlier chapters being a medley of confused traditions and fanciful imaginations."

Writes AL Basham,[22] "In the 12th century AD, a Kashmiri poet, Kalhana, thought fit to write the history of his native land in verse, but his *River of Kings (Rajatarangini)*, although of great value for the study of history of Kashmir, has little to tell us about India as a whole, and there is no good evidence that similar chronicles were composed elsewhere."

Writes Moriz Winternitz,[23] "He (Kalhana) endeavours to describe not only the long past times, but also the events of his own and near ages (sine ira et studio), and his opinion is mostly inspired by high moral cosmic philosophy."

Dale Hoibergand & Indu Ramchandani write,[24] "He (Kalhana) displayed surprisingly advanced technical expertise for his age in his concern for unconventional sources. He looked up a variety of epigraphic sources relating to royal eulogies, construction of temples, and land grants. He studied coins, monumental remains, family records, and local traditions."

According to Michael Lee Scott,[25] "The interest of Kalhana's *Rajatarangini* for Indian history generally lies in the fact that it represents a class of Sanskrit composition in character. Together with the later Kashmir Chronicles which continue Kalhana's narratives it is practically the sole specimen of this class."

According to KN Dhar,[26] "Among the galaxy of such writers, of historical Kavyas, Kalhana shines the brightest."

Kalhana

This celebrated author of *Rajatarangini* was the son of a great Kashmir minister, the illustrious Lord Canpaka. Canpaka was the Lord of the gate (Dvarapati) or commandant of the frontier defences in the latter part of King Harsa's reign. The high standards of Sanskrit displayed in his poetic expression shows that he belonged to a Brahmin family where learning atmosphere was rife. Kalhana and his family members were Shiva worshipers. It is a well-known fact that Kashmiri Pandits are known as Shaivites or the worshipers of Shiva.

Kalhana has not recorded his education and early studies. "In fact there is no record to tell us about the life of the scholar-poet to whom we owe our knowledge of the history of old Kashmir,"[27] says M A Stein. Kalhana seems to have been conscious of his genius in writing the chronicle. In his own words, "That man of merit alone deserves praise whose language, like that of a judge, in recording the events of the past has discarded bias as well as prejudice." What is apparent is that he was a voracious reader. He has mentioned the names of the works of some of the older poets. He had studied epics such as *Raghuvansha, Meghadootam* and he had carefully studied *Vikramankadevacharita*, a historical poem of the fellow citizens. Kalhana had thoroughly studied, Bhana Bhatt's *Harshacharitra*, a well-known historical romance describing the activities of King Harsavardhana. He had also studied *Ramayana, Mahabharata*, and other epic literature; also, he had gone through other literature such as *Srikanthcarita* poetry composed by Mankha. He had consulted the early chronicles, biographies, critically examined inscriptions of temples, coins, Tamrpatras issued to people, archaeological buildings and the inscriptions carved on them. According to E Sreedharan,[28] "To check these literary sources Kalhana used much more original authorities such as ordinances relating to religious foundations and land grants and other privileges, edicts, laudatory inscriptions, coins as well as ancient monuments. He was master of the topography of the Kashmir Valley. It is surprising that a medieval Indian chronicler should have regarded inscriptions and coins as legitimate sources of history."

Kalhana has been honest enough to acknowledge in his introduction of *Rajatarangini* that he had inspected eleven works of former scholars containing descriptions of the former kings.

The other sources of Kashmir history Kalhana collected and studied are—Kshemendra's *Nrapavali* and from Helaraja he got the 'lost list of Kings'. He had studied *Mahatmaya,* in which are contained important descriptions of Tirthas and it seems they are many in number and work as a guide for the pilgrims who come to Kashmir for pilgrimage.

The most important source of Kashmir history, however, is *Nilamatapurana*, which Kalhana had thoroughly studied and largely quoted. There is a legend about *Nilamatapurana*. It says that Nilanag, son of Kasyapa and head of the Naga tribe of Kashmir, had issued directions as to how to worship the many Tirthas of holy springs in Kashmir. And Kalhana is very particular about the construction of Viharas and temples, the kings, their queens or their ministers have built.

However, Kalhana has abundantly praised the women who committed Sati. He was a fanatical believer of Brahmanism and did not see a king above the Brahmins. The discussion between King Jayapida and the Brahmins indicate that Kalhana was a staunch believer of the Brahminical cult. Writes Moriz Winternitz,[29] "He (Kalhana) is wholly in keeping with the common Indian opinion, to the extent that he believes in magic and witchcraft. When he speaks about the kings, who were ruined either on account of witchcraft or due to the curse of the Brahmins, he does it with the same conviction with which he would narrate that they perished either with sword or on account of poison."

According to PNK Bamzai,[30] "He does not, for example, distinguish a legend from history. At places, there are serious gaps in chronology."

Jonaraja's *Dvitiya Rajatarangini*

Interestingly, the monumental work of Kalhana remained anonymously authored for 300 years. In fact, it was Jonaraja who first mentioned the name of Kalhana as the author of *Rajatarangini*. Jonaraja says, [31] "Then the Brahman Kalhana, with lucid words imparted the freshness of youth to the old accounts of the king down to the reign of Jayasimha." Jonaraja began writing his *Dvitiya Rajatarangini* from 1127 AD onwards from where Kalhana had left, completing the reign of Jayasimha ie 1127-1420 AD. Jonaraja says,[32] "Let my work which is mingled with that of Kalhana Pandit be accepted, for even the water of a reedy marsh is taken for drink when it has mingled with the river water."

In his narrative poem, *Rajavali,* in Sanskrit, Jonaraja covers the period from 1150 AD to 1459 AD. Srivara, in *Zaina Rajatarangini* pays compliments to Kalhana and Jonaraja and calls them "Princes amongst the poets."[33] The couplets say, "The prince amongst the poets are fit to be adored, whose command over letters is heart-captivating; who can tell water from the milk and whose fame is established by virtue of their having used the words replete with aesthetic pleasure."

Srivara's *Zaina- Rajatarangini*

Srivara completed *Zaina Rajatarangini* from where Jonaraja left giving details of the events and conditions of Kashmir in his narrative *Zaina Rajatarangini* during 1459-1484 AD. According to Kashi Nath Dhar, who has translated *Zaina Rajatarangini*,[34] "Here we can infer that Srivara, besides being a poet and historiographer, had command over astronomy and astrology also. Actually, this Pandit combined in himself all the talents in respect of Dharmashastras, language, rhetoric, astronomy and astrology and even medicine."

Srivara in *Zaina Rajatarangini* has written 2241 Shlokas. He is said to have translated the famous Persian work of *Yusuf and Zulaikha* authored by Mulla Abdul Rahman Jami, the Sufi poet of Afghanistan. The translation was titled *Katha Kautuka*. The book was written for the benefit of Muhammad Shah.

Prajyabhatta/Sukha's Rajavalipatika/Rajatarangini

Prajyabhatta-authored *Rajavalipatika* is the fourth important chronicle whose composition took place in 1486-1587 AD. His student Sukha completed it with 398 Shlokas. He started his work from the period when Akbar annexed Kashmir.

Two
A Paradise on Earth

The Kashmiri landscape is called 'Bhusvarga' (heaven on earth). "It indeed occupies a unique position in India, not only in the panoramic scenic beauty, salubrious climate, but also in the realm of Indian culture," writes S C Banerji in his book *Companion to Tantra* [1].

It is, therefore, no exaggeration to say that nature has been extremely lavish in bestowing Kashmir with utmost bounty. Stunning lakes with sparkling waters in the heart of Srinagar and many more outside it are nature's extraordinary gift to the valley. Some of these are Manasbal Lake, Wular Lake, Sheshnag, and Kausarnag. Not just lakes, the beautiful springs that people worshipped as nags are also a part and parcel of Kashmir's charm. Vethvatur, Verinag and Nilanag are worshipped with the same reverence. In fact, these three names are the source of river Vitasta (now called Jhelum). Till today, Hindus worship these nags as serpent deities. In olden days, people composed verses and sang in praise of nags. The famous love story of 'Hemall Negara' continues to be a testimony to this.

Nilamatapurana makes a mention of this in the initial chapter—of the origin of the enmity between Kadru and Vinata, the two wives of

Kasyapa, and their descendents. The naga (literally means snakes or springs) children of Kadru being persecuted by Garuda, son of Vinata, flee to the Satisar, where Vishnu grants them asylum. A mention may be made of Kunsar Nag and Cheshma Shahi springs. The water of these two nags is not only crystal clear but also very healthy. So many reasons why Kashmir is truly a paradise on earth.

Topography of Jammu & Kashmir

S C Banerji in *Companion to Tantra*[2] describes the topographical anatomy of the State of Jammu & Kashmir as divided into three distinct regions, namely Kashmir,Jammu and Ladakh.

Kashmir Valley

'Kashmir' means 'desiccated land' (derived from Sanskrit: Ka = water and shimeera = desiccate).

According to Muhammad Haydar Duglat, "Kashmir is among the most famous countries of the world, and is celebrated both for its attractions and its wonders." He further writes, "… In short, I have neither seen nor heard of any country equal to Kashmir, for charm of climate during all the four seasons."[3] Sir Francis Edward Younghusband[4], a British Army officer, explorer, and spiritual writer, remembered mainly for his travels in the Far East and Central Asia, wrote, "Kashmir is more beautiful than Greece." The valley of Kashmir forming the temperate zone of Jammu and Kashmir state of India, lies between 32-30 and 34-30 degree of North Latitude and 74 to 75-30 degree East Longitude. It is about 5000 feet above sea level. The valley is about 80 miles long and 40 miles wide, consisting of the districts of Anantnag,Srinagar, Kulgam, Budgam, Shopian, Pulwama, Ganderbal, Bandipora, Kupwara and Baramulla. These have mostly purely Kashmiri speaking people. Muzaffarabad, which is situated at the confluence of Jhelum and Neelam rivers, reflects a blend of various cultures and languages. The main language spoken here is a form of Hindko, which is part of the Lahnda subgroup of Indo-Aryan languages spoken by Hindkowans in Pakistan and northern India, some Pashtun tribes in Pakistan, as well as the Hindki people of Afghanistan.

During the days of *Rajatarangini*, Sanskrit was the official language in which everything was written. People not only studied Sanskrit but also made their contribution towards Vedic literature, grammar and philosophy, and also towards Buddhist philosophy. Says Andre Wink[5],

"It was the classical land of the Vedas and Mahayana Buddhism; and it almost looks as if the restoration of Brahmanism began from the secluded valley of Kashmir."

Panini was one of the greatest grammarians, and his monumental work on Sanskrit grammar, *The Astadhyayi*, drew in great comments from *Patanjali* in the *Mahabhasya*. Panini flourished during the second century and lived in village Gudar in Kulgam Tehseel.

The other noteworthy authors who contributed towards art and science are Kayyatacharya, known for his contribution to Sanskrit grammar, Vagbhatta, disciple of Charka and also author of Sanskrit grammar, Charka, author of medicine. Vasugupta, who lived near the end of the 8th century of the Christian era, was the founder of Shaiva philosophy. Kalhana, Jonaraja, Srivara, Prajyabhatta and Sukha were all renowned contributors to *Rajatarangini* writing. However, despite this entire awakening in the field of writing, no one has written about the people of Kashmir valley—their customs, lifestyles, eating habits, and, above all, their economic activities. KM Panikkar, a scholar, journalist, historian, administrator and diplomat, says, "Walled off by high mountains and endowed with unequalled natural beauty, Kashmir remained an inviolate sanctuary of Indian culture till at least the 14th century."

Such is the pristine beauty of Kashmir that French writer Francois Bernier[6] called it the paradise of the Indies, with its towering pine forests, deep lakes, flower carpeted meadows, and fields of iridescent saffron. In fact, the 17th century Mughal Emperor Jahangir sighed on his deathbed that his last wish was to be buried in Kashmir. Jahangir also wrote in *Tuzuk-i-Jahangiri*[7] that "Kashmir is a garden of eternal spring or an iron fort to a palace of kings—a delightful flower-bed, and an expansive heritage for seers. Its pleasant meads and enchanting cascades are beyond all description."

According to E F Knight,[8] "It is not strange that the invaders, who came upon this sweet oasis after months of travelling among the fearful and arid mountain regions that lie beyond waxed enthusiastic over its fertile beauty and hailed it as the first paradise."

Writes W Wakefield in his book, *The Happy Valley*[9], "Kashmir is a theme well worthy of a poet. Nowhere in Asia, not even perhaps in the remaining quarters of the globe, can the parallel be found of such an earthly paradise; a paradise in itself as formed by Nature, but made doubly beautiful by its surroundings."

Jammu Region

"Jammu as a political concept," writes Sukhdev Singh[10],"came to be attributed to the territory and it had gradually evolved into the 'Jammu Raj', the boundaries of which gradually but constantly extended all around."

Originally, Jammu was known as Jambu and finds its mention in the Puranas. The region consists of Kathua, Udhampur, Riasi, Mirpur, Chennai, Poonch, Rajouri and Jammu main. The Jammu region is situated beyond the mountainous range that surrounds the Kashmir valley and extends to the plains of Punjab. Mountains and moors and sloping ridges give Jammu a beautiful landscape. At present, Jammu, as the winter capital of Jammu & Kashmir, is also called the gateway of Kashmir. It is considered a land of temples and Rajputs. The people of Jammu are called Dogras. The name Dogra comes to them because Jammu has two famous lakes, Mansar and Siroensar. Thus, the inhabitants were known as Dogirath, meaning two lakes. The people of this place were subsequently named Dogras. Writes Ashok Jeratha in *Dogra Legends of Art & Culture*[11], "Dogras were the erstwhile Kinners who were fond of music and dance. They were beautiful people; the womenfolk especially fascinated the Devas (angels) by their charm of beauty and music."

It is baffling that some chroniclers claim Jammu traces its traditional history to 6000 BC. Shri Ganesh Dass Wadehra, working in the revenue department during Maharaja Gulab Singh's period, wrote his famous work *Rajadarshani* in Persian. He has stated that the foundation of Jammu took place in 3650 BC. However, according to Bhumesh Sharma, Deputy Transport Commissioner of the state of Jammu and Kashmir[12], "Little is known of Jammu's subsequent history until in 1730 AD, it came under the rule of the Dogra King, Raja Dhruv Deva. The Dogra rulers moved their capital to the present site and Jammu became an important centre of art and culture, especially the Pahari school of paintings."

The legend: When Bahu Lochan, the king of Jammu, died issueless, his younger brother Jambu Lochan ascended the throne. It is, in fact, Jambu who founded the city of Jammu. There is an interesting legend surrounding his decision to make Jammu his capital. Though Jambu extended his territory up to the Chenab, he wanted to have the capital town of the principality at some other place.

One day, on a hunting expedition, he found himself near a pond and was astonished to see a lion and a goat standing next to each other drinking water. He found the place ideal, with animals also living in peace and harmony. That was when he decided to make it his capital and named it after his name Jambu.[13] According to Sukhdev Singh Charak[14], "Jambu Lochan is said to have ruled during the sixth century of Kaliyuga, ie in about 2500 BC. His only son, Purana Karan, became the ruler of Jammu. He probably shifted his capital from Bahu to the newly founded Jammu, and is said to have been the first ruler of Jammu. Purana had two sons, Daya Karan and Dharam Karan. It is interesting to note that Daya Karan became the ruler of Kashmir."

Jammu traces its history from the date Alexander invaded India. It is also during that time that the Rajputs of Rajasthan and Delhi came to Jammu to reside permanently. Tradition says that during Timur's invasion of India in 1398 AD, Jammu was engaged in small skirmishes with other principalities in which it was divided. During the Mughal rule, it seems that the Jammu Raja accepted the supremacy of Mughal kings. Raja Ranjit Dev, son of Raja Dhruv Dev[15], ascended the throne of Jammu in 1728 AD and ruled for 53 years.The most powerful of all the kings, Raja Ranjit Dev, had to face many hurdles as soon as he was crowned the king. However, during his reign, there was stability in the state and the people enjoyed peace and prosperity. With the opening of the Banihal Road (B C road or Banihal Cart road) it became the mandi (main market) for Kashmiri goods. Ranjit Dev tried to conquer the valley but Afghan forces that ruled the valley then, repulsed the attack and he had to withdraw.

After his death, his eldest son, Brij Raj Dev, became the King of Jammu after defeating his brother Dalil Singh. However, he could not continue to remain in power against the onslaughts of Sikh armies. Mahan Singh, father of Ranjit Singh of Punjab, defeated Brij Raj Dev, who had to pay Rs 50,000 annually as tribute to the Sikh kings of Punjab. Finally, Jammu came under the Sikh rule until Maharaja Gulab Singh managed to get back Jammu as well as Kashmir.

Maharaja Gulab Singh was the son of Kishore Singh, a Jageerdar of

Samba, a place some twenty-five miles away from Jammu. After getting necessary training in handling arms and warfare, Gulab Singh took service under Maharaja Ranjit Singh as the commander of a small unit of forces. After some time, he was sent to Jammu to fight Mian Dido who had raised a revolt against Sikh rule. Gulab Singh defeated Dido and Maharaja Ranjit Singh gave Jammu as jageer to him.

Sukhdev Singh writes,[16] "Like several other political units of India, Jammu also experienced ups and downs in the political arena of the country before it emerged as the leader of the traditional twenty-two hill states."

Poonch: Poonch is popularly known as mini Kashmir with a long history. Poonch's tryst with history began with the arrival of Alexander the Great who invaded the lower Jhelum belt to fight Porus. This region was known as Darvabhisara. In olden times, the capital of Poonch was known as Lohara, a town to the south east of Poonch. While travelling from Kashmir, Chinese traveller Yuan Chwang (633 AD) visited Poonch then known as Pruntsa in Kashmiri dialect. However, during Yuan Chwang's time, it came to be known as Parnotsa. According to Sukhdev Singh Charak[17], "Pruntsa or Poonch was probably the first state to be founded in the Abhisara Tract and may have existed much earlier than the visit of Yuan Chwang. Its capital in ancient days was Lohara, a town to the south east of Poonch."

It was in 850 AD that the region became a sovereign state with Raja Nar ruling over it. Raja Nar was basically a horse trader. Poonch was a haven for tourists with its seven lakes and several waterfalls. One of them was known as Noori Chamb, named after Noor Jahan, the queen of Mughal emperor Jahangir.

Rajouri: An important hill state, Rajouri has been a gateway to Punjab. MA Stein has said:[18] "Owing to its position on the most direct route to the Punjab, Rajpura (its early name) was necessarily often brought into political relations with Kashmir." We find a mention of Rajouri in *Mahabharata* where it is referred to as Raja Vari. Kalhana has also written about it. And *Rajatarangini* has mentioned that Rajouri's first ruler was Raja Prithvi Paul in 1003 AD. According to Abdul Majid Mattoo [19], "A fort was built by Akbar during his first visit to Nowshera, a principality of Pargana Rajouri."

Doda-Basohli-Bhadarwah Kishtwar: The important towns of Jammu and Kashmir are Doda, Basohli, Bhadarwah and Kishtwar. Kalhana has made mention of these towns in his book *Rajatarangini*. Basohli was known as Vallapura and features during the reign of Ananta Deva of Kashmir (1028–1063). Similarly, Bhadarwah was known as Bhadravakasa, which literally means Happy Region, and Kishtwar was known as Kashthavata.
Doda: The district derives its name from a utensil-maker known as Deeda, who set up his work in a village near Kishtwar on the instance of the King of Kishtwar. With the passage of time, the name Deeda changed into Doda. The river Chenab flows from this district.
Basohli: Basohli is a tehseel (town) in Kathua and is about 80 km away from Kathua. The fort of Basohli is a magnificent piece of art. Basohli paintings are known for bold vitality of colour and line. These paintings have their own style and evolved into the Basohli School of Painting, and are famous the world over. Their uniqueness lies in the fact that it is known as the first school of Pahari paintings and one of the finest gifts to the world of art. It is believed that this art flourished even before the Mughal period in Jammu and Kashmir.
Bhadarwah: About 200 km from the city of Jammu, the Bhadarwah valley is a hill station of Doda district. Bhadarwah offers a variety of beautiful landscapes.
Kishtwar: Popularly known as Chota Kashmir (Little Kashmir), Kishtwar is a small hill town of Jammu and Kashmir. It is about 232 km from Jammu city. The story goes that the place was an abode of Rishi Kishat, thus, it came to be known as Kishtwar. It has Bhadarwah on the east and the Chenab on the west. The river is locally known as Zumpa. The place is also known as 'Land of sapphire and saffron'.

According to *Tuzuk-i-Jahangiri* [20], "In Kishtwar there is much of wheat, barley, lentils, millet, and pulses. In comparison with the rest of Kashmir, it produces little rice. Its saffron is finer than that of Kashmir." Kishtwar has been a safe haven for fugitives and political assassins.
Ladakh: Ladakh, which literally means 'many passes', is the northern extremity of India. Situated east to the valley of Kashmir, Ladakh is often referred to as the 'Kha-chan-pa', 'Little Tibet', or the 'Last Shangri-La'. It is the trans-Himalayan region, which separates the western Himalayan peaks from the Tibetan plateau.

The earliest records suggest that around the 10th century, the Thi Dynasty was ruling Ladakh. With their capital at Shey, Thi rulers had built many forts. Around the same time, Tibetan Buddhism invaded Ladakh, as the region witnessed a surge of construction. Around 100 Gompas or monasteries were built.

This fascinating region consists of Ladakh, (at the height of approximately 5000 meters above the sea level), Astor, and Gilgit. Until recently, this area was cut off from the valley by mountain ranges of Karakoram. This area was part of Kashmir but due to lack of metallic roads and communication facilities in the valley, it remained socially cut off from the outside world.

The people of this place belong to three ethnic groups such as Mons, Dards and Bot-pa of Mongolian origin. They are short and sturdy. Buddhism might have spread in Ladakh during second or third century AD. It was during Namgyal's rule that Islam was also accepted, though it was introduced in the 14th century during the period of King Zain-ul-Abidin. Later on, Mirza Haydar Duglat also spread Islam in the region. However, Christianity is believed to have spread in 1855 AD, which was propagated by Moravian missionaries.

The climate of this place is very hot during the day and very cold during the nights. The rarefied air could well leave you gasping for breath. The rainfall is very scarce and so is the snowfall. The people of Ladakh cultivate in the fertile areas of this region where the irrigation is easily facilitated by the rivers. It is indeed a very picturesque place like the Karakoram valley with towering mountains touching the sky—colourful and captivating. .

In Ladakh, we find very rare animal species such as Mountain Goat, the Snow Leopard, Wild Yak, Large Horned Sheep, Musk Deer and Tibetan Antelope. The famous shawl *Shah-toos* (Shah is King and Toos means nature), is made of Tibetan antelope fur. But that product is strictly banned now.

The majority of people in Ladakh are Buddhists. According to Alexander Cunningham [21], "The faith (Buddhism) was first introduced into Ladakh during the reign of Asoka, upwards of 2000 years ago when that great follower of Buddha was propagating his new religion with all the zealous ardour of a proselyte."

There are only three tehseels of Ladakh, namely Leh, Kargil and Skardu (Skardu and Gilgit are under the unlawful occupation of Pakistan). The people of Kargil and other adjoining places are recently converted Muslims. Until recently, polygamy was rampant as the number of girls was less than boys. If a family had five sons, the daughter-in-law that was brought into the family was the wife of all the five brothers.

Until recently, the road route was not available nor was wheeled traffic. Despite this difficulty, Walter Lawrence writes,[22] "Long distances and difficulties of terrain were no bar to free movement and constant travels of the people over the Himalayas, for they had sheer economic pressure to maintain the lifeline of commerce. It is natural that the inhabitants of an alpine country, surrounded by the difficult mountains, are accustomed to travel long distances, and have developed marching powers."

According to S R Bakshi,[23] "Printing has long been known in Ladakh. Several years ago, when most people in Kashmir were quite unaware of what a newspaper was, Ladakh had a newspaper published in the Bodhi language. The first newspaper in Kashmir state was a monthly known as the *Ladakh News*."

The people of Ladakh are agrarians. They grow various crops such as wheat, rice and cereals. They also grow apples, mulberries and apricots. The apricots are dried and exported. Wonderful animals such as Yak are reared there. Yaks carry the loads in the difficult mountain regions.

Muzaffarabad

Since ancient times, Muzaffarabad, previously known as Udabhanda alias Yagistan, was part of Kashmir. Situated at the confluence of the Jhelum and Neelum rivers, it is about 118 km from Rawalpindi, Pakistan and is a breathtaking lush green spot. Sardi and Nardi, two mountain peaks cradle an important Hindu shrine known as Sarada[24] in Yagistan. According to Stein[25], "The Tirtha here referred to is the ancient shrine of Sarada, traced by me in September 1892 at Sardi in the upper Kisanganga Valley. The upper Kisanganga Valley was practically independent territory or Yagistan during the Pathan and Mughal rule". The distance of Sardi from Kashmir proper and the inaccessibility of the road and transport leading to it explains why the Tirtha has become less known among the Brahmins of the capital.

For long, this state of seclusion remained until the 'Treaty of Lahore' signed on 9 March 1846 between Maharaja Gulab Singh of Jammu and the Sikh government. Under the treaty, Kashmir valley was transferred to Maharaja Gulab Singh. Subsequently, on 16 March 1846, 'The Treaty of Amritsar' was signed which as per Article-I says, "The British Government transfers and makes over for ever in independent possession to Maharajah Gulab Singh and the heirs male of his body all the hilly or mountainous country with its dependencies situated to the eastward of the River Indus and the westward of the River Ravi including Chamba..."

Politically, the geography of Kashmir during the Sikh rule was very different from what it is today. Across the Sindhu Valley in the east was a territory generally under the joint control of the Sikhs and the tribes residing there; actually the latter had the sole control. However, to the north west, the case was different. The bold and warrior tribes of Bombas and Khakas, who, now and then, carried out looting incursions into the valley were a constant source of anxiety for the Sikh administration there. The language, customs, lifestyles, food habits, dress, culture and cultural heritage were different between the people of Kashmir and Muzaffarabad. The people of Muzaffarabad are more closely connected to the people of NWFP (North West Frontier Province) and Punjab than to Kashmir. The main language spoken there is known as Hindko. The upper Kishanganga Valley above the famous shrine of Sarada was, in olden days, and at present, peopled by Dards.

Satisar: the Hindu legend

Among the legends about Kasyapa Rishi, there is one that says that once the Rishi was on a pilgrimage to north India and he saw a beautiful place with a glorious lake. He wanted to reclaim the place and therefore prayed to God Shiva (some say he prayed to God Vishnu). Shiva called Balbhadra, Lord Krishna's brother, who came with his plough and made a hole in the mountain at Baramulla and the water gushed out and thus appeared the valley.

Kalhana traces the history of Kashmir to the King Gonanda-I who ruled Kashmir during the period when Yudhisthira, the eldest brother of Pandavas, was coronated. According to *Nilamatapurana*, Kasyapa Rishi went on a pilgrimage to Pushkar, Prayaga, Kurukshetra etc. and then his son Nilanag ruled Kashmir[26]. *Nilamatapurana* describes the coronation of Nilanag.[27] *Nilamatapurana* also describes Nilanag's excellent administrative acumen in dealing with and subduing the violent tribes such as Pisacas and framing rules for new immigrants such as Danavas, Yaksas, Daityas, Pisacas, and Raksasas[28]. His descriptive tales surrounding Kasyapa Rishi or Nilanag should have been given historical status, but for reasons of being legendary, they have not found their due place in the pages of history. Charles Hugel Baron says,[29] "If there were any truth in the tradition that the valley has been drained by human ingenuity, the Herculean work must have been undertaken at this part. But the height of the mountain, and the breadth of the bed of the river, precludes the possibility of such a conclusion, except in legendary presumption: others attribute its execution to their gods." However, after the valley was drained, the land became fertile. Immediately people from other places migrated to the valley.

The Buddhist legend

There is another legend about Kashmir, which tells us of the Buddhist connection. According to the legend, the valley of Kashmir was a huge lake. Yuan Chwang has mentioned in his travels *On Yuan Chwang's Travels in India* [30], that "according to native records, Kashmir was originally a dragon-lake. The Buddha having subdued the wicked dragon of Udyana had arrived above Kashmir on his way through the air to Central India...." He further writes that, "Ananda's disciple, the Arhat Madhyantika, perfect in spiritual attainments, having heard of Buddha's prediction (that Kashmir would be a seat of learning for Buddhism) was delighted. He accordingly came hither and took his seat in a forest of a great mountain. Here he made miraculous exhibitions and the dragon seeing these asked the Arhat what he wanted. 'I want you to grant me room for my knees in the lake', was the reply—'I want to have as much dry land in the lake as will enable me to sit cross-legged.' The dragon thereupon proceeded to grant the Arhat's request by withdrawing water from the lake but Madhyantika by the exercise of his supernatural powers enlarged his body until the dragon had drawn off all the water of the lake."

The Islamic legend

We have yet another legend which the Muslim community believes in. According to George Foster[31], "The legend of the country asserts that Solomon visited this valley, and finding it covered, except the eminence now mentioned with noxious water, which had no outlet, he opened a passage in the mountains, and gave Kashmir its beautiful plains. The Tucht (Takht) Suleiman, the name bestowed by Mahometans on the hill, forms one side of a grand portal to the lake and on the other stands a lower hill, which in the Hinduee is call Hirney Purvet, (Hari Parvat) or green hill, a name probably adopted from its being covered with gardens and orchards."

It is strange how Solomon could have come here. And there are sceptics of the theory too. According to Godfrey Thomas Vigne[32],"I know of no miracle attributed to him (Solomon) in the vicinity of the towering monarch of the Sulimani range, through which I passed with the Lohanis: many may exist, but I never heard of them. In Kashmir, on the contrary, Solomon is supposed by the Musalmans to have done wonders and to have drained the valley, through the instrumentality of one of his servants, a Deo or Gin, named Kashuf, who is the Kusyapa of the Hindu history."

Francois Bernier has also mentioned in *Travels In The Mughal Empire AD 1656 -1668*, that [33], "A third is the common tradition that Solomon visited this country, and that it was he who opened a passage for the waters cutting the mountain of Baramoule (Baramulla). A fourth, the belief that Moses died in the city of Kachemire, and that his tomb is within a league of it. And a fifth may be found in the generally received opinion that the small and extremely ancient edifice seen on one of the high hills was built by Solomon; and it is therefore called the Throne of Solomon to this day."

Surprisingly, Kashmir is not the only place said to have been under water. There are other places believed to be submerged with water. Writes J Vogel[34], "It is curious that in Nepal we find a very similar tradition. There, too, it is believed that the country was originally an enormous lake inhabited by Nagas, and therefore called Naga-brada or Naga-vasa. By divine agency, the mountains to the south were pierced and the water rushed out carrying the Nagas along with them. The deity who thus delivered the country was Manjuari, or according to another version, Vishnu. Here too, there remained a lake of moderate dimensions and this was assigned to the Naga Karkotaka (the only one who had stayed) for his habitation."

Tribes

The Nags

The history of the nags begins with ample description in *Nilamatapurana*, which says Nilanag was placed by ancient tradition as the head of all Nags or springs of deities of the land. He was considered a son of Saint Kasyapa from his wife Kadru, daughter of Daksa. Kasyapa's other sons were Devas, Daityas, Danavas, the Khasas, Bhadras, and Garudas. His residence is the famous fountain near the village Verinag situated in the Shahabad Pargana at the foot of Banihal Pass. The *Nilamatapurana* describes the origin of the enmity of Kadru and Vinata, wives of Kasyapa and their descendents. The Nags, the children of Kadru, persecuted by Garuda, son of Vinata, fled to Satisar where Vishnu granted them asylum. This particular legend has it that after the Satisar Lake was drained, Kashmir came under the occupation of the Nags. The other tribes such as Pisacas and Manavas (Manavas had come from different parts of the country) also made Kashmir their home. Among various tribes the Nags were most likely more civilised and lived near lakes and springs.

In the words of MA Stein[35], "Allusion has been made already to the fact that the Indian mind has never learned to divide mythology and the legendary tradition from true history." True enough, the veil of myth and legend peeps out "to identify the nags—at one time as reptile snakes, at other time as human beings."

According to J Fergusson[36], "Be this as it may, Cashmere has always been considered, in historical times, as one of the principal centres of Serpent Worship in India, and hitherto it has been principally from her legends that what little was known of the Nags has been gathered." He further says, "Although from the context there is a strong presumption that Snake Worship prevailed in the valley from a very early period, still we have no direct testimony to the fact till the century before the Christian era, when the King Damodara (Damodara-II) having, it is said, offended some Brahmin was converted into a snake, and still it is said, haunts the spot."

K R Subramanian in his *Origin of Shaivism* mentions that the nags belong to Shaivism, and it is claimed that South Indian Shaivism migrated to Northern India leaving in the south its remnant in the Nagaras or Nayars. It may be true, as the South Indian Shaivism even today is based on dualism. However, on reaching Kashmir, Abhinavagupta, one of the most outstanding acharyas of the Shaiva philosophy, gave Shaivism a new concept of monism. Further, the tribes of Nags had powerful kingdoms in different parts of India. According to Sham Lal Sadhu[37], "Another race named Nagas is supposed to have lived along with the Pisacas, or soon after their decline. The Nags were, probably, more civilised than the Pisacas, as few unpleasant memories are associated with them. They lived near tarns, lakes and springs which carry the suffix nags along with their names: Shisharamnag, Kausarnag, Nilanag, and Taksaknag… Some tales like *Heemal Negara*, depict them as being equally at home, on land and in water."

It is probable that after the arrival of the Aryans into India and subsequently in Kashmir, the Nags might have merged with them. Perhaps, where people must have initially settled they named these springs as Verinag, Kukarnag, and Kausarnag etc. Even the womenfolk of Kashmir would dress themselves in such a fashion that their headgear resembled the shape of a cobra hood. The headgear (Taranga) covered with cloth (Pootch) would appear like a snake's body and was attached from head to toe. While walking, the movement of the piece of cloth would resemble the movements of a snake.

It is said that with Nagarjuna's preaching of Tantric Buddhism, the traditional Naga cult almost vanished from the country. However, a Brahmin named Chandadeva, a Kashmiri Shaivite and a descendant of Sage Kasyapa, revived it. It is still prevalent among Hindus in the valley. There still remain even today some families of Kashmiri Pandits settled in India, whose family name is derived from Nag, now known as Nagu. The Nagus trace their migration to India when Muslim king Sikandar (Butshikan) persecuted their ancestors. According to Walter Lawrence[38], "He (King Sikandar) gave them three choices—get converted to Islam or get killed or leave Kashmir for good."

Writes Pandit Jawaharlal Nehru, "The Nags vary greatly in education and general intelligence. Many Nags are, I think, better material than most non-tribal people in India."

Tribal Immigration

Much of tribal immigration took place in Kashmir. For a long time, Nags were considered as tribal immigrants who were serpent worshipers.

However, later on, it was established that they were a tribe who lived in the mountains even before the Aryans came in to Kashmir. Another tribe known as Pisacas, who came to reside in Kashmir, had migrated from Central India. With the immigration of the Pisacas tribe into the valley, the relations between Nags and Pisacas became hostile. But the relations between these two rival tribes improved later on, as per *Nilamatapurana*.

Other Immigrants

King Asoka brought with him 5,000 Buddhists who came to live permanently in Kashmir to study Buddhism. These Buddhists tried to spread the faith to the people of Kashmir. With the coming of Buddhism to Kashmir, a great social change took place. One of the most significant changes was that people discarded the caste system which was prevalent in India. The other immigrants who came into Kashmir were from Persia, Greece, Afghanistan and Turkistan. With the advent of Islam, about 700 Sayyid came from Persia and Central India to propagate Islam in Kashmir.

Three
Early Kings of Kashmir

To begin with, it is important to distinguish between authentic history and legends. Keeping this in view, it is said that the initial period of *Rajatarangini* is a legendary account. Legends can be termed as happenings that are outside the realm of possibility. Though they may be attributed to imagination, on account of non-availability of authentic records, we cannot, at the same time, reject the episodes mentioned in *Rajatarangini*. Legends may have been transmitted orally from person to person, but perhaps there are chances of legendary history becoming history someday.

3102 BC: Kashmir clan is named in the *Mahabharata*. According to the *Mahabharata*, (Vana Parva, the book of the forest) the Pandavas travelled to the Vrashaparva Ashram in China via Kashmir. During the 12-year exile of the Pandavas, they spent some time in the valley of Kashmir.

2629-2564 BC: Rule of King Sandiman. Tradition says that King Sandiman built the Jyeshtia Rudra, present Shankaracharya Temple or Takht-i-Suleiman hill.

Raja Ramdev

Though Kalhana has not made any mention of the King, the story, however, goes that Raja Ramadev was one of the 35 lost kings. Tradition says that a King known as Raja Ramdev was a great warrior and he ruled Kashmir in 3000 BC. It is said that he built the temple at Matan.

Sunder Sen

King Sunder Sen is said to have ruled Kashmir from 2082-2041 BC.

Gonanda-I

According to *Rajatarangini*, Kashmir's history can be traced to the rule of Gonanda-1(2448 BC) who conquered Kashmir in 653 Kali, (a traditional date of the coronation of King Yudhisthira, eldest of the Pandava brothers). According to Jyoteeshwar Pathik,[1] "Gonanda I is said to have conquered the Kashmir valley, and was then said to be ruled by small feudal lords known as Kutrajas." This was the time when the Pandavas established their kingdom. Jerasanda, the father-in-law of Kansa and relative of Gonanda-I, was the king of Magadha. The animosity between Jerasanda and Krishna stemmed from Krishna slaying Kansa. Perhaps to avenge Kansa's assassination, Jerasanda had laid a siege against the forces of Krishna, but fearing defeat, he asked Gonanda-I for military help. Gonanda-I left Kashmir with a large army and reached Mathura to help Jerasanda in the fight against Krishna.[2] Krishna and his brother Balrama killed Jerasanda and Gonanda-I as described in *Nilamatapurana*. Kalhana says,[3] "Eventually, with his limbs wounded by weapons in the battlefield, the king of Kashmir embraced the earth while the Yadava King embraced the goddess of victory."

Damodara-I

The death of king Gonanda-I came as a rude shock to the people of Kashmir. His son, Damodara, who was immediately sworn-in as the king, vowed to avenge the death of his father. It so happened that once Lord Krishna was attending a Svayamvara (marriage ceremony) arranged by Gandhara on the banks of River Indus, and Damodara took the opportunity to fight Krishna to avenge his father's death."Accompanied by his four-fold armies, the king went to the Svayamvara to fight with Madhava, the son of Vasudeva,"[4] says *Nilamatapurana*. In the ensuing battle, Damodara was killed leaving behind his pregnant wife Yashovati.

Queen Yashovati

Yashovati, as per tradition, wanted to become sati. But on Krishna's behest agreed to become the ruler of Kashmir. Yashovati was made the ruler. Krishna showered the highest praises on her, says the *Nilamatapurana*. She was a successful and popular ruler who fully understood the art of running the kingdom. Prem Nath Bazaz writes[5], "No detailed account of the queen's activities has been preserved but it is known that those who were prone to disbelieve that a woman could possess the intelligence and energy to rule competently over a realm, had to admit that they were wrong."

Gonanda-II

Yashovati gave birth to a son named as Gonanda-II. The infant child was crowned the King of Kashmir. During his childhood, all the ministers took great care for him. Yashovati became the ruler of Kashmir against the wishes of the courtiers, for whom it must have been difficult to see a woman on the throne. Brahmins must have connived to dethrone her, but since she had the blessings of Krishna, they must not have succeeded. Hurriedly, all formalities such as baptism etc were taken care of, and the child was named after his grandfather, Gonanda-II. The infant child was installed as King on the throne. Kalhana says that when he was crowned his legs were dangling from the throne. However, Yashovati became the regent of the infant King.Meanwhile, preparations for the epic war of Mahabharata had started and since the Kashmir King was an infant, neither the Pandavas nor the Kauravas asked for Kashmir's participation in the Great War.[6]

Writes Jyoteeshwar Pathik,[7] "During his rule (Gonanda- II), Hardev, a descendant of Pandavas came to Kashmir. The ruler took pity on his poverty and took him into his service. He rose to the position of Dewan earning favours from the King." It is said that one day Hardev killed the king.

The Other Lost Kings

Prior to Gonanda-I, there were 52 Kings who ruled over Kashmir but any information on them is lost. During the rule of Gonanda-I and Gonanda-II, Kalhana has not been able to give us any insight into the condition of the state and her people except that the two kings participated in the battle against Krishna, the epic hero of Mahabharata, and were killed. How long Gonanda-II ruled Kashmir is also not known. After his death, about 35 kings ruled Kashmir. The description of those 35 kings is either lost or destroyed. Sukhdev Singh Charak in his book *A Short History Of Jammu Raj* mentions that 22 Kings of Jammu ruled Kashmir for 650 years.

Lava

In the absence of reliable information about these, Kalhana started with King Lava who became the King of Kashmir. Kalhana's description of Lava is[8], "After them (the lost 35 kings), Lava, an ornament of the earth, a favourite of victory that wears the flowing robe of fame, became the King." The King was very brave and fought many battles. Kalhana says[9], "The din of his army which was enough to cause sleeplessness to the world consigned his enemies to a long slumber." Lava constructed 84 stone buildings and people seemed to have been prosperous during his rule. He constructed a Vihara for the Brahmins on the banks of river Lidar and named it Lavara. He also founded the city of Lolau (presently known as Lolab Valley) and then died. Kalhana has not described Lava's antecedents nor have we any information available about the date when he became the King and when he died.

Kusa

After the death of Lava on the banks of river Lidar, his son Kusa succeeded him and ascended the throne. About Kusa, it is said that he was quite handsome and people respected him. He granted Agrahara (Jageers) to the deserving people of Kashmir. He built the city of Kurushara.

Khagendra

The succession story continued. After King Kusa died, his son Khagendra, and grandson Surendra became the kings of Kashmir. There is nothing extraordinary about these three kings except that they strengthened the country subduing the enemies of the state. Khagendra is said to have destroyed his enemies sending an array of elephants. Khagendra belonged to the Garuda community who were known as destroyers of Nag tribes.

Surendra

With the death of Khagendra, his son Surendra succeeded to the throne of Kashmir. He is known as the 20th king, a descendant of Hardev. He was a pious king with great qualities and was even compared to God Indra. He constructed a Vihara called Narenderbhaoond Savra. After the death of his father, he made a kund. Surendra, who died childless, was also said to have been the first Buddhist ruler of Kashmir. He erected the first Vihara in Kashmir (presently known as Soura) on the Anchar Lake, north of Srinagar. It is said that during his rule Kashmir experienced a great earthquake.

It is an accepted fact that Buddhism came to Kashmir during Asoka's period in 250 BC. However, there is a great belief that Buddhism had already set foot in Kashmir during Surendra's reign.

Godhara

After Surender's death, the management of the country passed in the hands of the scion of another family, Godhara. Godhara was an able king who protected his country well from his enemies. No date is available as to when he became the king and when he died.

Suverna

Suverna, son of Godhara, was crowned the king of Kashmir. According to Kalhana, Suverna was a humanitarian and was known as 'giver of gold'. He distributed gold to the needy. He constructed canals that irrigated the lands for cultivation.

Janaka

Suverna's son Janaka ascended the throne after the death of his father. He built a Vihara at Jalora, which is modern Zohlar, and gave Jageers to the poor. It is not known how long he ruled Kashmir. He was considered as good and philanthropical as his father.

Sacinara

After Janaka, his son Sacinara ascended the throne. He seemed to have inherited the genes of his parents and grandparents and was indeed a noble king. He built a Shiva temple at Vijayeshvara. Unfortunately, he died issueless. Then came a pious and religious king known as Asoka. It is said that saffron cultivation was introduced during his reign.

Asoka

Asoka, who then ruled the valley, was the great-grandson of Sacinara. He was considered a pious king. He laid the foundation of the town of Srinagari (Srinagar) near present Pandrethan. It had about 96 houses. He also built 500 monasteries for Buddhist monks. This was the time when Mleechas came to invade the country but Asoka subdued them. He gave a fillip to Buddhism. He constructed many stupas at Vitasta.

He also built two temples at Vijayeshvara, and named them Asokesvara. The name and antecedents of Asoka and the subsequent four kings, says Stein[10], "are taken by Kalhana from the author Chavillakara." According to Stein[11], "It has been assumed that the Mleechas referred here are perhaps the Greeks." Asoka had prayed for a son and God granted him a boon—a son named Jalauka.

If we go by the dates given by Kalhana, then, Asoka ruled somewhere before 1182 BC but history suggests Asoka was born in 304 BC. Also, it is difficult to say whether King Asoka of Kashmir was different from King Asoka, the greatest emperor of the Mauryan Empire of Patliputra who actually was the ruler of whole of India including Kashmir. There are a lot of similarities which point to the fact they are not different individuals, and that it was the Mauryan king who also ruled Kashmir.

Tradition says that Asoka was the son of a Greek princess, the daughter of Seleucus, who became the wife of Bindusara, the father of Asoka. The alliance was in accordance with the terms of peace between Chandragupta, Asoka's grandfather, and Seleucus. Again, we have no evidence to prove this. However, it is also said that Asoka was the son of Bindusara and Rani Dharma, who belonged to a Brahmin family. King Asoka's coronation took place in 269 BC. After the Kalinga war, King Asoka converted to Buddhism and preached the religion far and wide. So did King Asoka of Kashmir, who gave a boost to Buddhism. King Asoka visited Kashmir twice.

Writes J Fergusson in *Tree and Serpent Worship*[12], "Kashmir was in Asoka's empire. A bhikku (a Buddhist monk) named Majjhantika, was sent to Kashmir and Gandhara by Ashoka (Ashoka the great) after the third Sangiti (council) at Patliputra in 253 BC. Aravaalo, the Naga king ruling in Kashmir then, tried to terrify the bhikku, but was ultimately converted to Buddhism."

The legend: In his memoirs, Yuan Chwang narrates that during the reign of Asoka, an ordinary man known as Mahadeva impressed the king with his ability as a Buddhist monk. So impressed was the king by him that he did not tolerate the other monks. Chwang says,[13] "the king summoned all monks to the Ganges with the intention of causing them to drown. But the Arhats (500 head monks) finding their lives in danger used their supernatural powers and flew through the air to Kashmir." After some time, the king realised his mistake and begged them to come back but they refused. Chwang further says, "...So the King built 500 monasteries for them and gave up all of Kashmir for the benefit of the Buddhist Church." According to Thomas Watters, the translator of Yuan Chwang's Travels [14], "Those 500 Arhats introduced and propagated the Sthavira School in Kashmir, and the majority of inferior brethren at Patliputra began the Mahasanghika School."

Jalauka

After the death of Asoka, his son Jalauka became the King of Kashmir. Jalauka was considered a heavenly person with supernatural powers. The tradition goes that he could transform metals into gold. He made the country prosperous and shining. Legend says that he used to go to Wangat and bathe there in the spring every morning. One day he was very late. The deity felt compassion for him and so willed that another spring arose in the city, called Sahodara (born of the same parents). Thus, he was saved the great trouble of making a long journey every morning to the holy spring.

It was during that period that some Mleechas (foreigners, perhaps Bactrian Greeks) incursions occurred in Kashmir and they oppressed the people. Jalauka, being a great warrior, freed the land of these oppressors. He not only annihilated the Mleechas but also invaded other countries such as Kanauji and Gandhara. He is said to have constructed stone temples with rich endowments. According to MA Stein, Jalauka undertook a pilgrimage to Sharda.[15] "These references make it clear that Sharda is but the ancient name of the sacred spring now called Narran Nag." He exhibited great courage.

King Jalauka was traditionally a fervent worshipper at the shrines of Shiva, and initially an opponent of Buddhism. Subsequently, he adopted a friendlier attitude towards Buddhists and stopped the killing of animals. The bringing of the king closer to Buddhism is said to have been due to the efforts of an elderly, courageous member of the Buddhist cult known as Krityadevi, who in the garb of a beggar, asked the king for human flesh.

The legend: There are many legends surrounding Jalauka. As per Kalhana,[16] "Once upon a time, when the king was preceding to Vijayeshvara, a woman, whom he met midway on the road begged for food. When he promised to give her food as she desired, she changed her form and disclosed a desire for human flesh. King Jalauka, who had renounced the killing of living beings, gave her permission to please herself with the flesh from his body. She thus addressed him, 'O King you must be Bodhisattva."

Jalauka also demonstrated great administrative capabilities and created a systematised working of the government. He was the first king who established a council of ministers who were answerable for the problems of their respective departments.

The talented queen Isanadevi

His talented queen, Isanadevi, as recorded by Kalhana, inspired much of what Jalauka did in his lifetime. When Jalauka turned his attention to building temples and raising other structures for the material and spiritual well-being of the people, the queen lent her support. "She was well versed in the philosophy of Kashmir and could easily discourse on religious topics with learned men,"[17] says Prem Nath Bazaz. She founded Matri Chakras (Circles of Mothers) in the frontier town and different parts of the kingdom." It is also believed that Jalauka and Isanadevi jointly built the temple on the crest of the Shankaracharya hill at Srinagar. An ardent devotee of Rudra (Shiva), he sent 100 girls from his seraglio[18] who danced every day before the deity at the Jyestharudra temple built by him. According to Vincent A Smith[19], "But the story of Jalauka, notwithstanding the topographical details is essentially legendary, and no independent corroboration of the Kashmir tradition has been discovered."

Damodara II

The throne of Kashmir came to Damodara II after Jalauka's death. No date is available as to when he ascended the throne. He belonged to Asoka's race. Damodara II was considered as a jewel among kings. He was a Shiva worshipper who was granted good fortune. He is said to have constructed dams and even built a canal routed to an unirrigated plateau named Damodara-Suda.

The legend: Once King Damodara wanted to take a bath in the river Vitasta, but unfortunately some Brahmins had taken a bath there. When the Brahmins saw the King, they asked him for food. The king told them that he did not give food as charity until he took a bath. He further told them not to coil around him like a snake. Angry at this remark, the Brahmins cursed him. "Be you a snake." Instantly Damodara was transformed into a snake. The king begged the Brahmins to remove the curse. They then told him that when he listened to the recitation of the whole of *Ramayana*, the curse would be eased one day.

J Fergusson substantiates this story[20], "King Damodara having, it is said, offended some Brahman was converted into a snake, and still, it is said, haunts the spot."

According to MA Stein[21], "The legend of King Damodara's transformation into a snake goes that when the king was unable to take the canal to the plateau, he went to pray at a place named Damodara (Damodara Suda). He may have constructed a spring after which a legend has spread that the king turned into a nag, which means snake or a spring."

Huska/Huvishka

Kashmir had three kings named Huska/Huvishka, Juska and Kanishka. These three kings were very powerful and they laid the foundation of three towns named after them. According to S R Bakshi[22], "The fall of the Mauryan empire ushered in a period when the north-west of India fell victim to foreign invasions from which Kashmir was not immune. The political stability of Kashmir was revived by the rulers Huska, Juska and Kanishka..." Huska built 'Caitya-cum-Vihara' where pilgrims would spend their nights during their onward journey. "The town was called after his name as Hushkapura. The town has been located by Cunningham at a small village known as Uskur about two miles to the southeast of Baramulla."

Juska

Juska built a town and a Vihara known as Jayasvamipura. It is located at the northern side of Srinagar in Zukur.

Kanishka

Kanishka, who flourished during the second century (127-151 AD), was known as a great patron of Buddhism. He is celebrated in the Buddhist annals as a second Asoka. He was the fifth and famous king of Kushan dynasty, who ruled over a huge territory of North India including Gandhara (Eastern Afghanistan). The territory extended from the Amu Darya (Oxus River) in Central Asia in the West to Varanasi and Mathura in the east, and from Kashmir in the north to the coast of Gujarat. Kanishka was known as a violent, brutal and faithless ruler. However, a Buddhist bhikshu brought complete change in him and he accepted Buddhism as his faith. His contribution to Buddhism is enormous. He constructed a huge stupa in Peshawar (now in Pakistan), which was roughly 286 feet in diameter and more than 650 feet high.

Kanishka built Kaniskapura, which is located at the road from Srinagar to Shupiyan named Kampore. The Turuskas Kings—Huska, Juska and Kanishka—had faith in Buddhism. Kanishka strengthened the roots of Buddhism in Kashmir. In fact, it was during his reign that the Mahayana doctrine came into being. Kashmiri scholars too contributed a lot in the emergence of the doctrine. According to Stein[23], "*Rajatarangini* says that Kanishka's and Huska's rule has been confirmed by the coins found but Juska's rule was not confirmed." According to Mark S G Dyczkowski[24], "Remarkable as Kashmir has been as a seat of Hindu spirituality and learning, it was no less so as a centre of Buddhism, possibly introduced into Kashmir as early as the third century BC."

As per Yuan Chwang, Kanishka who ruled India was also ruling Kashmir. It was during his period that the fourth and the biggest Buddhist Council at Kundala Sadarhadvana (present day Harvan) was convened in Kashmir. Kanishka gathered 500 Buddhist monks, headed by Vasumitra, to systematise the Sarvastivadin Adhidharma texts, which were translated from earlier Prakrit vernacular languages (such as Gandhari in Kharosthi script) into the classical language of Sanskrit. It is said that during the council, three hundred thousand verses and over nine million statements were compiled, a process which took 12 years to complete. Yuan Chwang says,[25] "When leaving to return to his own country Kanishka renewed Asoka's gift of all Kashmir to the Buddhist Church." During the Buddhist Council at Kaniskapura in Kashmir, great scholars such as Asvaghosa and Vasumitra were supposed to have attended. For six months, the scholars discussed various aspects of the doctrine of Buddhism.

It was during Kanishka's rule that a Kashmiri famous physician, Charaka, the principal contributor to the ancient science of Ayurveda, flourished. Tradition says that Charaka was the Prime Minister of Kanishka.Kanishka's date of succession is controversial. Some of the chroniclers have placed him at 58 BC, others at 278 AD.

Abhimanyu I

King Abhimanyu I was a great king and a fearless warrior who knew no enemies. It is not known how he became the king. However, he was kind-hearted and gave jageers to the needy. He founded the town of Abhimanyupura in his own name. Abhimanyupura is the place presently known as Bemenu area of Srinagar. The town was affluent.

It seems that King Abhimanyu I wanted to popularise education. To make it easy and to re-interpret the Mahabhasya for the people, he appointed scholars of that time. According to Stein[26], "I understand it is intended to say that Candracharya and other grammarians under Abhimanyu's instructions set again on foot the study of Mahabhasya, which, owing to the absence of competent teachers or a correct text had become difficult and disused."

It was the time when Nagarjuna spread Buddhism in Kashmir and the practice of religious rituals such as Bali (sacrifices), which was very common amongst the people, were stopped. The legend goes that the Brahmins also offered oblations and sacrifices and as such stopped the destruction caused by a great snowfall in which many people perished. There was peace and prosperity in Kashmir during King Abhimanyu's time. It was during his period that the great grammarian Candracharya founded a school of grammar. However, the latter part of his rule was affected by the menace of Yaksas who plagued the land.

Four
Gonanda Dynasty

Gonanda III

Prior to the rule of Gonanda III, Kalhana laments the loss and destruction of the names and account of the reign of the 52 kings of Kashmir. He has also not been able to mention the duration of the reign of any king of Kashmir. In this respect, King Gonanda II's rule is significant for the reason that Kalhana is able to indicate the length and time of individual reigns. With King Gonanda III's rule begins, in fact, a continuum in the list of kings, which Kalhana professedly obtained from the earlier chroniclers.

Gonanda III's re-introduction of Nag worship: Tradition believes[1], "The kings whose only object is to oppress their subjects, perish together with their descendants, whereas royal fortune attends the race of those who will repair what has been destroyed." Thus, his rule is important because he chose the path of tradition and repaired the wrongs done by other kings. There was development all around. Gonanda III ruled Kashmir for 35 years.

Writes Michael Lee Scott[2], "Kalhana's narrative distinctly names

Gonanda III as the first of the Gonanda race, and the founder of that dynasty. It is difficult to believe that some connection had not been established between Gonanda III and these earlier rulers of identical name if the latter had been known to genuine tradition whether of the people or the learned. It is possible that the first two Gonandas are only reflex images, as it were, of the recognised founder of the oldest Kashmir dynasty, projected into a higher antiquity in order to provide Kashmir contemporaries for the heroes of the Mahabharata."

Vibhisana

Vibhisana, the son of Gonanda III, became the king of Kashmir. But not much is available which can tell us about the condition of the people at that time. It seems that his rule must largely have been peaceful because he could not have ruled for such a long period otherwise. He ruled for 53 years and six months.

Indrajit

In the chronology of rulers of Kashmir, it is not known if Indrajit was the son of Vibhisana. He was a god-fearing king and worked for the betterment of the people. His rule lasted 35 years.

Ravana

Ravana ruled the country for 30 years. The ancient Kings had a prime duty of appeasing Gods. Ravana introduced Linga worship. He built a Linga which was named Vatesvara and he performed his puja (worship) there every day.

Vibhisana II

Vibhisana II was the second son of King Ravana. He ruled Kashmir for 35 years and six months. Apart from the fact that he was a strong ruler, nothing else has been documented about his rule.

Nara I

Vibhisana's son, Nara, who was named Kinnara, also ruled the country for 41 years and three months. The early years of his reign were marked by efficiency, but later he succumbed to some vices and fell prey to lust and greed. People resented him for it. They felt the king's misdoings were the cause for the natural calamities which befell the people of Kashmir. It was also the period when Brahmanism and Buddhism were each struggling to establish their supremacy. King Nara, who was powerful, was devoted to Hinduism. Obviously, he resented the fact that Buddhism was flourishing.

But what led him to destroy Buddhism was an incident involving his queen. There lived a Buddhist bhikshu by the name of Siamana who was living alone in Kimnaragrama Vihara. Nara's queen used to visit the Vihara. On one occasion, the bhikshu seduced the queen. This created a ruckus in the kingdom. So infuriated was King Nara that he burnt thousands of Buddhist Viharas. Not only this, he also cancelled the jageers given to the Buddhists and gave them to the Brahmins instead.

Some of the chroniclers believe that King Nara created this ruckus to stop Buddhism from enveloping Kashmir. According to Suresh K Sharma,[3] "The reason assigned for this conduct (burning of monasteries) is that a Buddhist had eloped with the King's wife; but this seems unlikely and false, and has apparently been got up by later Brahmins to blacken the character of Buddhists." King Nara undertook the construction of new markets on the banks of the Vitasta. These were full of supplies. The gardens were full of fruits and flowers and the valley looked as if it were a paradise. It is not definitely known how long Nara ruled over Kashmir but presumably he did for 41 years and three months.

The legend of Nag girls: The legend about Nara's destruction comes with this story. Two Nag girls, Iravati and Chandralekha, who were living at Susravas Nag, were infatuated with a Brahmin boy, Visakha. Writes Sham Lal Sadhu,[4] "He (the Brahmin boy) saw before him two exceedingly beautiful damsels draped in blue shawls. They wore rubies on their ears and a thin line of kohl marked their elongated eyes. These moon-faced, lotus-eyed maidens further amazed the Brahmin when he discovered them eating pods of Kacchagucha grass. When he asked them why they ate grass befitting the humble they told him that their father would appear at Taksaknag (Zevan) on the twelfth day of the dark half of *Jeshth* (month) and would explain everything." Prof Sadhu has written a note on this story. "This pool of water exists even now at Zevan. In Akbar's time, cultivators worshipped there and poured milk into it to enlist the aid of the deity for a good crop."

After some days, the girls took Visakha to their father, who in turn gave this boy wealth and then allowed him to marry these two girls. Both girls were virtuous and faithful to their new husband. The reputation of their beauty reached the ears of the king, who sought them out. Accompanied by his soldiers, King Nara approached one of the girls for satisfying his lust. The soldiers were instructed that in the event of her refusal she should be lifted force and brought to him. The girls came to know this and stealthily left the place with their husband from the backdoor of the palace and reached the home of their father, Prince Susravas. On hearing their plight, the father became so furious that he inflicted heavy losses on King Nara. Susravas burnt the whole town of the king in which perished thousands of people. Ramanya, the third sister of the Naga girls, threw a boulder from the mountain and dropped it to block the river from flooding the houses of the people. A boulder at Ramanyatavi, (present Rembyar) is attributed to this story. King Nara perished along with his force while defending himself. After the carnage, the Naga himself felt great remorse and he went on a pilgrimage. Kalhana laments that a small error of the king brought destruction to the people and the country.[5]

Siddha

At the time when there was death and destruction caused by Prince Susravas, father of the Nag girls, in his fight against King Nara I, the son of King Nara, known as Siddha, was a child and was being looked after by the maidservant. Fearing that his father's sins may cause misery to the young prince, she took him to Vijayaksetra (modern Bijbihara) where it is said that the prince was protected from any kind of misery.

After the death of King Nara, Siddha was made the king. He proved a very good king.[6] "This King called Siddha then revived the thoroughly exhausted nation as the clouds revive the mountain which has been parched by a forest fire," says Kalhana. Siddha, was surprised to know the story of his father. Leading a pious life himself he practised humility and inherent goodness. He also realised the futility of the mundane life associated with wealth and riches. He renounced the jewels and ornaments and started devoting himself to the worship of Shiva. He had realised that giving in to lust and greed was not only bad for himself but for the kingdom on the whole. Siddha ruled the country for 60 years. At his death, even his attendants expressed their love for him by joining him on the funeral pyre.

Utpalaksa

Utpalaksa was the son of Siddha, who then ruled Kashmir. His name Utpalaksa is attributed to his beautiful lotus like eyes. Like his father, he was also a virtuous king who looked after his subjects well. He ruled the country for 30 years and six months.

Hiranyaksa

Hiranyaksa, son of Utpalaksa, ruled the country for 37 years and seven months. He built a town, Hiranyaksa, and named it after himself.[7] The town is situated on the Srinagar to Ganderbal road. According to Stein, there is a Naga (a spring) near the village which is visited by the pilgrims before proceeding to the Haramukuta Tirthas.

Hiranyakula

Hiranyakula was the son of Hiranyaksa, who founded the town of Hiranyotsa. He ruled for 60 years. According to MA Stein,[8] "Wilson has already pointed out that Hiranyaksa figures in Somadeva's *Katha-sarit-sagara* as the hero of the fairy tale. His father Kanakaksa was called King of Kashmir, and said to reside in Hiranyapura, the capital of the country."

Vasukula

Vasukula, the son of Hiranyakula, also ruled for 60 years. There is nothing much known about his rule.

Mihirakula

Mihirakula is known as the most controversial figure in the history of Kashmir. There are two versions of Mihirakula. One of the versions is given by Kalhana and the other by Yuan Chwang, the Chinese traveller.

Kalhana's version: Mihirakula was the son of Vasukula, who was enthroned as the king of Kashmir. He is known as a man of violent actions. Kashmir was already suffering death and destruction in the hands of the Mleechas tribe who had invaded the country. Its new ruler Mihirakula added to the devastation and woes of the country. The magnitude of the death inflicted by him was so great that people could see thousands of vultures hovering in the sky over the dead bodies floating in the Vitasta river. Mihirakula, the terrible enemy of humankind, spared no pity or respect for children, women or the aged. He had no compassion for human suffering and no conscience for any of his bad deeds. He was a man troubled by only trivial things. Seeing his wife dressed in a robe made of silk from Ceylon, that had the foot impression of the King of Ceylon, annoyed him so much that he declared war against that country.

Mihirakula's Sadism: After defeating the king of Ceylon and other kings,

Mihirakula returned to Kashmir. It is said that as soon as he reached the gateway to the valley, an elephant fell down the gorge. While falling, the elephant let out a terrified cry. This shriek of the elephant so amused the king that he ordered 101 elephants be thrown down the precipice. The echo of their dying cries gave the king great thrill and sadistic pleasure.

Mihirakula's Religion: As he grew old, a sense of guilt engulfed him. In order to seek atonement for his sins, he gave jageers to Brahmins belonging to the land of Gandhara, which was also under his rule. There is an interesting legend about the king. He tried to divert a river called Candrakulya for irrigation purposes. But a stone rock in the middle hampered the process. At this point, King Mihirakula performed penance and was told by the Gods in his dreams that a powerful Yaksa, who observed the vow of chastity, was living in the stone. If chaste women were to touch the stone, it would not cause obstruction. The king ordered many women of high repute to touch the stone. But they all failed. Finally the huge rock was moved by the touch of a poor potter's wife. Mihirakula ruled the country for 70 years. In his old age, he was afflicted with many diseases, especially skin diseases which gave him great pain. Unable to bear the pain, he committed suicide by hanging himself.

Yuan Chwang's version of Mahirakula

Yuan Chwang's account of Mahirakula seems identical to that of Mihirakula given by Kalhana. According to Yuan Chwang, Mahirakula was a white Hun. He was the son of Tokamina who ruled over territories from Kabul to Central India. In the year 515 AD[9], when Mahirakula moved to Central India, Baladitya of Magadha defeated him. Mahirakula was forced to retreat and take shelter in Kashmir in 530 AD. Mahirakula's territory was Afghanistan, Punjab, Malwa and Rajputana. Sialkot was his capital.

Tradition also says when he took refuge in Kashmir, the then King of Kashmir received him warmly and made him incharge of a small territory. But Mahirakula, after consolidating his position, ousted the king who had offered him shelter, and started ruling the land. Yuan Chwang's records[10] of Mahirakula show similar cruelties inflicted by Kalhana's Mihirakula. Yuan Chwang says[11], "kings prior to Mahirakula were patrons of Buddhism. However, when Mahirakula succeeded as the king of Kashmir, he killed the Buddhist monks and destroyed their sacred buildings. He also beheaded the 23rd head priest of the Buddhists and broke Buddha's bowl."

According to Yuan Chwang,[12] Mahirakula was the king of Sakala. He once desired to learn Buddhism from the head priest but the priest declined and that angered the king. He then invaded Magadha, which was ruled by Baladitya. When defeated, he was released by the orders of the queen of Baladitya. His younger brother fled to Kashmir and took possession of the throne there. He followed the footsteps of his elder brother and continued the destruction of Buddhism. He destroyed 1600 stupas and monasteries. But then he died suddenly. After his death Buddhism flourished again in the valley.

However, Stein has pointed out in the introduction of *Rajatarangini*, that studying the rule of the two kings—Yuan Chwang's Mahirakula and Kalhana's Mihirakula—there is a difference of 1200 years. Hun Mahirakula ruled during the first half of the sixth century AD, whereas Kalhana's Mihirakula ruled around 704-634 BC. Also, there is some difference in the name. For Kalhana it was Mihirakula, and for Yuan Chwang it was Mahirakula. However, the truth about the two kings is still not known.

Baka

After the death of Mihirakula, his virtuous son Baka was made the king. Unlike his destructive father, his reign was peaceful. Law and order was maintained. This great prince founded a new town named Lavanotsa, somewhere near Padampura (modern Pampore), constructed the shrine of Shiva and named it Bakesa. He also dug up the Bakavati canal which helped people to irrigate their land. He ruled the country for 63 years and 13 days. According to a legend, once Baka came across a very beautiful woman having magical powers. She met the king one evening and spoke to him, leaving him mesmerised. When she invited him for a sacrificial ritual, he gladly accepted. Next day, Baka, accompanied by his 100 sons and grandsons came to see the sacrificial feast. Little did anyone realise the woman was making the king, the sacrificial offering to the circle of the goddesses.

Ksitinanda

Ksitinanda, the son of Baka, ruled Kashmir for 30 years. Kalhana says that of all the sons and grandsons of Baka sacrificed, the Goddess had spared only Ksitinanda so that he could be the next heir to the throne.

Vasunanda

Vasunanda, the son of Ksitinanda, ruled for 52 years. He composed a well-known work of erotic (Smarasastra) writings on lovemaking, It explores all matters related to sexuality, from setting the mood to explicit instructions on techniques.

Nara II

Nara II was the son of Vasunanda and ruled for 60 years. Details about his rule remain unavailable. However, tradition says that his rule was, by and large, peaceful, and the people were happy.

Aksa

Aksa was the son of Nara II. He also ruled the country for about 60 years. He founded a town known as Aksavala, the modern Achbal.

Gopaditya

Kalhana has mentioned the name of Gopaditya as king of Kashmir without giving any indication as to who he was or where he came from. It is said that Gopaditya ruled the country for 60 years and six days. It was a reign that seems to have earned him much appreciation and goodwill. He constructed a shrine 'Jyesthesvara' on the Gopadri also known as Shankaracharya and now Takht-i-Suleiman. According to M A Stein[13], "Gopadri, the ancient designation of the conspicuous hill, now popularly known as Takht-i-Suleiman" He also constructed shrines at Valur and Nagam Pargana.

According to *Tarikh-i-Jadul*, the temple on the hill was known as 'Zishi Shore', and Sandiman (Suleiman), as minister of Gopaditya, had been deputed to repair the temple. Pirzada Gulam Hasan[14] also mentioned that the repairs of the temple were carried out during the reign of Raja Gopaditya. Gopaditya bestowed the title of Gopa-Agrahara on the Brahmins born in Aryadesa. Many poets exalted him highly in their poems. One of the poems written in his praise was *Prasasti*. He practised pure vegetarianism where even eating of garlic was not allowed. He ruled Kashmir for 60 years and six days. If the dates are correct, then Alexander invaded India in 327 BC during Gopaditya's period. Alexander marched from Taxila to the Hydaspes (Jhelum) along with his forces, touching the valley of Kashmir.

Gokarna

Gopaditya's son Gokarna ruled the country for about 58 years. For many of these rulers, their greatest achievement lies in their appeasement of the Gods by constructing temples or founding a new town in their own name. Gokarna was no different. He also constructed a Shiva temple and named it Gokarnesvara. Coins were issued in his name. His name occurred on a coin found by A Cunningham.

Narendraditya-I

Narendraditya, son of Gokarna, became the king after the death of his father. His second name was Khinkhila He was a saintly man and a Shaivite by faith. He constructed a shrine in the name of Shiva Bhutesvara. His Guru, Ugra, was bestowed with divine powers. The Guru also constructed a Shiva temple, Ugresa. Narendraditya founded a permanent place for the board and lodging of Brahmins. He ruled the country for 36 years and 100 days.

Yudhisthira I

Narendraditya's son, Yudhisṭhira I, succeeded his father and ruled Kashmir for 34 years. He was nicknamed Andha-Yudhisthira for his eyes were small. For some time, he ruled the country with great care like his predecessors. However, mesmerised by the regal splendour of the life he was enjoying, he fell into evil company. In the words of Kalhana,[15] "The wise whom he had deprived of their dignity by treating them alike with his ignorant attendants shunned him in his depravation. True, for a yogin, it is right to see the same in every person but for a King it is a great fault and the source of disgrace. By parasites who turned faults into virtues and virtues into faults, he was gradually deprived of his intellect, and rendered like a slave of women."

Another bad habit of Yudhisthira I was that he would praise a person in public but say bad things about him behind his back. He seemed to have formed a caucus of flatterers around him. The people surrounding the king were all ignorant and foolish but he revelled in their company. He always listened to them, and, as a result, the country fell into disorder and confusion. When the country suffered on account of mismanagement, people revolted against the king. Frightened and overcome by the public outcry, the king ultimately had to bow to the will of the people. Sparing his life and avoiding any bloodshed, he was asked to leave the country, which he was forced to do. When he left the palace, his enemies looted his treasure and the women of his harem. However, the king along with his few attendants and the lamenting royal ladies, left the city and took shelter in some other country.

After some time, he returned to Kashmir with the intention of reclaiming his kingdom but his own courtiers had turned against him. They imprisoned him and put him in captivity at Durgagalika (presently called Drugjan near Dal Lake). Meanwhile, the ministers decided to put Pratapaditya I, a relative of King Vikramaditya of Ujjain on the throne of Kashmir.

Five
Vikramaditya Dynasty

Pratapaditya I

After King Yudhishthira I was unseated by the people, the throne remained vacant for some time. The people's successful revolt led to a complete power vacuum. It is not known how long Kashmir remained without a king. The people were unaware that the country could be run without a king, that the country could become a republic, and then there would be no need to install a king. However, being used to monarchy, the people earnestly tried to find a king. So, Pratapaditya I, a relative of King Vikramaditya of Magadha, was brought from Central India and crowned the king of Kashmir. While Pratapaditya was spellbound by the scenic beauty of Kashmir, it is not known if the people benefited from his ascending the throne. What is known, however, is that he ruled the country for 32 years. After his death, his son Jalaukas took over.

Jalaukas

The name of Jalaukas resembles the name of Asoka's son Jalauka. Jalaukas, the son of Pratapaditya, ruled Kashmir for 32 years, the same period as his father. He was a benevolent king and treated his subjects with compassion. Kalhana has not said anything extraordinary about Jalaukas except that he treated his subjects as his own children. He earned the title 'Ornament of the Earth.' Such lavish praise from the people shows that he was a benevolent ruler. During his reign, the people were affluent and devoted to cultural activities. G L Kaul writes,[1] "Music had attained perfection in the time of Jalaukas whose queen also danced."

Tunjina I

After the death of King Jalaukas, his son Tunjina became the King. He is known as one of the most important kings of Kashmir. Even today, he is remembered for the sacrifices he made for his subjects. Shaivites by faith, the king and queen built temples and a town called Katika. Such was their consideration for the people that they even planted trees to provide them relief from the fierce heat of the sun. It was in Tunjina's reign that a poet, Candaka, descendent of Vyas Muni, composed a play which was popular with the people. In short, the people were happy and the kingdom prosperous.

The great famine: There was a sudden famine which brought death and destruction. According to Kalhana,[2] "Then came a terrible famine due to the untimely snowfall when the paddy fields were ripening, and destroyed the rice fields which resembled a kind of hell with the masses of starving people (moving about) like ghosts. Tormented by hunger, everyone thought only of his belly, and forgot in his misery the love for his wife, affection for his children and regard for his parents."Tunjina and his wife Vakpusta opened the treasury of the kingdom and bought food for the people. The king and his queen also emptied their personal treasury and distributed the wealth to the people. Even then, people were dying like flies.

Desperate king's decision to commit suicide: Unable to cope with the tragic scene of his people dying, the king, helpless and frustrated, thought it was the result of his own sins. He wanted to sacrifice himself to please the Gods. He decided to commit suicide. When the queen heard this, she was in a state of shock and anger, but she was a strong-willed woman. She tried to stop him with a mild rebuke and tried to impress upon him that kings who have the ability to face challenges are the real kings and that they have the right to rule. Those who cannot face difficult situations do not deserve to be kings. She urged him to struggle against the misfortune. According to Kalhana, the queen told the king,[3] "Devotion to their husbands is the duty of wives; faithfulness is the duty of Ministers; the duty of kings is to have no other aim but the protection of their subjects." She assured the king that she had an intuition that the worst was over. This worked as magic for the king who devoted himself once again to the task of relief operations. But the situation worsened; once again, the royal couple were on the verge of desperation. The tearful king and queen spent one whole night praying at the royal temple.

"Then something miraculous happened. The legend goes that the next day, the rooftops of all houses were full of dead fowls. People cooked these and satisfied their hunger. Soon food must have arrived from their friendly neighbouring countries and the people were saved. Not a single starving man was left unfed.[4]"

Vakpusta stands alone as the only queen with great humanity in the history of Kashmir. Her story is incredible. While many women found sanctity in the confines of their kitchens, Vakpusta moved beyond that and showed strength of character and bravery in tackling a colossal problem. In fact, she deserves complete credit for the miraculous reversal of her husband's decision to end his life by making him committed to restoring a fallen land. This is one of the finest examples of how a woman of Kashmir saved the country from disaster. Given the enormity of the tragedy, had the King sacrificed himself there would have been largescale disaster all around and nobody would have been able to save the people or the country from such a calamity. There are many such examples in the history of Kashmir where women have saved the country from disasters.

Tunjina died after ruling the country for 36 years. But he was fortunate that by that time, the destruction of the famine was over. The anxiety faced by the king and the queen was over. When the king died, the queen could not bear the separation from her husband and she committed sati on his funeral pyre. This royal couple left no heir to the throne of Kashmir. So heart-rending and remarkable was Tunjina's desperation to save his subjects from the disaster, that his name has found a place in Kashmiri lingo when expressing desperation. Today *Tunjina Chhukh Logumut* means someone who has become utterly desperate.

Vijaya

With the death of King Tunjina, the throne of Kashmir once again became vacant. A certain Vijaya, who belonged to some other family, became the king of Kashmir. It is not known which family he belonged to. The only thing known about him is that he built a town which surrounded the shrine and named it Vijayeshvara (modern Bijbihara).

Jayendra

Jayendra, the son of King Vijay, followed the natural order of succession. He was highly religious and worshiped Shiva. The people loved him. He appointed a minister called Samdhimati who was a great sage. However, some powerful people poisoned the ears of the king against the sage as they feared his wisdom. That led to his banishment. However, the sage was not disappointed but was happy and lived a humble life thereafter. Interestingly, there was a sudden upsurge of news in the kingdom, spreading from house to house: "To Samdhimati will belong the kingdom." The confidants of the king told him that the rumours had some base and they made him believe that Samdhimati may become the king some day. The king was furious; he saw his own uselessness as a threat from the sage. He decided to put him in prison. Samdhimati was not unhappy. He saw prison as the place where he could continue his prayers to God Shiva without any hindrance. Meanwhile, the king was burning with hate and anger. Not satisfied with the punishment given to Samdhimati, he gave orders for his death. Says Kalhana,[5] "When the pain-worn king heard of his impalement, the sting of anxiety first left him, and then his life." Ten years passed; the king remained morose for he was issueless and subsequently died issueless.

The legend: According to Kalhana, some supernatural powers revived Samdhimati, the saintly man, after he was killed. The legend goes that when the guru Isana saw the dead man eaten by the wolves, he saw something written on his forehead. He translated it and found that Samdhimati had to become the King, but he left the limbless skeleton of Samdhimati there. After midnight, an army of witches came and made a huge noise. At this, the guru went back to see the skeleton. Hiding behind a tree, he saw that the witches had encircled the dead sage and were enjoying their drinks. In their state of intoxication, they offered their own limbs to Samdhimati. They then applied some ointment on his body and with magic brought him back to life. The night was fast turning into day. Fearing that the witches would soon take their limbs back from the body, Guru Isana immediately went near the body and shouted loudly. All the witches vanished. Kalhana writes,[6] "Then their voice was heard: 'may you not be in fear, O Isana, we miss no limb, and do not defraud him whom we have chosen as our lover.' Dressed in a magnificent attire and priceless ornaments, Samdhimati got up and greeted his guru. Overwhelmed, the guru embraced the sage. For some time, the guru took care of him."

Meanwhile, there was no one to take over as king of the country. Jayendra had ruled for 37 years. It was then that the people requested Samdhimati to accept the throne of Kashmir. He reluctantly agreed and became the king.

Samdhimati Aryaraja

King Samdhimati's reign was titled Aryaraja. He was an intelligent king, but he ruled the kingdom briefly.[7] He was well acquainted with the rules and regulations of administration and overhauled the system. In spite of his religious inclinations, he devoted himself to the development of the country. His royal engagements kept him so busy that he even gave up going to temples for worship.

Gradually, things changed for him. Samdhimati Aryaraja's style of working was quite novel and fascinating. He spent the months of spring in the forests enjoying the beauty of nature and worshipping. During summer, he went above the forest ranges and enjoyed the snow that accumulated on mountain peaks. He prepared Lingas made of snow and worshipped them. Eventually, his initial religious fervour took over and he began spending more time in worship. He gave up looking after the day-to-day work of the administration of the state. He also vowed to pray before 1000[8] Shiva-lingas every day.

Ultimately, he abandoned the throne, became an ascetic and lived on alms. Fed up of his ways, the people began looking for another king. They found him in Meghavahana, a great grandson of Yudhisthira and son of Gopaditya.[9] Meghavahana constructed a temple named Isesvara after the name of his Guru Isana.

Six
Gonanda Dynasty Restored

Meghavahana

After King Aryaraja abandoned the kingship and started living on alms at the sacred site of Bhuteshwara temple, the throne of Kashmir remained vacant for a while. Left with no alternative, a minister of Aryaraja guided the people, went to Gandhara (Afghanistan) and brought Meghavahana, who was a descendent of the Gonanda family. He was the son of Gopaditya, a great grandson of Yudhisthira. On being approached to become the king, Meghavahana, who was famous for his valour, accepted the offer and was crowned the king of Kashmir. He was a staunch Buddhist, and, therefore, believed in non-violence and protection of all forms of life. As soon as he became the king, he issued his first proclamation to stop killing of animals. He compensated butchers paying them from the state treasury for their livelihood. He wanted to make the 'Prohibition of Killing' universal. For this, he was willing to go on a conquest of the world. Though Meghavahana was a Shaivite by religion, and a Buddhist by faith, he had respect for all religions. He also freed the Nag tribe from being prosecuted. They had inadvertently been arrested under his orders.

There is a legend about their arrest and subsequent release.

A legend has it that King Meghavahana was once spending some recreation time outside his palace when he heard people shouting "thief."[1] The king shouted back, "Arrest him." Thus, on his orders, some Nags were arrested and put in prison. The wives of the Nags decided to meet the king. A few days later, when he was going out on his horse, the Nag wives approached the king and told him that the farmers believed the Nags travelled on clouds. They informed him that the farmers were also afraid lest the Nags bring a hailstorm over their ripe paddy crop. They requested mercy and prayed to him for the release of their husbands. The kind-hearted king, having heard the women, ordered the release of the Nags, who remained thankful to the king.

Prior to Meghavahana's rule, human sacrifice was common. There was an incidence once of a person who wanted to sacrifice a man in order to appease the deity, to protect his ailing child. The king, on hearing it, offered himself to be sacrificed instead of the man. His offer turned the tables. No one was killed. The sacrifice to the Gods was not performed by sacrificing any living animal but the effigies[2] of animals made of pastry. The great coincidence was that during the night, the child recovered from his illness.Meghavahana maintained the precept of Buddhist faith by disallowing animal or human sacrifice.

He is known for having constructed a vihara. His queens, in their bid to outdo each other, built viharas and Stupas. One of the queens, Amritaprabha, a princess of Assam, built a vihara in her own name as Amritabhavan.[3] She also built a stupa in the name of her father's spiritual guru, who hailed from Loh (present Leh). Another queen Yukadevi, constructed a very beautiful and spacious stupa at Nadavana (Narvor in Srinagar). She placed an unmarried bhikshu in one half of the stupa, and a married bhikshu in the other half. Another queen of Meghavahana, known as Indradevi, built Indradevibhavana Vihara. Another queen, Khadana, also built a vihara in her name. The village was also named as Khandanyara. Queens, Yukadevi and Samma, also built viharas in their names. During Meghavahana's rule, both Buddhism and Shaivism flourished despite their apparent differences. People worshiped Buddha with the same reverence as they worshiped Shiva. Another legend about Meghavahana, this time pertaining to his conquests, is that he conquered Lanka.[4] King Vibhisana, the ruler of Lanka, received him warmly and gave him a lot of presents. Meghavahana ruled Kashmir for 34 years before he passed away.

S'resthasena Pravarasena

After the death of Meghavahana, his son, S'resthasena, became the king of Kashmir. He was a very brave and affectionate king. People found him like King Tunjina and he received the sobriquet, Tunjina, affectionately[5]. He constructed shrines and founded a town known as Pravarapura. He also constructed various holy shrines at Puranadhisthana, currently Pandrethan. One of his ministers by the name of Moraka also built a convent after his name. Pravarasena ruled Kashmir for 30 years.

Hiranya & Toramana

S'resthasena died leaving behind two sons, Hiranya and Toramana. Hiranya the elder brother became the king. But there was hostility between the two brothers. When the younger brother issued coins in his own name, Hiranya was infuriated and put him in prison. Toramana's pregnant wife Anjana feared that her brother-in-law would also persecute her. She went to a potter's house under the cover of darkness and gave birth to a son who was named Pravarasena II. Hiranya died issueless after ruling the country for 31 years. However, Pravarasena II did not make any claim for the throne. He preferred to serve his mother who was weak and ill.

The throne of Kashmir was without a king. The people became desperate and helpless because they could not raise the slogan "Long Live the King." It was then that a poet named Matrgupta recommended the name of Vikramaditya as king. He also assured the people he would make Vikramaditya agree to accept the kingship of Kashmir.

Vikramaditya

There is an interesting anecdote mentioned about Matrgupta. Being a poet of great repute, he was keen to impress King Vikramaditya with his poetic skills. He went to Ujjain. It is said that for six months he could not get an audience with the king. One night as he wandered near the palace, he heard the king calling his gatekeeper to light the lamps. All the palace lamps had run short of fuel and there was darkness. Strangely, no gatekeeper or attendant was available at that time. Hearing the king's voice, Matrgupta rushed to comply with the king's orders. While he was lighting a lamp, the king started a conversation with him. Matrgupta found his chance to relate the whole story to the king and requested him to take up the kingship of Kashmir.

King Vikramaditya read the letter sent by the ministers of Kashmir requesting him to take Kashmir under his rule. He replied to the ministers recommending Matrgupta as the best choice as the future king of Kashmir.He sent Matrgupta to Kashmir with instructions to the people that the poet was able and intelligent, and brave too, and that under his leadership the country would be prosperous and peace would prevail. Thus, Matrgupta became the king of Kashmir.

Matrgupta

People accepted Matrgupta as their king and were quite happy with his rule. He was a wise king who liked the company of wise people. Kalhana says,[6] "This king here is endowed with merits and is a friend of the virtuous. To comprehend his perfection turn (one must turn) to the king of the old times." Once, a poet known as Mentha, recited in honour of the king, a poem *Hayagrivavadha* describing the killing of the demon Hayagriva Vishnu. The King did not comment over it until the whole poem was finished. At the end when the poet began folding his book, the king placed a golden dish below it saying this was done to preserve the fragrance of the poem, which was excellent. Matrgupta was himself a great poet and wrote a commentary on Bharat Muni's *Natyashastra*. He is also regarded as the Kalidasa of Kashmir.

Matrgupta ruled Kashmir for about five years. He proved a successful ruler. He built a shrine of Madhusudhan and named it Matruptasvamin. Meanwhile, Vikramaditya passed away and when Matrgupta came to know about his death, he was overcome with shock and grief. He left the throne and went to Varanasi to adopt an ascetic life. When Pravarasena II heard this, he met him and persuaded him not to abandon the throne. Matrgupta instead persuaded Pravarasena II to take over the throne as he was adamant to go to Banaras for renunciation. According to Kalhana,[7] "Therefore, you being the foremost of the virtuous and praised by the wise, are truly, a tested jewel, highly valued by the righteous.... Hence do me (this) favour, do not abandon the throne. May it be also to my credit that I have sided with the virtuous."

Pravarasena II

Prior to Matrgupta, King Hiranya ruled Kashmir, but he had died issueless. Pravarasena II was the son of Hiranya's younger brother Toramana, whom he had imprisoned for issuing coins during his rule. Pravarasena II was, in fact, the real heir to the throne but he had chosen to live in obscurity and serve his ailing mother, who had escaped to give birth to him fearing the same treatment from his uncle. But Matrgupta ensured that the throne went back to him.

Pravarasena II became the king of Kashmir and is placed in the sixth century. But, curiously enough, he sent Matrgupta the yearly revenue that was collected from the kingdom. It must have been under an agreement that both made prior to him becoming the king. Pravarasena II made various conquests and subdued many other kings. He also invaded Saurashtra and destroyed his enemy. He helped Pratapasila alias Siladitiya, the son of Vikramaditya, to secure his throne after he was dethroned. He also brought back the throne of Kashmir, which was carried away by his enemies. He defeated King Mummuni seven times but pardoned him everytime. He was a great builder. He constructed a new town after his name, known as Pravarasenapura, and later it came to be known as Srinagar. He also constructed a wooden bridge and named it Brhatsetu on the river Vitasta near Maksikasvamin (presently Maisuma).

The legend goes that he killed a demon known as Vitala who lived in a village called Saritaka (Sharika of Hari Parbat). The demon, while dying, told him to build a town which Pravarasena did and named it after his own name. The king worshipped Hindu Gods—Lord Shiva and Vishnu, as well as Buddha. He built a vihara for Buddhist monks and his maternal uncle Jayendra constructed a huge statue of Buddha. How long he ruled Kashmir is not known. According to the *Imperial Gazetteer of India, Kashmir*,[8] "Pravarasena II reigned in the sixth century and, returning from his victorious campaigns abroad, built a magnificent city on the site of present capital of Kashmir. The city was known as Pravarapura, and is mentioned by Yuan Chwang at the time of his visit (AD, 631) as a new city."

Yudhisthira II

Yudhisthira II was born to Pravarasena II and his wife Ratnaprabha. After the death of his father, Yudhisthira II became the king of Kashmir. He ruled for 39 years and three months. During his rule, not only did he carry out many noble works but his ministers too constructed viharas and looked after the people of Kashmir. Writes Lal Mani Joshi,[9] "During the reign of Yudhisthira II, son and successor of Pravarasena, his ministers were Buddhists who constructed Viharas and Caityas. One of these (Viharas) is Skandabhavana vihara, built by the minister named Skandagupta."

Narendraditya/Lahkhana

The rule of King Yudhisthira II was mostly peaceful. After his death, his son Narendraditya from wife Padmavati became the King. He was also known as Lahkhana. He had trusted and pious ministers known as Vajra and Kanka, the sons of Vajrendra, who was a minister during the period of his father. King Narendraditya was married to Vimalaprabha. He ruled for 13 years.

Ranaditya

Ranaditya, brother of King Narendraditya, became the king of Kashmir. He was a brave and wise king and was ever ready to help his subjects. In return, he also earned the affectionate nickname of Tunjina, a former king much loved by his subjects for his inherent goodness. Cloaked in supernaturalism, there are many legends woven around Ranaditya and his wife Ranarambha. It was said that Queen Ranarambha was the shakti of Hindu Gods such as Vishnu and Shiva. According to SR Bakshi,[10] "One of Ranaditya's queens was a patron of Buddhism. She placed an image (probably Buddha's statue) in the vihara built by Bimba, a queen of Meghavahana." Another queen Amrtaprabha constructed a shrine, known as Amrtesvara where she placed a fine statue of Buddha in the vihara.

Legend of Ranaditya's previous life: A legend goes that Ranaditya was a gambler in his former life. Once he had lost everything including all his property. He was on the verge of committing suicide when he thought of going to meet Goddess Bhramaravasini whose abode was in a mountain cave. Covered with clay, cow-dung and metal armour, he entered the cave with great difficulty and was bitten by killer bees. Somehow, he managed to reach the goddess. Battered and bruised, he fell down. The goddess appeared in person, touched him, and transformed herself into a beautiful maiden. She then asked him to request one boon. He said he wanted to have a sexual union with her. The goddess was annoyed and surprised at his wish. She told him to ask for something else as it was an improper demand, but he was adamant. Ultimately, the goddess said, "So be it," but added it could not be in this life but in another life. With that, she disappeared. The gambler killed himself and was reborn as King Ranaditya and the goddess as Ranarambha.

He ruled over Kashmir with love and compassion for his subjects. Kalhana compared his love for his subjects with that of Rama of Raghuvansha. Ranaditya built the temple near Martanda. The royal couple also built Ranarambhasvamin, Ranarambhadeva, and a math for Pasupata. The famous Sun temple, Martanda, was however constructed by Lalitaditya during 8th century. It is difficult to say where the temple constructed by Ranaditya is.

His last days were also a fanciful legend, which says that his wife granted him magical powers. He crossed River Chandrabhaga, the modern Chenab, and reached the cave of a demon Namuci. Followed by all his people, he entered the cave where he breathed his last. Another legend about his reign, as described by Kalhana, is that he ruled the country for three hundred years. Commenting upon Kalhana, Maurice Winternitz writes,[11] "He is Indian in this respect as well that his chronology of earlier ages is often improbable. He makes King Ranaditya rule for 300 years – a thing that is not credible." P N K Bamzai wrote,[12] "Hasan, however, on the authority of Ratnakarpurama says that actually six kings were on the throne of Kashmir during that period – namely Tunjina, Sarabsena, Gandharsena, Lachmana, Surrka and Vajraditya." PNK Bamzai has nothing more to say about the administration of these six rulers. In this connection, Dr Pandita's translation of a Persian Chronicle of an unknown writer says,[13] "After him (Ranaditya), his son Onta Dev reigned for forty years...' However, how far this is true is not known."

Ranaditya's son Vikramaditya

Ranaditya's son, Vikramaditya, is supposed to have ruled Kashmir. He was a brave king who conquered many places. He also constructed a shrine known as Vikramesvara dedicated to God Shiva. He had two trusted ministers, Brahman and Galuna. Brahman built Brahmamatha, a vihara in his own name and Galuna constructed a vihara in the name of his wife

Ratnavali. King Vikramaditya ruled Kashmir for 42 years and then died. After his death, his elder brother Baladitya became the king.

Baladitya

Vikramaditya's eldest brother Baladitya ruled Kashmir for 37 years. This king was fearless and pious as well. He defeated the Vankalas [14]. He also founded an old-age home known as Kalambi, where the old, the sick and also travellers could be accommodated. He and his wife Bimba constructed this accommodation and other rest houses for the travellers of Kashmir.[15] The queen Bimba derived her name from the red lips she had, just like the Bimba fruit. She built the shrine of Shiva Bimbesvara in Aristotsadana. It was said that the temple could remove the misfortunes of the people.

The king's reaction to an astrologer's prediction: There is a story about Baladitya's daughter Anangalekha, who was considered exceptionally beautiful. Once, an astrologer saw her and told the king that his daughter's husband would be a conqueror of the world. Baladitya did not like the idea of his son-in-law becoming such a great conqueror that he could usurp his own kingdom. Therefore, instead of marrying her off into royal blood, he got her married to an employee who was in-charge of fodder for the horses—a handsome man named Durlabhavardhana. Little did the king know that the handsome man was a descendant of the Karkota dynasty. As per Kalhana,[16] "The king did not know that he was really born to the throne, (being the son) of the Naga Karkota who had cohabited with his mother when she took her purifying bath."

So, destiny had something else in store. Durlabhavardhana's good deeds earned him high positions in the kingdom to the extent that the king bestowed on him the title of Prajnaditya.

Anangalekha's paramour: Princess Anangalekha's marriage to Durlabhavardhana was not one based on fidelity. After marriage, she showed little regard for him. Gradually, she enticed a minister named Khankha. One night, when her husband entered his wife's chamber, he found her asleep with her paramour in a compromising position. He took out his sword to kill both of them but he did not do so. Instead, he left a note on the minister's dress: 'Remember that you have not been slain, though you deserve death.'

Khankha read the message Durlabhavardhana had written on his dress, and he was brought to his senses. He was desperate to redeem his status in his eyes and do something to subdue his anger. He refrained from meeting the princess. Gradually, the princess also suffered remorse and felt ashamed for straying outside her marriage. This episode marked the dawn of a new era in the history of Kashmir. Prem Nath Bazaz writes,[17] "The incident proved a turning point in her life and made her famous in history." Baladitya died without a son. That was the end of the Gonanda dynasty in Kashmir.

Seven
Beginning of Karkota Dynasty

Durlabhavardhana, 598-634 AD

King Baladitya's death marked the end of the Gonanda dynasty and the beginning of the Karkota-Naga dynasty after the minister Khankha, as a sign of gratitude to Durlabhavardhana, impressed upon the other ministers to make Anangalekha's husband the king of Kashmir. The suggestion was accepted and Durlabhavardhana became the king. He never spoke to anyone about the misdeed of his wife but gave her all the respect even after he took over as the king of Kashmir.

Queen Anangalekha constructed a vihara in her name called Anangabhavana. The King was blessed with a son, whom he named Malhana. Unfortunately, the astrologers predicted that the child had a short life. This made the king construct a shrine for Vishnu in the name of his son, Malhanasavamin. He also built another shrine of Vishnu and named it Durlabhasvdmin. After its completion he breathed his last. He died after ruling Kashmir for 36 years.

Durlabhavardhana was a benevolent person with true royal blood. His rule was marked by peace and prosperity. According to Ram Shankar

Tripathi,[1] "Durlabhavardhana had a long reign of 36 years. He won the friendship of Harsavardhana by giving him a prized tooth-relic of Buddha for enshrinement in Kannuaj." Politically, he became powerful. He captured all the adjacent territories including Parnotsa, (modern Poonch), Rajpura (modern Rajouri), Urasa or Hazara, etc. During his rule, Buddhism also flourished. The main language was Sanskrit. People from far off places came to Kashmir to study. According to Mark S G Dyczkowski,[2] "The first king of Tibet, Srong-Bcan-Sgampo, sent Thon-mi Sambhota to Kashmir during the reign of Durlabhavardhana (616 AD). He learnt Sanskrit from Devatitasimha and returned to Tibet with a modified thirty-letter version of the Kashmiri script. Kashmir continued to play a role in the transmission of Buddhism from India into Tibet."

According to James Hasting,[3] "Among the most famous pilgrims are Fa-Hien, who started his journey in AD 399; Sung-yun, whose travels took place between AD 518 and 522; I-Taing, who lived from AD 613 to 713; and particularly Yuan Chwang, who was absent from his home from AD 620 to 645." It must have been during 620 to 645 AD that Yuan Chwang visited the Valley. Anand Kaul[4] has mentioned that travellers from China visited Kashmir to study Buddhism. Yuan Chwang visited the valley in 631 AD and Ou-Kong, in 759 AD. Thomas Watters, translator of *Yuan Chwang's Travels India*, also confirms that Hiuen Tswang and Yuan Chwang, were in Kashmir from May 631 to April 633.

Yuan Chwang has given a detailed account of his visit to the Kashmir Valley. It is written that the then king of Kashmir extended them a warm reception. Writes Thomas Watters, the translator of *Yuan Chwang's Travels in India*,[5] "His majesty was attended by his grand ministers , and certain Buddhist monks from the capital, and he had a magnificent retinue of above 1,000 men." He further writes, "Neither the record nor the life gives the name of the king of Kashmir who so hospitably entertained our pilgrim." The period in question happens to be the time when Durlabhavardhana was ruling Kashmir. It is perhaps during this period that Yuan Chwang visited the Valley and stayed for two years. He relates [6] that from the capital of Kashmir he travelled to Poonch and then to Rajouri. In both cases, the towns were dependent on the king of Kashmir.

It was during Durlabhavardhana's rule that some of the books on Ontology were written. According to Andre Wink,[7] "Pancaratra ontology and ritual are enshrined in the Vishnudharmottara Purana, a text which is undated but on good grounds can be presumed to have been completed at the Kashmir court in the eighth century. Its composition was preceded by the *Nilamatapurana*, which is also of Kashmir (one of Kalhana's sources)and was completed probably at the court of Durlabhavardhana, the founder of Karkota dynasty, and the first king to constitute, in accordance with the text of the Purana, a state as a Pancaratra theophany…" (Pancaratra, literally meaning five nights, is Vaishnava Agama, the revelation of God Vishnu)

Durlabhaka Pratapaditya II, 634-684 AD

Durlabhaka-Pratapaditya II, son of Durlabhavardhana and Queen Anangalekha, ruled Kashmir for 50 years. He was a strong king and his glory and fame would chill the spine of his enemies.

He built the town of Pratapapora. During his rule, business flourished in the land. "Pratapapora is identified with the modern Tapar situated on the high road from Baramulla to Srinagar. It is confirmed when we read Sussala's retreat from Srinagar to Lohara," writes MA Stein[8].

A Merchant's Story: There is charming anecdote about the king. A merchant named Nona of Rauhitaka (present Multan) had constructed a math for the benefit of the Brahmins of Kashmir. The king came to know about it and he invited the merchant to his palace. Reciprocating the kind gesture, the merchant also invited the king. As soon as the king reached the merchant's house, he saw the merchant's beautiful wife Narendraprabha and fell in love with her. The attraction was mutual. However, the king refrained from expressing his desire to her. The king, according to Kalhana, said,[9] "If the King himself takes away the wives of the subjects, who else could punish the trespass of the law."

For a while, the king exercised restraint but the attraction did not wane. He could not forget the woman and at the same time could not forget his duties as a king. Frustrated, he fell ill. All the treatments given to him proved futile. The merchant came to know the cause of the king's illness. He took his wife to a temple and coaxed the king to marry her. But the king did not agree. At this, the merchant told the king that he was going to abandon Narendraprabha in the temple as she was a good dancer, and hoped that the king might accept her as a temple dancer. This worked. The merchant left her at the temple and the king accepted her as his queen.

He married Narendraprabha and had three sons from her—Chandrapida alias Vajraditya, Tarapida alias Udayaditya and Muktapida alias Lalitaditya. It is said that Narendraprabha gave birth to seven sons but Kalhana mentions only three She constructed a huge structure dedicated to Shiva known as Sri Narendreshvara.Durlabhaka Pratapaditya II was an efficient king. He would not depend on his ministers but would guide them in the working of the administration. During his tenure trade flourished in the country.

Chandrapida, 684-692 AD

Chandrapida Vajaraditya was crowned as the king of Kashmir after the death of his father since he was the eldest son. It was the time when Muhammad-bin Qasim, an Arab invader, threatened India including Kashmir. According to Sailendra Nath Sen,[10] "When Kashmir was threatened with an Arab invasion led by Muhammad-bin Qasim, Chandrapida sought the assistance of the Chinese emperor sending an envoy to him. Although no help came, Chandrapida was able to beat back the Arabs."

Chandrapida was an accomplished man, and completed all the work left by his predecessors. He was an illustrious, brave king known for dispensing justice to his people. His judgment was dispassionate and resolute. For him, everyone was equal before the law. He saw to it that people got justice even if it was a low-caste person fighting against the king himself. Kalhana[11] records that once the king had ordered the construction of a temple Tribhuvanaswamin at a certain place. While clearing the area for construction, it was found that the hut of a poor leather-tanner was in the way. When asked by the officers of the king to leave the hut and settle somewhere else, the tanner refused. The king came to know about it and shouted at his officers to "stop the building, or have it constructed elsewhere." The tanner then sought the king's audience outside the court and told him that if he personally came to his hut to ask for it, "in accordance with propriety," he would part with it. The king accepted and went personally to the tanner's hut, paid the price for the hut and purchased it from the owner.

Believer of Human Rights: During Chandrapida's eight-and-a-half-year reign, recognition of human dignity and human rights was the most important aspect of the rule of law. His sense of justice was considered impeccable. There are many stories wherein justice was intelligently disbursed by the king. It is said that once he awarded punishment to a Brahmin who had secretly committed the murder of another Brahmin by means of witchcraft. The Brahmin was very angry and wanted revenge. So he joined hands with Tarapida, the king's younger brother and both of them manipulated and killed the king with the use of witchcraft.

It is difficult to believe that the king died of witchcraft. Perhaps, some other way such as the use of poison could have led to the king's death. However, Kalhana says it was the first instance when witchcraft was used to slay a king, and from then onwards, other princes resorted to witchcraft to claim or secure thrones.

According to Ram Shankar Tripathi[12], "Chandrapida, the second predecessor of Muktapida, received investiture as king from the Emperor of China in 720 AD." During his rule, the caste system seemed quite prevalent. For example, when the tanner sought the king's audience, he was not allowed to enter the king's court but had the audience outside the palace court. When he vacated his hut for construction[13] of the temple, the place was purified. Chandrapida did his best to improve the condition of the people and during his short tenure there was improvement and affluence all around. His queen Prakashadevi built the Prakasha vihara. His Guru Mihiradatta also built a temple of Vishnu at Sangam near Khannabal, where three rivers meet.

Tarapida, 692-696 AD

Tarapida /Udayaditya acquired the throne of Kashmir by the cruel means of fratricide—killing his brother in connivance with the murderer Brahmin. He ruled Kashmir for a very short period, a little more than four years. But his rule, according to Kalhana, was the darkest period in the reign of kings. It created uneasiness everywhere. People were horrified by the terror he created; they could not escape the wrath of the king and were subjected to severe hardships and miseries. Tarapida also started punishing the Brahmins although it was a Brahmin who helped him become king. As a consequence, the Brahmins used their witchcraft to kill him. The irony of fate is that he died with the same weapon which he had used to kill his elder brother.

Lalitaditya Muktapida, 696-733 AD

Lalitaditya means 'the beautiful Sun'. King Lalitaditya immortalised himself into the annals of the history of Kashmir. In fact, one can safely say that his brilliance shines not only in Kashmir history but also in Indian history. He always puzzled his contemporaries. To some, he was a brave soldier, to others he was an admirer of intellectualism, and yet some others thought he was a great architect. King Lalitaditya is a name worth mentioning for the reason that he was a man of valour who conquered almost the whole of Northern India up to China. Kashmir, under his rule, was the most powerful state. The boundaries had extended from Tibet in the east to Iran and Turkey in the west, and from Central Asia in the north to Orissa and the seashores of Dwarka (Gujarat) in the west. According to MA Stein,[14] "The name of Lalitaditya or Muktapida is found in the Chinese Annals of the T'ang dynasty. These record the arrival of an emissary from Mu-To-pi, King of Kashmir, during the reign of the Emperor Hiuen Tsang, AD 713 – 755 and after the first Chinese expedition against Po-liu (Baltistan), which took place between the years 736 – 747 AD. They had requested an alliance against the Tibetans, and the dispatch of a Chinese auxiliary force, which was to encamp in the midst of his (Lalitaditya's) country on the shore of Mahapadma lake (Wular Lake)."

His vision was not limited only to the valley of Kashmir but spanned the mountain peaks beyond Kashmir to the places where he wanted to assert his authority. It is evident, that in addition to his excellent command over planning war strategies, he had a strong and dedicated army. The glory of his valour and conquests was adored by Kalhana[15] who wrote, "Then the illustrious King Lalitaditya became the universal monarch, he who was far beyond the conception of fate which creates only rulers of limited territories." He made a conquest of modern Turkey, a victory which was celebrated by the people of Kashmir at the end of the month of Chaitra. Says Alberuni[16], "Such was the king's fury against his enemy that it only eased and was over when the enemy kings folded their hands at their defeat."

"Early in the eighth century, an important name Yasovarman established an empire at Kavyakubja(modern Kannauj), who for a while controlled much of the north, but which soon fell to Lalitaditya, one of the few kings of Kashmir to play an important part in the politics of Gangetic plains,"[17] says AL Basham.

Writes RC Majumdar,[18] "But the best period of Kashmir history is the one in which she enjoyed a brief spell of imperialism under Lalitaditya. All that was good and bright in a nation brilliantly shone forth, and a petty provincial state was raised to the pinnacle of glory by succession of an eminent ruler. The history of Kashmir since that date is written in decay." He was a terror to the enemy. Kalhana says,[19] "At the sound of his drums (beaten) in attack, the dwellings of his enemies were deserted by the (frightened) inhabitants and thus resembled women dropping in fright the burden of their wombs."He further says, "He made the enemies wives, on whose face the ends of the (painted) forehead marks become detached, and whose tears were flowing, perform as it were oblations to the Pitrs (nivapa) with folded hands." (With folded hands, Hindus offer water to their ancestors). These are the attributes mentioned by Kalhana in *Rajatarangini,* about the great King Lalitaditya.

Lalitaditya's Expeditions: Lalitaditya was the third son of Durlabhaka-Pratapaditya II who took over the reins of Kashmir after the death of his elder brother Tarapida. Much of his glory is attributed to his great conquests leaving many of his enemies terror-stricken at the mere thought of his name. He spent 37 years of his life, during his reign, as a conqueror, and carried expeditions to different parts of the adjoining countries. He invaded and conquered many countries in Asia and India. The Punjab, Kannuaj, Tibet, Ladakh, Badakhshan, Iran, Bihar, Gauda (Bengal), Kalinga (Orissa), South India, Gujarat, Malwa, Marwar and Sind were all conquered by him. It was he, who finally broke the power of the Arabs in Sind. He had a great desire to conquer the world. The logic he gave was that he wanted to conquer all the countries through which flowed the rivers originating from his land until they reached the sea. For conducting these invasions and conquests, he needed a well-trained army and seems to have successfully undertaken the training of soldiers who could not only invade but also conquer the enemy. One remarkable thing about him was that unlike the Muslim invaders, he would not destroy or loot temples, nor would he kill people.

Writes RC Majumdar,[20] "He (Lalitaditya) entered into an alliance with Yasovarman and defeated the Tibetans. Like Yasovarman, and probably for similar reasons, he sent a diplomatic mission to the Chinese emperor in order to induce him to make common cause against the Tibetans. This mission was received with honour by the emperor who recognised the king of Kashmir as his royal ally, but no military assistance was sent from China. But even unaided, Lalitaditya succeeded in defeating not only the Tibetans but also the mountainous tribes on the north and north-west frontier of his kingdom such as Dards, Kambojas and Turks." However, Reynaud[21] seems to have serious doubts about Lalitaditya's conquests particularly at the time when Arabs began coming from the north to India.

The story of a faithful minister: Once, on an expedition, a man came and prostrated before the elephant the king was riding. The king saw blood dripping from his hands and asked the man to relate what had happened to him. The man informed the king that he was a minister in the kingdom of Gauda (Bengal) near the desert and that he was very faithful to his king. He said that when he told his king to submit to the powerful King Lalitaditya to save the kingdom from destruction, the king punished him by cutting off his hands.

King Lalitaditya was furious and assured him that he would punish his master. The injured minister was looked after well. After a few days, the minister again told the king that he wanted to avenge the insult as early as possible. He said that the normal route to his kingdom would take more than three months; however, he knew a shorter route that would take only fifteen days. He cautioned the king that the route was sandy and there was no water. Therefore, the king ordered that water be carried on the expedition. The march started through the desert. After three days, King Lalitaditya found that his soldiers were exhausted by thirst. He wanted to know from the minster how much more time it would take to reach the kingdom as the army was on the verge of death. The minister laughed and told the king sarcastically that the route he was taking would lead them to the kingdom of Yama (the God of death). He informed him that he was loyal to his king and that is why he had sacrificed his life to save him and his kingdom. Hearing this Lalitaditya was aghast, and enraged. Without losing time, he ordered his men to dig the earth to find water. To their good luck, they found water and the army was saved. They returned and took the proper route to the kingdom. Subsequently, King Lalitaditya punished the minister and his master.

He received many tributes from the kings and wore the turban of victory in the Antarvedi, the region between river Ganga and Yamuna. The land of Kannuaj, from the banks of Yamuna to the banks of the Kalika came under his sway. He went on conquering one kingdom after another. Having conquered Bharatvarsha, he turned his march towards the north — Porushpura, Taxila and Gandhara. He proceeded to Bokhara and Turkistan defeating all the rulers of the region. He also conquered small kings adjoining the valley of Kashmir such as Kishtwar, Parnotsa and Rajouri. He not only conquered these small rajas but annexed their kingdom with Kashmir state. He annexed Ladakh with his kingdom.

His Machiavellian wisdom is reflected in his policy towards his progeny and towards his subjects. He imparted his views on administration by giving instructions to his ministers before he started his expedition towards the north. He cautioned them against the Carvakas tribe, an atheist sect that came up around Kashmir at that time. When Lalitaditya went on his expeditions to the north, he felt he might not be able to return for a long time. So, he ordered his ministers that they should continue to rule over Kashmir but he laid down some instructions. An instruction to the agriculturist of the country was that the ministers should not be given more rice than they needed for the whole year, otherwise they would become lazy.

He instructed his ministers that of his two sons—Kuvalayaditya and Vajraditya—the elder Kuvalayaditya be made the king in the event of his death and that no one should express grief. It is said that Lalitaditya disappeared on the Zojila Pass while he was returning from the expedition after conquering Persia. His period is treated as one of the best periods in the history of Kashmir. He was brave, intelligent and a good administrator too. However, his extraordinary trait was his respect for human rights.

The scholars of his period: Lalitaditya respected all religions. He patronised men of learning and invited foreign scholars. The vihara he constructed hummed with literary activities. He brought Artigupta, the ancestor of Abhinavagupta, to Kashmir. Artigupta was a great scholar of Kannuaj. The king gave him a mansion to live in near Chandramulisvara temple on the banks of River Vitasta. Dharmottaracharya flourished during his region. Dharmakirti was a great Buddhist scholar of Kashmir. Being a logician, he wrote treatises known as *Pramanaviniscaya* and *Nyayabindhu*. Vakpatiraja was a great scholar during Lalitaditya's period. He authored *Prakrit Kavya* and *Gaudavah*. Another scholar Jayanta was a minister in his cabinet. Artigupta was designated as 'Gopta' a title granted to a learned person by the king.

The architectural excellence of Lalitaditya: Lalitaditya evinced interest in other spheres of life besides his conquests. He had a penchant for architectural brilliance. Art and trade received importance during his reign. Religious festivals were rife. He provided special facilities and encouragement to paintings and sculpture. He was also a successful writer himself and a Veena player. Like Asoka, he is considered one of the greatest rulers of Kashmir.

Martanda the Sun Temple: Lalitaditya built Martanda, the most spectacular architectural marvel which has earned a place among the world's greatest architectural designs. Located about eight km from Anantnag town, the temple is dedicated to Bhaskara, the Sun God. It is an expression of Kashmir's pristine glory. Lalitaditya built several towns in the name of his wives. He constructed a vihara where literary discourses were held. The two architectural marvels by which he is remembered even today are the Martanda temple and the town of Parihaspura, also called the city of pleasure. Writes Charles Hugel Baron,[22] "The city (Parihaspura) was built by the great conqueror Lalitaditya, who reigned from AD 714 to 750. It was adorned with many fine temples and monuments; among others, with a pillar cut out of one stone, twenty four yards high, at the top of which stood the image of Garuda, half-man and half-eagle."

The legend: There is an interesting story about the discovery of two temples. Once, when the king went to train a horse, he left the city and reached a secluded place. Suddenly, he heard someone singing. Following the voice, he saw two very pretty girls. One was singing and the other dancing. When he asked them who they were, they replied that they were dancing girls belonging to a temple in the village of Suravardhamana. They explained that their mothers used to perform there as per tradition but did not know the reason why they too performed at that particular spot. The king ordered excavation of the place the next day and found two temples with images of Kesava. On the base was engraved that Rama and Lakshmana constructed these temples.

The king constructed two separate stone buildings by the side of the temples—Vishnu Parihasa on one side and the image of Ramasvamin on the other. The two girls were made in-charge of the temple. But Stein has not been able to find such a place or these temples. According to Younghusband,[23] "But it is at Martanda that there is the finest structure, typical of Kashmir architecture at its best, built on the most sublime site occupied by any building in the world—better than the site of Parthenon, or of the Taj, or of St Peters, or of the Estuarial...." Among the towns Lalitaditya founded are Suniscitapura, Phalapura, Lalitapura (modern Latpore), and Lokapunya. Among the temples he constructed, the most remarkable was the Martanda temple later destroyed by vandals. The other temples are: Kridaramaat in Parnotsa, Aditya shrine at Lalitapura, Parihasakesava, Muktakesava, Govardhanadhara, Jyestharudra, and Brhadbuddha. Cakramardika, the queen of Lalitaditya, constructed a town with 7,000 houses. Kamaladevi, the king's consort, got a large silver image installed and named it Kamalahatta.

Lalitaditya collected many wise men from various countries. From Tuhakara, he brought Cankuna, who became his minister and was a brother of the great magician Kankanavarsa. Cankuna belonged to the Tuhakara tribe of China. He was endowed with great qualities and gradually attained an important position in the court. Isanadevi, the wife of Cankuna, constructed a big pond full of water where invalids would take a bath and become healthy.

It would be worthwhile to state that the political conditions that prevailed in the adjoining countries helped in making Lalitaditya's conquests rather easy. For instance, the Guptas ruled northern India for three centuries but lost their sheen because of defections among the rulers, as well as misrule and corruption. Lalitaditya took advantage of these prevailing conditions. When he killed King Gauda, his irate soldiers wanted to avenge his death. They came to Kashmir on the pretext of making a pilgrimage to Sarada temple. On reaching there, the soldiers destroyed the temple, which was very sacred to Lalitaditya. Immediately, an army came from Srinagar and killed the enemy. Kalhana has praised the soldiers of Kashmir. If Lalitaditya is named as the Alexander of Kashmir, it would not be an exaggeration. He was an alcoholic like Alexander. Once in a drunken fit he ordered the whole city of Srinagar to be set on fire. Fortunately, his ministers saved the city by burning grass somewhere. The next morning, when he heard that the ministers had saved the city of Srinagar he was very pleased with them. Many questions regarding Lalitaditya's rule still await satisfactory explanation. However, it goes without saying, that he was an admirable king of enormous sagacity.

Kuvalayapida, 733-734 AD

Lalitaditya died far away from his home leaving behind his wives and sons to look after the country. Kuvalayapida, his eldest son from his wife Kamaladevi, became the king of Kashmir. He was a noble and god-fearing king. He gave equal powers to his younger brother in running the administration. Initially, the administration ran smoothly and people were very happy with their rule. But with the younger brother also assuming the same powers, there arouse a dual administration and a situation where ministers changed their loyalties from one brother to the other to benefit themselves. Being a decent, honest and straight-forward king, Kuvalayapida got fed up with the affairs of the administration and the games of his ministers. He gave up the throne and went to the forest to seek penance.

Before leaving, he wanted to punish the ministers in his anger. However, he remembered a parable from the Hindu scriptures where the Gods churned the sea and out came the poison and the nectar. Lord Shiva kept the poison in his throat to save mankind. Kuvalayapida's anger vanished and he immediately renounced the throne and went to a forest named Plaksaprasravana. However, before he left for the forest he wrote on the throne, "Go straight to the forest, O my good friend. Devote yourself to the austerities. Such fortune like this is bound to decay and vanish in a moment." The king started his renunciation in the forest. However, on learning the news of the sudden death of his son Mitrasarman, he drowned himself in the river Vitasta in a state of shock. The queen also followed him. Kuvalayapida ruled for only one year.

Vajraditya, 734-741 AD

Vajraditya, the brother of Kuvalayapida, and son of Lalitaditya, was also known by the names, Bappiyaka and Lalitaditya. He was born to Queen Cakramardika. The death of his brother came as a boon to him and he became the king. He was very different from his brother and was a womaniser. His seraglio boasted of a large collection of women. He stopped all constructions in Parihaspura which had been started by his father and became engrossed in wine, women and wealth. To amass wealth, he even sold his own subjects to Arab Muslims as slaves.

After ruling the kingdom for seven years, this sinful king died of his excessive drinking. He left behind three sons – Prthivyapida born to

Queen Manjarika, Samgramapida-1 and Jayapida were born to Queen Mamma.

Prthivyapida, 741-746 AD

Like his father King Vajraditya, Prthivyapida was corrupt and sadistic by nature. During his tenure, he treated his subjects like animals. He ruled for four years.

Samgramapida I, 746 AD

Samgramapida I, son of Vajraditya, and younger brother of Prthivyapida, was born to Queen Mamma. He overthrew his brother and ruled the country only for seven days. His sudden death enabled Jayapida, the youngest among the brothers, to ascend the throne.

Jayapida Vinayaditya, 746-747 AD

Prior to Jayapida's coronation as king, Kashmir had plunged into great turmoil. The enemies had raised their heads and there was disturbance everywhere. Jayapida was a vindictive and ambitious ruler. He wanted to teach a lesson to those rulers who had been subjugated by his grandfather Lalitaditya but had now raised their heads. So he set out to fight his enemies. But he refused to take help from other princes and went with a handful of his men. While he was away on his expedition, his brother-in-law, Jajja, fraudulently captured the throne of Kashmir.

Jajja, 747-750 AD

Jayapida remained out of Kashmir for three years, and for those three years, Jajja ruled the country. When he came back, another battle awaited him for he had to fight Jajja's soldiers. Jajja was essentially a notorious and despotic ruler and had developed a reputation for cruelty and excessive brutality. He did not care for his subjects, and all along, he was haunted by the thought of King Jayapida's return.

When Jayapida returned to Kashmir, Jajja was ready with his forces. A fierce battle took place at a village called Suskaletra /Hukhaletro. It was to Jayapida's advantage that the subjects were unhappy with Jajja's misrule, so all the villagers joined hands with Jayapida.

A Candala known as Sridev went in search of Jajja. He asked the villagers about his forces. Since the villagers were disgruntled with the king, they informed Sridev about his whereabouts and pelted Jajja and his soldiers with stones. The king fell from his horse seriously wounded and his men fled from the scene of battle. It became an easy victory for Jayapida. An overjoyed Sridev said, 'There I have slain Jajja'.[24] That marked the end of Jajja who ruled Kashmir for only three years.

Jayapida Vinayaditya, 750-781 AD (Second Term)

Jayapida, the youngest son of Vajraditya ascended the throne after the death of his brothers, Prthivyapida and Samgramapida-1. He was an illustrious king. He wanted to tread in the footprints of his grandfather Lalitaditya and collected a force of 8,000 soldiers for his conquest of other countries.

But much time had passed since Lalitaditya's reign; the kings of Kashmir had hardly made any conquests since then, The soldiers were slack and lacked experience in warfare. The Arabs had better facilities for warfare. Jayapida had to cope with tired soldiers who were restless to return home. Allowing his soldiers and officers to return to their homes, he went alone further until he reached Paundravardhan, (capital of modern Bengal). There he remained under the protection of Prince Jayanta of Bengal.

Romantic twist: There is a beautiful story about the good luck that came to Jayapida in Bengal. He was the royal guest and was known as Rajaputra Kallata as he had concealed his true identity. He met a court dancer Kamala and fell in love with her. He was a strong-willed man and resisted the dancer although he became friendly with her. While at her palace, she wanted to make love with the charming prince. Without offending her, he told her that he had vowed not to indulge in any pleasure until he finished his incomplete task.

One day, Jayapida went to the riverbank to say his prayers. He sat there until it was dark and returned to his beloved dancer. He found her in a state of nervousness. He asked her the reason. She told him, "No one here roams until so late as a lion was found roaming around. The lion has killed many people. No one has been able to kill the beast." The next night, Jayapida went into the forest and waited for the lion. The lion came and pounced upon the prince. With great swiftness, Jayapida put his elbow into the mouth of the lion and with his other hand tore its belly with a dagger. The lion was killed. When his host King Jayanta came to know about the extraordinary feat, he was very impressed. He subsequently came to know that his guest was none other than Jayapida of Kashmir. He decided to marry his only daughter

Kalyanadevi to him. In this way, Jayapida became the king of Bengal after the death of Jayanta. He annexed many countries to his territory in Bengal and then went back to conquer his birthplace Kashmir. In this fight, the state army opposed Jayapida but the people and villagers came to his aid in his fight against his brother-in-law Jajja, who had usurped the throne during his three year absence.

Jayapida's dare-devilry: Once Jayapida went stealthily into the fort of Bhimasena, king of the eastern region, who lived the life of an ascetic. Siddha, the brother of Jajja, was there and he recognised Jayapida. He alerted Bhimasena and poisoned his ears. Jayapida was imprisoned but managed to escape from the prison using a novel trick. At that time, Bhimasena's country was hit by plague. Jayapida ate a broth which gave him high fever. He manipulated his jailors into believing he was struck by plague. Knowing how infectious plague was, they let him escape.

Jayapida's Nepal expedition: Jayapida launched an expedition to Nepal subjugating the other kings along the way until he reached Nepal. When he saw Aramudi's army, he was furious. Both armies faced each other on the two banks of the river. Jayapida attacked the army of Aramudi with full force and tried to cross the river. When his army was midway, a sudden swell in the river swept off all his soldiers, elephants and horses. The water was only knee-deep when the invaders stepped into the river, but the Nepalese troops let out the water that was harnessed by a dam. Suddenly, the river was flooded and the enemies were washed away. Jayapida was arrested and imprisoned but very cleverly escaped from prison.

According to Perceval Landon,[25] "A certain king of Kashmir, named Jayapida, flushed with other conquests, attempted to subdue Nepal also. The Nepalese sovereign, Aramudi, went to meet him and, as usual, secured a notable victory. The army of Jayapida was cut to pieces, and the intruder himself was shut up in a remote tower on the edge of the Black Gandak. But one of his ministers, wandering in search of his master, heard the songs of Kashmir dolefully intoned from the barred windows of the tower, and at the cost of his own life enabled Jayapida to escape."

However, according to MA Stein[26], Aramudi of Nepal does not appear in the list of kings of Nepal nor is anything about Bhimasena known.

Jayapida respected learned people. He brought learned people to Kashmir from outside who taught him *Ramayana* and *Mahabharata*.

These learned people became his advisers. A great patron of learning, he appointed Ksirasvamin, a well-known grammarian commentator on *Amarakosa* (Sanskrit Dictionary) and *Nirukta* (Vedic Dictionary). Udbhata alias Bhattodbhata, the sabhapati of King Jayapida, earned a salary of one Lakh dinars. Writes Jeffrey Moussaieff Masson, M V Patwardhan,[27] "It was under King Jayapida that the school of literary criticism in Kashmir originated. The sabah to which Udbhata was appointed as director was doubtless a panditasabha rather than a political body." Also Vamana, author of *Kavyalankara Sutra*, is believed to have been a minster of King Jayapida but later he migrated to the court of King Govinda III. King Govinda III was very powerful and had his territory from Cape Comorin to Kannuaj and from Banaras to Broach.

Damodaragupta, perhaps the most original and classical Sanskrit poet and author of *Kuttanimatam*, was Jayapida's chief adviser. Other poets who flourished at that time were Manoratha, Sankhadanta, Cataka and Samdhimat. According to Jia Lal Kilam,[28] "He (Jayapida) was a great conqueror and lover of learning. Katayana's commentary on Panini was re-compiled. Vasugupta, the founder of Shaiva philosophy, belongs to that era; and so do many other philosophers and poets of great renown." Jayapida was also a lover of music and dance and architecture. According to AM Shastri,[29] "King Jayapida, is said to have gone to the temple of Skanda at Paundravardhan in order to witness a dance performed in accordance with Bharat's instructions."

Jayapida the builder: Jayapida built a city named Jayapura near the Wular Lake. He also built a strong fort there around marshy land so that no enemy could come. His two queens, Kalyanadevi, and Kamaladevi founded the towns of Kalyanpura and Kamlapura respectively. The king's mother Amrtaprabha, built a temple in her name as Amrtakeshava.

Jayapida had respect for Buddhism and helped Buddhists by giving them grants. According to Sunil Chandra Ray in *Early History and Culture of Kashmir* [30], "Jayapida Vinayaditya, another celebrated monarch of the Karkota family set up three images of Buddha and a large Vihara at his newly founded town Jayapura."

Jayapida's Oppression: Given his long expeditions, it was but natural that the treasury of the kingdom had almost become empty. Jayapida displayed excellent valour and great tenacity against all odds but showed great weakness when he saw his treasury empty. To finance his conquests of other lands, he collected copper from copper mines and minted enormous coins in his name, but that destroyed the financial management of the country. He, therefore, became a tyrant. In order to fill the treasury, to maintain his army, as well as run the administration, heavy doses of revenue tax were announced, to the extent that cultivators were given nothing for their produce. He also targeted the Brahmins inviting their wrath. Kalhana writes,[31] "The greedy officers of finance such as Shivadasa and others excited his desires for treasure beyond measure and he became prey to avarice." The poets wrote satires about him. The refrain of the satires was that Jayapida, who was holding a glorious position, had come down to becoming a killer of Brahmins.

The legend: In his bid to fill the coffers, the king wanted to confiscate the land around Tulamulla, a sacred worship place for Brahmins. But when he heard that ninety-nine Brahmins were ready to die for that place, he refrained from confiscating the land. Instead, he tried to humiliate the Brahmins who told him that no king had so far disrespected them. They warned him that if he continued to humiliate them they could curse him. At this, the king laughed, and, according to Kalhana, haughtily asked them,[32] "Who art thou then? Vishvamitra or Vashistha or perhaps Agastya, treasure of asceticism." This added fuel to the fire. A Brahmin said,[33] "If you are Harishchandra, Trisanku, or Nahusa too, then I singly can be more than Vishvamitra and the other Rishis." One of the Brahmins tapped the earth and said, "Let the staff of Brahmins fall." Just then, one of the golden poles attached to the canopy, broke and fell on the king and wounded him. The wound decomposed and the limb had to be amputated. Soon the pain increased and the king died of pain.

Lalitapida,781-793 AD

After the death of Jayapida, his son Lalitapida from Queen Durga became the king. He squandered the wealth collected by his father through frivolous activities. Unlike his father, he respected the Brahmins and did not confiscate their wealth. He married Jayadevi, the daughter of Uppa Kalyapali, a spirit–distiller and a trader whom people looked down upon. Jayadevi, being quite pretty, the king took her as a concubine. According to Prem Nath Bazaz,[34] "King Lalitapida took as his spouse Jayadevi a courtesan and the great Avantivarman was born of a girl whose parents were spirit-distillers." Lalitapida's rule was not smooth. People were miserable and the king was busy with his own wicked activities. However, he granted the Brahmins, the jageers of Suvarnaparsva, Phalapura and Locanotsa. He ruled for twelve years and then died.

Samgramapida II, 793-800 AD

After Lalitapida's death, his younger brother, Samgramapida II, also known as Prthivyapida, born to Queen Kalyanadevi took over the reins of Kashmir. After ruling for seven years, he was replaced. His rule was short and devoid of any extraordinary event.

Cippata-Jayapida 800-812 AD

Cippata-Jayapida was the minor son of Lalitapida from Queen Jayadevi, who was the concubine of the King. When he was young, he was guided by five ministers, his maternal uncles—Padma, Utpala, Kalyan, Mamma and Dharma. Lalitapida had squandered most of Jayapida's wealth, and whatever remained was squandered by Utpala and his brothers. Suddenly these brothers grew very jealous of their nephew who was emerging as a grown-up man. He had started taking independent decisions in the administration of the country. Kalhana says,[35] "These low-born persons, who knew no restraint in their actions, feared their fall as the king, their nephew, gradually emerged from childhood." In order to capture the throne, they connived to kill him.

Cippata-Jayapida ruled for twelve years with the help of his uncles. After the death of their nephew, the brothers began fighting each other for the throne. Hence, no one became the king. However, Utpala played an important role in choosing the next king. Tribhuvanapida who was the eldest son of Vajaraditya was not accepted as the king of Kashmir but Utpala managed to make another son of Vajraditya named Ajitapida as the king. He had his own evil designs for choosing Ajitapida. During his rule, Cippata-Jayapida's mother, Jayadevi, though daughter of a spirit distiller, was magnanimous and very much respected. She constructed a temple and named it Jayeshvara.

Ajitapida, 812-849AD

Ajitapida, son of Vajraditya, was born to Queen Jayadevi (not Cippata-Jayapida's mother) and remained a puppet in the hands of Utpala and his brothers Padma, Mamma and Dharma. For all practical purposes, the country was ruled by Utpala and his brothers while the king remained one only in name and was provided with living expenses. These thugs appropriated all the revenue of the country. They spent state money in building towns, temples and edifices. Utpala constructed a temple named Utpalasvamin at his town Utpalapora; Padma built a Vishnu temple Padmasvamin at Padampura. Kalhana says,[36] "The dynasty of the kings from the Karkota race was almost destroyed and the family of Utpala's descendants obtained great might."

Utpala and his brothers virtually ruled Kashmir for 36 years and nine months. They almost emptied the state treasure building temples and towns in honour of their names. But the jealousy-ridden Mamma and Utpala became hostile towards each other. There was a big fight between the soldiers of the two in which Yasovarman, Mamma's son came out victorious. Both Mamma and his son then removed the king and placed Anangapida, son of Samgramapida-II, as the king. A famous poet of that period known as Sankuka wrote a poem called *Bhuvanabhyudaya* (The Rise of the World) giving details of the period. During this period Padma laid the foundation of a town known as Padampura (modern Pampore)

Anangapida, 849-852 AD

The change of guard with Anangapida replacing Ajitapida irked Sukhavarman, Utpala's son. However, he could do no harm to Anangapida who remained king for three years. Meanwhile, Sukhavarman, the son of Utpala, became powerful. He collected an army and defeated Mamma. After that, he dethroned Anangapida and made Utpalapida, son of , the king.

Utpalapida 852-854 AD

Utpala's son, Sukhavarman, succeeded in ousting King Anangapida and making Utpalapida the king, as per Stein.[37] Kalhana in a satirical remark has compared these kings to Pisachas as mentioned in *Nilamatapurana*[38] who were ordered by Nila-Nag to live around Satisar for six months and leave the palace for six months. The *Nilamatapurana* says, "For six months, he lives happily on the Himacala (present day Himachal). From today, I have allotted to him a dwelling-place here for six months (of each year). You shall have to live here for six months with him along with his armies and for six months, after his departure, in the company of men."

Nonetheless, some ministers could attain sufficient powers even during these unsettled times. For instance, Ratna, foreign minister during

Utpalapida's reign had assumed great powers. Nara and another minister also wielded power in the kingdom. Such activities contributed to the destruction of the Karkota dynasty. There were puppet kings placed on the throne and, therefore, came the end of this dynasty. Meanwhile, Utpalapida's own relation, Suska, killed Sukhavarman out of sheer hatred. Suska was considered a wise man and an able prime minister. Disgusted by the working of the puppet kings, he worked for a direct accession of Sukhavarman's son named Avantivarman to the throne of Kashmir. Avantivarman ousted King Utpalapida and declared himself as the king of Kashmir. With this came the end of the Karkota dynasty.

Eight
Dawn of Utpala Dynasty

Avantivarman 855-883 AD

A man of wisdom and culture, Avantivarman was the son of Sukhavarman and grandson of Utpala. He was made the king of Kashmir with the help of Suska, the wise and able prime minister. He is believed to be the first Vaishnavite ruler of Kashmir. He was also good looking and debonair. Unlike Jayapida, or for that matter Lalitaditya, Avantivarman did not take any expeditions of conquests to any neighbouring or far off countries. Previous expeditions by kings had emptied the treasury. So, Avantivarman concentrated on looking after the people and made every attempt to improve the financial condition of the state. He succeeded in restoring the financial health of the country and started giving alms to the poor.

He initially had to face many battles. He even had to fight his own brothers. However, not only did he manage to subdue them but he also succeeded in maintaining law and order and brought peace in the state. Being wise and intelligent, he bestowed on Suravarman the honour of Yuvaraj, the prince or heir to the throne. Yuvaraj Suravarman, his stepbrother, was a pious and accomplished person. He constructed an agrahara in the village of Panachasta (modern Panzath) in the Devasar Pargana. In this village, there is a large spring named Pancahastakanaga (the name is mentioned in *Nilamatapurana*),[1] from where the Vitasta originally flowed. There are no remains now in the neighbourhood which could be identified as a math (where people could learn religion) as recorded by Kalhana. Suravarman granted jageers to the needy and built maths (pilgrimage centres). Kalhana lists many temples and towns built by the king or the Yuvaraj. Even Mahodaya, Suravarman's doorkeeper built a shrine of Vishnu in his own name as Mahodayasvamin, and appointed Ramata for the recitation of shlokas at the temple. Ramata was famous for his work on grammatical sciences.

Passion for art and literature: During Avantivarman's period, literature also flourished in the country. Anandavardhana was the poet. He is the author of two works *Dhvanyaloka* and *Devisataka*. Ratnakara was also a poet who authored the great Kavya called *Haravijaya*. Muktakana and Shivasvamin were the other poets. Krtamandara was the court-bard whose songs reminded the ministers to do good deeds. According to Jia Lal Kilam,[2] "Culturally, Kashmir witnessed great advancement. Kayyatacharya, Somananda, Muktakantha, Swamin, Shiv Swamin and Anandavardhana and Kallata, the great Shiva philosophers and authors, flourished during this period."

During Avantivarman's time, scholars and learned people were given place in his council of ministers. His magnanimity towards the Brahmins is exemplified in an incident when he was once distributing gold dust to them. In a fit of joy, one of the Brahmins exclaimed, "O Avantin well done," instead of "Well done O king."[3] The king did not take offence. On the contrary, he gave him more handfuls of golden dust.Believing that the ornaments and wealth in the treasury had been misused by previous kings, Avantivarman thought it proper to give all this in alms to the needy and the Brahmins.

Avantivarman's respect for human rights : He was a great believer in human rights. He would protect people from any political, legal and social excesses. Once during his trip to the temple of Bhutesvara, he found that the priest of the temple had placed an offering of a wild plant named Utpalasaka. Shocked, the king questioned the priest. Prostrating before the king, the priest said someone, known as Dhanava, was exploiting the friendship of the minister Sura. This Dhanava was controlling the village and the temple and taking all the earnings of the village meant to be spent on the temple. Because of this, the priests were reduced to abject poverty. The king left the temple and pretended to the ministers that he was unwell. Sura, the minister, realised the displeasure of the king. He went to another temple of Bhairava (usually Hindus offer a living being to this deity), called for Dhanava and ordered the soldiers to behead him.

Suyya, lord of the food: Right from the days of Jayapida, the valley of Kashmir was tormented by frequent floods and famines making only a small portion of land cultivable. During the famine, the price of rice became 1050 dinars. This made the king very worried and he wanted to get rid of these calamities plaguing the land.

Once, while he was discussing the situation of floods in the valley with his ministers, the famous poet Anandavardhana was also present. When the poet found that the discussion was reaching nowhere, he broke his silence with, "Sire, in Parihaspura I heard of a man who has been saying for years, 'I have a plan to save Kashmir from floods. I would work it out if I had the resources.' People say he is a madman." Avantivarman felt interested and said, "Tell us more about him."

"I know no more, Sire," confessed Anandavardhana, "but I can have the man traced."A man named Suyya appeared before the king. The king secured the services of this engineer to help in the prevention of the floods and famines. About Suyya, it is said that he was the illegitimate son of an unfortunate woman who threw the child away at the time of his birth in a raw earthen pot. A Candala (outcast) woman adopted him. He grew up very intelligent and attained education. He had deep knowledge of irrigation and flood control.

Suyya generally used to be surrounded by wise people. He was brought before the king who asked him about his knowledge. Suyya replied, "I know how to banish the famine." The engineer told the king that the catchment areas in the state caused the floods. "In many places, landslides also block the flow of the rivers and change their course. The very same waters become the source of destruction in the shape of floods in villages and towns. It is necessary to remove these bottlenecks and I know how to remove them."

In order to test his ability, the king told him, "I will keep my treasury open for you; show me how to banish the famine." Sailing in a boat down the villages in Madavaraja (Maraz area above Srinagar), submerged under flooded river in the southern district of the valley, Suyya took many pots full of coins and threw them in the river. He cruised down the Vitasta to Kramarajya villages (Kamraz below Srinagar) and found that with the course of time, boulders had fallen from the mountainous banks and bottled up the neck of the river. This made the waters of Jhelum river gush back into the valley. He threw a pot of money at a village called Nandaka (Nandi, on the Vishnu River, which was submerged with flood water). The remaining money he threw in the river near Dyar-gul near Khadnyar in Baramulla district. Initially, people took him as a man of unsound mind. Those who saw him throwing the coins cleared the beds of the river from rocks which had choked it while looking for the coins. In two or three days, the riverbed was cleared and the water flowed down the river. The money that Suyya had thrown in the river was visible. Previously, the uneven flow of the Vitasta river had turned large areas into swamps. However, Suyya regulated the course of Vitasta, and, as a result, these swamps were dried up and the land was available for cultivation. He reclaimed many villages by raising embankments around the swamps to stop the water coming out.

This arrangement to remove the accumulated mud and stones from the bed of the river enabled the Vitasta river to flow freely. In addition to this, he constructed diversions from it which lowered the water level thus avoiding flooding the land meant for cultivation. He also constructed a dam across the Wular Lake which enabled the lake to collect water during the rainy season when there was a possibility that the river Jhelum could be flooded. Suyya claimed to be a flood prevention expert. He was very resourceful and found permanent solutions for floods and their destruction.

He studied the confluence of the Vitasta and Sindhu rivers at Trigram, the main place from where the floods took their course. He planned to change the course of these two rivers and directed their confluence at Shadipur, at present near Srinagar. This helped in the eradication of floods in Kashmir. The swamp areas dried up and people began living there. He also constructed a canal by which water was made available for the people and helped irrigation. Before this development, the price of one

Khar (measure) of rice was 200 dinars but with these developments, the price was reduced to 36 dinars.

Suyya, the angel of prosperity, was the greatest engineer of medieval Kashmir. He was given the title of Annapati 'Lord of Food'. His great engineering feats are even remembered today. He also built the present town of Sopore on the banks of Jhelum in his own name.

Avantivarman was a large-hearted King. He had no jealousy for anyone. He granted permanent royal prerogatives to Sura, his minister who remained loyal to him, and his son. He was a bird lover also. He had two domesticated parrots and birds from outside also visited the palace.

Avantivarman a great builder: Avantivarman was a great builder. He had an innate aesthetic sense and keen appreciation of beauty which is visible in many of his constructions. He built a town named Avantipura. In the words of MA Stein,[4] "That the town of Avantipura remained a place of importance is known by the numerous references made to it by Kalhana and in the later chronicles. The extant of the town is attested by the remains of ruined buildings which can be traced along the slope of the hill rising to the east of the present Vant'pora for a distance of over two miles. From Kalhana's account it seems that the whole family of the King was builders." He also built a temple and named it Avantisvamin. The temple is small in size compared to the Martanda temple. His brother, Samara, built a temple called Samarasvamin where Kesava (Krishna's image) was placed.

Avantivarman's prime minister Shura had a wife who was very religious. She built a temple Kavyadevishvra and dedicated it to Sadashiva. The Avantisvamin temple was occasionally subjected to sacrilegious treatment even during Hindu times. The tyrannical Kalasa (1081-1089) confiscated the villages around it. Its military possibilities do not seem to have escaped anyone.[5] "In the 14th century, Sikandar But-Shikan completed the destruction which had already begun in the troubled times which followed the reign of Avantivarman. Avantivarman's emotional mind had a special attraction for natural wealth. That is why there are many instances which speak of his sympathy and love for mountains, rivers, forests, birds and animals," says Narendra Sahagala.[6] He had prohibited killing of animals or sacrificing them to propitiate the gods. His rule was marked by law and order and prosperity of the people. The king passed away listening to a Bhagavad Gita recital.

Avantivarman, though not of a glorious lineage, was an illustrious king and the most beloved of monarchs. He was chivalrous, humane and courageous—truly a messiah of the poor. He is the most celebrated king of Kashmir and increasingly admired in the annals of Kashmir's history.

Samkaravarman, 883-902 AD

With the death of Avantivarman, there were many aspirants in the Utpala dynasty to the throne of Kashmir. Many staked their claim but it was with the help of Ratnavardhana, the chamberlain, that Samkaravarman, the son of Avantivarman, became the king in 883 AD. At the same time, a councillor named Karnapa, manipulated and designated Sukhavarman, the son of Suravarman (the king's brother), as the Yuvaraj. But this was done against the wishes of the king and thus began the misunderstanding leading to enmity between the king and the Yuvaraj. This complicated the problems of the people. At one time their loyalty was to the king, at another to the Yuvaraj. The tension grew so much that war broke out between the king and the Yuvaraj wherein many valiant men of the king lost their lives. Finally, though with great difficulty, Samkaravarman defeated the Yuvaraj.

Samkaravarman's conquests: Having freed himself from the home-grown enemies who wanted to capture the throne, Samkaravarman, like some of his predecessors, started conquests and subjugated the adjoining areas of Kashmir. Because of famine and the domestic war, the population had thinned and the financial condition of the country was strained, yet the king continued with his conquests. Write RC Majumdar and AK Warder [7], "He (Samkaravarman) first of all conquered Darvabhisara and Trigarta, and thus recovered the hill tracts immediately to the south of Kashmir, which were lost during the last days of Karkota dynasty. But the greatest victory of Samkaravarman was against the king of Gurjara (Between the Jhelum and Chenab near Punjab) which extended the territories of Kashmir in that direction." Samkaravarman was very eager to conquer Gurjara. He went with a large army and conquered it without any resistance from the its King Alakhana. According to Jia Lal Kilam,[8] "Gurjara was then under the rule of one Alakhana, who by his name appears to be a Muslim, though till then Islam had not yet set foot in the Punjab."

Samkaravarman collected a large army as he wanted to make sure that he was able to conquer Gurjara. According to *Imperial Gazetteer of India, Kashmir,*[9] "He (Samkaravarman) was able to lead an army of 900,000 foot soldiers, accompanied by 300 elephants, and 100,000 horses." Another expedition that he undertook was against Lalliya Shahi, son of Toramana, but could not defeat him. However, his conquests extended up to Multan.

Samkaravarman, the builder: After the conquests, the king came back to Kashmir and built a town Samkarpura in Pattan Pargana. In his bid to make Pattan very famous, he plundered all that glorified Parihaspura. Pattan was famous for weaving of woollen clothes and it was also a big cattle market. But that town never became popular. People considered his name a bad omen. Samkaravarman's own son Gopalavarman was unhappy with the deeds of his father. In the words of Kalhana,[10] "When the people were thus cruelly suffering, the king's son Gopalavarman by name who was touched by compassion on one occasion addressed his father with the following words,[11] 'From these exactions which your majesty has introduced at the instigation of the Kayasthas (civil servants) breathing is the only vital function which nowadays remains (free) for men'."

Chroniclers have expressed their anger at his destroying another city to build his own. Even Kalhana has described Samkaravarman as one, 'who possessed but little character' as he carried away all that was valuable in Parihaspura. Kalhana says[12] that this was the time when kings were like those poets who augment their own works by taking from others works.

Samkaravarman constructed Samkaragaurisa and Sugandhesa, temples of Shiva and appointed a Brahmin by the name of Nayaka, who was well versed with all the four Vedas, as in-charge of the temple. Desh Bandhu has stated,[13] "There are two large stone temples on the roadside at Pattan. These, which bore the name of Shankara-Gaurisha and Sugandheshvara, were built by Samkaravarman who reigned in Kashmir from 833 to 902 AD and his queen Sugandha."

Samkaravarman's oppression: The King, on account of his conquests, restored the glory of the Karkota dynasty, but after some time his mind became fully engrossed in avarice. He could not raise sufficient revenue for the expenses of the country. Therefore, he became oppressive towards the people. He made deductions in the temple grants and imposed fines on villages for no reason. Through these measures, he amassed revenue for the administration. He introduced Begaar (forced free labour), by which labourers would not get cash or kind for the work done by them. What is more, there was no time frame for a labourer under Begaar. It could continue for days or months.

Gopalavarman, though a young boy, resented his father's exploitative nature and told him to stop. The poor were already fighting all odds such as plagues and famines, he told his father, and as if that was not enough, they had to work free for the king. He reminded his father that his avarice was making him unpopular with the people. He requested him to abolish the new tax known as Rajasamvahana (the king's revenue). The king instead chided the prince.

Cultural vicissitudes: Samkaravarman was jealous of men of letters. He discontinued the allowances of a famous poet known as Bhallata, and made him live in abject poverty. Bhallata, a protégé of King Avantivarman, had authored *Bhallata-Sataka* (collection of hundred stanzas).

"During this period, though very much disturbed by political vicissitudes, Kashmir was culturally quite alive. Pradyumana Bhatta, Utpalacarya, Rama Kantha, Prajnarjuna, Lachmana Gupta and Mahadeva Bhatta have made enormous contributions to Shaivite thoughts and some of them have been given a very high place of honour amongst ancient Indian philosophers," says Jia Lal Kilam[14]. It was during Samkaravarman's period that Jayanta Bhatt flourished and he wrote a play *Agamadambara* in four acts which satirises various religions in Kashmir. Jayanta's great grandfather was a minister during Lalitaditya Muktapida's period.

Samkaravarman's death: Samkaravarman met a violent death. One of his relatives was the Dvaradhipa (Lord of the Gate). He was killed through sheer negligence in Viranaka, a place at the bank of the Vitasta below Baramulla. The king himself went to avenge his death. Queen Sugandha also accompanied him. He was ruthless in crushing many lords on the bank of Indus River along the way and reached Urasa. Kalhana has not mentioned what exactly happened between his soldiers and the inhabitants of Urasa. But a fight arose. A person belonging to a low caste was fighting from a hill top. He pulled the string of his bow and sent an arrow, which unfortunately pierced the neck of the king. Though medical help arrived on the scene but as the arrow was being pulled out, the king died.

Queen Sugandha

King Samkaravarman was infatuated with his queen Sugandha Devi, who was a very beautiful woman. She was the daughter of Svamiraja, the ruler of the northern region. She, too, was devoted to her husband. His death was a tragic and disastrous blow to her. Shattered, she stood by the dying king who told her to take care of their son Gopalavarman since he was young and there was no male relative to take care of him. It was to Queen Sugandha's credit that the king's death was kept top secret. Had the king's army known the fact, they would have been dispirited and demoralised. Similarly, had the enemy known about the death of the king, they would have created uncertainty and confusion amongst the army of the king and perhaps even captured the country. The queen played an important role in organising the march of the dead king. The trusted ministers of the king, Sukhraja and others carried the king and placed him on an elephant. His body was tied with cords. The cords were pulled to make the dead body work like a puppet and coordinate the wave of his hand or the nodding of his head to the greetings of the soldiers and the people who had come to pay homage to him. After the sixth day, they reached a place called Bolyasaka,[15] the territory of their kingdom. According to Stein, Bolyasaka is the place of Duiravati near Varahamula, the present Baramulla. On arrival, the trusted ministers hurriedly conducted the last rites of the king and announced the coronation of Gopalavarman, his son.

It is surprising that an exactly similar episode took place in Spain where a military general met the same fate as King Samkaravarman. The exact date of the brave Spanish military leader El Cid's birth is unknown. However, most historians believe that El Cid was born in the year 1040 AD in Vivar (Bivar), a small town about six miles north of Burgos, the capital of Castile of Spain. Legend has it that during the war, an arrow hit El Cid and he could not survive. After he died, his wife Jimena got his body strapped to his horse and sent it back into battlefield, believing that his absence from the battlefield would demoralise his troops and lead to defeat. The troops, thinking that their leader was riding to fight beside them, rallied once more. The opposing army was so afraid of what appeared to be an invincible fighter that they retreated to their boats. Like King Samkaravarman, El Cid is thus said to have won his final battle in spite of his death.

Gopalavarman, 902-904 AD

Gopalavarman, though still a child, became the king of Kashmir. He was virtuous and had compassion for the people. He had shown his resentment towards his father for harassing the people. Initially, he ruled the country under the guardianship of his mother. He ruled only for two years after which he died. During this period, his mother Sugandha, a widow, was enamoured by a minister Prabhakaradeva and fell in love with him.

After the death of King Samkaravarman, some of the disloyal chiefs tried to raise their heads. Sensing the danger, Sugandha ordered Prabhakaradeva, the minister in-charge of Kosadhyaksa (treasury), to quell the uprising. He succeeded in killing the disloyal Hindu Shahi of Udabhandapura. After crushing the rebellion, he installed Kamaluka as the new chief. This enhanced the prestige of Prabhakaradeva in the court. As per Prem Nath Bazaz,[16] "The incident enormously raised the prestige of Prabhakaradeva at the court and being a paramour of the queen, he began to give airs to himself." He looked down upon other ministers. He plundered the riches of the queen and made the treasury empty. Gopalavarman came to know about the misdeeds of the minister and took him to task. Sensing that the king was very angry and that could prove detrimental for him, Prabhakaradeva hatched a conspiracy and got Gopalavarman killed by Ramadeva who was well versed with witchcraft. Nanda, the wife of Gopalavarman, belonged to an aristocratic family. She founded a temple and named it Nandakeshava. Sugandha Devi also constructed a temple and named it Visnugopala Kesava.

Samkata, 904 AD (10 Days)

Gopalavarman's brother Samkata was crowned the king of Kashmir. Unlike his brother, he did not seem to have any good traits and loved to commit crimes. Though some ministers resented this move and advised Sugandha against it, the Queen had no choice but to install Samkata on the throne. Unfortunately, he died after ten days of ascending the throne. After his death, there was no legal heir to the throne.

Sugandha Devi, 904-906 AD

With the death of Gopalavarman and his brother Samkata, the lineage of King Samkaravarman ended. With no one to make a claim to the throne and no dearth of self-seekers, there was widespread restlessness. As per Prem Nath Bazaz,[17] "...influential representatives of the public acted and a meeting of the people was called to choose the future ruler of the country. It speaks of the popularity of Sugandha that in this public gathering she was unanimously voted to the throne."

However, there was one hope for the continuity of Samkaravarman's lineage as Jayalaksmi, the wife of Gopalavarman, was pregnant. But unfortunately, while she did give birth to a son the child died just after his birth. So, all the chances of retaining the rule of the king ended. The only hope left was Queen Sugandha. She was asked to rule the country. According to Dilip Kumar Ganguly,[18] "The case of the queens being the de-facto and de-jure rulers of States, though rare, is also known from other parts of India like Kashmir where queens like Sugandha, Suryamati, Didda and Kotadevi ruled with distinction as full-fledged sovereign monarchs..."

The affairs of the state went on smoothly as soon as Queen Sugandha ascended the throne. People were relieved as there was peace. She devoted herself to the betterment of the people. She built a town Gopalapura in the memory of her son and another town in her own name. Unfortunately, this situation was shortlived. The cold war between Tantrins and Eknagas was brewing. The Tantrins, in fact, did not like a woman ruling them. They felt that her gaining full control of the kingdom could destroy them and so they started creating trouble in the smooth functioning of the state. Sugandha became aware of the situation and decided to put up a male heir to the throne. She wanted to pass the throne to her relative Nirjitavarman, who was the son of Sukhavarman. But the Tantrins did not allow that to happen. On the contrary, they allowed Sugandha to rule. She ruled the state for two years only after having earned the goodwill of the Tantrins.

Who were the Tantrins ? According to Stein,[19] "The Tantrins so frequently mentioned in the account of the succeeding reign appear to have formed in Hindu time, an armed military caste of strong organisation." They brought Partha, son of Nirjitavarman to the throne of Kashmir. At the time of Partha becoming the king, Queen Sugandha Devi went away from the scene. Writes Prem Nath Bazaz,[20] "Despite her heroic endeavours to restore order, to organise the government on stable foundations, and to regain prosperity for the people; she could not remain in power for more than two years." After Partha was put on the throne, she left the capital and went to live in Ushukur near Baramulla. The animosity between the Tantrins and Eknagas intensified. A battle broke out in which the Tantrins defeated the Eknagas. And because the Eknagas were loyal to Sugandha, the Tantrins captured Sugandha alive and imprisoned her.

Partha,906-921 AD

King Partha was only 10 years old when he was crowned the king of Kashmir. The Tantrins had selected him. However, his rule was full of intrigues and internal fights. Some of the ministers were not in favour of his becoming the king. Nirjitavarman, the father of Partha, became his guardian. But the Tantrins were against Nirjitavarman. Thus, there was a tug-of-war between the two. Consequently, the Tantrins exploited the king and got bills for encashment from the treasury. This made the treasury empty. During Partha's rule, his minister Meruvardhana built a temple of Vishnu and named it Meruvardhanasuamin.

Queen Sugandha's Death

Meanwhile in 914 AD, Queen Sugandha was secretly trying to make a comeback. She succeeded in organising another body of soldiers. Backed by the Eknaga troops, she fought a battle against King Partha and the Tantrins but was defeated by their combined forces. She was caught, imprisoned, and then put to death in April 914 AD. Says Kalhana,[21] "Deprived of her sovereign power, she left the royal palace, making her tears take the place of a necklace of pearls." Queen Sugandha, a brave woman, had a spectacular career, but she died unsung.

The sons of the ministers: The Tantrins had taken complete hold of the administration, to the extent that the sons of the minister Meruvardhana had accumulated riches by oppressing the people. His eldest son Samkaravardhana, joined with another person Sugandhaditya, and together both robbed the palace.

Great Famine

A terrible famine occurred in 917-18 AD. Food grain prices rose so alarmingly that one Khar of rice was sold for 1000 dinars. Thousands of people are said to have died of starvation. Then, floods caused great devastation. It is said that thousands of corpses flowed down the Vitasta. The people who were wealthy at the time were the ministers, Nirjitavarman, and the Tantrins, who sold the rice at a very high price. The king saw the death and destruction of the people and removed his father for his anti-people actions. The period was unusual. There were intrigues and malpractices all around. Nirjitavarman, in league with the Tantrins, ousted his own son Partha, and declared himself the king. Moral degeneration was rife and the queens of the palace offered their bodies to ministers and to those who mattered, to satisfy their lust and sought help in getting their sons secure the throne of Kashmir.

Nirjitavarman, 921-923 AD

In the year 921 AD, Partha was overthrown and Nirjitavarman became the king. He remained in power for two years only after which he died. The king's apparently dissatisfied wives bribed a minister known as Sugandhaditya with lots of riches for the satisfaction of their carnal desires.

Cakravarman, 923-933 AD

After the death of Nirjitavarman, his son Cakravarman, still a child, was made the king. Meanwhile, there was division in the ranks of the Tantrins. Cakravarman ruled initially under the guardianship of his mother, Bappatadevi. However, later on, he remained under the guardianship of his grandmother Ksillika. This child king proved as wicked as his father and was soon dethroned by the Tantrins. In his place, another person Suravarman was made the king. According to Kalhana, the two women, Bappatadevi and Ksillika, 'did not know that the egg they were fondling had a snake in it.'

Suravarman I, 933-934 AD

Suravarman was by nature a good king. His uncle became his enemy and with the help of the Tantrins managed to overthrow him. He remained king for only a year.

Partha, 934-935 AD(Second Term)

The Tantrin soldiers dethroned Suravarman and expecting lavish financial help from Partha, they restored the throne to him. This time, the Tantrins had become kingmakers.The rule of the kings depended upon the favour they could win from the Tantrins. During Partha's rule, his mistress, a courtesan named Sambavati, was able to construct a temple of Shiva in her name on the bank of Vitasta.

Cakravarman, 935 AD (Second Term)

In 933, the Tantrins ousted King Cakravarman due to the fact that the king ignored them, and the people did not like the king. Having realised the importance of the Dammars (powerful feudal lords), Cakravarman came back as the king with their help.The Dammars collected a huge army and Cakravarman was made its head to capture the throne of Kashmir. In order to bribe Sambhuvardhana and Samkaravardhana, sons of Meruvardhana, Cakravarman offered the post of Court of Justice to the latter and office of Grahakartya (Domestic Affairs) and Attapatibhaga (Revenue Collector) to the former.[22]

In spite of getting a lucrative and honourable assignment as a revenue collector, Samkaravardhana conspired against the king. Meanwhile, some bills from the Tantrins were pending with the king who could not pay them for want of sufficient funds in the treasury. Remembering the Pampore defeat, Sambhuvardhana enticed the Tantrins to his side. Before the clash, King Cakravarman fled leaving the throne vacant.

Sambhuvardhana, 935-936 AD

After Cakravarman fled, Samkaravardhana and his elder brother Sambhuvardhana wanted to capture the vacant throne. In order to succeed in this attempt, Samkaravardhana sided with his elder brother to negotiate with the Tantrins. The negotiation was successful and they began the preparations to capture the throne. Cakravarman's escape was most strategic. After leaving the throne, he straightway went to meet Samgrama , chief of the Dammars and convinced him of his love and loyalty. He sought help to defeat the two brothers. The Dammars agreed and a war broke out. It continued for almost a year during which Sambhuvardhana declared himself as the king. It was his plan to send his elder brother Samkaravardhana to fight against the Dammar forces where he got killed. When the Tantrins heard the news of his death, they ran away from the battlefield. That gave victory to Cakravarman who became the king for the third time.

Sambhuvardhana tried to flee but was captured by Bhubhata who chained him and brought him before the king only to kill him in his presence. Kalhana shows his anger with Bhubhata as he writes, [23]"This wretched man, to show his faithfulness, killed like a Candala before the king the prisoner, who, from fear of the stroke, had closed his eyes."

Cakravarman, 936-937 AD (Third Term)

It was for the third time that Cakravarman became the king after defeating the Tantrins and killing his enemies. He heard praises of himself everywhere, which made him egoistic. He began thinking of himself as God and started indulging in all sorts of evil actions. In those days, the caste system was prevalent in Kashmir. Low caste people were not allowed to enter the court of the king. One day, a Domba caste woman named Ranga wanted an audience with the king so that she and her troupe could put up a performance before him. The audience was arranged in the outer portion of the court. The whole place was decorated, and to witness the show even the ministers and the royal women were invited. The Domba woman was accompanied her two daughters — Hamsi and Nagalata. While dancing, Hamsi won the heart of the king.

The king made Hamsi the chief queen. She was a low caste girl who used to sing in the courts of the kings. But with her elevation to the status of a queen, Domba women and men became very important in the court. At their behest the king began killing Dammars with whose help he had acquired the throne. Ultimately, the Dammar robbers killed the King. The death of Cakravarman was dramatic. Soaked in blood he went inside the palace, fell into the lap of Queen Hamsi, and died.

Unmattavanti, 937-939 AD

Unmattavanti became the ruler of Kashmir. He was helped by a minister Sarvata and some others. This son of Partha proved not only immoral but also wicked and evil. His team of ministers were rogues and ruffians. Initially, his prime minister Parvagupta, was very close to him. Parvagupta, in order to amuse Unmattavanti, even danced naked in his court. But he harboured secret ambitions of capturing the throne of Kashmir. To realise his ambitions, he connived with other ministers Bhubhata, Sarvata, Choja, Kumuda and Amrtakara, and they assured him help to dislodge the king.

Parvagupta misdirected the king and induced him to commit crimes which were reprehensible. Unmattavanti killed his own brother, Partha's younger son by imprisoning him and starving him to death. He then got his father, who was living with his family in modern Srinagar on the charity of Buddhist monks, killed. He got hold of Parvagupta and killed him too. Writes RC Majumdar in *Ancient India*[24], "King Unmattavanti or Mad Avanti was one of the worst despots that ever disgraced a royal throne. The first acts of this depraved king were to starve his half-brothers to death and then to murder his father Partha. The horrible brutality that accompanied this act has no parallel in either history or fiction. The old man was dragged away from his crying wife and children, and pulled along the streets by his hair...."

A sadist by nature, Unmattavanti would enjoy killing and took pleasure in it. He would chastise people with poisonous reptiles. When his father was killed he went to see the dead body and was overjoyed to see his father and brothers dead. He would also rip open the wombs of pregnant women. Kalhana writes,[25] "He had the womb of pregnant women cut open in order to see the child and also cut off limbs of labourers to test their power of endurance." But soon he became ill, contacted a deadly disease and suffered terrible pain. Kalhana says, [26] "Not only were his subjects delighted by these sufferings of his, but also the fourteen queens of his own seraglio." Eventually he died in July 939 AD.

Suravarman II, 939 AD

The concubine of King Unmattavanti had brought an unknown child and declared that he was the son of the king. He was installed on the throne. Kamlavardhana, the commander-in-chief, was very eager to capture the throne. He came with a huge army from Madavaraja and fought the Eknagas, the Tantrins and the Dammars and entered the palace. The mother of King Suravarman ran away along with the child king to a safe place.

Despite having overpowered the king's forces, Kamlavardhana did not occupy the throne immediately and the throne remained vacant. The foolish commander-in-chief, in order to make his occupation of the throne legal and constitutional, collected all the Brahmins to discuss and decide in his favour. The Brahmins did not accept him as king and, on the contrary, they voted in favour of Yasaskaradeva.

And with that came the end of the rule of Utpala dynasty in Kashmir.

Nine
Other Kings

Yasaskaradeva, 939-948 AD

Yasaskaradeva did not belong to any dynasty of kings, nor did he share any lineage with previous kings. He was the son of Gopalavarman's treasurer, Prabhakaradeva. He had returned to Kashmir as a learned man after staying outside the country. Being wise and intelligent, he managed the affairs of the government efficiently and brought law and order to Kashmir. In the words of Kalhana,[1] "The land became so free from robbery that at night the doors were left open in bazaars and the roads were secured for travellers."

Yasaskaradeva's next step was to free the country from corruption. During his rule, it was found that people belonging to various occupations remained busy with their vocations. The Brahmins devoted their time to reciting the religious books and studying. They did not carry arms nor did they consume alcohol. The ascetics abstained from marrying and procreation. The farmers looked after their land. The kingdom had peace and prosperity because the king was not interested in reckless wars and there were no external and internal troubles.

Believer of justice: King Yasaskaradeva was known for dispensing justice. Relating an example of a man who went to the king for justice, Kalhana gives a beautiful account:[2] "I was once a wealthy citizen," said a man who sought to commit suicide out of starvation because a merchant cheated him. Seeking justice, the man narrated his story of how he became financially bankrupt. The creditors who were demanding money started pestering him. Ultimately, he thought that the only way of clearing the debts was to sell off his property and go abroad in search of employment. Therefore, he sold his house to a merchant. Now, there was a well attached to the house which yielded rent from vegetable growers. He retained the well for the sustenance of his wife while he was away.

After several years, he returned with a small fortune. He found his wife eking out her existence working as a housemaid. He knew that he had left enough for her sustenance, so her plight surprised and shocked him. She told him that the merchant who had purchased the house had taken away the well too, saying that the well was also a part of the house. The man then took recourse of the law but they also dismissed his claim. So he informed the king that he was going to put an end to his life. The king called the merchant and some judges and all of them examined the sale deed. To their surprise, they found that the sale of the well was also included in the agreement. However, the king became suspicious, but he kept quiet. Secretly, he sent out a messenger to the house of the merchant and got the account book in which the deed was finalised, from the merchant's accountant. The king examined the account book carefully and found that one letter was altered—instead of *ra* it was made *sa*, which made all the difference. For this forgery, the king restored not only the well but also the whole house to the complainant.

The poor brahmin's story: Another complaint came to the king from a poor Brahmin. He said that he had gone abroad, worked there and earned one hundred gold coins. While coming back to his native place, the hundred gold coins, which were his entire savings, fell into a well. He was about to jump into the well but the onlookers prevented him. From among the crowd, a man came out and told him, "What will you give me, if I get you this money out of the well?" The Brahmin replied,[3] "I in my helplessness, what power have I over that property? Whatever seems right to you, let that be given to me from it."

The man brought out the money from the well and gave two coins to the Brahmin keeping the remaining 98 coins with him. When this man was brought before the king, he explained that he did what the complainant had told him to do—"Whatever you like you give me". In this case, the king made a classical judgment saying that the man had not acted according to the words of the complainant who had told him, "Pay me what you like." The complainant had asked him to pay him the gold coins that the man liked. The man liked ninety-eight coins, which he kept for himself. Thus, 98 coins should be given to the Brahmin and the person who brought them out of the well should keep the remaining two coins. The story has found a place in *Ain-i-Akbari*.

While Yasaskaradeva ruled over the country justly, he became an object of ridicule on account of his own blemished conduct. However much he purified his body every day with earth and water like other Brahmins, he did not hesitate to associate himself with Domba and other low caste people—something his subjects did not like. The other factor was that he showed great relief at the death of his brother, which gave rise to the suspicion that the king's brother had been poisoned. The king constructed a math where students from within and outside the valley could learn various subjects. He also constructed 50 Agraharas on the bank of the Vitasta for the Brahmins. Yasaskaradeva became afflicted with a deadly disease and he therefore declared Varnata as the king. He did not make his own son Samgramadeva the king as he thought that his son came from a low caste. He designated Varnata, the son of his paternal granduncle Ramadeva, as the king. After handing the throne to him, he wanted to leave the palace. Unfortunately, Varnata did not come to see the dying king.

Varnata, 948 (One Day And Night)

With the disease spreading to every part of his body, King Yasaskaradeva appointed Varnata, and not his son, as the next king. This hurt his greedy ministers. A minster, Parvagupta, played a trick and vanished from the scene. After the coronation, the new king did not go to the dying King nor did he ask about his condition. Yasaskaradeva, who was still in the palace, was so upset that he regretted not crowning his own son as King. He ordered that Varnata be arrested. As per his orders, the new king was kept locked in a hall and was ousted the next morning. Fortunately, the ministers helped him in reconsidering his decision. The dawn came as a boon for Yasaskaradeva's son Samgramadeva. In the morning, he was crowned the king. Parvagupta the minister was instrumental in installing Samgramadeva, the young child, on the throne. After the ceremony, Yasaskaradeva left the palace..

He had taken two-and-a-half thousand gold coins for the maintenance of the math. His ministers robbed him, took away the whole amount, and poisoned him, making him die penniless. Among all his queens, only Trailokyadevi became a sati.

Samgramadeva, 948-949 AD

Parvagupta, an important minister of Yasaskaradeva, had set his eyes on the throne. Kalhana aptly called him an "evil-doer..." Since Samgramadeva was only a child when he was made the king, he made Samgramadeva's grandmother his guardian while he himself wielded the real power. Subsequently, he dismissed all others who could interfere, including the grandmother, and established himself as the sole master in the palace. While doing so, he gave the title of 'Rajanaka' to himself. According to M A Stein,[4] "The title Rajanaka, literally meaning 'almost the king', was given for services rendered to the king." According to Prof Buhler, "The title has survived in the form of Razdan as a family name occurring very frequently among the Brahmins of Kashmir."

Parvagupta put on the robes and grew his beard as if he was the king. Initially, he did not dare to kill the child-king. Later, being overly tempted by his ambitions, he tried witchcraft on the king. When that did not work, he took the opportunity to slay the king on a day of heavy snowfall. Along with his forces, he went inside the palace. A fight broke out with the minister Ramvardhana who was guarding the king. After killing Ramvardhana, Parvagupta succeeded in killing the young king by tying a cord with flowers around his neck. He then threw the body into the Vitasta at night tying it to a boulder. Then he declared himself the new king.

Parvagupta, 949-950 AD

Parvagupta, belonged to a humble family of accountants. His status as a king, which he had attained by treacherous means, did not last long. He was instrumental in robbing king Yasaskaradeva and leaving him to die lonely. He had a hand in denying the throne to Varnata whom king

Yasaskaradeva had chosen. He murdered the child king Samgramadeva and declared himself as the king. During his short rule, he collected money forcibly from the people and constructed a temple of Shiva called Parvaguptaesvare.

Kalhana says,[5] "The malevolent princes, Eknagas, chiefs, ministers, officials and Tantrins were afraid of him and showed nothing but only treason." The courtiers were scared of him. Once, a person known as Madanaditya who was a descendant of Suyya inadvertently played a large drum in the court of the king. Parvagupta tore his dress, got his head shaved and insulted him. The shocked man left the palace and became an ascetic.

An incident worth mentioning is that of a queen of Yasaskaradeva, whom Kalhana compares with the virtuous Gauri, wife of Lord Shiva. The queen, of royal lineage, was a beautiful woman. Parvagupta had the audacity to propose marriage to her. At this, the queen played a trick on him. She promised to marry him on the condition that he would complete the half-constructed temple made in the name of her husband. So bewitched was Parvagupta by her beauty that he got the temple constructed as early as possible. When the queen saw that the temple was ready, she burnt herself to save her honour. Kalhana says, "by this action and other wicked acts, Parvagupta had earned great disrepute, even ignominy. People hated him and he soon died afflicted with a disease."

Ksemagupta, 950-958 AD

On the death of Parvagupta, the people must have heaved a sigh of relief, but his son, Ksemagupta, installed as king must have dismayed them as he seemed to inherit many of his father's vices. Ksemagupta engrossed himself in wine and women and remained in the company of parasites and drunkards. The royal court became a den of gamblers, drunkards and womanisers. Kalhana writes,[6] "The king, wholly bent on mischief, was sharp in laughing at others, fond of love for wives of the subjects. He spat at the beard of venerable men, poured abuse into their ears and dealt blows on their heads." At another place, Kalhana writes,[7] "The royal assembly, filled with whores, villains, idiots and corrupters of boys was unfit to be visited by the wise." The king had for company a certain Jinsu and his rogue sons. They made the king dance to their tunes. They would take the king to their home and introduce him to their wives who were made to keep their breasts exposed. The king was lavish in his gambling with them. Some of them even went to the shameless and degrading extent of offering their mothers to please the king.

Ksemagupta burnt the famous Jayendra vihara only because a famous Dammar named Samgrama had taken refuge in it. When the vihara was completely burnt, the king collected the brass stupa of Buddha and got it melted. He collected stones from crumbling temples and erected a Shiva temple.

Didda marries the King

The only good thing that came into Ksemagupta's life was that the great Lohara, Lord Simharaja, gave his daughter in marriage to him and this changed the very course of Kashmir history. With this marriage, Kashmir came under the rule of the Lohara family. According to R C Majumdar,[8] "After the death of Toramana, also known as Kamaluka and Kala, Varman, his son ascended the throne under the title of Maharajdhiraj Paramesvara Shahi Sri Bhimadeva. The famous queen Didda of Kashmir was the granddaughter of Bhimadeva..." Following the marriage of Didda, Bhimadeva visited Kashmir and stayed there for some time. During his stay he built a temple in Bumzu near Matan, dedicated to Vishnu and named it Bhimakeshava.

In the words of Zimmerman, "Beauty is worse than wine, intoxicating both holder as well as beholder to the exclusion of most other objects of interest." Ksemagupta was so smitten by Didda's beauty that he would do nothing without her consent. His behaviour got him a nickname 'Diddakshema'. Says Prem Nath Bazaz,[9] "Nothing could be done without her consent and permission; she was the real power in the kingdom. Her influence over the king was so much that in the coinage her name in abbreviation was made as a prefix to the king's name. As if born ...and acquainted with the statecraft, Queen Didda almost took charge of the administration ...her husband becoming more and more irresponsible. She took care of the armed forces also." Just after the marriage, Queen Didda became jealous of Phalguna, the prime minster of the country. Phalguna had also given his daughter Chandralekha in marriage to the king.

King Ksemagupta had constructed maths and named them Srikanthamatha and Ksemantha near Hushkapura in Baramulla. While on a hunting expedition, the king was infected with a serious disease. He proceeded to these maths and died there.

Abhimanyu, 958-972 AD

Abhimanyu was still a child when his father Ksemagupta died. He was made the king under the guardianship of his mother, Queen Didda. With the assumption of the guardianship, Didda had reasons to be suspicious about the intentions of Prime Minister Phalguna. In accordance with the Hindu custom, the Queen wanted to die a sati placing herself on the burning pyre. Kalhana says,[10] "After the death of her husband, upon seeing the co-wives follow him in death, she, through ostentation, began to prepare to commit sati and the prime minister gave her his consent readily." Though Phalguna gave his consent, Naravahana, another minister, dissuaded the queen from committing sati. Commander-in-chief, Rakka, also poisoned the ears of the Queen telling her that Phalguna wanted her to die with her husband as he was determined to usurp the throne. Didda, therefore, decided not to commit sati.

Immediately, there arose an internecine fight between Phalguna and Didda. When Phalguna came to know what Rakka had told the queen he decided to leave Kashmir and go to Poonch with his huge army. However, he decided to stay until the return of his son, Kardamaraja, who had gone to the Ganga to immerse the remains of the king. Didda sent her soldiers after him. When Phalguna saw them, he changed his mind and returned to the valley to collect his army. Didda got worried about his intentions. Phalguna had not only contemplated a conflict but was also preparing for a civil war. Suddenly he changed his mind and went to Baramulla where he placed his sword before the image of God Varaha.

With the assumption of guardianship, Didda had to face a lot of difficulties. A great fire broke out near the Shiva market which spread slowly to other parts of the valley destroying large number of houses. Apart from the natural calamities, the Queen had to face a well-planned revolt from Parvagupta's two grandsons named Mahiman and Patala, born of his two daughters. These two grandsons, during the time of Parvagupta, were residing in the palace and they, with the help of some disgruntled ministers, raised a revolt to usurp the throne. When Didda came to know of the conspiracy, she at once asked them to leave the palace. They collected an army and a battle took place at Pampore. But Minister Naravahana remained faithful to Didda, and with his help, the Queen showed her extreme statesmanship and grit using a befitting and subtle diplomacy like that of old Greek hero Odysseus who diplomatically worked the Trojan war. She corrupted some people of the enemy who mattered and thus the revolt was stopped.

Didda, being a keen observer, found out that Yashodara, a man of valour, if won over, could prove very useful for the running of the state. She called him and appointed him commander-in-chief of the defence forces. To show his valour, Yashodara even led an expedition against Sahi, ruler of Thakkana. He defeated him, captured Thakkana and returned as a victorious commander. Nevertheless, backbiters were plenty and they poisoned the ears of the Queen against him, They told her that Yashodara was planning to overthrow Abhimanyu and capture the throne. A surprised Yashodara, who was expecting royal recognition of his victory, was banished from the capital. In this way, she created another enemy who turned rebellious against her. This time Didda mobilised even the common man, and with herself in the vanguard, inflicted a crushing defeat on the rebels. Rebel Himmaka was slain while fighting. Yashodara and Eramantaka were captured and imprisoned. Eramantaka was drowned in the Vitasta River. In this revolt also, Naravahana the minister helped Didda.

Queen Didda understood the importance of Naravahana who had given material and administrative assistance in fighting off the various disturbances and rebellions. She conferred the royal title of 'Rajanaka' on him. In gratitude, he invited the queen for dinner at his house. Sindhu and Bhuyya, the two sons of a litter carrier were employed in the palace. Sindhu, who was promoted to the post of a treasury chief, became jealous of Naravahana and he poisoned the ears of the queen telling her that he would imprison her in his house. The queen got terrified at this and she went back without eating anything. Then she tried to humiliate Naravahana who got so frustrated that he committed suicide. In his death, Kashmir lost a very great, straightforward and wise man. Writes Prem Nath Bazaz,[11] "In the death of Naravahana, Kashmir sustained an irreparable loss and, as we shall see, the country plunged into turmoil." Without Naravahana, Queen Didda had no choice but to recall Phalguna. Though he had decided not to work with her, he reluctantly started working for the administration of the country. Kalhana's description of Queen Didda was that she was a foolish woman. By her foolish actions, she made her most loyal and trustworthy ministers her enemies.

On the home front, the queen's brother, Udayaraja, had a friend known as Jayagupta. He somehow got associated with Abhimanyu and introduced him to alcohol. Kalhana, given his faith in supreme powers, thinks it was divine justice for Didda's errors of judgement. He writes[12] "And at that time, Abhimanyu, whom the sins of evil conducted by his mother rendered miserable, fell into consumption." Soon the alcoholic habit overpowered Abhimanyu, and in 973 AD he died. It was during Abhimanyu's reign that a famous Buddhist, Rinchen Zangpo, came to Kashmir to study Buddhism, Tantric history and Indian languages. He undertook several trips to Kashmir. After attaining perfection, he spread Buddhism in Tibet.

Nandigupta, 972-973 AD

Abhimanyu was a very handsome man with eyes the shape of a lotus. He was also an intelligent man. His death shattered Queen Didda. His son Nandigupta was made the king. But Queen Didda's grief over the death of her son was so great that she no longer remained the cruel Didda but turned mild and gentle. She constructed a temple of Vishnu called Abhimanyusvamin and a town known as Abhimanyupura. She also founded a town in her name, Diddapora, and a math of Vishnu, Diddasvamin. She did not forget her husband and constructed Kankanapur.

It took about a year for Queen Didda to overcome the shock of her son's death. However, after the lapse of a year, she forgot all her grief and began to work as a hard taskmaster.[13] Kalhana says that she killed her grandson Nandigupta by witchcraft. She never tolerated opposition, however right and reasonable it was. She was authoritarian and felt insecure.

Tribhuvanagupta, 973-975 AD

Queen Didda was the guardian of both Nandigupta as well as Tribhuvanagupta, who was the other grandson. She killed them both by witchcraft. Kalhana believed that[14] "In the same fashion she destroyed her grandson Tribhuvanagupta, on the fifth day of the bright half Margasirsa in the year (of the Laukika era four thousand) fifty-one (AD 975)."

Bhimagupta, 975-980 AD

"Then the cruel queen put without hesitation her last grandson Bhimagupta on that path of death which bore the name throne," says

Kalhana, adding[15] "It was during this period that the great minister Phalguna died and this queen began doing all the things, which she had so far concealed because of some regard for him. She fell in love with a buffalo herdsman named Tunga, who had come from Poonch for employment. He was employed as a letter carrier." Bhuyya, a pious man, had induced the queen into giving up all bad actions. She secretly poisoned Bhuyya and got rid of him.

Meanwhile, Bhimagupta attained adolescence and realised that the actions of his grandmother were not good. This woman put him into prison where he was tortured to death. AL Basham says about Queen Didda,[16] "The wicked tenth century queen of Kashmir managed to retain control of the state acting as regent for her sons and putting them to death one after the other before they reached their maturity."

Didda 981-1003 AD

After the death of Bhimagupta, Queen Didda took over as ruler of Kashmir and ruled the country like a diplomat who suppressed all types of rebellions, separatist movements and corruption.

Didda's romance with Tunga: Tunga was a herdsman who lived in Baddivasa, a village somewhere in Pir Pantsal. Along with his five brothers, Sugandhisiha, Peakata, Naga, Aittayika and Sanmukha, he came to the capital for employment. He soon found employment in the palace and was appointed as Lekhaharkara (letter carrier). When Didda saw him it was love at first sight. Patronised by her, Tunga became her loyal security guard. He even went to the extent of killing Bhuyya. As long as Phalguna was alive, Didda did not meet Tunga openly. but after his death, she openly flaunted her love for Tunga. However, she did not turn into a love-sick queen or neglect the country. In fact, there was progress all around. Says Prof KN Dhar in his article for Sri Parmananda Research Institute, [17] "Among the powerful women who changed the course of history of Kashmir by their irresistible personality, Didda deserves full mention. Actually, being the consort of Ksemagupta, she wielded the real regal power, as her consort was a weakling given to licentious habits. She tried to give a clean administration by getting rid of corrupt ministers and even the Prime-Minister Phalguna. Many rebellions took place, but were quelled by her without any mercy."

After the death of her last grandson Bhimagupta, Didda made

Tunga the prime minister. But this infuriated all the ministers. They, with the help of Vigraharaja, the son of Didda's brother, rose in rebellion. Fearing the revolt, Didda hid Tunga in her own apartment for some time. Meanwhile, she used a tactic to help win over the enemies. She started distributing gold lavishly among Brahmins who had links with her enemies. In no time she won over the enemies and the revolt fizzled out.

This was not the end of Didda's adversaries. Prithvipala, the king of Rajpura attacked Kashmir. But Tunga, with his brothers, attacked Rajpura and burned the country completely. This led to Prithvipala's defeat.

Hunt for successor

Didda's control gradually weakened on account of her advanced age. She wanted to nominate her brother, Udayaraja's son as the crown prince. She used a novel method of selecting him. She brought all the sons of her brother and asked them to collect as many apples as possible from a heap of apples kept in the palace. Among them, it was Samgramaraja, who collected the maximum number. When she enquired from the child how he had collected so many apples, he said that he got all those apples by making all the brothers fight for them. He said he stood aloof and was thus unhurt and able to collect all the apples. Stunned by the answer, Queen Didda decided to make him the Yuvaraj (heir to the throne.) Queen Didda died in 1003 AD and Yuvaraj Samgramaraja was made the king.

Ten
Rise of Lohara Dynasty

Samgramaraja, 1003-1028 AD

With the death of Queen Didda, the rule of the Utpala dynasty over Kashmir ended[1]. Sensing there was no one from the dynasty fit for accession to the throne, the Queen, during her old age, had chosen Samgramaraja, her brother's son, as the king. Samgramaraja's accession to the throne of Kashmir ensured the ascendancy of the Lohara dynasty. People had thought that after her death, her paramour Tunga would fall and die along with her. However, that did not happen. Instead, two ministers, Candrakara and Bhimatika, died along with her. According to Kalhana[2], "Candrakara was an able and efficient minister who deserved to be the prime minister but he chose to remain faithful to the queen and died along with her."

The new king was unable to bear the burden of the work of the kingdom. He entrusted the work of administration to Tunga while he indulged in the pleasures of life. It was also a time when the country faced a severe financial crisis. He was desperate for help. He sought financial help from a wealthy person known as Preman—a superintendent of

Diddamatha. The king went to the extent of marrying Preman's daughter, Lothika, which people thought was an unequal matrimonial alliance. The Brahmins had started revolting against Tunga. They even started a fast and the ministers too joined them. Kalhana says,[3] "Then the Brahmin councillors, in order to bring about the fall of Tunga made the Brahmins and Purohits of sacred shrines (Parisadya) start a solemn fast (Praya) at Parihaspura."

Mahmud Ghazni/Mahmud-e-Gaznavi, led a number of violent attacks against India. The great wave of invasions, which swept across the Indus Valley and along the Punjab plains, in the early decade of the eleventh century, however, did not go beyond the mountain ramparts protecting Kashmir. The several expeditions, never seriously threatened the independence of the valley. Gaznavi, the Muslim plunderer, was not only spreading Islam by forcible conversion of non-Muslims, but also looting, killing and destroying Hindu temples of great architectural beauty. So there was no respite in terms of progress or peace for the unfortunate people of Kashmir. They witnessed bestiality and savagery of low-born adventurers who misgoverned the country. The quick succession of brief and oppressive rule of kings, palace intrigues, rebellions, civil wars, political murders and natural calamities weakened the Hindu rule over Kashmir.

Tunga's excesses: The appointment of Samgramaraja and the earlier part of his rule did not make much difference to Tunga's powers, which remained unchecked. Rival Brahmins were even ready to overthrow the King. Kalhana says,[4] "The Brahmins who were ready to depose the sovereign were somehow placated and induced to consider the expulsion of Tunga as an expiatory offering." But then the king, Tunga and others promised them money instead. When the Brahmins did not accept Tunga's offer, he tried to suppress them. The Brahmins then brought a dead body claiming it to be of a Brahmin and wanted it cremated at Tunga's residence. That became the cause of a revolt. The mischievous Brahmins involved Rajakalasa, probably a minister, and then ran away from the back door. Rajakalasa was defeated and Tunga imprisoned him. Another minister named Bhutikalas too was defeated.

Absolute power made Tunga careless about administrative measures and extravagant expenditure drained the state's treasury. In order to meet the financial deficiency, people were heavily taxed, a move that made Tunga very unpopular. The king secretly sent emissaries to kill him but they were defeated. This also led to the death of Mayyamanataka, who had attained an important position in the court. He was the able son of Candrakara. Kalhana says,[5] "Thus every crisis which was believed to bring about the downfall of Tunga, in turn, owing to favourable providence on the contrary, enhanced his reputation." Tunga became the invincible, uncrowned king of Kashmir. But his fall became evident when he employed Bhadresvara, a Kayastha belonging to a low caste, as his assistant to look after the state. [6] Bhadresvara stopped paying people for genuine work. Meanwhile, two of Tunga's brothers died. This devastated him.

Invasion of Mahmud Gaznavi

Mahmud came from Gazni by the valley of Banu. He crossed the Indus near Isakhel and the old town of Rori, and passing the Sindh-Sagar Doab, (between the Indus and the Jhelum in Punjab, now in Pakistan), through Mitta Tiwana reached Bhera by way of Khushab and Shahpur. On his fourth invasion of India, he attacked the Shahi King Trilochanapala via Tosamaidan. According to Alberuni, Mahmud's historian, he was the last independent prince of the Hindu Shahi dynasty. Kalhana has not noted the actual date of this invasion when the king of Kashmir sent Tunga to the assistance of Trilochanapala. From Mohammedan historians, we get indications that the war fought by Mahmud against Trilochanapala and Tunga was in the year 1013 AD. Trilochanapala had fought Mahmud with his father Anandpala and he was acquainted with the new techniques of the Arabian warfare where horses were mostly used. After the death of Anandpala, Mahmud invaded his son who asked the king of Kashmir for military help to oust Mahmud. When Tunga came to help, Trilochanapala cautioned him that Mahmud Gaznavi was not an ordinary foe. The warning proved true. The struggle was grim. Though Trilochanapala and Tunga showed strong resistance, both were defeated. This defeat marked the downfall of the Shahi dynasty. Tunga was crestfallen and he returned humiliated. Writes Ram Shankar Tripathi,[7] "Samgramaraja (1003-28) proved a weak king, and during the earlier part of the reign Tunga continued to be the real power in the State. The latter went to the help of Trilochanapala Sahi in 1014 AD against the aggression of Mahmud, who, however, utterly routed the combined Hindu army."

Alberuni, who had witnessed the events which led to the annihilation of the Shahi dynasty says,[8] "This Hindu Shahi dynasty is now extinct, and of the whole house there is no longer the slightest remnant in existence. We must say that in all their grandeur, they never slackened in the ardent desire of doing that which is good and right, that they were men of noble sentiments and noble bearings." This shows that in his mad zeal, Mahmud used jihad for destroying a decent and humanist Hindu king of Shahi dynasty.

With this defeat, near the River Tohis of Pruntsa, the Shahi Kingdom was overthrown, and the subsequent death of Tunga became certain. Though King Samgramaraja was not angry at the defeat, he became doubtful of Tunga's strength. A point which irked him was that Tunga's son Kandarpasimha had amassed riches and was behaving like a king. The last nail in the coffin of Tunga was a warning the king received from his brother Vigraharaja.

Meanwhile, Mahmud Gaznavi tried to invade Kashmir via the fort of Lohkot on the southern slopes of the Pir Pantsal, quite near the Tosamaidan, that was the barrier to conquer the Kashmir Valley. Bad weather and heavy snowfall seemed to have compelled him to retreat. According to Tripathi,[9] "The Sultan made an attempt to conquer the valley in 1021 AD, He advanced up to the foot of the hills but being unable to storm the fort of Lohkot, he withdrew to Lahore."

Tunga's tragic death: One day, the king called Tunga and his son and when both of them arrived at the palace, Parvasarkara and others attacked Tunga with swords. Simharatha, a devoted attendant of Tunga, tried to save him throwing himself on him but the stroke of the sword had done the job and Tunga breathed his last. Gradually, the followers of Tunga were also slain. Tunga's brother Naga had in fact connived with the king to kill his brother. He was awarded for his loyalty to the king and was made the chief commander of the army.

When the followers of Tunga saw his severed head, in a pool of blood, most of them turned their head the other way. Kalhana had praise for some of his followers.[10] "The troops, when they saw their master's head, turned away dispirited. Some of Tunga's followers brilliantly displayed the character of (true) servants. Bhujamga, the son of a Brahmin feudal chief (Samantha), who had arrived from his home was not merely angry but made King Samgramaraja flee from one apartment to another." He then killed twenty royal soldiers in the assembly hall.

From a humble herdsman to becoming the prime minister—Tunga had made systematic progress in Queen Didda's government. He had shown exceptional brilliance, fearlessness and valour and had faced several critical situations. According to Kalhana,[11] "After Tunga, whose conduct had been free from treachery, had been slain together with his son by the king, it was chiefly the miscreants who having secured a rise began to aggrandize themselves in the royal palace." Tunga's wife Mankhana left the palace along with her two grandsons, Vicitrasimha and Matrsimha, born of Kandarpasimha, Tunga's son. She was also accompanied by her daughter-in-law. They settled in Rajpura (modern Rajouri). Naga, the brother of Tunga, who had connived with the king to kill him, developed illicit relations with the beautiful Ksema, the wife of Kandarpasimha. Tunga's wife did not commit sati but his daughter-in-law, Bimba, one of the wives of Kandarpasimha did.

After Tunga's death, the condition of the state did not improve. The king himself was not a good administrator and failed to select able ministers. He also removed Naga from the post of chief commander of army and appointed Bhadresvara in his place. Bhadresvara plundered the treasury and many temples. The other appointments made by the king also proved disastrous. The whole country was in a state of anarchy. Minister Partha developed illicit relations with his brother's wife. Matanga, Sindhu's son was made the fiscal commissioner. He exploited the people to fill the treasury of the king. Queen Srilekha, the daughter of Yasomangala, began having illicit relations with many people. Tribhuvana, son of Sugandhisiha, developed relations with the queen. With these conditions prevailing in the country, as well as in the palace, and the king doing nothing, some Dards and Dammars came into the limelight. Suddenly, the king handed the kingdom to his son, Hariraja. He died in 1028 AD. His daughter Lothika,[12] born to Queen Tillotama, constructed a monastery in the name of her mother and she also constructed a convent Lothika after her own name.

During the reign of Samgramaraja, there lived a prolific scholar known as Kshemendra, a household name in the literary world of India. He was essentially a satirist. His poem entitled *Samyamatrika* depicts the wandering of a courtesan in the valley.

Hariraja, 1028 AD (22 days)

Samgramaraja died in 1028 AD, and his son Hariraja from Queen Srilekha became the king of Kashmir. In fact, Samgramaraja had nominated Hariraja when he was alive. Hariraja is said to have been a young man of good nature who sought the company of wise men. On his succession to the throne, the people were so delighted that they illuminated their houses. As soon as he took over as king, he got rid of the thieves in the kingdom and prohibited people from closing their doors at night. He ruled the country for only 22 days.

He was not happy with his mother. Her licentious conduct annoyed him. Also, she wanted to become the ruler herself. Hariraja is said to have been killed by his mother through witchcraft.

Ananta Deva, 1028-1063 AD

After the death of Hariraja, Queen Srilekha was to be the ruler of Kashmir. She had made elaborate plans for her coronation. Before the coronation she went to take a bath. But when she returned for the ceremony in the assembly, the nobles of the country such as Eknagas and Sagara, decided to make her son Ananta Deva, the king of Kashmir. Thus her dreams of becoming the ruler were thwarted. But there were others who were also eyeing the throne at that time. Vigraharaja, the paternal uncle of Ananta, and the ruler of Lohara, attempted to oust Ananta to become the king himself. He burnt down the gate and entered the city but the forces of Ananta retaliated and Vigraharaja took refuge in a house, which was burnt with him inside along with his other followers.

Shahi princes and king Ananta: King Ananta was married to the sister of Rudrapala's wife, known as Suryamati. Meanwhile, two Shahi princes named Rudrapala and Diddapala, perhaps from the Shahi dynasty that Mahmud Gaznavi had destroyed, became friends of the king. The king had outgrown his childhood, developed some vices and became extravagant too. Says Kalhana,[13] "Through the companionship of Rudra (pala), who pleased his ears, the king was led into evil habits, just as Sudyodhana through that of Karna..."

In the company of these two princes, the king's extravagance went to such an extent that he spent the entire revenue of the state. Of the two, Rudrapala was closer to the king and was given a huge salary. Diddapala also got a large salary which exhausted the treasury. Yet, he was greedy.

Along with Anangapala, another favourite of the king, he planned to rob the golden statues of Gods, melt them, and take the gold away. Rudrapala developed such proximity to the king that he was able to influence him a great deal. He married Asmati, the daughter of Induchandra, king of Jalamdhara (Raja of Kangra) and he also prevailed upon King Ananta to marry Suryamati, the younger daughter of Induchandra.

Sensing the worsening condition of the country, Tribhuvana, the commander-in-chief, revolted against the king. King Ananta himself led the army to face the attack. He hit Tribhuvana with his sword and wounded him. Tribhuvana and his followers fled from the battlefield. Kalhana says that the hand (of King Ananta) holding the sword could not be opened until it was washed with milk.[14] King Ananta's friendship with Rudrapala brought him more woes than he could imagine. He had appointed one of his relatives known as Brahamaraja as the treasury-in-charge but he could not function independently as time and again he was bothered by Rudrapala. There arose an enmity between the two. Brahamaraja was so disgusted that ultimately he left the job and went away.

Meanwhile, the king of Dards known as Acalamangala wanted to wage a war against Kashmir. He allied himself with the Mleechas princes and confronted King Ananta's army. Rudrapala proved heroic in that war. He cut the head of Acalamangala and brought it before the king. The king got a lot of treasure from this war.

Queen Suryamati's intervention: Despite the victories in these wars, King Ananta was a weak king. He did nothing to prevent his state treasury being looted by his unscrupulous companions. Even Dullaka, protector of the state funds was party to the embezzlement of the treasury. These activities resulted in the king becoming poor. When the princes started hatching petty intrigues and causing disturbances, they incurred the wrath of the queen who objected to their disorderly conduct. The king also developed a habit of chewing beetle leaves. Meanwhile, with the death of the two princes, Rudrapala and Diddapala, the king came under the direct influence of his virtuous wife Suryamati. The history of Kashmir has witnessed great upheavals due to kings losing their sanity or self control. And at such critical junctures, it was the queens who acted as God sent angels to save the country from utter ruin.

Gradually, Suryamati put an end to the problems caused in the country by the king's habits. The king had pawned his diadem and throne to Padamaraja, a businessman who supplied him with beetle leaves. Suryamati gave Padamaraja her personal treasure to settle the huge debt the king had incurred. She also got the diadem and throne back from Padamaraja. And she took complete charge of the administration. Troublemakers such as Dullaka and others like him were removed from service. Everyone in the palace and the people of the country admired the steps taken by the queen. No one blamed her for making her husband submissive to her.[15] "The wife-like submission on the part of the husband and her triumph over her lord owing to their stainless character did not become a matter of reproach for either party," says Kalhana. Queen Suryamati succeeded in changing her husband who became like a saint and earned great praise from the people. The state treasury became full and there was peace and happiness in the country. Queen Suryamati was also known by the name of Subhata.

Watchman's son, the prime minister: There was, during that time, a Vaishya security guard in a temple, known as Bhuti. He had three sons, Haladhara, Vajra and Varaha. Haladhara was appointed in Suryamati's personal service. Soon, this intelligent son of a security guard rose to the position of the prime minister of the country.

King Ananta's expeditions: King Ananta, through his wife's intervention, had attained so much self-confidence that he led expeditions to the territories adjoining Kashmir on the south and asserted his authority over them. He defeated King Sala of Champa (modern Chamba) and placed a new king on the throne. In addition, Darvabhisara also acknowledged Ananta's authority. However, his expeditions against Urasa and Vallapura proved a failure. Prem Nath Bazaz says,[16] "He successfully led the armies on the battlefield and having humbled the enemies he generally forgave them."

After correcting the affairs of the administration, Queen Suryamati devoted herself to construction of public buildings. She constructed Gaurisvara and a math, Subhatamatha. She constructed maths in the name of her brothers and her husband. Through Padamaraja, the importer of betel leaves, Bhoja the king of Malwa sent a lot of money for construction of a kunda (pool) at Kapatesvara. Kapatesvara was on the Achbal Kishtwar road as described[17] by RC Kak.

During that period there were two great literati known as Bilhana and Somadeva. These shining stars of the literary field, occupied high positions. Bilhana flourished under King Karna of Chalukya dynasty and Vikrama VI. The famous court poet of Ananta was known by the name of Somadeva. According to Prabhakar Narayan Kawthekar,[18] "Bilhana only mentions the existence of the Chaitya. Ananta, king of Kashmir, was a great devotee of Lord Shiva. His queen named Subhata had built a big temple of Lord Shiva, on the bank of the Vitasta." Somadeva's famous work *Katha-sarit-sagara* (Ocean of Stories) is a monumental work. It is compared with medieval European fairy tales with magic, demons, vampires and high adventure. Evidently, it was written sometime between AD 1063 and 1089, when Kalasa was on the throne and Suryamati was still alive. According to ML Varadpande[19], "He compiled the work for the amusement of Suryamati, daughter of king of Kullu Kangra, and wife of King Ananta of Kashmir." There is no doubt that Suryamati was a very wise person but there was also a romantic side to her. She had a soft corner for her prime minister, Haladhara, who was always in attendance on her, to the extent that King Ananta became annoyed. Although Kalhana has not mentioned it but it seems that the King was jealous of Haladhara because of his constant presence. The king even got him imprisoned once. However, he was released on Suryamati's intervention.

Kalasa's coronation: Suryamati's efforts to bring peace and prosperity earned her great admiration from the people of the country. But her weakness destroyed everything she achieved. It started when she prevailed upon the king to abdicate kingship in favour of her son Kalasa. After some hesitation, the king agreed, and it was in 1063 AD that Kalasa's coronation took place. The ministers were surprised and unhappy over the decision. Wise Haladhara also tried to dissuade the king. Kalhana says that when the prime minister was presenting the prince to the new king, he presented Ananta also to the new king and said,[20] "Your Majesty, this is Prince (Rajaputra) Ananta." The angry king turned round and looked at him. The prime minister laughed sarcastically and told Ananta,[21] "Where the rulers of Kanyakubja (modern Kannuaj) are introduced in this manner why should there be another procedure followed with you who have resigned the royal power."

King Ananta met an unfortunate end. Suryamati was ready to go to any extent for her son Kalasa. She always protected him. Perhaps it was on account of the anguish of the death of their first son, Rajaraja. At that time, both the king and the queen were so depressed that they left the royal palace to live near a shrine of Sadashiva. Because of the loss of Rajaraja, she wanted to fulfil every demand of Kalasa.

After Kalasa was coronated, Suryamati became jealous to see the queens of her son in command. Suddenly, she commanded her husband Ananta to resume his powers. She was candid in saying that she regretted her decision of making Kalasa king. She did not spare her daughters-in-law and ordered them to work like slaves. Unfortunately, everything went wrong. Ananta had to leave the palace and he tried to settle at Vijayeshvara (modern Bijbihara).

Kalasa wanted him to leave Vijayeshvara and go to Parnotsa. Ananta was angry at this. The queen intervened and persuaded the king to agree to Kalasa's proposal. This enraged Ananta and for the first time he stood firm. According to Kalhana,[22] "The son who resembles not in figure and manners, he who is hostile to the kindred, and who is without affection for the father may be known to be alien seed." The queen was angry at Ananta's unwillingness to move and like a wounded tigress attacked him,[23] "This lack-lustre, anchorite, dullard, who has slurred reversal of fortune and who has grown old to no purpose—the fool does not know where and what to say... He is stupid, superannuated, banished from the country by the son, and is deserted even by the wife, of such calumny the fact is that I have a horror." This was a blow to the honour of a man who was once a king, who had fought his enemies with valour and subjugated them. Ananta Deva did not expect such behaviour from his wife whom he loved more than his life. He rushed to a place where he had kept his dagger (presented by Suryamati) and pushed it into his abdomen. The blood gushed out and he fell down and died. The queen was left stunned, shocked and terrified. She too ended her life by committing sati along with her dead husband.

Kalasa, 1063-1089 AD

Though King Ananta Deva had abdicated the throne in favour of his son Kalasa, he took care of the country's administration for many years. In the meantime, Kalasa fell into bad company and indulged in excesses. Like his father, he too befriended wicked people from the Shahi family such as Bijja, Pittharaja, and Paja who became his advisers. He made friends with Jayananda, the son of treasurer Naga. Jayananda taught him wicked things. The king had, among his company, a religious teacher, Pramadakantha, who taught him to ignore the difference between a mother, sister, wife or a prostitute. He taught him that women, irrespective of the relation, were only meant for men's pleasures. This abhorrent teacher, according to Kalhana, was in fact having sexual relations with his own daughter.

All these things had their impact and King Kalasa become shameless. He was so blinded that he saw virtues in his vices. He even molested his aunt Kallana and her daughter. There have been instances in history where some kings disguised themselves and wandered around to know the actual condition of the people. They would dig out the injustice done and punish those responsible. In the case of Kalasa, he would roam the city at night disguised but only to fulfil his sexual passion. On one occasion, the immoral daughter-in-law of Jinduraja, hobnobbed with him. She was preparing to receive him. As soon as the king reached the gates, the dogs started barking and the guards mistook the king and his men for thieves. They came with swords to attack. Fortunately, the king's men threw themselves on him and saved him. In spite of this, he received many blows. With great difficulty, his friends whisked away the battered, bruised king to the palace.

The unfortunate parents heard the story. They wept the whole night, and finally decided that they would enthrone Harsa, the eldest son of Kalasa from queen Bappika. Both Ananta and Suryamati spent sleepless nights. Then came a gloomy morning when King Ananta called his son Kalasa. Says Kalhana,[24] "As soon as he entered his father slapped him in the face, and thus addressed him 'You wretch, give up your dagger'." Bijja, the bodyguard of King Kalasa saved the situation and took him to Queen Dilha, who hid him in a chamber and told everyone that the king was unwell.

Shaking with anger, frustration and desperation, King Ananta, with his attendants, rushed towards the chamber where he was hiding. But once again, Bijja, prevented Ananta from entering the chamber. An infuriated Ananta left the capital in a huff accompanied by Suryamati. When the people came to know about this, they wept bitterly, "They cried," says Kalhana, "O mother, O father! Where do you thus go?"

When leaving the palace, King Ananta had taken most of his wealth with him. This annoyed Kalasa who found his treasury empty. The financial difficulties forced him to take part in the governance. He made quick changes in the administration and appointed his friend Jayananda as prime minister. He deputed Varahadeva as 'In charge of the Gate'. The post of commander-in-chief was given to Vijayamitra. Ananta's feelings for his son began to soften, but the latter was raising an army with the help of the ruler of Nilapura to take on his father. Ananta chose to live with Harsa, Kalasa's elder son. This displeased Kalasa. He raised more forces and declared war against his father.

Kalasa's war against Ananta: Kalasa and his forces were set to storm the temple of Vijayeshvara where Ananta was residing. When Queen Suryamati came to know this, she sent him a message asking him to refrain from such a misadventure. She warned her son that Ananta was not a person he could take on lightly. She reminded him how powerful he was. Surprisingly, Kalasa accepted his mother's advice and retreated. Ananta was shocked when he came to know his son had planned to attack him and he decided to make his grandson Harsa the ruler of Kashmir. When Harsa came to meet his grandparents, they could not contain themselves. All three wept bitterly. King Ananta prepared Prince Harsa to revolt against his father. Kalasa came to know about it and he again set out for Bijbihara. He asked his soldiers to burn the temple where Ananta was living. It was burnt down. With that Ananta lost everything.

He took out his dagger and stabbed himself. While dying, he warned that the people should not know the exact cause of his death. The death of her husband opened Suryamati's eyes to the wickedness of her son, albeit a bit late. She prepared one hundred equestrian soldiers for the protection of her grandson, Harsa. She made them take an oath to protect the future king of Kashmir. She also had a piece of advice for the young prince. As per Kalhana,[25] "With his head placed at her feet, the grandson was weeping; kissing him on the forehead she gave him the sacred libation and he was warned by her thus, 'Do not trust your father'." In fact, it was during his lifetime that Ananta had anointed Harsa and declared him the king of Kashmir. Says Kalhana,[26] "On arrival, he fell at the feet of his grandparents, who, with streaming tears of joy, performed the Abhisheka upon him."

She then proceeded to the pyre. Before entering the flames, she cursed those people who had created a gulf between father and son. "May those who have caused the fatal enmity between us two and our son quickly be destroyed together with their descendants.[27]" Kalhana says that Suryamati's curse did work. Queen Jayananda and the minister Jinduraja who were instrumental in creating a rift between all of them died early. With a smile, Suryamati entered the flames and committed sati on her husband's funeral pyre. Others who joined her were Gangadhara, Takkibuddha and the litter-carrier Dandaka. The female servants, Uddi, Nonika and Valga also joined her on the burning pyre. Some of the close relatives of Ananta, who did not have the courage to jump into the burning pyre, renounced the world and started meditation in Bijbihara.

Harsa's anger against his father: Harsa, son of Kalasa and the grandson of Ananta and Suryamati, who was witness to the whole episode, seethed with anger against his father. He remained at Vijayeshvara. However, Kalasa sent his representatives to appease him. After much persuasion, the son agreed to come back. Kalasa went personally to Vijayeshvara and brought back him.

Return of the prodigal son: The death of his parents was a turning point for Kalasa. There was a complete metamorphosis in his behaviour. He regretted the destruction that had been caused by the civil war that prevailed in the country. The after effects of the war between him and his father made the political conditions in the country uncertain. The first thing he did was to remove differences with his son Harsa who had great admiration for his grandfather Ananta. Then he assumed the role of a benevolent king who took care of his subjects. He did away with the corrupt officers and punished them. In order to have first-hand information of the economic, political and social conditions of his kingdom, he moved around the country incognito. To make his subjects happy, he took the help of wise and efficient ministers and commanders of the army. After a long time, the country experienced peace and prosperity.

Although the king turned very good for the people, he did not leave his old habit of womanising as well as some of his other vices. Little wonder then that there were seventy-two women in his harem. Nonetheless, these did not come in the way of his efforts to improve the life of his subjects.

Expansion of territories: After the death of Sahajapala, Samgramapala, though a child, was the legal heir to the throne of Rajpura. However, his uncle Madanpala tried to usurp the throne. The sister of Samgramapala approached King Kalasa for help. Kalasa undertook an expedition which was not to annex Rajpura but to help the child King, who was installed as the king of Rajpura. In this expedition, Kalasa deputed two important commanders—Jayananda and Bijja—who were the main persons to inflict a crushing blow to Madanpala. After the defeat, Bijja remained in Rajpura along with his troops under the pretext that the security of the state had to be maintained. The fact is that he had grown suspicious of the ministers of King Samgramapala. When Bijja began to live like a king, people in turn began feeling suspicious about him. They brought him gifts and requested him to go back to Kashmir. Bijja, much against his wishes, went back to Kashmir along with Jayananda but left his troops behind citing security reasons.

While returning to Kashmir, Jayananda developed a fatal disease. Once they reached Kashmir, King Kalasa came to inquire about his health. In the course of the conversation, Jayananda told him that he wanted to talk to him in secret. When everybody including Bijja was leaving, Jayananda told him [28], "Clearly the kingdom does not belong to you since Bijja has come to power." After learning all the facts, King Kalasa became indifferent towards Bijja. Sensing the king's displeasure, Bijja asked his permission to leave the capital and retire. The king gave his permission. The remaining ministers advised the king to confiscate Bijja's property. But Bijja was an innocent man and he always remained faithful to his King.

Kalasa extended his territory to some principalities of Jammu also. During his rule, there lived a hill chief by the same name of Kalasa. He was the ruler of Vallapura. As per Kalhana,[29] "In the presence of the king appeared Kirti, the ruler of Baddhapura Asta, King of Champa and Kalasa, Tukka's son, lord of Vallapura; King Samgramapala, too, lord of Rajpura; Utkarsa, Lohara's ruler; Sangata king of Urasa; Gambhirasiha chief of Kanda, and the illustrious Uttamraja, the ruler of Kashthavata (modern Kishtwar)." This clearly indicates that he subjugated many principalities of the Jammu region. During this period, Raja Sangram Dev was ruling Jammu (1053 – 1094 AD).

According to Rose Hutchison[30], "Kalasaha (Kalasa), son of Ananta Deva, like his father asserted the claim of suzerainty of Chamba, and other hill states. That this claim was widely acknowledge is proved by the fact that the rulers of seven other hill principalities, from Chamba to Urasa or Hazara were present in Kashmir at the same time as Asta Varman (King of Chamba in 1080 AD)." The success of Kalasa's foreign expeditions decidedly enhanced his status among many neighbouring rulers as well as among his subjects. He organised an assembly of the neighbouring kings and rulers in the year 1087-88. In that meeting, kings such as chief of Chamba, the chief of Nilapura, Samgramapala, Utkarsa, Kalasa's second son, Sangata, the king of Urasa, Gambhirasiha the ruler of Kangra and Uttamraja the ruler of Kashthavata (modern Kishtwar), were present. What deliberations took place in the meeting is not known.

King Kalasa the builder: Kalasa rebuilt the temple of Vijayaksetra which he had burnt down. He also constructed a temple of Shiva at Tripuresvara, north-east of the Dal Lake. The idol was decorated with a golden garland. He also constructed another temple dedicated to lord Shiva known as Kalasesvara. The roof of the temple was adorned with gold plates.

Harsa arrested: After the death of his parents, Kalasa had made peace with his son Harsa. The young prince was given a monthly allowance, which did not meet his extravagant needs. Prince Harsa had developed his talent in the arts. He could speak many languages, write and recite poetry, and had a melodious voice to sing his compositions. Often, his father would ask him to sing in the presence of other kings who showed great appreciation for his talent. Prince Harsa also used this talent to put forward his arguments before his father. Through poetry he would get across points such as the allowance being given to him was insufficient.

Unfortunately, the prince had inherited the trait of keeping bad company from his grandfather and father. It was not surprising that his companions took advantage of his gullible nature and even poisoned his ears against his father. King Kalasa had to order Harsa's arrest to save him from these people. Meanwhile, a queen of Kalasa, Queen Bhuvanamati, became a mediator between the King and his son. She was the woman who ensured that the contact between father and son was maintained. She looked after the needs of the prince personally. When the prince was sent to prison, the queen could not bear the separation, so she slit her throat and died.

A strange love-hate relationship between father and son was developing. The love of the father wanted his son to reform. But when this seemed impossible, Kalasa degenerated and saw it as a form of revenge to enjoy some of Harsa's wives. Kalhana says he enjoyed them as if they were the wives of his enemy. One of them, Sugala, was the granddaughter of Tukka. Sugala developed a close relationship with King Kalasa, her father-in-law. She then connived with Nonaka, a minister, and tried to kill Harsa by poisoning his food. It is a common saying that "whom the Gods protect no one can harm." Perhaps that was true of Harsa. Prayaga, a cook loyal to Harsa, came to know about the conspiracy and informed the prince who did not touch the food but gave it to two dogs. The dogs died. When King Kalasa heard about the conspiracy, he was shocked. He immediately changed the cook. But Prince Harsa lost his trust and ate food only brought by Prayaga.

Kalasa meets same fate as his father: The differences between father and son grew so much that an angry Kalasa once went to a famous temple and destroyed the statues of the God. However, despite the animosity there still remained parental emotion in Kalasa. When he fell seriously ill, he had a burning desire to see Harsa who was under house arrest. This instinct was so strong that in the words of Kalhana[31] "He now longed to see his eldest son but as the servants ignored his order, the ailing man suffered greater misery because of his yearning." He repeated his name many times. Not finding him near aggravated his pain. Suddenly he started vomiting blood. The king knew that he was dying. He started for the Martanda temple on a Tirtha (Pilgrimage). Though he wanted to install Harsa on the throne of Kashmir, all the ministers opposed the proposal. On account of his illness, Kalasa had no energy to argue the case of his son. Nevertheless, so intense was his love for his son that he asked some singers to sing the songs composed by him. He then asked that his second son Utkarsa be made the king. Utkarsa came but as soon as Kalasa started giving instructions to Utkarsa, his tongue stopped moving and he lost his speech. The king died in the premises of the Martanda temple. His queen, Mammanika, and six other queens joined the king and became sati. Kayya, the prime queen, refused to commit sati. She left the palace and started living with a commoner at Vijayaksetra.

Utkarsa, 1089 AD (22 Days)

When the ministers observed that Kalasa's death was not only sure but was fast approaching, they ignored the claim of Harsa who was the eldest son and heir apparent to the throne. In this connection, Kalhana in *Rajatarangini* (Translated by RS Pandit) writes,[32] "The right of the ministers to oppose the succession of Harsa raises an important point of constitutional law. That Harsa had been guilty of treason and disloyalty was a good ground for supersession. The researches of learned German scholars show that monarchy in the Vedic period was elective. In the epic period, hereditary monarchy appears to have been well established but the practice of excluding a member of the ruling family to make room for a person better qualified existed subject to sanction by the people."

At the approach of the death of King Kalasa, Utkarsa was sworn in as the king. All the ministers joined the coronation except Vamana who performed the funeral rites of the King. It was a strange scene—on one side, there was happy music of coronation of the new king, on the other sad music was played for the king who was dead. Utkarsa had another brother, Vijayamalla, born of Queen Padmasri. To avoid any confrontation with him, Utkarsa promised him that he would henceforth get all the allowances that their father had given Harsa. Prince Harsa was still in prison. King Utkarsa did not release him. Lamenting and weeping, Harsa had requested his younger brother that he should be permitted to join the last rites of the father and be permitted to go to a foreign country to live there. However, Utkarsa rejected all his requests. He kept promising him an early release but delayed it as he sensed a threat. He was sure that the minute Harsa breathed the fresh air of the land he could become his enemy.

King Utkarsa was a miser. He would not spend money to even feed the queens of his father with good meals. Instead, he ordered that only Mudga, (a rice dish) be prepared and served to the queens, who hated it. "Mudga," writes Lawrence, "is pulses (Mung Dal).[33] Dal made with Mung is not regarded as a favourite dish among well-to-do families." Gradually, the atmosphere started becoming hostile for Utkarsa.

Revolt of half-brother Vijayamalla: Utkarsa was not a brave person. He always felt insecure and in order to feel safer he won the sympathy of Vijayamalla. However, in spite of the promises, Vijayamalla was not given his fixed allowance. Feeling dissatisfied with the treatment meted out to him, he openly revolted. In this revolt, he got the support of numerous disgruntled people. Prince Jayaraja joined him. Some soldiers, too, who were unhappy with the king also joined him. The respected people of the city also revolted against Utkarsa. They wanted Harsa to be crowned the king.

Harsa told the soldiers who were guarding him that in case they did not release him, Utkarsa would destroy him. While they were discussing this, around fifteen soldiers knocked at the door. Harsa opened the gate for them. The soldier-in-charge instructed that as soon as anyone came with the orders to kill Harsa, they would do it provided the person had the seal with him. A tormented Harsa waited for the orders. But he was a man of grit. He started befriending the soldiers, offered them betel leaves and made them sit with him.

King Utkarsa knew that till Harsa was alive, he posed a danger for him so he ordered his messenger to kill him. Unfortunately for Utkarsa, he did not give the messenger the seal of authority. By that time, the soldiers had become followers of Harsa. Vijayamalla was gaining grounds for a revolt. At one point Vijayamalla thought Harsa was dead. In a fit of anger, he tried to burn the palace but was stopped by the king's men who assured him that Harsa was alive. King Utkarsa asked one of the queens of Harsa to go to Vijayamalla and show him an earring of Harsa. Only on seeing it was Vijayamalla pacified and he stopped burning the palace. The ministers and Vijayamalla then went to the prison and freed Harsa.

Harsa escapes death to become king: Harsa's alertness and flair for diplomacy saved him from the jaws of death. The king's plot to kill him failed. His continued imprisonment had made him very alert and wise. When he came out of the prison, Vijayamalla was excited to see him. He ordered the throne to be brought and asked Harsa to sit on it. Harsa took advantage of the rebellion of his half-brothers,Vijayamalla and Prince Jayaraja, against King Utkarsa and succeeded in capturing the throne of Kashmir, of which he was the legal heir.

Completely defeated, the King hid inside the palace along with his concubine, Sahaja. He lied to her that he was going for evening prayers. He went alone inside a room and cut his throat with a pair of scissors.

Sahaja heard a noise, rushed into the room and saw the gory and gruesome scene.Harsa entered the palace to be crowned as the king of Kashmir.

Harsadeva 1089 - 1101 AD

Harsadeva has been the most controversial character in the history of India. He had unusual powers of perception, and therefore, could see far beyond the walls of the prison. His was an interesting journey—from prison to the throne of Kashmir. There can be two reasons for the attention Kalhana gives Harsa. One is that Kalhana's father, Canpaka, was a minister during Harsa's reign and therefore it would be obvious to assume that Kalhana got all his information first hand. Secondly, perhaps Kalhana had access to the palace where the servants would tell him everything. One wonders how a person such as Harsa with such artistic talents could degenerate to the extent that he is termed an iconoclast.

Writes Ram Shankar Tripathi,[34] "Harsa, who began well as an administrator, military leader, and liberal patron of the softer arts of music and poetry, later degenerated into a profligate, cruel-hearted, and irreligious man. His extravagant expenditure and unbound immorality soon led him into deep waters. He employed 'Turuskas' (Muslim generals) in the army, and devised a systematic policy of plundering the temples and defiling the images."

Harsa was a man of extremes. One could see his fun and frolic, wit and wisdom, and levity and license. Kalhana says,[35] "At the palace gate (Simhadvara) he hung up great bells in all four directions to be informed by their sound of those who had come with the desire of making representations. And when he had once heard their plaintive speech, he fulfilled their desire (as quickly) as the cloud in the rainy season (fulfils) that of the Cataka birds."

At other times, Harsa seemed earnest and Machiavellian, candid and obsessively taciturn, decisive and ambivalent, self abnegating and greedy, accessible yet aloof. Kalhana writes,[36] "How is it to be related that story of King Harsa which has seen the rise of all enterprises and yet tells of all failures; which brings to light all settled plans and yet shows the absence of all policy; which displays an excessive ruling power and yet has witnessed excessive disregard of orders; which tells of excessive abundance of liberality and equally excessive persistence in confiscation; which gives delight by an abundant compassion and shocks by the superabundance of murders; which is rendered charming by the redundancy of pious works and soiled by the superabundance of sins; which is attractive on all sides and yet repulsive, worthy of praise and deserving of blame; which sensible men must magnify and deride, regard with love and yet feel aggrieved at; which is to be blessed and to be condemned, worthy of memory and yet to be dismissed from the mind." Harsa possessed these qualities and he could display these any time he wanted. He was as good as any actor in enacting them.

Harsadeva's efficient administration: In the beginning, his rule was commendable. He made many changes in the administration of the kingdom. Vijayamalla's opinions were taken very seriously. Sunna, the son of Vajra, was given an important portfolio of a minister. Jayaraja, was given a very important position. King Harsa, whose rule began from 1089 AD, seems at first to have come to Kashmir during a period of consolidation, prosperity and peace, but subsequently the country was victim to his Nerolike, propensities. He also issued coins in his name. The golden coin had an elephant on one side and Harsa's name on the other.

Revolt and death of Vijayamalla: Meanwhile, Vijayamalla, who was responsible for getting the kingship for Harsa, felt disgusted with his ways of working. He, therefore, revolted and decided to kill him. But the king came to know of this plot and ordered his soldiers to be ready. Vijayamalla stole the horses of the king and tried to pounce upon him but he was met with soldiers prepared to take him on. He fled from the scene. Taking his wife, he jumped into the swollen river Vitasta. However, he succeeded in crossing the mountains of the valley and reached the territory of the Vidyadhara Sahi, ruler of the Dards. After some time, he went for an expedition, where an avalanche killed him.

Harsa's compassion: In a rush of compassion, Harsa forgave his enemies —ministers such as Nonaka, Silhara, Bhattara Prasastakalasa and the rest who were imprisoned because they had helped Utkarsa in the war against him. He released them and even appointed them as ministers in his court. This proved very helpful for him as these people became loyal to him and helped him in administering the country efficiently. Harsa was himself a poet and respected learned people. He brought back Bilhana, a poet who had left Kashmir, and made him chief Pandit. He was neither superstitious nor had he faith in idol worship. He was, in fact, to a great extent, an iconoclast. He was well versed in Botany, animal and bird science.

Interestingly, Kalhana,[37] while describing Harsa, has also given an account of his physical features and appearance. He says, "Surely he must have been born from atoms of light...." He has further explained that he wore earrings which flashed like the image of the sun. His looks resembled a happy lion. His beard was bushy, his shoulders were like those of a bull, his complexion was swarthy, and his voice was loud with a base like that of thunder.

Commenting on his administrative abilities, Jia Lal Kilam has mentioned,[38] "Harsa enlisted Muslims and organised the army on a new model. Each group of hundred soldiers was placed under the charge of a Muslim commander thus making it impossible for his soldiers to hatch plots, or run away from the battlefield. From Harsa's time onwards, the Muslims, as a class, appeared in the political field."

With the appointing of Muslims in the country, it seems some change came in the dress code also. MA Stein has tried to analyse these changes, "Can the change of fashion referred to here have had something to do with spread of customs from the Mohamadian West?" Harsa instructed his prime minister Jayananda and his commander-in-chief Madana to change their dresses.

Harsa a Hindu iconoclast: According to ML Gupta in *Kashmir: A Wailing Valley*,[39] " this time, India from Gazni to Sirhind (in Punjab) had come under Muslim invaders of foreign origin. Harsa, thus, had become disenchanted with idol worship practiced by Hindus and even desecrated many idols in the temples." He destroyed many Hindu and Buddhist temples, thus earning the sobriquet of a Hindu iconoclast. Charles Allen writes, "It was because of this persecution, several centuries before the arrival of Islam that the philosophy of the Buddha, once a serious rival to Hinduism, virtually disappeared from India. Harsa Deva, a single Kashmiri raja, for example, boasted that he had destroyed no less than 4,000 Buddhist shrines." Along with this destruction, Harsa began to slowly degenerate from being sublime to becoming ridiculous. His lavish lifestyle and love for ostentatious dressing, not only himself but also the whole palace, and his other multifarious extravagances soon landed him in great debt. In order to meet this expenditure, he levied all unimaginable taxes and yet the treasury remained empty.

Writes AL Basham,[40] "The dissolute king Harsa or Harsadeva (AD 1089 – 1101), when in financial straits, was advised by his evil counsellor Lostadhara to restore his fortunes by looting the temples and melting down the images of gods." He further says, "MA Stein, in a footnote in his translation of this passage, suggests that the use of the epithet Turuskas (modern Turks), in respect of Harsa may be taken with the fact of his iconoclasm as evidence of his leaning towards Islam. Harsa, while favouring Turkish mercenary officers, remained personally un-influenced by Islam."

With a vengeance, a bankrupt Harsa began to take away the golden statues of Gods and precious stones from temples.[41] "There was not one temple in a village, town or in the city which was not despoiled of its image by King Harsa," says Kalhana. He adds, "Harsa appointed Udayaraja for seizing divine images. In order to defile the statues of Gods he had excrements and urine poured over their faces by naked mendicants whose noses, feet and hands had rotted away. Divine images were dragged along with ropes around their ankles." Despite collecting all the money through villainous and sadistic methods, the king's expenses still increased manifold on account of excessive profligacy and debauchery. He taxed people more and more. He also levied a tax on night-soil. The people were burdened with these heavy taxes. He became very unpopular with his subjects. According to Sailendra Nath Sen,[42] "The reckless extravagance of the king exhausted the treasury. Harsa began to impose oppressive taxes and appropriated images of temples for the valuable metal of which they were made." Kalhana uses the epithet of Turuskas (Mohammedan) while referring to Harsa's idol breaking.

Writes K Jamnadas in *Kashmir Problem Has Origin In Buddhism* (Article) [43], "Two big Buddha images installed in the capital Parihaspura by previous kings were the objects of adoration for Buddhists even in eleventh century. These two images escaped destruction at the hands of King Harsa (1089-1101 AD), who was keen on destroying temples." Harsadeva has been called the 'Nero of Kashmir'. In the tradition of iconoclasm, Harsa stands unique. Some of the chroniclers have mentioned that he had employed Muslim soldiers in his army and was perhaps influenced by them. It is difficult to believe that he had regular discourses with the Muslim soldiers. It is also unlikely that those soldiers had made such a great impression upon him. According to Romila Thapar[44], "Temples controlled an income that included the revenue received from their lands and endowments, the wealth donated to them in gold and precious stones by wealthy donors, as well as the offerings of the many thousands of pilgrims. All this added up to a sizeable sum. Some temples invested in trade, and the profits from this activity came to the temple treasury. Not surprisingly, therefore, they were targets for greedy kings."

The stupidity or pretence of Harsa: Writes SL Sadhu [45], "Harsa was credulous and indiscreet. One day his courtiers brought to his presence a dignified woman, befittingly dressed and bejewelled. They told him that she was Bappika, his mother, who had come from heaven and she desired something from her royal son. Harsa at once fell at her feet and rewarded her with great wealth." On yet another occasion, some good-looking women were brought before him and he was told that they were goddesses. The king gave them suitable gifts. Such was his stupidity or maybe he pretended to be stupid. He was no doubt one of the most controversial characters, yet his ability to run the country's administration efficiently does not qualify him to be called stupid.

Harsa the artist: Harsa was not only a poet but a singer also. He learnt singing from Kanaka, the uncle of Pandit Kalhana, the brother of Canpaka. Canpaka was appointed as a minister during his rule. Harsa was married to Vasantalekha from the Sahi family. She founded a math and an Agrahara in the holy city of Tripuresvara, (modern Jyesthyer). Harsa learnt music from Ranaka, who was a strict and tough teacher. He presented him one Lakh gold coins. Kanaka was also instrumental in saving the statue of Buddha in Parihaspura.

Harsa non-traditionalist: Harsa's extraordinary high expenses were due to his extraordinary activities. For instance, he had collected 360 women of ill repute in the seraglio, in addition to his queens and concubines. This was his recurring expenditure. Next was his growing hatred for his father, who had imprisoned him in the Martanda temple.[46] "In order to avenge the enmity shown by his deceased father, he plundered the math and other endowments of the latter which bore the name of Rajadhani. In his liberality, he squandered right and left the riches which his greedy father had accumulated and called him the name of Papasena (whose army was one of villains)."

Another costly activity was the humbling of the King of Lohara,

Samgramapala, who had shown signs of indifference towards him. Harsa's military chief Kandarapa went with an army to subdue the Lohara King. In the meantime. the king got very angry with the Raja of Rajpura (Rajouri) and went himself with a force to subdue him. His attempts ended in failure. A similar fate awaited him in the fight against Dugdhghatta. It is for the first time that in these campaigns the two brothers, Sussala and Uccala, were seen fighting valiantly for the king. These two brothers descended from the Lohara family and were claimants to the Kashmir throne after the death of King Harsa.

Plague and Famine: In 1099 AD, fresh calamities fell upon the people of Kashmir. While plague was spreading rapidly and taking its toll, robbers were busy looting. At the same time, the country had to face a disastrous famine because of great floods, which carried away all the paddy plantations. People became anxious and began criticising the government. To divert the attention of the people, King Harsa organised an expedition against the Dammars. Kalhana's descriptions of cruelties and casualties perpetrated on Dammars show how revolting these acts of Harsa were. He attacked numerous Dammars of Holada in Madavaraja and killed them.

Harsa's perversions: King Harsa's perversion and obsession for sexual activity became so acute that he did not use the slightest discretion when picking a partner. Disregarding tradition, he showed clear signs of a Freudian Oedipus complex. Kalhana says[47] that, "he indulged in incest having sex with his sisters and even with widows of his father. In the company of 'low natured parasites' whose advice he heeded, he vowed to obtain Candala (Chandralekha) the most beautiful wife of Parmadi, lord of Karnata. He had already earned notoriety for being a debauch." People began hating him.

Entry of Uccala and Sussala: Harsa became suspicious of his cousin brothers—Uccala and Sussala. It so happened that a neighbouring prince of Dard, who came to know the weaknesses of the king, annexed numerous villages to his territory. Harsa went to capture the fort of Dard. The Dard soldiers having vantage position threw boulders as missiles and it became very difficult to defeat them. The king's two cousins, Uccala and Sussala, were fighting on his side. Meanwhile, there were torrential rains and floods. A terrible confusion prevailed in the army and they began to leave the battlefield. But Uccala and his brother persisted and the war was won. Curiously enough, the king tried to get these two brothers killed but did not succeed.

The last days of Harsa: Surrounded by enemies, sycophants and hostility, King Harsa felt a growing sense of insecurity. Initially, when he became the king, he had shown all the skills of a strategist and the wisdom of a learned man, but his reputation dwindled because of his degrading actions. While some people suggested he run away to the mountains, others told him to fight to the finish. The palace, administration and the army were in a state of confusion. Wise people began deserting him. Activities of treason began to rear their head. In his state of nervousness, the king made blunders thereby losing everything. Going by the advice of his sycophants, he attacked and killed Malla, the father of Uccala and Sussala. Seeing her husband killed, Nanda, the widow of Malla, burnt herself in the campfire made by her son. This invoked a sense of revenge in Uccala and Sussala against King Harsa.

Sussala defeated the royal army at Vijayeshvara and started his onslaught upon Srinagar. Then Uccala began attacking the royal army from the north. However, Harsa took command personally to check the onslaught of these two brothers. But suddenly Harsa's elephant was wounded and it turned back throwing the royal army in confusion. Total disorder prevailed in which Harsa managed to flee crossing the river and reaching the palace. But the forces of Uccala and Sussala burnt the palace and the King had no alternative but to run away. In those fires, seventeen women, including the queens of the palace, were burnt alive.

Harsa's death: An army was sent to bring Harsa dead or alive. He, while loitering on the outskirts of the city, took refuge in the hut of mendicants. When the soldiers reached there, he wanted to fight back but in vain. The soldiers struck him twice in his chest. Though he was not religious, while dying he uttered, "Oh Mahesvara." King Harsa was killed and his head was taken to Uccala who burnt it. The rest of his body, naked like a paupers, was cremated by a wood-dealer known as Gauraka. There is a paradox in the life and death of King Harsa.[48] Kalhana notes that not one among this multitude of women in his seraglios shed a tear for him on his miserable death, nor did any of his sycophants even present himself at his cremation ground. A gruesome and lonely death was his end.

Eleven
Rise of Second Lohara Dynasty

Uccala, 1101-1111 AD

After the miserable death of Harsa following a civil war, Uccala, son of Harsa's cousin Malla, was chosen the new king of Kashmir. When King Uccala ascended the throne, the task of governing Kashmir was not an easy one. For one, the Dammar lords who had helped him and his brother Sussala in defeating Harsa were showing arrogance and did not allow him to assert authority and independence. They behaved as if they were the true rulers. Sussala, for whom the king had annexed the Lohara territory and made him and independent sovereign there, was not happy with his brother and wanted to invade the valley. When Sussala was given independent charge of that country, he had, in fact, taken with him everything—elephants, arms, foot soldiers, horses, treasure, councillors etc. Yet he was dissatisfied, for at the back of his mind was a greater greed—to be the king of Kashmir.

Meanwhile, Harsa's son Bhoja became the proud parent of a male child from Queen Vibhavamati after having lost all his other children. This child was named Bhiksacara, which means a beggar. This two-year-old child was not treated as an enemy and on the advice of Janakasimha, King Uccala made it a point to bring up this boy who was the legal heir to the throne.

But things were still not running smoothly for the King. Through his great resourcefulness, he used tactics to create an internal feud among the Dammars themselves. As a result, Dammars Janakasimha and Bhimadeva developed hostility towards each other. The forces of Bhimadeva struck and killed Janakasimha and cut his body into two. Gagga and Sadda, the younger brothers of Janakasimha, who had come to aid their brother fled. Slowly, but surely, Uccala managed to suppress the other Dammars too. King Uccala proved to be a very seasoned strategist in the way he used his skills to create infighting among the Dammars. He saw to it that all his enemies were destroyed and killed. He forced the Dammars to disband their forces. By taking such preventive measures, he steadily secured his position as the king.

The main irritant was his brother Sussala who continued to harbour the idea of waging war against him. Uccala was suspicious, and, therefore, vigilant. When Sussala finally declared war against his brother one day, he was easily defeated. But being a good strategist, Uccala, even after defeating Sussala, reconciled with his brother.

Jayamati was born in a poor family. Unable to bear the burden of raising a girl, her parents abandoned her in a street. A dancer known as Kanasravati brought her up. Because of her graceful figure, Jayamati was taught the art of dancing. Soon she started performing for princes and nobles. During one such performance, she saw Uccala and fell in love with him. Uccala also fell in love with her. Soon, they got married. Jayamati was destined to be the queen of Kashmir. As per Prem Nath Bazaz,[1] "In accordance with the ancient tradition Jayamati was crowned as his queen and as an inalienable part of the coronation ceremony the sacred water of Abhisheka (coronation) was sprinkled on her body."

Queen Jayamati used to occupy half the throne. She was very magnanimous and exuded the grace and dignity of a queen, despite her humble background. After some time, Uccala started disliking her and got married to Bijjala, the daughter of the lord of Vartula. Jayamati built two monasteries, one of which was in honour of her sister-in-law, Sulla. King Uccala showed the traits of a benevolent monarch. When famine struck, he tried to lessen the sufferings of the people by distributing his own store of food at very low prices. He helped reform bad people by encouraging them to mend their ways so that they would lead an honourable life in society. He was not greedy. He helped people financially when the need arose. He was very eager to know their difficulties. King Uccala's sense of justice as a king was commendable. He was aware of merchants cheating people. Once a case came to him for judgment: A man had deposited one lakh dinars with a merchant asking him to keep the money safely. After thirty years, the man asked the merchant to return the remaining money after deducting what he had spent. The merchant gave him a big list of items alleged to have been bought by him and his family which became more than the amount deposited. The merchant, however, offered some money to him.

The depositor made an appeal to the king for justice. The king was aware of the practice of merchants. In the words of Kalhana,[2] "The merchant who puts drops of sandal-ointment on his forehead, eye-holes, ears and heart, takes one's life in a moment, just as a dangerous scorpion would which is marked in six places." Uccala asked the merchant to bring a little money, some coins, out of the depositor's amount to examine it. The merchant brought coins minted in Uccala's name. Based on that, the king pointed out that the depositor had given money when King Kalasa was the ruler. Therefore, the merchant should pay interest for all those years to the depositor along with the remaining money.

According to Kalhana, the benchmark of a king's rule is measured by the standard of the people.[3] "Friendship which ought not look to interested motives; strength which ought to be free from arrogance; a woman's virtue which ought to be above rumour; propriety in speech which ought to satisfy all; learning which ought to command power; youth which ought to be free from irresolution; and royalty which should be without blemish—all these verily are found reversed in this last epoch." And Uccala's reign had all the trappings of a dignified society in place.

Construction of temples: The king did not waste his wealth pulling down buildings. He restored the temples of Parihasakesava and put up a new image in place of one which was desecrated by Harsa. He also rebuilt the temple of Tribhuvanaswamin and an old temple known as Visnu Cakradhara. He constructed a vihara in the name of his father Malamatha.

His queen Jayamati also built a vihara, Navamatha. He looked after the suffering Brahmins giving them relief in the form of cows, horses, gold and other gifts. King Uccala loved his people. A strict disciplinarian, he tried to root out corruption from the administrative machinery. Says Prem Nath Bazaz,[4] "Uccala discouraged flattery. He forbade flunkeys, back-biters and tale-bearers to approach him."

Beginning of the end: The king began finding faults in people who were connected to him. This created many enemies. Subsequently, he became sadistic. He organised combats between two individuals with matched weapons. Such fights often resulted in the killing of one of the contenders. He would then reward the winner. He would provoke his officers, soldiers and others to participate in such fights. Says Kalhana,[5] "The women, when their husbands returned alive after going to the royal palace, thought that they had gained a day, but otherwise never felt safe." The officers became scared to face the king. He was so unpredictable that in a fit of anger he would remove efficient administrators or military commanders and replace them with a commoner who did not have any expertise. He appointed sons of common soldiers as his ministers. It was not surprising that some of the good and experienced people left the capital and did not accept high posts in the government.

Meanwhile, Sussala suddenly planned an attack on his elder brother again. But the king inflicted him a crushing defeat. The king sent Gaggacandra with adequate military forces under Bhogasena's command and was able to capture Sussala's horses and make him flee. This way a great danger was averted. As usual, there were other attempts of rebellion made by the king's relatives with the support of the Dammars. But the king was able to quell all uprisings. Meanwhile, a development took place that infuriated the king so much against Bhiksacara, son of Harsa, whom he was bringing up, that he ordered his execution. The executors tied a boulder to his body and drowned him in river Vitasta. Luckily, strong winds floated him to shore and he was saved by a Brahmin. Bhiksacara remained with the Brahmin family safely outside Kashmir.

King Uccala continued to make enemies. A soldier by the name of Sadda had three sons known as Chudda, Radda and Vyadda, whom the King had given important positions such as lord of the gate. When Chudda, the police chief, along with Sadda, killed a soldier who was living as their neighbour, the king was not amused. Their mother, who was a widow but young and hot blooded, was believed to have had an illicit relationship with the soldier. The king heard about it and ordered that the woman be punished too cutting off her nose. This infuriated the brothers. On the other hand, the king's brother Sussala got a son who was named Jayasimha. His birth brought good luck to Sussala and he was successful everywhere. King Uccala gave up his enmity with him.

Radda, Chudda and Vyadda, the sons of Sadda, along with their followers, hatched a conspiracy against the king. Since the king had insulted Bhogasena, the lord of the gate, he also joined them in their scheme to kill the king. It was the routine of the king to have his evening meal and then head towards the apartment of Bijjala. The conspirators seized this opportunity to attack him, so they waited in the main hall and positioned themselves. As the king approached the hall, one of the conspirators, a Brahmin, Teja, pretended to kneel before him. He then held the king's hair and stabbed him with a dagger. At this, Sujanakara, the king's bodyguard, who was carrying the sword of the king fled the scene. The king was helpless. Somehow, untangling himself from Teja's hold, Uccala caught hold of a dagger. Like a wounded tiger, he first hit Teja, then Radda who was trying to attack him from behind and then he stabbed Vyadda and others. All of them were hurt. The injured king ran towards the hall's exit only to find the doors locked. He suddenly saw Bhogasena but could not catch his attention. He ran further and tried to scale a railing when a soldier came and cut his knees. The king fell to the ground. The final blow came from Sadda who slit his throat. The king died instantly.

King Uccala became a victim of a conspiracy hatched by Bhogasena. "The King anxious to gain Yama's land (death) did not exile those who had been insulted, who were full of aspirations, who had formed a league and had lost their subsistence,"[6] says Kalhana in *Rajatarangini*. The way Harsa's death was like a tragic scene of a play, similarly the death of Uccala came in a most tragic and heart-rending manner. The once benevolent and just king lost all dignity at his death and was even denied cremation with honour. Like a pauper he was dragged from the palace, his wounds still oozing blood. His body was taken to a place near the confluence of Mahasarit and Vitasta rivers. King Uccala also died unsung. However, after his death, his trusted minister Gaggacandra turned the tables on the enemies.

Queen Jayamati did not want to commit sati but in view of the tradition prevailing, she told Gaggacandra to prepare the funeral pyre. The pyre was made ready but before Jayamati could step on it, Queen Bijjala entered the pyre. Queen Jayamati also committed sati by entering the flames. Kalhana says,[7] "Then as she (Jayamati) was ascending the pyre her limbs were hurt by the pilferers who robbed her in eager desire of her ornaments."

Radda-Sankharaja 1111AD 8-9 December

With his clothes drenched in blood, Radda, brother of Chudda the lord of gates, sat on the throne and declared himself the king of Kashmir calling himself Sankharaja. However, his accession to the throne was shortlived. The friends and relatives of Uccala such as Gaggacandra came to fight with the conspirators. Radda, who was seated on the throne with the crown on his head, stepped down and fought bravely. Armed with a sword he went on a killing spree. After he had cut down many by his strokes and had repeatedly rendered the victory of his enemies doubtful, he fell at last in the combat.

Gaggacandra, a leading Dammar of Lar district and a very trusted supporter of Uccala, was able to defeat both the rebels killing Radda in the fight. PNK Bamzai writes,[8] "Radda, a brother of Chudda whose hands were red with the king's blood, crowned himself. Assuming the name of Sankharaja, he could retain it only for a night. Next morning Gaggacandra, leading Dammar of Lar district and trusted supporter of Uccala attacked the traitors and overpowering them with his force avenged his master's death in the blood of Radda and his fellow conspirators." Finding no immediate legal heir-apparent, Gaggacandra installed Salhana, a half-brother of Uccala, on the throne.

Salhana 1111-1112 AD

In the words of Kalhana,[9] "The shameless intriguing Tantrins, mounted soldiers and councillors collected again after abandoning the defeated conspirators and brought up the elder half-brother, Salhana. When Garga, who had not found anyone fit for the throne saw this he had him quickly consecrated as king." Salhana thus became the king of Kashmir. There was chaos and confusion. Says Kalhana,[10] "There were seen royal attendants who served in the evening King Uccala, in the morning Radda and at midday Salhana." King Salhana could not restore peace in the country. He was neither wise nor brave. Nor was he interested in the matters of the kingdom. He kept himself busy in the company of women along with his brother Lothana. He proved unfit and weak and this licentious king left the management of the kingdom in the hands of Gaggacandra.

Gaggacandra was unhappy with Uccala's brother Sussala, who was the king of the independent principality of Lohara. When he sent a messenger to Sussala and informed him about the death of his elder brother and the treacherous way he was killed, Sussala raised a small force and started preparations for conquering Kashmir and avenging the death of his brother. He also sent his foster brother Hitahita to win over Gaggacandra. In the evening when he returned, Hitahita informed him that though Gaggacandra did not decline the offer but his intentions were not honourable. Thus Sussala started his march to Kashmir. Gaggacandra came to know about it and he went to fight him in the battlefield. Sussala was easily defeated and many of his generals killed. Even his foster brother Hitahita was captured. Gaggacandra tied his hands and legs and threw him in the Vitasta river. Sussala escaped death as he succeeded in fleeing back to Lohara. Gaggacandra did not possess great administrative acumen and as such was not efficient. The country's law and order situation was so bad that robbers plundered people even during daytime. People were terrorised. Sadda, Hamsaratha and Nonaratha, Uccala's killers were tortured with sparks of fire, needles and had to undergo terrible suffering. This was done on the orders of King Salhana.[11]

The king foolishly plotted against the Dammara chief Gaggacandra. Unfortunately, Gaggacandra came to know about the plot, and in order to punish the king, he compromised with Sussala and invited him to conquer the kingdom. Aided by him, Sussala engulfed the valley like a wild fire. He entered the palace without any difficulty. The friendship between Sussala and Gaggacandra grew to the extent that the latter gave his daughter to Sussala in marriage. Some people had suggested he marry his daughter to King Salhana but he had refused. Meanwhile, King Salhana and his brother Lothana were captured and put under house arrest. Sussala achieved his dream of becoming the king of Kashmir. Salhana died while he was in captivity in the year 1112 AD.

Sussala, 1112-1120 AD

As soon as he ascended the throne, Sussala started weeding off treacherous elements. He exterminated the families of those who had betrayed his brother. He was aware of the wickedness of the people and was ruthless towards them; otherwise by nature he was a gentleman. He assumed a cruel persona so that his enemies and the people were disciplined. He had many similarities in character with his elder brother Uccala. Like his brother, he won the kingdom by violence and displayed the same hot temper.

During the time before Sussala, the Dammars had attained unrestricted power. But rivalries between Dammars, Prthvihara and Mallakostha, led to continuous fights between the two in the palace. In addition to this, the king's growing incompetence was causing instability —political and economic. Unscrupulous profiteers were cashing in on this. Items of daily use became scarce and costly. People were disgruntled and Sussala's own army revolted against him. He had to leave the palace and go to Lohara.

Bhiksacara, 1120-1121 AD

To divert the attention of the people from harsh realities, the then King Bhiksacara had directed his prime minister Bimba to lead an expedition to Lohara against Sussala. The most unfortunate period against the Hindu rule in Kashmir was brought by Bimba who secured the aid of Mohammedan soldiers under Sallara and Vismaya against Sussala. Bhiksacara was the first king who organised a cavalry force consisting of mainly Muslims. The king's forces attacked Sussala near Poonch. An unexpected situation developed there when the king's forces switched their loyalty to Sussala as they hated their king's style of governance that had brought much suffering to the people. This changed the course of the war in favour of Sussala who marched to Srinagar from Baramulla. Bimba retreated, and Sussala reached Srinagar unopposed and was successful in capturing the throne of Kashmir. Bhiksacara left Kashmir together with Prthvihara and the rest proceeded to the village of Pusyananda in Rajpura territory, near Pir Pantsal.

According to MA Stein,[12] "He (Bhiksacara) was a mere tool in the hands of rival Dammara factions, and the royal authority was so much reduced that Bhiksacara had difficulty in procuring food. The Prayopavasa (solemn fasts) held by the Brahmans in the capital and elsewhere showed the extremity to which the people were driven by the rapacity and violence of the Dammars and their allies in the official classes. The eyes of the populace turned once more towards Sussala. After successfully repulsing a Kashmirian force that had been sent against Lohara, Sussala came back to Kashmir, and owing to the Dammars disunion, recovered the throne."

Kalhana's portrayal of Kashmiris, including the nobility and the army's character during those times, which lacked consistency, physical and moral courage seemed surprising. With his humorous sarcasm, he exposed the inveterate cowardice and empty bragging of the Kashmiri soldiers, who shamelessly changed their loyalties from their master to their master's foe. Kalhana says,[13] "...The Kashmirian unabashedly deserted Bimba and went over to the king's (Sussala's) side." It was, he says, a strange scene as people bowed to those against whom they had rebelled the day before.[14] "That very Bimba, who had been the first to go over from the royal army to Bhiksacara, deserted the latter and joined the king."

According to Sukhdev Singh Charak,[15] "He (Bhiksacara) returned in order to make an attempt to recover his paternal throne, and on his way, while at Kurukshetra, he fell in with several hill chiefs who had come there on pilgrimage. Among these, there were three local chieftains and two heir-apparent of small principalities: Vajradhara (Chakra Dev), Lord of Babapura, Jasata of Champa (Chamba), Raja Sahajapala of Vartula, and Uvarajas, princes, Balha and Anandaraja of Trigarta and Vallapura (Balour) respectively. They entered into an alliance against Sussala and agreed to restore Bhiksacara to the throne of Kashmir." However, Bhiksacara did not succeed in capturing the throne.

Sussala, 1121-1128 AD (Second Term)

After his retirement to Rajpura Bhiksacara did not sit quietly. He made many attempts to capture the throne of Kashmir but failed each time on account of unreliable and fickle-minded soldiers. Ascending the throne of Kashmir was not smooth for Sussala. Kalhana vividly describes his re-entry into the capital of Kashmir,[16] "His sword was in its sheath as he rode on his bounding horse in the midst of his horsemen, whose drawn sabres formed a line. In all the directions the ground was covered by his wide spreading forces, shouting and screaming, accompanied by the music of kettledrums. Thus Sussala entered the city."

He entered the city in 1121 AD, after six months. The first thing he did was to search for Bhiksacara who had already fled the palace when he heard that the soldiers of Sussala were near the river. Meanwhile, Sussala captured Simha, a relative of Prthvihara. Bhiksacara had fled with Prthvihara bidding goodbye to the city of Srinagar. Sussala won over all the Dammars. Seething with anger, he could not sit on that throne that was once occupied by Bhiksacara. So he broke down the throne and gave a piece each to his servants in the palace as a present. Meanwhile, Bhiksacara did not take his defeat lying down. Remaining under the protection of Prthvihara, he prepared for revenge. He and Prithvipala led a contingent of Dammara soldiers and almost defeated Sussala's army near Vijayeshvara. However, this near-victory proved useless, as in their excitement, one wicked person from the Dammara community torched the refugee camp in anger. The fire developed into a great conflagration and destroyed everything that came its way. People had taken refuge in this camp because of the war. The tragedy alienated the people and they cracked indecent jokes about the soldiers.

To the misfortune of Bhiksacara, even though he had won many victories through guerrilla warfare, he failed in his fight against Sussala though he used the same tactics. On the contrary, his Dammara companions got suspicious of him and they began showing indifference towards him. Slowly Sussala gained his position and ultimately captured the throne of Kashmir. It seemed that the fight between Bhiksacara and Sussala would continue unless one or the other got killed. Meanwhile, owing to previous hostilities, King Sussala had developed a suspicious attitude even towards his followers. Another bad habit was that he used indecent language towards everyone. That was the reason, Yasoraja, his commander-in-chief, left him and joined the enemy.

In 1123 AD, a fresh revolt was organised by Yasoraja and Bhiksacara and they were able to lay siege to Srinagar city. Coincidentally, nature also seemed to be abetting the enemies as a severe dust storm accompanied by several earthquakes shook the country. The people were so scared and traumatised that they thought Doom's day had arrived.

It was a time when Sussala had to face a lot of misfortune in his life. That same year, yet another fire struck the city. Within no time, the whole city was in flames. As per Kalhana,[17] "On the Great Bridge (Brhatsetu) one saw as yet only the smoke that had risen from Maksikasvamin, trussing on like a herd of elephants, when at that very moment (the fire) fell with vehemence upon the Indradevibhavana Vihara. Thereupon the whole city was at once seen in flames."

The burning of the city brought the king's enemies out of their hiding. The king faced them bravely and tried to subdue the rebellion. Unfortunately, because of the fire, all the stocks of grain were burnt and there was a famine in Kashmir. The Dammars took advantage of the situation and burnt houses on the outskirts of Kashmir. "When all the food-stores had been consumed by the fire there arose a hard and terrible famine over the whole land. The people's savings were exhausted, their houses were burned, and outside (the city) the Dammars seized their produce and blocked their road,"[18] says Kalhana. Kalhana has given a grim and terrible picture of the conditions in the country. For a whole night, Prince Jayasimha kept awake and thought of remedies to all these problems.

Misfortunes never come alone. Or so it seemed with Sussala. The chief queen, Meghamanjari, who was long suffering from a disease, passed away. In fact, the king was awaiting her arrival and had instructed people to celebrate it as a festive day. But destiny had other plans. When the queen reached Phalapura village, she died. Queen Meghamanjari was a gentle, noble and magnanimous queen. She was very popular among people inside and outside the palace as she treated everybody affectionately. Tired and disgusted with life, King Sussala felt a sense of helplessness.Natural calamities and constant threats from his enemies made him sick, dejected and desperate. He decided to renounce the throne and brought his son Jayasimha back from Lohara hills after three years. Prince Jayasimha, who had now attained adulthood, was pained to see his father in distress and at the same time he was shocked to see the whole country burnt to ashes.

The King crowned his son Jayasimha as the king of Kashmir in 1123 AD. But he bestowed upon him only the insignia of sovereignty; he did not make him manage the affairs of the state. As soon as the prince was sworn in, like a divine intervention all the troubles started diminishing. There was no dearth of food and all the enemies were destroyed. The effects of natural calamities such as plague and drought disappeared. There was rich food production in the country. After earning his place as a prince, Jayasimha went on to destroy some enemies. But backbiters and palace intriguers poisoned the ears of the king against him. Sussala announced that he was a traitor. As a result, the prince was going to be arrested, but because of the good sense of Vijaya, the executer, only a guard was placed to watch the activities of the prince. This action by Sussala estranged relations between father and son. The King undertook an expedition against his enemies and defeated Bhiksacara and his men near Kalyanpura. Bhiksacara and his friend Lavanya fled to save themselves.

The king wanted to get Bhiksacara killed by any means and to do so he tried to employ the services of Utpala, son of a guard and cattle shepherd, who was also a trusted man of Tikka. Bhiksacara was living with Tikka and therefore Utpala, if he accepted the king's orders, had to kill Tikka. To entrap Utpala, the king sent costly presents to his wife who had given birth to a son. But Utpala's wife was a very intelligent and perceptive woman. She advised her husband not to undertake any such work because the king might later on kill him too, after the job was done. She advised him to kill the king instead, an act which would be liked by his master Tikka.

It was a curious paradox that King Sussala began having more faith in Utpala, the enemy's servant, rather than in his own son, Prince Jayasimha. Kalhana says[19] that the reign of Sussala brought sufferings, sorrow, terror, poverty, death of beloved persons and other calamities. When he saw that even his queens were feeling miserable, he agreed to abdicate the throne in favour of his son. In order to put pressure on Utpala to do the job of killing Tikka and Bhiksacara, the king took his son hostage. But Utpala had his own plans. He executed him when the king had taken a bath and was sitting on his bed. The king was killed treacherously. According to J Hutchinson and JP Vogel,[20] "Sussala had espoused two princesses of the Chamba family whose names were Devalekha and Taralalekha (Taralekha), both of whom became sati after the death of Sussala, in AD 1128."

Jayasimha 1128-1155 AD

Kalhana has mentioned the birth of Jayasimha when his father was ruling Lohara. Jonaraja has not written anything about this birth but mentions, [21] "O Wonderful! Prosperity always rested on Jayasimha. The goddess of learning brought him up, and he enjoyed the company of the goddess of fortune. They abided in him together like a mother-in-law and a daughter-in-law and did not display hostility towards each other." Jayasimha was a prosperous king and had complete faith in God.

The news of the death of his father, who was treacherously killed by Utpala and his men, reached Jayasimha through his cousin Preman. He was greatly agitated. Mourning the death of his father, he became nostalgic about his happy days with him. Kalhana says, [22] "Before me as it were, is the face you showed when looking at me, thrilled and smiling with tenderness and sweet with kind words." Sussala at the time of his abdication had called his son Jayasimha from Lohara to install him as the king. But after his death, friends of Jayasimha advised him to go back to Lohara for his safety. Others asked him to fight for the throne and stay in the capital.

Jayasimha declares amnesty: After Sussala's death, the next morning before being declared king, the first thing Jayasimha did was to declare amnesty with the beating of drums.[23] "Whatever a person may have taken to himself that is now forsaken me and amnesty has been given to those who have joined the enemy, guilty though they may be.... " With this act of his, the people became attached to him. But lust and hunger for the throne made the enemy soldiers led by Bhiksacara into the city. Tilaka, the son of Kaka, the chief commander of the army during Uccala's reign, addressed Bhiksu as the king and advised him not to make haste. Bhiksu and others such as Kosthesvara and other rebel leaders did not agree with Tilaka and ridiculed him. They decided to go ahead with the war. When they reached Padampura, a fierce fight broke out between the forces of Jayasimha and Bhiksacara. Initially, the commanders of Jayasimha were defeated. Meru and Sajjana, two brave soldiers, died. Malla, the son of Vatta, the Tantrin chief, was injured and died after a few days. [24]

It may be pointed out here that Poet Jonaraja has also mentioned the name of Malla during the period of Jayasimha but as per his version, [25] "Once upon a time he received into his court Malla born of the family of Susharmma the king of Trigarta. Malla had been banished from his country by his enemies and had come here with a view to obtain a livelihood." Jonaraja further says, "Malla became the favourite of the soldiers on account of his great valour. Strong in his courage, Mallachandra went at night to the camp of his enemy in order to ascertain the number of the king of Turuskas's soldiers that had survived slaughter. There, even a breath of wind could not enter as the palace was guarded by powerful soldiers, but Malla went in among the enemy's troops, no doubt by the force of incantations and charms. But afraid of committing a sin by any hostile act towards those who were sleeping, he did not kill the king of the Yavanas, but only placed a pair of shoes marked with his own name on the head of the king as his turban."

It may be clarified here that Yavanas were the Muslim warlords who had entered Kashmir during the period of King Harsa.[26] Then arrived on the scene Pancacandra, the son of Gaggacandra with his soldiers and this strengthened the position of Jayasimha. The soldiers attacked the rebels and Bhiksu, Tilaka and Prthvihara were unable to face the forces of Jayasimha. The panic-stricken rebel soldiers vanished from the arena.

Sussala's end: It is very tragic that the body of King Sussala was lying guarded by rebel Utpala, somewhere in the palace. Once the soldiers of Jayasimha learnt that the war was over, they took the body of the king and hastily put it on a funeral pyre just near the palace. Rebel Bhiksacara managed to take the head of King Sussala away. He sent the head to Rajpura. Saubhagyalekha, the daughter of Uccala, tried to kill the people who wanted to take the head of her uncle. Later on, Somapala, her husband and son-in-law of Uccala, took his head and it was cremated at Gopalapura, Rajouri. While these fights were going on, Jayasimha was busy subduing the rebellion. He succeeded to a great extent. The second thing Jayasimha did was to exercise his authority over the valley, and in this task he was helped by the unscrupulous and cunning Laksmaka. The King bestowed upon him the title of chief councillor.

Bhiksacara dies while fighting: Things were slowly changing for the better due to the fact that Jayasimha had gained the goodwill of the people. Heavy snowfall kept away the greatest enemy in the person of Bhiksacara, who was waiting for a chance to strike and defeat the king. He came again with a big force to defeat the royal forces, but, under the command of Laksmaka, they defeated him at Banasala. Even the Dammara forces deserted him and Bhiksacara died while fighting.

His death did not end the misfortunes of Jayasimha. His enemies put Uccala's half brother named Lothana into a prison at Lohara. When Lothana was set free, he got hold of the treasury helped by Sarada,

Sussala's wife, and declared himself the ruler of that place. A letter came to Jayasimha from Lohara informing him about Lothana's activities. Lohara was the stronghold of the king of Kashmir. Whenever Sussala became weak in the war, he would at once go to Lohara which was a safe resort for him. Similarly, Jayasimha too would go to Lohara when the Dammara lords threatened him. The letter contained very bad news. If Lothana succeeded in conquering Lohara, eventually the king of Kashmir would lose territory as well as the treasury. In order to save this stronghold, Jayasimha sent an army under the leadership of Laksmaka who went and laid a siege around the hill fort of Lohara. To Laksmaka's misfortune, the siege proved a failure because his soldiers got heat strokes, perhaps even malaria, which took a major toll on his army. He had to retreat. While retreating, he was captured by Sujji forces that were advancing against him. Sujji had a personal enmity with Laksmaka. It is said that Laksmaka was released after paying a handsome ransom.

Jayasimha vanquished Bhiksacara and applied the appeasement policy towards Lothana, Mallarjuna and Kosthaka. The rebellion was overcome to a great extent. However, Bhoja, the son of Salhana, proved a hard nut to crack. "Bhoja was courageous, self willed and sensitive; above all, he was self respecting,"[27] says Prem Nath Bazaz. Jayasimha wanted to make peace with the rebels. Making peace with Bhoja was a problem. So the King thought of his wise and skilful queen Kalhanika who could be the best ambassador for peace with Bhoja and others. Queen Kalhanika was sent to settle peace.

As per Prem Nath Bazaz,[28] "From the day she had arrived in the palace, Kalhanika had acted as a friend to Jayasimha's other wives bringing about reconciliation where there was any misunderstanding….." Her selection as goodwill ambassador by the king did not appeal to many. Some people saw making peace with Bhoja as a weakness on the part of the king. The noble and graceful Kalhanika went along with two ministers, Dhanya and Rilhana, who had already visited the place where Bhoja was camping. The queen reached Taramulaka. Tensions were high the whole night. Dammara chiefs from Nilasva, Devasarasa and Holada, who were neutral, sent their army to help Bhoja.

Bhoja, on the other hand, was happy to know that the ambassador, no less than the regal and majestic Queen Kalhanika, had come as the chief negotiator. The golden rays of the sun gave the whole atmosphere a joyous feeling. Perhaps, even the Gods knew that there was going to be a peace treaty between both the parties. Bhoja went personally to the camp of the Queen. The magnanimous queen received him as she would receive her son. Bhoja was very impressed by her frankness and graceful behaviour. The Queen took him to the king and both were happy about the reconciliation. When Bhoja touched the feet of the king and bowed before him, his turban fell on the ground. Kalhana says,[29] "Then, in the confusion caused the obeisance, the turban fell off from Bhoja's head, but as he rose the king invested him with his own head-dress."

King Sussala had employed Prajji as Lord of the Gate and Sujji as chief justice. The two brothers, Prajji and Sujji, belonged to a royal family. Sujji was a good fighter; he always fought on the side of the king. But when Laksmaka was made the commander-in-chief, there rose an immediate rivalry between the two, and, later on, Sujji changed his loyalty to the enemies of King Jayasimha. With the defeat of Laksmaka, Lothana consolidated the gains of this victory which was due to the valour of Sujji, who was made the commander-in-chief of Lothana's government at Lohara. Meanwhile, Utpala, the murderer of Sussala, came out of hiding and wanted to consolidate his forces. An army commander of the watch station, known as Pincadeva was searching for his horses when he saw Utpala. He captured Utpala and killed him. When the king passed through the watch station, Pincadeva showed the enemy's head to him. The sight of the murderer of his father killed brought great relief to the king.

When King Jayasimha, a successful diplomat, saw that the forces against Lothana were not doing well, he used diplomacy. He proposed that Mallarjuna, his half brother, would be made the ruler of Lohara. Lothana agreed to this proposal. But later on, he understood that Mallarjuna had conspired with King Jayasimha and arrested him. Mallarjuna was kept a prisoner in Lohara fort. Enmity developed between Mallarjuna and Lothana and Jayasimha succeeded in his policy of 'divide and rule'. In this fight, it was only Dammara chief Kosthaka, working as prime minister, who enjoyed everything. The feuds and fights between Mallarjuna and Lothana made them both weak before the forces of Jayasimha who was successful in influencing both Kosthaka and Sujji to his side. He then sent Sujji to conquer Lohara. Unable to fight Sujji's forces, Mallarjuna left the castle with his treasures. But on the way, he was plundered by dacoits. The enmity between Lothana and Mallarjuna continued for a while. Ultimately, with the help of Jayasimha's forces, Lothana was dethroned in the year 1131 AD. Mallarjuna became the king of Lohara.

Commander-In-Chief Sujji consolidated the victory of Lohara making Harsota the governor. He wanted to stay on in Lohara for some time to make that place peaceful. At the royal palace, some mischievous persons poisoned the ears of the king who became very angry with Sujji. At Lohara too, Sujji's high handedness in administration made people averse towards him. The people of the valley had great regard for Sujji as he had been able to get back the lost territory of Lohara. Kalhana laments that Sujji, a loyal person, was made the king's enemy and subsequently killed by his foolishness,[30] "That king who with dull senses mistakes a falsehood for the truth and truth for falsehood, foregoes his aims and is put to sufferings by misfortunes."

After the death of Sujji, there were small uprisings against King Jayasimha. Lothana had taken refuge in the Dard territory. He was encouraged by Dard chief Viddasiha to raise a revolt against Jayasimha and was helped by a powerful Dammara chief of Kishenganga Valley. Jayasimha's army was successful in compelling Alamkaracakra, the Dammara chief, to sue for peace against the siege laid by the forces of Jayasimha. As a result, the two pretenders to the Kashmir throne namely, Lothana and Vigraharaja, were repatriated to the Kashmir government.

Mallarjuna, who became the undisputed king of the Lohara kingdom, did not prove a sensible ruler. He had wealth, thanks to King Sussala who had heavily taxed the people and sent the money there. Now Mallarjuna began spending the money quite lavishly and ended up spending the entire wealth.

Jayasimha decided to punish Mallarjuna. So he sent his army to subdue him. But when that failed, he defeated the Lohara king by sending his mother for peace. Mallarjuna had to pay tribute to Jayasimha. Kalhana says that there was nothing good about Mallarjuna except his good-looking face and good rhetoric. Finding all the pretenders vanquished, Jayasimha utilised all his energies and time in the development of the country and saw that the people benefited. He employed methods by which the financial position of the state improved and the treasury remained full.

Kalhana has given a long list of the king's developmental works by which the people were happy with the king. At Kasyapagara, he constructed a bridge where the river water was rising from Nilanaga He performed various religious activities and gave lavish 'dakhshina' (offerings in cash or kind) to the priests. He constructed houses for the learned and encouraged learning. He constructed a shrine of Shiva named after himself and a math, which contained a large number of Shivalingas. According to Kalhana's observations of Jayasimha's activities,[31] "The king whose mind is all-pervading and steadfast has obtained fore-rank among the virtuous by his pious actions. As if he possessed perfect enlightenment like a Buddha, he has helped the enemy in distress, just as the sandal tree while burning gives delight to the person who has set the forest on fire." At another place he writes,[32] "This jewel of a king attained a pleasing character in the course of his development just as the vine attains greater sweetness as it grows to maturity." For the benefit of educated people Kalhana writes,[33] "He has made scholars and their dependents owners, as long as the planets, the sun and moon should last. The houses he has constructed for men of learning, raise their terraces to such heights that the seven Rishi come to see them as they are towering above their heads."

Mention Yvonne Yazbeck Hadad and Ellison Banks Findly,[34] "Cinta, wife of Jayasimha's commander Uhaya adorned the bank of Vitasta by a monastery consisting of five buildings, and Dhanya, one of the ministers, commenced the construction of a Vihara in honour of his late wife. Evidently, therefore, the reigning period of Jayasimha (1128-1149 AD), marked a revival of the Buddhist faith in Kashmir."

Jayasimha's eldest son Gulhana was appointed ruler of Lohara. Queen Raddadevi gave birth to four other sons who were noble and very clever. Among these four sons, Aparaditya grew up at Lohara as he could not live without Gulhana. The youngest son Jayapida remained with his elder brother Lalitaditya who was very wise and noble.

Queen Radda gave birth to four daughters also—Menila, Rajalaksmi, Padmasri and Kamala. The Queen was a very religious woman who undertook visits to Tirthas many times. She constructed a math Rudresvra and decorated it with gold.

Twelve
Jonaraja's Rajatarangini

It is believed that Kalhana wrote his *Rajatarangini* sometime during 1147-1149 AD. The period in question is after King Harsadeva, and alludes to Jayasimha's reign.Kalhana's father was a minister during Harsa's rule. It is possible that Kalhana had direct access to the material available about the royalty since he has given such detailed descriptions.

He has described people, both royal, and ordinary citizens who faced death on account of palace intrigues, civil war and claims for the throne. The death of Jayasimha marks the end of historian Kalhana's *Rajatarangini*—one of the greatest and monumental accounts ever written in the subcontinent. Historian Aurel Stein has fixed Jayasimha's rule from 1128 to 1150 AD. But according to Jonaraja, who wrote *Dvitiya Rajatarangini* three hundred years after the death of Kalhana, and continued from where Kalhana had left off, Jayasimha continued to rule over Kashmir for five years more. Accordingly, Jayasimha's rule should be from 1128-1155 AD. Jonaraja says Jayasimha ruled Kashmir from 1127 AD, for 26 years, 11 months and 27 days, coming very close to 1155 AD.[1] Since it is known that after the death of Jayasimha, his son

Paramanuka Deva ruled over Kashmir for ten years, his rule commences from 1155-1164 AD. It is surprising that Kalhana has not mentioned Paramanuka Deva as the son of Jayasimha. He has mentioned the names of his other sons—Gulhana, Aparaditya, Jayapida, Lalitaditya, and Yasaskara.

Paramanuka Deva, 1155-1164 AD

While describing the death of Jayasimha, Jonaraja states,[2]," In the month of Phalguna, on the twelfth day of the dark moon, the king dies in the midst of prosperity, and greatly gladdened the eyes of celestial damsels."

The people of Kashmir crowned Paramanuka Deva, the son of Jayasimha, as the king of Kashmir. He proved to be very lazy and neglected his duties towards his subjects and the state. He was also always in the company of wicked ministers, who feigned false affection for him, at the same time planting seeds of fear in his mind that a demon was out to kill him. According to Jonaraja,[3] the ministers once connived and dressed up one of the servants as a demon in a dress made of grass. He appeared before this simple king. The ministers told the king to offer all his jewellery to the demon. The king did so. This way his ministers, particularly Prayaga and Janaka, robbed him. Says Jonaraja,[4] "But the wealth of the king was like that of a Brahman who follows the injunctions of the Vedas—he could neither give it away to others nor enjoy it himself, and it was robbed by two cheats Prayaga and Janaka."

There is nothing extraordinary about the rule of Paramanuka except that he managed to fill the treasury of the country. He was helped by the two ministers, Prayaga and Janaka in accumulating wealth. The construction of a temple at Thapar was his pastime. The king ruled the country for nine years, six months and ten days. He died in 1164 AD.

Vartti Deva/ Vantideva 1164-1171 AD

Vantideva was a foolish king. In the seven years that he ruled the country, there is nothing significant that took place. With the king's death in 1171 AD, the Lohara dynasty's rule over Kashmir came to an end as Vantideva died issueless and there was no heir from the Lohara dynasty to succeed him.

According to ML Gupta,[5] "The social and moral conditions of the people were at their lowest ebb due to continuous infighting for the throne and years of misrule. The ministers preferred a puppet on the throne."

Vopyadeva, 1171-1180 AD

Vantideva's death put an end to the Lohara dynasty and also made it difficult to choose a king under the conditions that prevailed. The throne remained vacant. So the people of Kashmir selected Vopyadeva and made him king. Nothing is known about Vopyadeva or his parentage.

It is not difficult to imagine the miserable plight of the people of Kashmir who had suffered for hundreds of years on account of ruthless oppression by greedy kings. There is only a brief record of the kind of life these unfortunate people in the valley may have lived for two centuries. As Kalhana has depicted,[6] "There were seen royal attendants who served in the evening King Uccala, in the morning Radda and at the mid-day Salhana." Frequent murders, suicides, plots, conspiracies, rebellions, oppressions, extortions, and corruption, black marketing of essential commodities, civil wars, fires and famines were the order of the day. In the words of Francis Younghusband,[7] "it was a state of perpetual intrigues and assassinations, of struggles with brothers, cousins, uncles before a chief even came to the throne: of fights for power with ministers, with military, with the nobles, when he was on it, of wearying, internecine wars of general discomfort, uncertainty and unrest."

In such a depressing scenario, the dignitaries, nobles and people who mattered most, assembled to select a successor to the vacant throne of Kashmir, and Vopyadeva was anointed king. To the misfortune of Kashmiris, this man proved a very stupid king. His foolishness can be gauged by the fact that Jonaraja describes him as the very model of a dunce.[8] "Once this foolish king felt happy at the sight of large blocks of stones and ordered his minister to increase the size of the smaller ones, making them drink milk of beasts." (This King's puerile acts disgusted the people so much that Jonaraja called him "Rakshasa chief covered with grass.")[9] At another time, travelling in a boat, he saw his reflection in the water.He started making faces at the reflection. Suddenly he was angry and hit the water with his hand with the result that the royal ring fell in the water.

Jassaka, 1180-1198 AD

King Vopyadeva died issueless so his younger brother Jassaka was made the king. He ruled Kashmir for 18 years but even his rule was not marked by any notable event worth mentioning.

Jagadeva, 1198-1213 AD

Jagadeva's rule was comparatively better than his predecessors. He was the son of Jassaka. He wanted to rule the country in a better manner and give the people a good life. As per Jonaraja,[10] "He was well versed in science, and as a surgeon extracts a dart, he rooted out the evil laws of the country." He tried to end corruption which annoyed the administrators and they raised a revolt. The king was compelled to quit the throne by his own ministers.

It was at the behest of his trusted minister, Gunakararahula that he came back to rule again fighting his enemies with his help. The people were very happy to see the king and the minister back. However, his enemies did not relent and they fought a vicious battle. The whole of Kashmir was plunged into gloom. But the king succeeded in crushing his enemies. After he re-conquered the kingdom, he brought the country back on track courageously. Says Jonaraja,[11] "...the enemies fell under the devices and the prowess of the king and his minister, as insects fall into the fire."

Rajadeva 1213–1236 AD

Jagadeva's death (caused by Padma, the lord of the gate) shattered his son Rajadeva who secretly went to Kashthavata, (modern Kishtwar) as he was feeling insecure in the valley. The death of Jagadeva caused significant hardships for the population too; the environment and the economy of the country suffered and a civil war broke out. People arose against those who had killed their King. The Brahmins brought Rajadeva back to Srinagar and helped him become the king.

After Rajadeva occupied the throne, there was still unrest in the country. Padma, the lord of the gate and his father's killer, wanted to capture the throne. He laid a siege around Rajadeva's forces in the fort of Salhana. However, fortunately, a Candala killed Padma, and with his death, his forces got demoralised. Rajadeva was anointed the king with all the fanfare and rituals of coronation. Rajadeva was afraid of palace intrigues and became overcautious.

Baladhyachara had, now, established himself as a very powerful lord of Lohara collecting a large number of soldiers with his eyes on the throne of Kashmir. He captured half of Srinagar and the king could do nothing. King Rajadeva tried to be friendly with the Lavanyas (part of Dammara tribe who practised agriculture for their living). When the Bhattas, (a community known as Kashmiri Pandits) saw the king quite favourably drawn towards the Lavanyas and Dammaras, they became restive. So, the Brahmins wanted to replace the king.

Suspecting that the Bhattas (Hindus) were deluding him, the king took his revenge against the community by turning cruel towards them. People became traumatised as the king's troops started killing Hindus mercilessly. According to Jia Lal Kilam[12], "This is the first onslaught recorded in history against the Brahmans of Kashmir." The revenge was so severe that this community was heard saying, "I am not Bhatta, I am not Bhatta." After a rule of twenty-two years, Rajadeva died in 1236 AD as per Jonaraja[13].

Sangramadeva, 1236-1252 AD

Sangramadeva alias Samgramadeva was the son of Rajadeva. After the death of his father, he became the king. He was brave and energetic. He wanted to get rid of the powerful barons who would not allow the rulers of the state to function effectively. At the outset, he appointed his younger brother Suryya as his viceroy. Tunga was the Lord of Shamala. But Suryya joined hands with the powerful barons upsetting the king. He sought refuge with Tunga. The king fought both Tunga and Suryya, who lost the battle. In the events that followed, Suryya was captured and killed. Meanwhile, the Brahmins had risen in strength under the leadership of Kalhana (not the author of *Rajatarangini*), and his sons forced the king to retire. According to Jonaraja[14], "...and the king, who was anxious to save his royal state, feared them as serpents." When the king lost all hope, he fled to Rajouri. There prevailed chaos and confusion in the state. In this confusion, the Dammaras made hay. When the king came to know that his country was in shambles, he became restless. He started collecting forces and was successful in defeating the Brahmins. Sangramadeva became the king again.

He had great respect for Brahmins, so he forgave the sons of Kalhana. He also constructed a house named Shrivishala at Vijayeshvara. The house had twenty-one rooms and was used to shelter Brahmins and cows. Despite being forgiven, the ungrateful and mischievous sons of Kalhana wanted to plunder the royal treasury. They hatched a conspiracy and got the king killed. On his death, a poet Yhshaka wrote a poem praising him,[15] "like the necklace, an ornament of learned."

Yhshaka flourished during this period. He was one of the famous poets of the time. He composed a long poem wherein the king was shown as a warrior and a just king.

Ramadeva 1252-1273 AD

After the death of Samgramadeva, his son Ramadeva became the king. On assuming power, the first thing he did was punish the murderers of his father. He brought peace and prosperity and his wife Queen Samudra helped in the development of the country. He also had a trusted and faithful minister, Prithviraja, who helped him bring changes.

The king built a new fort Sallara on the banks of the Indus and repaired an old Vishnu temple Shamala at Utpalapora. Queen Samudra also constructed a matha on River Vitasta in her own name. The king did not have a son. So he adopted a Brahmin boy named Lakshmanadeva and constructed a town known as Bhisyakapora. He ruled for twenty-one years and died in 1273 AD.

Lakshmanadeva 1273–1286 AD

Lakshmanadeva succeeded to the throne of Kashmir. He was a very wise and learned king and loved to acquire all kinds of knowledge. He worked hard to contribute to the development of science and philosophy, perpetuating classical knowledge.

He was married to a pious and cultured woman known as Mahila. She built a math just by the side of her mother-in-law's math. While Lakshmanadeva was a learned man, he lacked the vigour of a Kshatriya soldier. Yet the people had great love and regard for him.

When Kajjala or Khajlak, a fierce Turkish Muslim warrior, invaded Kashmir, Lakshmanadeva failed to defend the country and was defeated. Kajjala plundered the country and went away. The king died and there was confusion and misery everywhere. Did Lakshmanadeva die without any offspring? No one knows.

Simhadeva 1286–1301 AD

After the death of Lakshmanadeva, Simhadeva ascended the throne. It is not known whether Lakshmanadeva and he were relatives. When Simhadeva ascended the throne, he was faced with internal rivalry from Samgramachandra, lord of Lohara, but the latter died and Simhadeva declared himself ruler of the country.

Initially, he was a pious and religious king. He constructed a temple and set up an image of Narisimha at Dhyanoddara. So religious was the king that one day he ordered that the idol of Vijayeshvara be bathed in milk purchased with one Lakh pieces of gold[16]. Also, Shankarasvami, the religious priest, who performed these duties, earned eighteen maths (place of worship) as his fee. Every morning, when the king awoke, he recited the couplet,[17] "I bow to Shankara the lord of Gauri, whose eyes are pure as fire, whose feet are worshipped by the learned, and who is bedecked with the crescent of the moon." The king was so pious that once he sought to punish a man for the wrongdoings of his daughter. According to RK Parmu,[18] "To end the vice, Raja Simhadeva had decreed that a father shall be punished for his daughter's misconduct. But it appears that the Raja had issued the order in a state of drunkenness, because shortly afterwards he revoked it at the instance of his own favourite dancing girl Idagali and the evil progressed unchecked."

The king did not remain religious for long; he soon fell into the company of bad men and lost faith in God. The change in the king made the people angry. In fact, the king's death came when he lusted after the beautiful daughter of his nurse. He fell for her and approached her but the young woman informed her husband Darya, who succeeded in conniving with other rebels and killed the king. Darya struck at the opportune time when there was a rebellion in the country as the people had become sick of the king. His death was a relief for the people. Simhadeva too died issueless.

Islam In Kashmir

Muhammad bin Qasim invaded Sind in the year 712 AD. His rule touched the borders of Kashmir. Since then, neighbouring countries such as Iran, Afghanistan, Turkistan and Sind have remained under Arab Muslims. Nothing could withstand the furious onslaught of the Arab Muslims who rose from the deserts to establish their supremacy in many countries. Kashmir had remained substantially unaffected from Islamic conversion. However, Muslims were frequent visitors to the valley. Some of the visitors even joined the army and other professions. The immigrant Muslims retained their distinctness and avoided merging with the Hindu majority. Meanwhile, Mahmud Gaznavi also began preparing the ground for Islamisation at various places. Gaznavi had so far succeeded in destroying the Sahi dynasty and even brought permanent presence of Islam in the valley but he still could not penetrate the valley despite trying many times. The topographic and climatic conditions at that time were not conducive making him give up his plans ultimately. However, there was a threat from Central Asia with the Turks trying to invade Kashmir. According to PNK Bamzai,[19] "Muhammadanised Turks were becoming more aggressive and were seeking new fields for their activities. A small force of these Muslim Turks, under their leader, Sallara Vismaya, appears to have extended its influence to the outskirts of the valley during the troubled days of civil war between Sussala and Bhiksacara."

Political disturbances, internal feuds, discrimination, cruel social injustice and cold apathy of the custodians towards their subjects added to the spread of the new faith. It was, however, from the period of Suhadeva that many foreigners came to Kashmir and Islam began to spread its wings and gain prominence in the Kashmiri society and polity.

Suhadeva 1301-1320 AD

After Simhadeva was killed, Suhadeva claimed the throne. He was the brother of Lakshmanadeva and became the king in 1301 AD. During his reign, many foreigners came to Kashmir. Prominent among them were Shah Mir and Rinchan whose role in Kashmir affairs is important. Shah Mir was "a Muslim adventurer from some village near Riasi, or some say from Swat Valley," says Prem Nath Bazaz, [20]. *Baharistan-i-Shahi* says, [21] "Shah Mir, now known the title Shamas-ud-Din, was a ruler of Swadgir (Swat)." According to Malik Haydar Chadora, "Shah Mir came to Kashmir in 1312 AD as a Darwesh which seems to put his royal ancestry in doubt."[22]

The second man who came to Kashmir in 1318 AD to live permanently was Rinchan who came along with a band of followers from Tibet. A Buddhist prince from Tibet known as Bottas, visited Kashmir. According to Jonaraja [23], "At this time, Kalamanya Bottas had become the enemy. He was deceitfully killed Vakatanya along with his friends and relatives. But one of the his sons named Rinchan, respected for his great intellect, escaped the massacre."

Rinchan reached Kashmir to seek asylum. He approached Ramchand (Ramachandra) the commander-in-chief of Suhadeva's army who gave him shelter at Gagangir,[24] says *Baharistan-i-Shahi*. Rinchan also sought military assistance from Ramchand.

Around that time, another man who came to the valley was Lanker Chak. The exact date of his arrival is not known. According to *Baharistan-i-Shahi*, [25] "One Lanker Chak, the forbearer of the Chaks, abandoned the lands of Dardu and moved to Drav because of family feud. He then migrated to Kashmir with his wife and children and settled in the Valley of Trihgam at Gagangir." Incidentally, the same village he settled in became the seat of Chaks later on. Kashi Nath Pandit, in his notes in *Baharistan-i-Shahi*, says [26] "Lanker Chak is a corruption of Alamkaracakra." It is true that Alamkaracakra is mentioned in Kalhana's *Rajatarangini*. But by and large, as we have seen, during this period Lanker Chak had no role in the affairs of the state. According to Prem Nath Bazaz, [27] "Lanker Chak was another Buddhist of royal birth from the principality of Dardistan in the north whose enemies were at his heels to annihilate him."

As per the traditional hospitality of Kashmiri Hindu rulers, when Suhadeva heard about Shah Mir's arrival in Baramulla he directed that arrangements be made for his stay there and provided him with means of living. In fact, Shah Mir's presence was appreciated by Prime Minister Ramachandra, who saw it as a form of security, given the very disturbed conditions because of invasion by Dulcha/ Dalcha into the valley. In the early spring of the year 1323 AD, a cruel commander, Dulcha/ Dalcha by name, invaded Kashmir from Baramulla. He led a troop of seventy thousand Mongol and Turk soldiers and cavalry and they entered the valley. Once the troops were in the valley, he instructed his men to carry out mass massacre of the inhabitants of every town and village. Whosoever fell into the hands of these barbarous, cruel soldiers between the boundaries of Maraz and Kamraz fell to the sword. These soldiers were ferocious men who insulted and killed men who were huddled in their houses. Nor did they spare their wives and daughters. Those who could run fled and hid themselves in the mountains and forests. It was a tragedy of immense proportions—men were killed; women and children made captive, and some of them enslaved and sold to the merchants and traders of Cathay who had accompanied the troops. The ruthless soldiers did not stop their acts of savagery there. They went on to torch the city and the villages creating an inferno that reduced the homes of people to ashes. People cried but there was no one to listen to their cries. The

Dulcha troops,[28] "consumed as much of food grains as they needed and whatever remained they destroyed. The whole of Kashmir was subjected to destruction by their ungodly acts."

There are conflicting views about Dulcha/ Dalcha's status in the country of his origin. Kashi Nath describes him as a "military officer under the Mongols." Dulcha/Zulju alias Dhu'l-Qadr Khan, was King Karmmasena's commander of the army. He was as ferocious as Genghis Khan, the Mongolian emperor. He was cruel and had no qualms about using deceit and treachery. When he marched towards Kashmir, Suhadeva fled to Kishtwar and left the Prime Minister, Ramachandra, his father-in-law, and his wife Kota Devi to face the enemy. According to Sukhdev Singh Charak, [29] "After about six months when the invader (Dulcha) had left the country (Kashmir), Jodh Dev (the king of Jammu including Kishtwar) helped Suhadeva to return to the valley, but meanwhile Ratan Ju (Rinchan Bottas), the ruler of Tibet (Tibet), had occupied the valley and had been accepted by the Kashmiris as their Raja. Sah Dev (Suhadeva) came back to Kishtwar and the Raja of Jammu made provision for his sustenance." Jodh Dev ruled Jammu from 1310–1361 AD. Before he fled, the king had tried to strike a deal with Dulcha giving him subsidy with the result that he imposed heavy taxes on the people. The Brahmins were angry. Upset by the king's timidity, they decided to die fasting

Dulcha remained in the valley for eight months. This exhausted his provisions for feeding 60,000 soldiers. He reached a point where he could not find food to feed them. As winter approached, he decided to leave the country. He carried with him the loot he had collected and also the men and women as slaves. As soon as they started their journey, it started snowing heavily. They faced the hardest winter at a mountain called Devasar Pass (probably Anantnag side). All of them along with their leader Dulcha, perished on account of the cold. It is said that Dulcha asked some slaves to guide them through the shortest route from the valley but the slaves knowingly directed them towards the longer and more difficult route, Nature took revenge on this ferocious plunderer with the result that the entire army perished. As per Prem Nath Bazaz, [30] "Those humiliated and brutally treated Kashmiris, getting a chance to avenge national honour, advised him to take the most difficult and dangerous of the passes in the south of the valley. While attempting to cross the mountains the entire Tatar army together with their commander perished under a heavy snow storm...." *Baharistan-i-Shahi* further adds, [31] "On reaching the top of the mountain, God's wrath hurled upon them a rain of destruction. Thunderbolts were let loose. Such was the onslaught of rain and snow that all the soldiers, the Turks and prisoners met with their death and nobody survived." Fifty thousand Kashmiri captives perished in the disaster.

With Dulcha's death, there remained Rinchan, and later on, Shah Mir whose role in the events in Kashmir is important. According to Jonaraja, Rinchan also came with his small band of soldiers and entered the valley when Dulcha raided it. [32] "Dulcha and Rinchan blockaded the town in the east and in the north, and the people first fled towards west and then in the direction of Yama (south). Dulcha was like a billow in the water, and on the hill, Rinchan was like a tempest..." Interestingly, even after Dulcha left Kashmir, Suhadeva, who had fled to Kishtwar, did not return to reclaim the throne. Nobody knows how his end came. However, the people of Kashmir were happy and did not miss the king. They were only worried as to who would be crowned the next king of Kashmir. The choice fell on Ramachandra.

Ramachandra 1320 AD

Dulcha went away from the country says Jia Lal Kilam (33) "But his visit had upset the whole social and economic fabric of the country. People were in distress, lawlessness was rampant, and marauding bands infested the highways. The people had lost all faith in their ruler. All they wanted was a strong man who could establish peace with a resolute will. Such a man they found in Rinchan, who had previously repulsed an attack of Khasi tribe where he showed a great deal of military prowess and valour." Ramachandra was an able, kind-hearted and trustworthy Prime Minister and commander-in-chief and administrator to King Suhadeva. During his reign, Ramachandra looked after the affairs of the country.

He administered the country to the best of his ability. In this task, his beautiful daughter named Kota assisted him. To fight Dulcha he took help from Rinchan who had a few hundred soldiers at his command. Ramachandra also sought the help of Shah Mir. That was the time when he needed all kinds of help to repulse Dulcha's invasion. Seeing the throne vacant, Ramachandra declared himself as the king of Kashmir. But it was a move that made both Rinchan and Shah Mir jealous. They began conspiring and raised a rebellion against him taking the royal army by surprise.

Unable to fight an unexpected foe, Ramachandra managed to escape and took refuge in the Lohara fort. But Rinchan's army, knowing that they could not fight the royal army in the open, entered the fort in the guise of cloth merchants. When inside, they mercilessly killed Ramachandra. With his death, the throne of Kashmir fell into the hands of Rinchan who declared himself the king. He managed to save his throne from his adversaries subduing them successfully. However, there remained a potential adversary in the person of Ramachandra's brother who had also fled at the time of Dulcha's invasion.

Prince Rinchan 1320-1323AD

Rinchan declared himself the king of Kashmir. Taking a pragmatic view of his position as the king, he believed that he had to win the cooperation of the people of Kashmir who were Hindus in majority, as also the sympathies of Ravan Chandra, son of Ramachandra, and his sister Kota Rani. Rinchan developed interest in Kota Rani who was very beautiful. He wanted to marry her. But his treachery towards her father whom he had killed had forfeited her love. Jonaraja says, [34] "The queen Kota was as the Kalpa creeper in the garden of Ramachandra's household; but now the strong armed Rinchan planted her on his own breast." Rinchan was very shrewd and he managed to entice her by appointing her brother, as a minister. He then succeeded in marrying Kota.

He was a wise and alert king. He tried to bring prosperity to the people of the state. He also tried to give justice to his subjects to the best of his ability. There is a story which illustrates his wisdom in administering justice. There were two mares belonging to two different owners. Both the mares gave birth to young colts. Unfortunately, one colt died and the other enjoyed the affection and milk of both the mares. Suddenly, there arose a fight between the two owners about the ownership of the colt. The quarrel ultimately reached Rinchan who told them to bring the mares and the colt on a bridge. He went in a boat and threw the colt in the water. One of the mares jumped into the water and saved the colt. Thus, the real mother of the mare was discovered. People were happy with the justice "....they thought that the golden age had returned,"[35] says Jonaraja.

Rinchan was a Buddhist, and to win over the cooperation of the Hindu majority, he decided to convert to Hinduism. When he made his request to be converted to the Hindu head priest Devasvami, it posed a tricky problem for the Brahmins. Since Kashmiri Hindus had firm faith in the phenomena of predestinations and in the sanctity of their ancestral lineage, which they traced from some ancient Rishi, they refused outright. According to Jonaraja, [36] "The king asked Shri Devasvami to initiate him in the mantras of Shiva. But he was a Bottas (of Mongolian tribe), and Devasvami feared that the king was unworthy of such initiation and did not favour him."

Unfortunately, this became a turning point in the history of Kashmir. For this denial of admission—a small error on the part of an orthodox Brahmin, Hindus for centuries were penalised. The refusal caused mental distress to Rinchan. Then there came a Muslim priest, Sayyid Abdul Rahman, popularly known as Bulbul Shah who converted the king to Islam. According to *Baharistan-i-Shahi*, [37] "Rinchan was the first ruler of Kashmir to be admitted to the Islamic faith. He got a Khanqah built for Baba Bulbul Qalander."

Lamenting over Rinchan's conversion to Islam, Narendra Sahagala writes,[38] "But the then Kashmiri Pundits, even being great scholars, had lost understanding of the basic elements of religion because of prolonged unrest. As such, lacking farsightedness they were incapable of interpreting religion as per the requirements of the era. They straightway refused to initiate Rinchan into Hinduism, when Buddhism is a branch of Hindu religion."

"Bulbul Shah, was a disciple of Shah Niamat Ullah Wali, a Khalifa of Suhrawardi Tarikh (a Sufi sect)," [39] writes Jia Lal Kilam. According to Mohammad Ishaq Khan,[40] "Even as a king, Rinchan is reported to have spent sleepless nights in the quest for truth. It was his spiritual cravings which prompted him to hold a religious discussion with Devasvami, a Brahman priest, who lived in the city of Srinagar. Disgusted with the spiritual pretensions and the caste-consciousness of Brahmans, Rinchan rejected Shaivism."

After accepting Islam as his religion he was named as Sultan Sadr-ud-Din. The name was given to him by Bulbul Shah. According to GMD Sufi, [41], "Rinchan embraced Islam at the hands of Bulbul Shah and assumed the name of Sultan Sadr-ud-din, and claims our attention as the first Muslim ruler of Kashmir."

Rinchan proved a good administrator. He knew the terrible sufferings of the people, made worse by Dulcha's eight months of loot and wanton destruction of life and property. He wanted to provide comfort to the people. Jonaraja writes, [42] "The country was weary of trouble and disorder, and Rinchan gave it rest under the shelter of his arm. When the dark days disappeared, the people of Kashmir witnessed again all the festivities which they had celebrated under the former kings."

Meanwhile, Udyanadeva hatched a conspiracy to assassinate the king. He took the help of a local influential Sardar Tukka and his trusted men. He then directed Tukka, the Shukkalankitas (a tribe) and other disgruntled courtiers and military commanders to kill the king. The opportunity came when one day Rinchan was travelling on a highway and his attackers struck him. Vyala, one of the conspirators, hit the king with a sword and the others fought with his bodyguards who later fled from the scene. The king fell down and fainted. The enemy thought he was dead but he had regained consciousness and remained in the same state to mislead the enemy. On reaching the capital, they tried to plunder the palace but suddenly they found that the king was still alive. The king destroyed them one by one. Jonaraja writes, [43] "The angry king ripped open by the sword the wombs of his enemy's wives in the fort, who were with child, as one tears open beans by the finger nail."

During Rinchan's rule, the administration was the same as it was under Ramachandra. He was strict in administering justice and could tame troublemakers such as Dammaras, Ekangas and Lavanyas. He adopted a policy of divide and rule. But Rinchan's wounds worsened and he did not live long to reap the fruits of his policies. He died in the year 1323 AD. Perhaps the king had some premonition of his own death because he had called Shah Mir and entrusted his son Haydar and wife Kota Rani under his care.

Udyanadeva 1323-1338 AD

Rinchan died and Kota Rani desperately tried to prevent a Muslim from becoming the king of Kashmir. Instead of installing Haydar, her son, as the king she called Udyanadeva from hiding and offered him the throne. Udyanadeva got not only the throne but also Kota Rani as his wife and the marriage was performed with great pomp and show.

It seems that Kota Rani was not happy as the wife of Rinchan. She did not acknowledge Islam as her religion when her husband converted to Islam. In Islam, the marriage between two people having different faiths is not valid. However, in Kashmir, Muslims had to adjust themselves to the local culture. In this connection, Prem Nath Bazaz has written, [44] "...in Kashmir, Islam to be a popular religion had to adapt itself to the demands of local culture." He has further said, "In their religious views, the Kashmiris have through their long chequered history been liberal and tolerant." In the same vein, Lawrence says, [45] "If a comparison be made between customs of Hindus and Muslims it will be seen that there are many resemblances." At another place, he writes [46], "The indifference shown in the matter of mosques and mullahs may be accounted for by the fact that Kashmiri Sunnis are only Muslims in name. In their heart they are Hindus and the religion of Islam is too abstract."

The majority of the population in the valley, at that point of time, were Hindus. So Kota Rani played a major role in preventing Kashmir from becoming an Islamic country. However, Udyanadeva did not prove to be the right choice. Though he ruled the country for 15 years, he proved to be a very weak king. He spent his time worshiping, in penances and prayers and neglected the administrative activities. He also spent money in charities. He did not raise a strong army to safeguard the country from outside invasions. He neglected the agricultural sector which would otherwise have made the people of Kashmir self-sufficient.

In 1330 AD, Kashmir had to face another attack from outside. A Persian Tatar or a Turkish (Turco-Mongol) named Urwan alias Urdil alias Sardar Achala, attacked Kashmir and reached Bhimanaka. The moment the news of the invasion spread in the valley, Udyanadeva, believing that Dulcha, the Tatar invader, had come again, fled to Tibet, leaving the country and the people at the mercy of Kota Rani. She became the flag bearer of Kashmir. She took charge of the situation and convened a meeting of all her officials, commanders and Brahmins too. She told them to face the enemy united.

She knew that fighting the huge army of Achala would annihilate her side but she was courageous and knew that military manoeuvring would stand her in good stead. She spoke to the people and told them if they did not stand united against this invader, the country was going to be ruined forever. She hatched a plan and used diplomacy to win Achala's trust. She sent a letter to him through a minister saying that the kingdom was without a king and therefore he could become the king of Kashmir. She advised him to send his army back as they were not locals and their presence could intimidate the people. Foolish Achala agreed and sent his army back. The ministers arrested him, telling him he was being taken to be part of a festival celebration.

Kota Rani was not in favour of employing Shah Mir as the prime minister. She was feeling insecure and slowly resenting the fact that he was getting very popular among the people and the ministers. Therefore, she had no alternative but to invite Udyanadeva again and install him as the king despite the fact that he had deserted her at the time of Achala's invasion.

Without a doubt, Kota Rani played a heroic and important role in ousting Achala from the country. Her diplomatic move paid off and she succeeded in unifying the people. According to Narendra Sahagala,[47] "Achala was engrossed in the imaginary enjoyment of beauty. Kota Rani reached there like a roaring lion and with one stroke of her sword beheaded Achala. The same fate awaited his colleagues. Kota Rani emerged victorious."

In the middle of all this, Udyanadeva passed away in 1338 AD on the day of Shivratri. Kota Rani did not declare the death of the king for four days as she was aware that Shah Mir would capture the throne. After four days, when she had settled every detail of the next ruler, she declared the death of the king. She decided to rule the country herself.

Kota Rani 1338–1339AD

After the death of Rinchan, his son Haydar had the right to occupy the throne of Kashmir but Kota Rani was determined not to transform Kashmir into a Muslim country. Her love for Kashmir was greater than the personal agenda of making her son king. She knew that Shah Mir was playing a very treacherous game. Though he had played an important role in defeating Achala, resulting in his popularity among the nobility, she was not in favour of the Kashmir throne going into the hands of Muslims again. But choosing Udyanadeva as the king also proved a wrong decision. In the words of Prem Nath Bazaz [48], "Udyanadeva did not prove worthy of the trust that the courtiers, nobles and grandees had reposed in him. He remained on the throne for more than fifteen years but lacked all the virtues of a wise monarch. He was chicken-hearted and good-for-nothing..."

According to Narendra Sahagala,[49] "Udyanadeva was simply a twinkling lamp in front of the resplendent glory of Kota Rani. With the help of her attraction, beauty and wisdom, the queen held Udyanadeva in her political clutches." After his death, she ascended the throne. She also appointed Bhikshana Bhatta as her prime minister. Both these moves hurt Shah Mir. Kota Rani had another son, Bhola Rattan, from Udyanadeva. The upbringing of the child was handed over to Bhikshana Bhatt just as the upbringing of her elder son Haydar was entrusted to Shah Mir. Shah Mir's role in fighting the enemy had earned him laurels. He could have easily taken control of the kingdom but he was scared of Kota Rani. She was not only beautiful but wise and intelligent too. She efficiently managed the administration of the country and looked after her subjects very well. She was trained in the functioning of the government under her father Ramachandra who had virtually ruled the country under the kingship of Suhadeva. She had taken overall charge of the administration of the country even when Udyanadeva was king as he proved unfit, weak and timid. Jonaraja says [50] "As the canal nourished cultivated fields with water, so did the queen nourish the people bestowing much wealth on them. She was to the kingdom what the moon is to the blue lotus; and to the enemy she was what that luminary is to the white lotus." But she had an underlying fear of Shah Mir. She found him very cunning and unscrupulous.

Kota Rani was also bold and shrewd. On one occasion, the lord of Kampala disobeyed her. She personally went to dislodge him. However, he captured and imprisoned her. Her trusted minister, Kumara Bhatt, went to the prison along with a servant who resembled her. He made the servant wear the dress of the queen and the queen put on her dress. This way Kota Rani escaped from prison.

When Kota Rani made Bhikshana Bhatt the prime minister, it angered Shah Mir who was expecting that post. He pretended to be ill. She sent Bhikshana Bhatt and Avatar to enquire after his health. Shah Mir killed both of them and raised a rebellion against her. When she came to know about the assassinations, she hid herself in Kota fort after closing the gates to thwart enemy attack. Shah Mir imprisoned her in her own palace and declared himself the king of Kashmir.

He then sent her a note with the message that she should sit with him on the throne. He unabashedly proposed marriage to her. Says Husayn Ibn Ali, "For Kota Rani, death with dignity was better than life with humiliation." Humiliated, the queen committed suicide and with her death the Hindu period of Kashmir came to an end.

Some historians say that she lured Shah Mir and offered him the throne and herself, a proposal which he accepted. After that she dressed herself in a bride's attire and went to him. She carried a dagger to kill him but could not do so. Instead, when he came close to her she thrust the dagger into her own heart and killed herself.

Kashi Nath Pandita, the translator of *Baharistan-i-Shahi* says, [51] "The author of the chronicle gives the impression that the marriage of Koteh Ren (Kota Rani) with Shah Mir lasted for some time." Several prominent historians have refuted this. Malik Haydar says, "Koteh Ren rejected his marriage proposal because she did not want to marry her subordinate. But she was defeated by him; she committed suicide by driving a dagger into her belly."

However, Stein in *Rajatarangini* has said [52], "To it retired Queen Kota, the last of the Hindu rulers of Kashmir, and there she was murdered by her husband, the adventurer Shah Mir (AD 1339)."

According to Mohammed Qasim Firishta,[53] "The second day after his marriage Shah Meer imprisoned his wife, and proclaimed himself king, under the title of Shums-ood-Deen, causing coins to be struck, and public prayers to be read in his name, and he established the Hunefy doctrines of the Mahomedan religion throughout Kashmeer."

Hassan gives the same story, but with a slight difference. According to him, she was compelled by circumstances to agree to his proposal[54]. "On the day of their marriage, she clad herself in gorgeous robes but stabbed herself ripping open her bowels, saying to Shah Mir, 'This is my acceptance'."

Jonaraja writes,[55] "The fascinating Shah Mir sent word to the Queen through his messenger, stating that she might sit with him on the throne, and on his breast with the goddess of royalty, and that she might live in his heart with the virtue of forbearers. The queen was won by his assiduity, and he took possession of the country and Queen Kota. He spent one night with her in the same bed and when he rose in the morning he caused her to be captured by the Tikshnas. Then on the tenth bright lunar day, in the month of Shravana in the year, the queen dropped from her kingdom like a star."

PNK Bamzai says [56] "Shah Mir sent a word to present herself before him. Clad in the rich costumes and wearing her most precious ornaments, she entered his bedchamber. Triumphantly Shah Mir approached her. But before he could draw her into his arms, Kota Rani had stabbed herself to death"

According to Jia Lal Kilam, [57] "At this time began the real struggle between militant Islam and tolerant but static Hinduism of the day. Kota Rani represented the latter and Shah Mir became the rallying point of the forces of Islam."

The character of Kota Devi is unique by all standards—flawless and perfect. She was entirely unselfish and devoted to the cause of the betterment of the country. She became a legendary political symbol for the people of Kashmir.

Thirteen
Cultural Boom in Ancient Kashmir

The Indus Valley civilization throws a flood of light on the social, cultural and economic life of ancient India. Mohenjo-Daro and Harappa established that we had a very advanced civilization even at that early period.

The archaeological excavations took place at Kutbal, Zurhama (Kupwara District of Kashmir) and Rafiabad. The unearthing of unique bronze sculptures in these places has added a new dimension to Kashmir's history. Similarly, the ancient coins discovered at the Rafiabad area of north Kashmir have added a new leaf to Kashmir's rich history. These findings have baffled experts.

Compared to other ancient civilizations that had left enough written material by which we could know about them, the Indus people have left no written material. In this regard, Kashmir is no exception. Thus, for the assessment of ancient civilization, we have to depend upon archaeological remains, numismatic evidence etc. But again, these sources are not enough to study the complete life of these periods—the social, economic and religious life, the food and drink, dress, sports, weapons of war, medicines, agriculture, religion etc.

Despite these handicaps, there is, however, a refreshing situation in the case of Kashmir for chronicling the events, as there are literary works on various subjects in Sanskrit that give us a fair insight into the history of Kashmir during the ancient period. Among them are *Nilamatapurana* and *Rajatarangini*. While the author of the former is not known, the latter was written by Kalhana, son of an illustrious minister of Kashmir, Lord Canpaka. Both these literary works have thrown light upon life in ancient Kashmir. There are, of course, other notable writers who have contributed in literary works. Prof Buhler writes that "Suvrata wrote a handbook of the history of Kashmir to be committed to the memory in the schools." Another author of repute was Kshemendra, also known as Vyasadasa, who wrote *Nrapavali*, a list of kings. He lived during the time of King Ananta Deva (1029 -1064). Prof Buhler's report describes *Nrapavali* as "an important source of information on the secret antiquities of Kashmir." M A Stein says,[1] "Helaraja, who was a Kashmiri and lived probably in the 9th or 10th century, has written a commentary on Bhartrhari's Vakyapadiya." Pandit Kalhana has mentioned that Helaraja composed a list of kings *Parthivavali* in twelve thousand Shlokas.

Kashmir: A Seat of Learning

From early times, Kashmir earned the reputation of being a seat of learning. The tradition in India, and in some parts of South-Indian provinces was that a young boy, at the time of being baptised for acquiring knowledge and learning, was asked to move seven steps towards the north, maintaining that he had fulfilled the pilgrimage to Kashmir for learning. There were certainly sufficient reasons for students and learners to come to the valley. As a result of constant interaction with the outsiders such as travellers and intellectuals, the Kashmiri people attempted to study almost all the branches of learning and also made their own contribution to it.

Religion

Kashmiris trace their origin to the Aryans and believe they are their descendents. Through *Rajatarangini* and *Nilamatapurana* and other historical documents, there is evidence that Kashmiris believed in the mystical and metaphysical pantheism. Shiva and Parvati were the chief deities worshiped. Fate, predestination and transmigration of the soul are important beliefs. Most of the ancient kings had temple building as a pastime. The introductory verses of Kalhana contain prayers addressed to Shiva representing God in his union with Parvati. Kalhana refers to Kallata Bhatt as one of the chief expositors of Kashmiri Shaivism.

Curiously, Buddhism flourished side by side with Shaivism. For centuries, the orthodox creed of Vedic religion where animal sacrifices are allowed existed peacefully side by side with Buddhism. Buddha was not only considered as an incarnation of Vishnu but was also taken as one of the ten Avatars of Vishnu.

The Great Scholars of Kashmir

Abhinanda

He was a great poet of Kashmir who flourished during the ninth century. Like Abhinavagupta, Abhinanda's ancestors also migrated from Gaudadesa to Kashmir. Abhinavagupta has mentioned about Abhinanda in his work *Lochana*. Abhinanda's father Jayantabhatta was also a scholar who flourished during Samkaravarman's period. His work *Kadambari-kathasara* is an epitome of Bana's Kadambari in an epic form.

Abhinavagupta

King Lalitaditya brought Artigupta, the ancestor of Abhinavagupta, to Kashmir. Once in Kashmir, the king gave him a mansion to live in, which was near the Chandramulisvara temple on the banks of the Vitasta river. As per Mark SG Dyczkowski,[2] "his ancestors were distinguished scholars in the court of Kannuaj. They were brought to Kashmir by King Lalitaditya about middle of eight century. Abhinavagupta's grandfather was Varahagupta and his father Narasimhagupta was also known as Cukhala. Despite the Vaishnava connotations of his father's name, he was an adherent devotee of Shiva."

Artigupta was a great scholar of Kannuaj administering about one hundred villages and was designated as 'Gopta' a title granted to a learned man by the king. Says Baljinnath Pandit in *Isvara-Pratyabhijna-Karika*[3], "Some ancient ancestor of Artigupta may have been such an efficient and influential Gopta that the common people gave all the members of his family the surname Gopta. The word may have later been abbreviated as Gupta."

Abhinavagupta, born between 950-960 AD, was a polymath and wrote *Tantraloka* (the world of tantra), which contains the essence of all the scriptural works of Monistic Shaivism. It will not be an exaggeration to say that Abhinavagupta was the harbinger of social and cultural revolution in Kashmir. His *Tantraloka,* also known as Trika Philosophy, is based on Monism. It was a new approach discarding the existing dualistic system of religion. It also discarded the most popular belief in Mayavaad as taught in the Upanishads and Vedanta philosophy. He avoided including negativism of Mayavaad. His Trika philosophy does not hesitate to accept an objective reality of the universe, which Vedanta's Mayavaad had discarded.

When he was young, he authored a work known as *Bodha-Pancadasika* on Kashmir Shaivism. It consists of 16 verses of which 15 deal with the subject matter and the 16th explains the purpose of such a composition. It is designed to enable ordinary readers to have an idea of the basis of monistic Shaivism.

Abhinavagupta's mother, Vimala/ Vimalakala, died when he was just two years old. After his mother passed away, his father, Narasimhagupta led an ascetic life. His younger brother Manoratha was also a Shiva devotee.

Abhinavagupta has been one of the greatest thinkers and philosophers of Kashmir. As per Pandit Madhusudhan Kaul Shastri, the first teacher of Abhinavagupta was Narasimhagupta who taught him grammar, logic and literature.

Abhinavagupta was the pupil of Utpalacarya, an authority on the Pratyabhijna system. *Isvara- Pratyabhijna-karika* and his *Tika* are his two commentaries on Utpalacarya's work. He took advantage of many Shaiva masters and teachers of other branches of learning who lived in Kashmir. Even in his formative period, he shunned the company of the impious and lived a solitary life devoted to the quest for truth.

He seems to have had just a small group of close disciples, most of whom were members of his family. His brother Manoratha was one of his first disciples. Later, his sister Amba and her husband Karna joined him. Karna's premature death left Amba alone with their only son Yogeshwera, and she began devoting herself entirely to the worship of Lord Shiva and the services of her brother. The in-laws of Abhinavagupta's sister were devoted to him and accepted him as their sacred teacher and served him faithfully. It is said that one of his cousins was Ksemagupta who later became his most famous disciple Ksemaraja.

It was at the instance of his guru, Shambhu Natha of Jalandhara, that he wrote *Tantraloka*. He wrote it in his early forties. As per Mark SG Dyczkowski,[4] "Thus Mandra invited him to stay in his town outside Pravarapura (modern Srinagar) where, in the house of Vatsalika, aunt of Mandra, he wrote the *Tantra-Aloka (*Light on the Tantras)."

Abhinavagupta had attained enlightenment when he wrote *Tantraloka* for the benefit of his disciples, who wanted to gain a perfect knowledge of the Tantras.

He is perhaps the greatest genius of his time and a most prolific writer. His other famous works are *Tantrasars, Gitartha Sangraha* (Commentary on the Bhagavad Gita), and *Parmarthasara.*

He learnt grammar, logic, literature and music from his father Narasimhagupta. He learnt Monistic Shaivism from Shambhu Natha Jalandhara, Tantra from Vamnatha, Brahmavidya from Bhutiraja, Krama and Trika philosophy from Bhutirajatanya. He also learnt Bhvanyaloka from Induraja, the son of Bhutiraja, Dramaturgy from Tauta Bhatta. However, there were other teachers from whom he learnt the art of philosophy, such as Vasugupta, Kallata, Sumatinatha, Helaraja, Bhutiraja, Bhaltenduraja, Somananda, Utpaladeva, Lakshamangupta, and Bhairava.

Abhinavagupta popularised Kashmir Shaivism. His interpretation and commentaries on the works of Somananda and Utpaladeva are elucidative. He synthesised the systems of Kaula, Kula and Trika Schools. He was a great philosopher, mystic, aesthetician, theologian, logician, dramatist, poet and musician. According to Harold G Coward, and K Kunjunni Raja,[5] "Abhinavagupta also accepts Bhattanayaka's opinion regarding the similarity between aesthetic experience and the mystic experience of the Absolute."

One of his important contributions was *Abhinavabharti*, a commentary on Natya Shastra of Bharat Muni. His *Lochana*, a commentary on the *Dhvanyaloka* of Anandavardhana is still being studied in Sanskrit institutes of learning. In addition to his poetic excellence, he was also a great composer. Robert Kane in his Introduction to Sahitya-darpana of Vishvanatha says that the *Dhvanyaloka* is an epoch-making work in the history of Alankara literature. It occupies the same position in poetry as Panini's *Astadhyayi* in grammar and Sankaracharya's *Saririka-Mimamsa* in Vedanta.

Kashmir Shaivism is classified by Abhinavagupta in four systems, namely: Krama, Spanda, Kula, and Pratyabhijna. Krama deals with space and time, Spanda with movement, Kula with the science of totality, and Pratyabhijna with the school of recognition.

According to G N Devy, [6] "With Bharatamuni and Anandavardhana, Abhinavagupta (10th – 11th century AD) is among the very greatest in Indian aesthetics. He has a further distinction, which the two others do not have, namely, he is also one of the most important of the Kashmir Shaivite philosophers. His work is comparable to that of Immanuel Kant in Western tradition."

Abhinavagupta, the master of fifty philosophical works, died somewhere in 1025 AD. According to Kashmiri tradition, reciting Bhairava Stava along with his 1200 disciples, Abhinavagupta entered a cave in Birwa village near Magam from where no one came out.

It is strange that Kalhana has not mentioned anything about Abhinavagupta and his excellence. This great contributor to Kashmir's art and literature should have found a place in *Rajatarangini*. According to Triloki Nath Dhar, [7] "The silence of Kalhana about Abhinavagupta as such is intriguing. He mentions three 'Abhinavas' in *Rajatarangini* and the suffix 'Gupta' he has not appended with any of these. The first Abhinava is 'Divira' or a scribe. The second is foster-brother of Kayyamantaka in the reign of Samgramaraja, and the third, a Dammara, a landed aristocrat. Nowhere, the name of Abhinavagupta appears as a scholar of repute or a Shaiva philosopher; whereas he has at times referred to such names as Muktakana, Shivasvamin, Anandavardhana, Ratnakara etc."

Anandavardhana

A Vaishnava and a devotee of Vishnu, Anandavardhana flourished during Avantivarman's period in Kashmir. His epoch-making work is *Dhvanyaloka* in Sanskrit, principally a treatise on the science of poetry. It is also called *Kavyaloka* and *Sahridayaloka*. This is a basic book on the Dhavani theory (the poetry which reveals a deeper meaning or suggestive quality of poetic language is termed Dhavani). It is in the form of verses (Karika) with detailed commentary called Vritti. According to GN Devy,[8] "He has the distinction of introducing in Sanskrit poetics the semantics of poetic language, but more important is the contribution in terms of turning the focus of critical discussion from the outward linguistic style and poetic embellishment to the more complex issue of linguistic structure in poetry."

According to PNK Bamzai,[9] "Anandavardhana found the inspiration for his epoch-making theory. His works reveal the vast range of his studies. His interests were varied—poetry, drama, philosophy, theology, ancient lore and Buddhist classics. He was equally familiar with them all. Anandavardhana's masterpiece, *Dhvanyaloka* or the Light of suggestion, marks the beginning of a new age in aesthetics." His work *Visamabanalila* (Sports of Cupid) is a narrative poetry in dramatic form. *Tattvaloka* is yet another philosophical work which we know from Abhinavagupta's reference.

According to Gaurinath Bhattacharyya Shastri,[10] "There are four schools of poetics: Alankara (figure), Ritti (style), Rasa (aesthetic pleasure) and Dhavani (suggestion). These have been declared to be the essential factors of poetry. Dhavani School, however, has grown to be the most important of all schools of Alankara literature."

Bhallata

This celebrated poet was the author of *Beellata-Sataka*. Bhallata is said to have flourished under the patronage of King Avantivarman. But when king Samkaravarman took over from Avantivarman he discontinued all allowance to Bhallata. Writes Somadeva Vasudeva,[11] "King Shan-kara-varman discontinued his royal patronage and Bhallata and his poet peers were forced to support themselves with lowly work."

Beellata-Sataka, a satirical poem, consists of 108 stanzas of varied meters and deals with morality and conduct. Abhinavagupta and Kshemendra have mentioned about this work.

Bhamaha

The author of *Kavyalankara* flourished in 500 AD. Bhamaha is one of the earliest writers on poetics in Sanskrit. He is also known as the earliest exponent of the Alankara/Alamkara school. Born to Rakrilagomin, he was Anandavardhana's predecessor and a contemporary of Rudrata. Amaresh Data says,[12] "According to him (Bhamaha), the body of poetry consisted of express and meaning; he advised poets to avoid defect (Doshas) and attain excellence (Gunas) and described the poetical embellishments (Alamkara), which enhance the beauty of expression. He was very particular about the grammatical correctness of expression and the absence of flaws in logical arguments."

There was a controversy among historians that Bhamaha was a Buddhist but the controversy died down as it became certain that he was not. He was one of the earliest critics to systematise poetic criticism and present it in a condensed form. His work *Kavyalankara* has been translated into English under the title *Kavyalankara of Bhamaha* by Naganatha Sastry.

Bhasarvajna

Bhasarvajna, a logician, was the author of *Nyaya-sara, Nayaya-bhusana, Ganakarika,* and *Nityajnanaviniscaya*. This scholar on logic was supposed to have flourished during the second half of the tenth century AD. Among the numerous writers on Indian systems of Logic, he occupies an important position. He belonged to Pasupata sect of Shaivism.

Bhaskara Bhatta/Kantha

Bhaskara Bhatta is also well known for his commentaries on *Shiva Sutras*. He composed *Sutra-vartika*. He flourished probably in the ninth century and was noted for his views. Bhaskara Bhatta was the disciple of Srikantha Bhatt and son of Divakara Bhatta.

Bhatta Ahladaka

Ahladaka Bhatt, the author of *Delarama-kathasara*, is known to belong to Kashmir. *Delarama-kathasara* is a poetic composition divided into 13 sections and builds around two brothers leaving their home. They are engulfed by the ups and downs of their mundane life. Fate plays havoc with them and they get separated from each other. But then there is a happy ending and they get united again.

Bhatta Lollata

Famous for his interpretation of Bharata's *Rasa Sutra*, Lollata Bhatta flourished in the ninth century in Kashmir. The analysis is known as *Utpatti-vada*. Lollata is known to be the first and earliest interpreter of Rasa Sutra. The interpretation given by him regarding the actors role in a play has been refuted by many subsequent authors.

Bhattanayaka

Bhattanayaka has been one of the greatest commentators of Rasa School. He authored *Hrdaya-darpana* on poetics, but that work is lost though Abhinavagupta has mentioned it. Bhattanayaka flourished during the ninth century AD. According to Gaurinath Bhattacharyya,[13] "It is interesting to note that Bhattanayaka has recognised two additional powers of word—the power of generalisation 'Bhavakatva' by which the meaning is intelligible to the audience and the power of 'Bhojaktva' which enables the audience to relish the enjoyment of the poem." Kalhana has mentioned him during the reign of Samkaravarman.

Bhatta Tauta

Abhinavagupta pays tributes to Bhatta Tauta as his teacher. Tauta appears to have written a work on poetics called *Kavya-Kautuka* which is now lost. Says T Nanjundaiya Sreekantaiya,[14] "Bhatta Tauta's work *Kavyakautuka*, a text of poetics, is now lost. But the statements that Abhinavagupta and several other rhetoricians have quoted are enough to establish that it must have been an important work." Bhatta Tauta lived in Kulgam district of Kashmir and Abhinavagupta learnt Dramaturgy from him.

Bilhana

Kavi Bilhana, a Sanskrit scholar, was an 11th century poet of Kashmir. He is known for his erotic love poem, *Caurapanchsika*. The poem, in fifty stanzas, depicts the secret love between a robber chief and a princess. Bilhana was born in Zevan, Khonmusha (modern Khunmu near Srinagar). He left Kashmir at the age of 42 and travelled widely to various places such as Mathura, Vrindavan, Kannuaj, Banaras, Bundelkhand and Gujarat. He finally settled at Kalyana during the rule of Vikrama VI of the Chalukya dynasty.

His works contain *Karanasundari*, a play in four acts which presents the secret love affair of King Karnadeva Trailokyamalla of the Chalukya dynasty. The king's marriage with a princess is elaborated as a romantic story. *Vikramankadevacharita* is the biographical data of the Chalukya Dynasty, and King Vikramaditya VI Tribhuvanamala (1076-1127 AD). This work has great historical significance.

Bilhana belonged to a family inclined to learning. His father Jyasthakalsa, a Brahmin, performed the Vedic Agnihotra (Fire oblation) sacrifice, and also wrote a commentary on the *Mahabhasya* which is lost now. His mother was Nagadevi and his two brothers Istarama and Ananda were both scholars and poets.

According to Prabhakar Narayan Kawthekar,[15] "Bilhana has been rightly respected for his literary contributions to Sanskrit literature." He further says[16] "We must admit that Bilhana is independent in his expression and does not apply the demand and the supply rule in a crude sense. His expression of the Shringara is unreserved, but not shallow." The legend goes that Bilhana fell in love with the daughter of King Madanabhirama,

Princess Yaminipurnatilaka, and he had a secret love affair. When they were discovered, Bilhana was thrown into prison. While awaiting judgment, not knowing whether he would be sent into exile or put to the gallows, he wrote the *Caurapanchsika*, a fifty stanza love poem.

It is unknown what fate Bilhana met. Nevertheless, his delightful poem was transmitted orally around India. There were several versions, including some from South India about his love life which had a happy ending; the Kashmiri version does not specify the outcome of his clandestine love affair.

In his introduction, Bilhana says, "poetry and the saffron are the two beautiful creations of Sarada Desh (Kashmir) which I never found elsewhere." Bilhana's works mention the staging of plays in which beautiful actresses and amateurs presented the performance on the life of Rama. Bilhana flourished during the period of King Ananta, King Kalasa and Harsa Deva.

Candracharya

During the reign of Abhimanyu, there was a great grammarian by the name of Candracharya. He wrote *Chandra-Vyakarna*, the Sanskrit grammar. He participated in the great Buddhist council in Kashmir. However, he also worked towards the triumph of the Brahminical cult. According to Suresh K Sharma and S R Bakshi,[17] "Candracharya, of Kashmir, was probably the first of these apostles of modern Brahmanism; Shankaracharya of South India who lived and preached in 8th or 9th century after Christ was the last." It is believed that the works of Candracharya were as important as Panini's works.

Charaka

Charaka, the principal contributor to the ancient science of Ayurveda, was born to a Brahmin family. He is placed somewhere in 300 BC. It is interesting to note that some of the scholars have placed him about 1000 BC, while some place him in the 1st or 2nd AD. It is believed that Charaka was the prime minister of King Kanishka. It is presumed that he belonged to Kashmir. His famous work is *Charaka Samhita*, which contains about 8,400 metrical verses. He was the first physician to present the concept of digestion, metabolism and immunity. Charaka says, "A physician who fails to enter the body of a patient with a lamp of knowledge and understanding can never treat diseases." According to his treatise, in order to treat a patient a doctor must first have an exhaustive theoretical knowledge of the nature of all known diseases, since preliminary symptoms are often the same whether a disease is mild or severe. Charaka emphasises that the malfunctioning of the digestive process is the first symptom of all diseases. It is remarkable that he first defined insanity in a human being.

Charaka's works are considered not only the most ancient and authoritative writing on Ayurveda but they also elaborate on the logic and philosophy on which the system is based. Science, he says, is dependent upon 'Yukt', a quality of intellect.

Damodaragupta

Damodaragupta was a minister in the court of King Jayapida. His famous work is *Kuttanimatam*—Kuttani is the procuress, and Mata is advice, therefore 'advice of the procuress'. Damodaragupta composed *Kuttanimatam/Kuttanimata* before joining the court of Jayapida. Writes A M Shastri,[18] "In India, like most of the luminaries on the horizon of Sanskrit literature, Damodaragupta also maintains complete taciturnity about himself, except only once when he gives his own name and speaks of himself as the author of *Kuttanimatam.*"

The Story: There lived a young courtesan Malati in Varanasi. Though extraordinarily beautiful, she was unable to attract rich people. In fact, she did not know the art of enticing the rich. One day, she went to a procuress, Vikarala, who had retired from the profession. In her young days, Vikarala had befriended very rich clients. She was very happy to see Malati and decided to teach her the art. *Kuttanimatam* is the teachings of Vikarala to Malati on how she could entice Chintamani, the son of an influential government officer and others like him. The story of *Kuttanimatam* is full of satires and comic situations. The characters in the story portrayed by Damodaragupta are lifelike. The work is a piece of art. Writes AM Shastri, [19] "Damodaragupta has brought all the important aspects of contemporary life within the purview of this little poem."

Drdhabala

Drdhabala was a great physician who flourished during the 8th-9th century. The son of great physician Kapila-bala, Drdhabala belonged to Panchanandapura (the town with five rivers) of Kashmir. He revised the *Charaka-Samhita* of Charaka and made many additions to the treatise. He contributed as many as 17 of the 30 chapters of *Charaka-Samhita*. The additions made by him came to be known as *Kasmira-patha*.

Harivarman

He was a disciple of Acharya Kumaralata, who had mastered the school of Sautrantika, a school of Buddhism.[20] This Harivarman was a famous Buddhist and a famous Sarvastivadin teacher of Kashmir. The school of Sautrantika, a Hinayana sect of Buddhism, was in fact started by yet another Kashmiri Brahmin known as Bhadanta Srilabha. Harivarman wrote *Satyasiddhi Shastra* and gave the right interpretation of the various schools of Buddhism,

Helaraja

Helaraja, the great philosopher, has been placed in the latter half of the seventh century. He was the son of Bhutiraja, born in the family of Lakshmanadeva, minister of Muktapida. Helaraja has written a commentary on Bhartrhari and he is also credited with having written *Prakirnakaprakasha*. According to John A Taber,[21] "Bhartrhari himself, however, did not explain why he believes that the word is superimposed on the meaning. His commentator Helaraja, however, mentions the fact that a word seems to be identified with its meaning when it is taught. The elder instructs the child, 'This is a cow, this is a horse.' Where the words 'cow' and 'horse' may be taken as referring to themselves; for the Indian grammarians recognised, as have modern linguists, that words are often used to indicate themselves quo sequences of phonemes." He further says, "Helaraja also suggests that the word functioning as a revealing medium becomes indistinguishable from the thing it reveals. Just as the light of a lamp cannot be separated from the object it illumines, so a word overlays the meaning it makes known and cannot be distinguished from it." As per Kalhana, Helaraja also composed a list of kings, *Parthivavali* in twelve thousand shlokas.

Jayanta Bhatta

Born to a wealthy and respected orthodox Brahmin family of Kashmir, Jayanta Bhatta appears to have flourished in Kashmir in 883-902 AD. He was the son of Chandra and father of Abhinanda. Jayanta wrote the well-known *Nyaya-Manjari* (A cluster of flowers of the tree of justice), which is unique in the sense that it is an independent work, not a commentary on an earlier work *Nayakalika* (A bud of the nyaya tree), and *Nayapallava* (A twig of nyaya tree). His famous play in four acts called *Agama-Dambra* is a historical-philosophical drama. Jayanta, also a logician, has, in his satires, ridiculed the elite during Samkaravarman's rule, even hinting that Samkaravarman was interested in statecraft rather than the fine arts. Jayanta Bhatta was a brilliant student from very young age. He wrote a commentary on Panini's *Astadhyayi* and got laurels for it from scholars of the time. Jayanta's great grandfather was a minister during Lalitaditya Muktapida period.

Jeratha/Jayadratha

Rajanaka Jeratha/Jayadratha, son of Sringararatha, is the author of *Haracarita-cintamani*, which is based on Shaiva myths and practices. He flourished during the first quarter of the 13th century. He was a great grammarian of Sanskrit from Kashmir. According to some scholars, he was the younger brother of Mammata. While the scholar poets who followed Abhinavagupta could not interpret his works, it was Jeratha who interpreted Abhinavagupta's *Tantraloka*. Jeratha also wrote *Viveka* which is a storehouse of historical information of Kashmir Shaivism. His work *Vamakesvarimata* describes typical tantric practices.

Kaiyata

Kaiyata, alias Kayyata, alias Kajjata was the son of Jaiyata Upadhyaya and younger brother of Mammata. He was the pupil of Mahesvara from Kashmir and authored *the Pradipa* (The Light), a major commentary on Patanjali's *Mahabhasya,* elucidating the meaning of words and expressions in that work. The work is also known as *Kaiyatadipa*. He is believed to have flourished during the 11th century. According to Harold G Coward, Karal H Potter and K Kunjunni Raja,[22] "There is little scope for giving his (Kaiyata's) views about problems on the philosophy of grammar; still the importance of the *Pradipa* in elucidating the views of Patanjali and Bhartrhari is considerable."

Kallata Bhatta

Kallata Bhatta can be traced to the 8th-9th century and was the disciple of Vasugupta. He developed and popularised the concept of *Spanda-Shastra* as a commentary, a key figure in *Spanda-Karika* (Song of the sacred tremor/vibration) tradition. According to Baljinnath Pandita,[23] "The *Spanda-Karika* reflects the same knowledge as is dealt with in the Shiva Sutra, although it is a philosophical treatise and not an Agama. It also does not deal directly with such philosophical topics as metaphysics, ontology, and cosmology."

Kallata Bhatta has been the most controversial scholar regarding the originator of *Spanda-Shastra*. The diverse opinion is that Vasugupta himself wrote *Spanda-Shastra*. Ksemaraja and Rajanaka Jeratha have also mentioned that it is Vasugupta who wrote the Spanda system and Kallata Bhatta only popularised it. Even Kallata Bhatta himself mentions that the 'Nectar of Spanda' is extracted by Vasugupta. Kallata Bhatta's works are *Tattvavicara*, which is lost. *Madhuvahini* and *Tattvartha-cintamani* are two commentaries on Shiva Sutra. He is also known as the preceptor of the Kula system.

Kukkoka Pandit

Kukkoka Pandit or Koka Pandit, son of Tejoka and grandson of Paribhadra, flourished during the ninth century. He was a Kashmiri Brahmin and was under the patronage of King Vainyadatta. He wrote a treatise on erotica, *Koka Shastra,* meaning scripture of the Koka. It was also known as *Rati Rahasya* (Secrets of Rati). Rati, according to Indian scriptures, is the wife of Kamadeva, the God of Love. It is, in fact, a complete guide for sexual preferences, but more a guide for husbands rather than wives, while the Kama Sutra of Vatsyayana is for both. The work has 800 verses and is divided into eight chapters. It has also classified women into four groups such as Padmini, Chitrini, Shankini and Hastini. According to Gaetan Brulotte and John Phillips,[24] "*Koka Shastra* is a manual that equips a man with the knowledge and skill to master the arts and technique of love and empowers him with essential knowledge about various habits, preferences, customs and manners of women hailing from various regions within India, the different bodily types, gestures, positions and techniques appropriate to specific occasions and types of women, and the suitable times for coitus."

Ksemaraja

Ksemaraja flourished during eleventh century. He was a very well read scholar and brilliant pupil of Abhinavagupta. Like his master Ksemaraja wrote on poetics, Tantra and Shaiva philosophy. He asserts that the teachings from *Spanda Karika* are the fundamental secret text of Shivagama, that is, the doctrine of this spiritual system. He therefore wrote *Shiva-sutra-Vimarsini* and he also penned *Spanda Sandoha*, which is an abridgement of his larger work, *Spanda Nirnaya*. This author of *Pratyabhijna-hridayam* was also a disciple of Abhinavagupta and teacher of Yogaraja and Sura. Ksemaraja also wrote a commentary *Netrodaya*, and a commentary each on Abhinavagupta's *Bhairava-Sotra, Varnodaya-Tantra, Vijrina-bhairava*. He also wrote the commentary *Vimarsini* on Vasugupta's *Shiva-sutra* and vivrti (commentary) on *Swacchanda-Tantra* of Rajanaka Ratnakantha. The *Swacchanda-Tantra* explains the pure Monistic side of the Advaita System of the Shaiva philosophy. The *Utpalastotravali Tika* is also his work. His work *Uddyota* is a commentary on Netra-tantra, which refers to Krama as distinct system. His works are *Pratyabhijna-hridayam, Vijnanadhairavodyata, Spandasandoha, Spandanirnaya, Stavcintamanitika, Parapravesika,* and *Tattvasandoha.*

Ksemaraja lived in Bijbihara. He was the son of Gundditya, and flourished during late ninth or early tenth century.

According to Mark SG Dyczkowski,[25] "Pratyabhijna representation of the Shaiva absolute as Light (Prakasha) and reflective awareness (Vimarsa), terms which denote the pure light of absolute and its infinite appearing. The absolute is Shiva who is universal consciousness and man's authentic nature (atman) who, reflection on Himself, actively generates and discerns His own manifestations."

Kshemendra

Another household name in the literary world of Kashmir is Kshemendra who flourished during King Samgramaraja/Ananta's reign. Interestingly, his father Prakashendra belonged to the Shaivite faith and had installed many idols in the name of Shiva at Svayam in Handawara. But Kshemendra chose to be a Vaishnava. His son, Somendra wrote a commentary on *Avadana-Kalpalata.* According to Pandit Madhusudhan Kaul Shastri, [26] "He (Kshemendra) knew Mathematics, Astrology, Medicine, Surgery, Politics, and Erotica, Buddhist philosophy and creed and Mantrasastra. It is believed that he began to be called Vyasadasa after his composition of the *Bharatamanjari.*"

Kshemendra acquired knowledge from great scholars like Abhinavagupta, whose disciple he was, and learnt Shaivism and Vaishnavism. Indeed, Kshemendra's contribution to Sanskrit literature is laudable. He was essentially a satirist and wrote with humour and sarcasm. His poem titled *Samyamatrika* is in eight cantos. The story depicts a wandering young courtesan Kalavti who gets introduced by a barber to an expert old lady Kankali for further training in her profession.

Kshemendra also fought for the downtrodden and the common man and loathed oppression of these sections of people by the elite. In *Naramamala*, he attacked people who held high office and oppressed the people. His works find ample mention of the bureaucracy as he wrote against the social evils in a bold and lucid manner. Some of his works are *Dasavataracharita, Kalavilasa, Ramayanamanjaari, Desopadesa, Naramamala* and *Vatsyayanasutrasara*. According to Nilakantha Diksita in *Three Satires*,[27] "Many of Kshemendra's compositions may offend modern tastes, but a consequent vilification of his works literary merit may be premature (he fares better if his work is judged with literary criteria prevalent in his time and milieu.)"

Pandit Madhusudhan Kaul highlights Kshemendra's writing in *Desopadesa* and *Naramamala* thus:[28] "In the opening and the concluding verses of the Desopadesa, the author begs to be excused for his use of uncivil tongue and says that he has done so not because it was his nature to pick holes in the coats of others but because of his earnest desire to see the people dissociate themselves from unlawful occupations and ignoble manners and customs. He thoroughly understands the importance of using the humorous style, rather than the sarcastic and taunting language, for training the raw youths in morals."

Kshemendra has used lot of similes in his works. His keen study made him find some errors even in the works of Kalidasa. According to T Nanjundaiya Sreekantaiya,[29] "Kshemendra studied literature under Abhinavagupta. Kshemendra was a man of universal curiosity. From *Brihatkatha Manjuari* to the *Caturvargasangraha*, there is no topic which did not become a subject to his pen. His works number about thirty five."

Kshemendra also wrote the *Brihatkatha Manjuari*, a summary of Gunadhya's *Brihatkatha* in 7,500 stanzas. His famous works *Rajavali* and *Nrapavali* are unfortunately not available. He also wrote a number of plays, which are lost. His two prominent plays are based on the epic stories — *Ramayana* and the *Mahabharata*.

Ksirasvamin

Tradition says that Ksirasvamin was the son of Isvarasvamin and flourished in Kashmir in the eight century during the period of King Jayapida. In fact, the king himself took grammar lessons from him. Ksirasvamin's commentary on Amarakosa and Nirukta called *Amarakosodghatana* is the oldest and most important commentary on the celebrated lexicon titled *Namalinganusasana*. He has also written a commentary on Panini's *Dhatupatha* tilted *Ksiratarangini*. Ksirasvamin is a Kashmiri grammarian but his book on grammar is not available.

Kuntaka

Essentially belonging to Kashmir, Kuntaka was one of the greatest scholars of Indian aesthetics, mainly in the realm of poetics and drama. His famous work is *Vakrokti-jivita*. He is known as the originator of the Vakrokti School. The theory portrays a critical analysis of poetic expression in terms of the language. He lived at a time when literary criticism in India was acquiring great sophistication.

Lagadha

Perhaps the first man to systematise astronomy, Lagadha's compilation named *Vedanaga Jyotisa* is the text on Vedic Astronomy which describes rules for tracking the motions of the sun and the moon for performing rituals. He is said to have flourished somewhere during 1350 BC to 900 BC, while others trace him back to the 5th century AD.

Laksmana Bhatta

Laksmana Bhatta was the teacher of Abhinavagupta, who learnt important philosophies such as Pratyabhijna and Krama from him. From Abhinavagupta we learn that he was a great philosopher. According to Abhinavagupta, Laksmana was the author of *Sri Shastra*. Nothing much is known about him except that he lived in Kashmir.

Mammata

Acharya Rajanaka Mammata, son of Jaiyata and brother of Kaiyata, is amongst the most famous Sanskrit scholars. This Kashmiri Brahmin lived in Balahom village of Pampore during the end of 10th century or the beginning of the 11th century AD. His famous work on poetics, *Kavya-Prakasha* comprises ten chapters. Hundreds of commentaries have been written on his work. Mammata has synthesised the earlier poetic doctrines into Dhavani school.

Mankha

Mankha was the son of Visvavrata and he had three brothers Srigara, Bhanga and Alamkara. Alamkara was the minister of King Jayasimha of Kashmir. He was a pupil of the critic Ruyyaka. Mankha composed mahakavya (a long poem) known as *Srikanta-carita* during 1135 -1145 AD. When he had completed the poem, he recited it to many court officials. He mentions the names of thirty of them. Among the listeners was a minister of King Jayasimha. Mahakavya is an epic poem that narrates the story of how the demon Tripura was overthrown by Shiva. However, the fascinating part of the poem is the description of seasons, including sunrise and sunset.

Matrgupta

An illustrious king of Kashmir, Matrgupta was also a poet himself. He is said to have written a commentary on the *Natyashastra* of Bharat Muni. He has been at times confused with Kalidasa. Kshemendra quotes the opinions of Matrgupta in one of his works.

Mentha

After Vikramaditya installed Matrgupta as the king of Kashmir, Mentha went to Kashmir and became a court poet. He composed the mahakavya *Hayagrivavadha*, describing the killing of the demon Hayagriva Vishnu.[30] When King Matrgupta heard the recitation, he presented a golden plate to be placed below it so that the flavour of poem did not vanish. Kshemendra has mentioned this poem in his *Suvritta-tilaka*. The poem is unfortunately lost. Mentha also wrote a poem on the story of Ramayana. He has been treated at par with Valmiki, Bhavabhuti and Rajashekhara. He is also treated as master of Rasa of Vakrokti.

Mukula

Mukula flourished during the period of Avantivarman in the ninth century. He wrote *Abhidhavrtti-matrka*, a grammatical-rhetorical treatise. He was the son of the famous Shaivite, Kallata Bhatta, who also flourished during the same period.

Panini

The historical record of linguistics begins in India with Panini, the fifth century grammarian who formulated 3,959 rules of Sanskrit morphology. Panini was a great Sanskrit grammarian who gave a comprehensive and scientific theory of phonetics, phonology and morphology. A treatise called *Astadhyayi,* and two poems *Patala-Vijaya* and *Jambavati-vijaya* are his major works.

Most Kashmiri scholars have authoritatively asserted that Panini was a Kashmiri but the claim has been refuted. According to Hiuen Tsang, a statue of Panini existed in Salatura. It is said that Panini was born in Salatura, a place on the banks of Indus River near Attok in Punjab. It is believed that he flourished somewhere in the fourth century BC. His mother's name was Dakshi and he was also named after her as Dakshi-Putra.

Pradyumana Bhatta

Pradyumana Bhatta was a Shaivite scholar of Kashmir. He flourished during Avantivarman's period. He was the disciple of Kallata Bhatta and was his cousin. Most thinkers appreciated his thesis but Somananda has criticised his Sakta predisposition inside the Shaiva fold. Pradyumana imparted his scholarly art to his son Prajnarjuna. His work is *Tatvagarbha-stotra* which eulogises Goddess Shakti.

Ramakantha

Ramakantha flourished during the 10th century (925 AD). His ancestors had come from Kannuaj and settled in Kashmir during the period of Lalitaditya. He was the disciple of Utpaladeva, the great teacher of Abhinavagupta. His commentaries on the Bhagavad Gita, known as *Sarvatobhadra* are lost. Ramakantha wrote *Spanda-Vivrti*. His interpretation is based on *Spanda-karika* of Kallata Bhatta. He called the commentary *Spanda-Vivrti*. He is said to have been born in Narayan in Kashmir and his father's name was Trivikrama.

Ratnakara

Ratnakara/Rakamala Ratmalara Vagisvari essentially belonged to the Vaishnava school of thought. He is the author of an enormous epic, a mahakavya called *Hara-Vijaya* which contained fifty cantos. Son of Amrtabhanu, he flourished under Ajitapida in 832-844 AD and Avantivarman (844-855 AD). He also wrote two small poems—*Vakrokti-Pancasika* and *Dhavanigathapancika*.

Rudrata

The son of Vamukha Bhatta, Rudrata was also known as Satanada. He wrote *Kavyalankara* and flourished during Samkaravarman's period. His works are divided into 16 Adhyas (chapters), which review the whole field of politics. Later, many writers commented on his works. Rudrata represents the Alankara School which is opposed to the theory of Vamana, that Ritti is the soul of poetry. In fact, he made Rasa and Ritti subordinate to Alankara.

Ruyyaka

Ruyyaka/Ruppaka/Rucaka flourished during the 12th century in Kashmir. His works on Alamkarasastra are *Alamkara-manjari, Alamkaranusarni,*

Alamkara-sarvasva, Alamkara-vartika, He also wrote *Harshacaritra-vartika, Nataka-mimamsa* and *Shrikantha-stava*. He also wrote commentaries on Mammata's *Kavya-Prakasha*.

Shambhu

Shambhu flourished during the reign of King Harsa in the 11th -12th century. He was the author of *Rajendra-Karnapura*, a poem in praise of King Harsa of Kashmir. His other famous work is *Anyokti-muktalata* in 108 verses.

Sankuka

He wrote a monumental work titled *Bhuvanabhyudaya* which describes a fierce battle for ascendency between Mammata and Utpala. Unfortunately, Sankuka's great work is lost. Kalhana has made mention about him. He flourished during the period of Ajitapida of Kashmir early in the ninth century. Sankuka's interpretation is known as *Anumiti-vada*.

Sarangadeva

His famous work on music and dance entitled *Sangeeta-ratnakara/ Sangita-Rahlakara* is considered the most important work on music after *Natyashastra*. The text is also known as Saptadhyayi as it is divided into seven chapters. The first six chapters deal with music and musical instruments while the last chapter deals with dance.

Sarangadeva was the son of Sodhaladeva of Kashmir and grandson of Bhaskara Sarangadeva. He flourished during 1210-1247 AD. His ancestors were from north Kashmir and his grandfather migrated to Devagiri (in Karnataka) which was later renamed Daulatabad, near Aurangabad and which later on became the famous capital of Mohammad bin Tuglaq. Sarangadeva worked as an accountant in the court of the Yadava King Singhana. So Sarangadeva was a Kashmiri whose family had migrated to South India where he wrote his book.

Sarangadeva, among other things, defined almost 264 Ragams, including some Dravidian and North Indian ones. He also described the various kinds of microtones and how to produce them. He classified them into various categories. He defined something called 'Kaku' (a term that is hardly used these days) as a blending of melody and Shruti.

Sangeeta-ratnakara is the first work to discuss the ragas in detail and it lists 264 of them. It also outlines the system of notation and goes into details about Swara, Shruti, Jatis, Taan, Grammas, Murchanas and musical instruments. According to Sarangadeva, 'Nada' is the basis of the art of music.

Srikantha/Srikanthanatha

Srikanthanatha who flourished perhaps in the 2nd century BC, is considered amongst the founding fathers of Shaivism. It is said that he wrote *Srikanthanatha Sutra* and *Srikantha Sutra. Srikantha Sutra* is said to be the basis of Trika system of Kashmir Shaivism. Swami Laksmana Joo, the Shaiva scholar of Kashmir believes that Srikanthanatha was Lord Shiva incarnate.

Silhana

A Vaishnavite by faith, Silhana, a Kashmiri, believed that Vishnu was the supreme God. He flourished in the early 13th century. His famous work is *Santi-Sataka*. According to Maurice Winternitz, [31] "The *Santi-Sataka* is a piece of pure religious poetry in which the hollowness of life and the grandeur of renunciation of the world and of the life of ascetics have been described in a considerably monotonous manner."

Shivasvamin

The son of Arkasvamin, a Buddhist philosopher, Shivasvamin wrote a mahakavya, the *Kapphanabhyudayam*, which contains an ornate poetry on a story of King Kapphana of Daksinapatha who invaded the territory of King Prasenajit of Sarvasti (Uttar Pradesh). Shivasvamin became a Buddhist and flourished during King Avantivarman's period and was his court poet.

Somadeva

This son of Rama was a famous minister and court poet of King Ananta. He compiled the famous work *Katha-sarit-sagara* (ocean of stream of stories), containing 2,13,88 stanzas in 18 Lambhakas (books) in 124 Taranga (chapters) for the amusement and edification of Queen Suryamati of Ananta Deva. In his introductory note, C H Tawney, the translator of the *Katha-sarit-sagara*, writes, "This is the Ocean of Story; this is the mirror of Indian imagination that Somadeva has left as a legacy to posterity." According to K M Panikkar, "Somadeva's *Katha-sarit-sagara*, one of the undisputed masterpieces of the world, may well be claimed to be the epic of the middle classes."

Queen Suryamati and Ananta had a very tragic life. To take her mind off the unhappy situations, the queen asked Somadeva to write for her. He, therefore, initially took help from the *Brihatkathaslokasamgraha* (Great Tales) composed by Gunadhya (from Andhra Pradesh), who was a poet in the early Christian era. While the original work is lost, Somadeva has preserved them though his monumental work *Katha-sarit-sagara.* Somadeva's work is a masterpiece, though some are tales of exotic sexual pleasures. His works are compared with medieval European fairy tales replete with magic, demons, vampires and high adventure. Evidently, it was written sometime between AD 1063 and 1089. This great piece of literature is a collection of stories that have ethos, romance and drama. It is difficult to translate or adapt the stories.

Writes CH Tawney,[32] "He (Somadeva) tells us that the Ocean of Story is not his original work, but is taken from a much larger collection by one Gunadhya, known as the *Brihat Katha*, or Great Tale. The manuscript of this Great Tale has not been found. In his first book, Somadeva gives us its legendary history, showing how it was related in turn by Siva, Pushpadanta (a great poet and author of monumental epic *Mahapurana*), Kanabhuti (a poet who helped Gunadhya compose *Brihat Katha*), Gunadhya (the composer of *Brihat Katha*) and Satavahana (the ruler of Andhra and great lover of literacy and architecture). The latter at first rejected it, and in despair Gunadhya began to burn it leaf by leaf—600,000 distiches are thus lost. Satavahana reappeared and saved the rest (100,000) which became known as *Brihat Katha*."

Shafi Shauq in the book compiled by Ayyappapanicker says,[33] "The great Sanskrit classics like the Purana, the Granthas, various chronicles, collection of tales such as *Katha-Sarit-Sagara*, amply reveal that the valley was inhibited by a people of great ideas and aspirations, centuries before the Christian era."

Somananda

Somananda (875–925 AD) was one of the greatest teachers of Kashmir Shaivism in the lineage of Trayambaka. As per legend, Sage Durvasa created a retarded son and named him Trayambaka. He created him to propagate the Shiva philosophy. Trayambaka married a Brahmin girl and got a son Sangamaditya from her. Somananda was the descendent of Sangamaditya. He was the author of the first philosophic treatise of this school, *Shiva-dristi*, which is the basis of Pratyabhijna-Shastra and tells us about the fundamental principles of Kashmir Shaivism. There are seven chapters and 700 verses in *Shiva-dristi.* It was, in fact, Somananda who systematised the concept of Shaiva Monistic Idealism in a philosophical form; rather we can safely say that he is the founder of Pratyabhijna. In the introductory note to Bhaskari, *The Doctrine of Divine Recognition*, KC Pandey writes,[34] "Vasugupta had recognized only three means or ways of final freedom of human beings: Sambhava, Sakta and Anava. All these meant life of detachment from the world and long practice of yoga, both extremely difficult in the practical world. Somananda represents an advance on Vasugupta. He shows a new way to the realization of the ultimate metaphysical reality, the Mahesvara."

A contemporary of Bhallata Kallata, the two formed the first wave of Kashmiri Shaivites to propose, in a rigorous and logical way, the concepts of non-dual Shaivism. Somananda was a philosopher who gave a rationalistic approach to the problem of the Ultimate Reality. He was the pupil of Vasugupta and flourished at the end of the ninth century. Like Abhinavagupta, Somananda's ancestors hailed from outside Kashmir, from north India. Somananda lived in Kashmir, most probably in Srinagar, where most of the later philosophers of the school lived.

Udbhata

Also referred to as Bhattodbhata, Udbhata was the Sabhapati of King Jayapida. The king engaged him at a salary of one Lakh dinars. His two works—*Kavya-lamkara-samgraha-Vritti* and *Bhamaha- Vivarnam*, a commentary on Bahama's Karyalamkar, are lost. *Kavya-lamkara-samgraha-Vritti*, a work on poetics, was divided into 75 Karika (cantos). He also wrote a poem called *Kumarasambhava*. The poem is now not available to us. In fact, Sanskrit literature produced between the ninth to twelfth centuries is more or less extinct. Udbhata exercised profound influence over the Alankara-samgraha. In his treatment of figures, Udbhata has followed in the footsteps of Bhamaha.

Utpaladeva

Rajanaka Utpaladeva/ Utpalacarya, one of the greatest philosophers of his times, belonged to the 9-10th century. There are opinions that the ancestors of Utpaladeva belonged to Gujarat. However, in Kashmir, he was the native of Guptapura (Kashmiri Gotapora, Vecharnag) in Kalaspur on the northern side of Srinagar. He was the son of Udayakara and the name of his mother was Vagisvari. His son was called Vibhramakara.

Surprisingly, Abhinavagupta calls him son and disciple of Somananda. He was attached to two great litterateurs of India—as a pupil of Somananda and teacher of Abhinavagupta. Utpaladeva is credited with the authorship of *Isvara-Pratyabhijna-Sutra* which is also called by the name of *Pratyabhijna-Sutra* and contains 104 verses. It is an authoritative work on the Pratyabhijna-Shastra of Kashmir Shaivism and of the *Shiva-stotravali*, written about 925 AD. It consists of a series of 20 short hymns in honour of Shiva. Writes Mark S G Dyczkowski,[35] "According to Utpaladeva, the man blinded by ignorance (Maya) and bound by his actions (Karma) is fettered to the round of birth and death, but when knowledge inspires the recognition of his divine sovereignty and power (Isvara), he full of consciousness alone, is a liberated soul."

Utpaladeva's great work *Isvara-Pratyabhijna-Karika-Vritti* is the most valuable philosophical work of Kashmir Shaivism. It is one of the best treatises which can be compared with the *Shiva-Dristi* of Somananda. According to Baljinnath Pandita,[36] "Although presenting an all-round comparative study of the subject at hand through a highly developed method of subtle logic—silencing the arguments of the contemporary schools of thought—the *Shiva-dristi* did not become as popular with scholars as did the *Isvara-Pratyabhijna* of Utpaladeva."

Utpaladeva is also the author of the *Siddhitrayi Vritti* on *Shiva-dristi*. He also wrote *Utpala-stotravali*. Though emphasising on the devotional love for God, he utilises subtle logical arguments aimed at establishing the existence of Atman as the basic re-collector. He counts only three aspects of Shakti as primary, in which the other two, Chit and Ananda are merged. According to Utpaladeva, says Baljinnath Pandita,[37] "The relationship between a cause and its effect can be established only when one and the same knowing subjects see both of them as necessarily being together." Utpaladeva was the guru of the great Tantrin Lakshanadesika/ Laksmana who lived in 10th –11th century.

Utpalavaisnava

Yet another important Shaiva scholar who belonged to Kashmir, Utpalavaisnava, was born in Narayanasthana, known presently as Naristan, a village in the Traal valley of Kashmir. He was a contemporary of Abhinavagupta and produced *Spandapradipika*. He practiced Pancaratra system of Vaishnavism.

Vakpatiraja

A great scholar during Lalitaditya's period, Vakpatiraja authored *Prakrit Kavya* and *Gaudavaho* and talks about King Yasovarman's' victory over the Gauda King. According to S Bhatt,[38] "Vakpati Bhatta gets mentioned in many accounts concerning a debate with Adi Shankara."

Vamana

A great poet and a minister during the period of Jayapida, Vamana further developed the Margi-Ritti style started by Dandin. His *Kavyalankararsutra*, a work on poetics, is considered to be one of the very earliest texts in literary theory. The treatise is divided into five chapters and deals with the whole sphere of Alamkara-Shastra. He boldly asserts that Ritti is the soul of poetry. His work is divided into three Adhyas comprising 319 Sutras.

Vasugupta

The greatest thinker, philosopher and teacher, Vasugupta, was the father of Shaivism. His famous *Shiva Sutras*: *The Yoga of Supreme Identity Translated* by Jaideva Singh, speaks of the essence of Shaivism,[39] "The Highest Lord is omniscient, omnipotent and omnipresent. As I have characteristic of Shiva, I am that very Shiva. With this strong conviction, one becomes Shiva himself."

The legend: Vasugupta (825 AD) is said to have lived near Mahadeva Mountain in the valley of the Harvan stream behind the Shalimar Gardens near Srinagar. Tradition goes that he received the command from Lord Shiva who came to him in a dream and instructed him to overturn a certain rock at the foot of Mahadeva mountain, on which he would find the teachings inscribed. He started searching for the rock, and one of the rocks turned up erect facing Vasugupta. He found the inscriptions on it and copied them. When he finished copying them the rock turned back to its original position. This rock called Shankaropala is still visited by devotees.

Shiva sutras are of divine origin or revelation and are not considered the product of the human mind. Highly refined and artistic, Vasugupta was the first to discover and explain the Agama teaching of Shaivism in a systematic form. He explained these sutras in the form of *Spanda-Karika*. Bhatta Kallata, a pupil of Vasugupta, gave publicity to his master's work and wrote *Spanda-sarvasva*.

Trika Philosophy

Kashmir has been the place of learning for science, social and religious philosophies of Hinduism, Buddhism and Islam. It has produced many scholars, thinkers and philosophers. The rich, spiritual and intellectual climate of Kashmir helped to foster various philosophies. Among these, the Trika system of Kashmir Shaivism tops the list and Shaivism is even now one of the widely practiced religions. According to Upendra Fotedar,[40] "In fact, the great philosopher and saint Shankaracharya is known to have prostrated himself in the Chakreshawri Temple at the Hari Parbat and declared that the Kashmiri Brahmins were great scholars and their philosophy was of the highest order."

Kashmir Shaivism provides an extremely rich and detailed understanding of the human psyche, and evinces a clear and distinct path of Kundalini-Siddha yoga (Kundalini is coil of a snake) to the goal of self realisation. MG Chitkara says,[41] "The power of Shiva that pervades the universe is also called Kundalini. Kundalini is the force or power of consciousness vibrating in the form of the whole universe."

According to MK Kaw in his article in the book *Kashmiri Scholars* [42] "Adiguru Shankaracharya claimed that Brahman was the only reality and the universe was Mithya. It was creation of Maya, the power of the Brahman to delude us into a mistaken belief that the universe was real." Vedanta philosophy describes the manifestation of the universe to be false—Mithya (Illusion). However, in Kashmir Shaivism the manifestation is based on Shakti (Energy). The system says that the universe is part of Shiva. The world, in this philosophy, is an object of enjoyment. Shaivite scholars have stressed that it is Shakti that is the active participant in the process of manifestation. The people of Kashmir recite Bhavaninamashasra, Indrakshi, and Panchastavi etc. Vaishnavite recitations such as Hanuman Chalisa are from the Ramayana. The people of Kashmir pray to Shiva and Shakti along with Vatuknath Bhairava who is treated next to Shiva, but Vaishnavites believe Bhairava is an obstacle in their worship. The Trika system of Kashmir Shaivism is therefore philosophy of divine consciousness divine blessings (anugraha) on the individual aspirant.

According to Hugh B Urban,[43] "Abhinava sought to create a grand synthesis and hierarchical ordering of all the known schools of Shaivism, ultimately placing his own school of Trika (Triad) at the summit, as their culminating goal." The Trika system of Kashmir Shaivism is the three-fold science of man and his world. The philosophy is open for any human being irrespective of caste, creed, colour or gender. Therefore, Kashmir Shaivism is a key to the mystery of existence and gives us knowledge of the supreme secret of life. Its purpose is to enable the practitioner to rise from individuality to universality. According to Prem Nath Bazaz, [44] "While synthesizing the previous systems of the Indian philosophy, Kashmir thinkers sedulously discarded the barren parts represented by Negativism, Escapism and Unemotional of the Upanishad Vedanta."

Trika philosophy has gone through many phases in the course of its long history. Shaiva philosophy has been 'self-correcting' faith for the Hindus of Kashmir as it has in-built correcting mechanism.

The origin of Kashmir Shaivism

The roots of Shaivism in India are presumed to go back into the pre-historic days. Evidence of worship of Shiva has been found in ancient archaeological sites such as Harappa and Mohenjo Daro. It is considered the highest, the most demanding, and the most transcendent yoga. According to Swami Shankarananda, "Kashmir Shaivism is more than an intellectual system. It springs from the direct visionary experience of the sages."

Though tradition says that Shaivism begins with Shiva himself, there has, however, not been any definite date of the origin of the Shiva Cult in Kashmir. The worship of Shiva, according to Kalhana, is as old as Asoka's time. According to some chroniclers, the temples were constructed in India as early as the Third Century BC. However, the numerous temples dedicated to Shiva are a testimony that the people worshiped him and hence practiced Shaivism. The difference between Shaivites and Vaishnavite is that those who worshiped Shiva became known as Shaivites and those who worshiped Vishnu were known as Vaishnavite. There were few Vaishnavites in Kashmir. "Brahmanism drew inspirations from Vedic scriptures like Upanishad, the school of Shaivism takes them from Shaiva Agama," writes BN Pandita in his book *History of Kashmir Shaivism.* Tradition says that Kashmiri scholar Narayan Bhatta, the son of Ratnakara Bhatta is known to have authored several Upanishads.

Earlier form of Shaivism and Agama

Though Shaivism was the religion of Hindus in Kashmir much earlier, its development took the shape of monistic philosophy during the ninth century. It was during this time that Agmic Shaivism started developing. The word "agama" means authoritative scripture. It was used by Panini, the Sanskrit grammarian, as a linguistic term to describe the formation of certain words. However, Agama Shastra is considered as being a direct revelation from Shiva. When Parvati asks the questions and Shiva answers them the treatise is called an Agama, and when Shiva asks questions and Parvati answers them it is called Nigama.

Tantra the spiritual science

These celestial writings/sayings shaped into Shastras or Agama Shastras. These are some of the famous Agama Shastras.

- Milinivijaya Tantra is the essence of doctrines of Kashmir Shaivism in mystic expression.
- Swacchanda Tantra is a store-house of information regarding the details of rituals of Trika system.
- Vijnanabhairava Tantra opens a vista to enter transcendental state of consciousness
- Netra Tantra speaks about the principles of theology,
- Mrgendra Tantra is about rituals
- Rudrayamala Tantra is union of Shiva with Shakti
- Shiva sutra Tantra, discourses between Shiva and Shakti. These revelations are passed on from teacher to pupil.

In fact it was practiced in dualistic form. According to Ganesh Vasudeo Tagare,[45] "It is regarded that there were ten Dvaita Agamas and eighteen Dvait-advaita Agamas. But these were amalgamated before the 9th century AD and this combine came to be known as Siddhanta (Dualist) or Siddhanta Shaivism." There were many scholars who contributed to Siddhanta Shaivism. Of them, Ramakantha II contributed greatly to the school of thought in the 12th century. He wrote *Nada-Karika*. Surprisingly, there were some differences among monistic thinkers. For instance, Adiguru Shankar's monism, non dualism Vedanta, *Kevaladvaita* is different from that of Trika.

Trika the three-fold system

In the midst of all this there appeared another school of thought in

Kashmir Shaivism that came to be known as Advaita (Monism). According to this school of thought, there is no difference between God and man as the world is one. Advaita developed into the Trika School. Trika in Sanskrit means three-fold and Trika system is about Shiva, Shakti, Nara or Shiva, Shakti, Anu (Matter).

Shiva means 'auspicious one', 'the pure one' or 'one who purifies everyone'. He is the unchanging consciousness, the ultimate reality. He is the subject and the object. He is the cause and the effect. According to Sarvepalli Radhakrishnan, "Shiva is the subject as well as the object, the experience as well as the experienced." He is attributed with as many as 1008 names including Rudra as mentioned in Rig Veda, which means 'the fierce one'. Shiva is the God of Transformation, the creation that comes out of destruction. He manifests, sustains, and finally withdraws all appearance back to himself. According to Mark S G Dyczkowski,[46] Abhinava prayerfully addresses Shiva with the words:

"When your nature expands, you, I and the entire universe come into being; when it is withdrawn, neither you nor I nor the universe exist. The universe awakes when you awake and is destroyed when you sleep. Thus the entire universe of being and non-being is one with you." Adiguru Shankaracharya in his *Soundarya Lahari* declares, "Shiva is able to function when united with Shakti; otherwise he is inert."

Shakti means 'to be able to do', a sacred force or empowerment. Shakti is the embodiment of power and upholder of the universe. It is also cosmic existence as well as liberation. Shiva is always associated with Shakti (power) which embodies the active feminine energy and plays a key role in the creative functions of the Lord. However, Lakshmi or Sri, in some schools of Vaishnavism, does not participate in great creation. Kashmir Saivism says that one can attain realisation of Shiva through Shakti. Shakti is the aspect of dynamic energy of Shiva.

Nara is the human being, struggling to get rid of the cycle of birth and rebirth.

The three primary energies

On account of the Shakti, the supreme energy, there are three-fold activities of the world such as: Para Shakti, Apara Shakti and Parapara Shakti. These are the three primary energies and can be described as follows:

- Para Shakti is supreme energy or in other words Shiva, Shakti and their union.
- Parapara Shakti is the combination of highest and the lowest.
- Apara Shakti is the lowest energy.

The Trika philosophy is also classified into three branches:

- Iccha: The will
- Jnana: The Knowledge
- Kriya: The Action

Shiva has himself revealed five energies:

- Chitshakti (consciousness)
- Ananda Shakti (Bliss)
- Ichhashakti (Will power)
- Jnanashakti (Knowledge)
- Kriyashakti (Action)

It tells us various aspects of knowledge of reality

- Abheda: Non-dual
- Bhedabheda: Non-duel and dual
- Bheda: Dual

Trika philosophy given by various philosophers is essentially based on three important Agamas: Namaka Tantra, Milinivijaya Tantra, and Siddha Tantra. These voluminous works are the discourses between Shiva and Shakti. Abhinavagupta took his cue from Milinivijaya Tantra. According to Baljinnath Pandita,[47] "*Malini-vijayottara-tantra* is said to be the most important scriptural work on practical sadhana of the Trika system. Abhinavagupta wrote a Voluminous work on the practical and theoretical teachings contained in this Tantra under the title *Malini-Vijaya-vartika*."

The meaning of Tantra

Tantra is a combination of two words; Tan is to expand and Tra is to liberate. The word comes from the root 'Tanu-Vistare', or 'to extend'. Tantra means 'what extends knowledge' and is a combination of two words 'Tattva' and 'Mantra'. Tattva means the science of cosmic principles and Mantra is the application of cosmic sciences with mystic sounds and vibrations. Tantra is fundamentally a spiritual science, a methodology to go into the sub-conscious mind. It is one of the potent powers for the spiritual regeneration. Kashmir Shaivism was taught by four great teachers namely Vasugupta, Somananda, Erakanatha, and Sumatinatha. These teachers have established four different schools which are: Spanda Karika, Pratyabhijna, Krama School and Kula School.

Kallata Bhatta's Spanda Karika

Spanda is derived from 'Spadi' which means to move a little. It can be translated as pulsation or throb and Karika means 'collection of verses on grammar, philosophical or scientific subjects'. Ksemaraja says Spanda Karika was the school of thought initiated by Vasugupta but it appears to have been written by Kallata Bhatta, a disciple of Vasugupta. However, Jaideva Singh in his book *Spanda-Karika* says,[48] "Regarding himself, Kallata only claims to have brought it to the notice of the people. However, *Vasugupta-padaihdrbdham* clearly shows that the Karika was composed by Vasugupta." Kallata Bhatta developed and popularised the concept of Spanda-Shastra as a commentary, even if originally composed by Vasugupta.

Spanda is divine creative pulsation and spiritual dynamism. It can also be defined as dynamics of consciousness, pulsation of ecstasy. Shivagama says that divine consciousness is not simply cold, inert intellectualism. It is rather active, dynamic, throbbing with life, creative pulsation, vibration or activity of Shiva. Vasugupta studied 64 Agamas and laid down three philosophies for liberation of man: Shiva or Patti or the ultimate reality; man or the individual soul or Pasu and; Pasa, the bonds that reduce the original Shiva-like individual soul to the position of a Pasu.

Spanda Karika has a scientific background. Scientists have discovered that the world was created from the vibration of the first explosion. The universe is still expanding. The absolute monism of the philosophy tells us that the nothing can exist without movement. Therefore Spanda Shastra is the science of the universe as an ever changing phenomenon.

Somananda's Pratyabhijna School

The Pratyabhijna School was propagated by Somananda and subsequently Utpaladeva. Pratyabhijna means 'science of recognition'. It refers to spontaneous recognition of divine nature. The philosophy tells us to realise the self. It is a spiritual discipline which leads the individual to get merged with the universal intelligence that is Paramashiva. It endeavours to dispel ignorance of the seeker after Truth. The Pratyabhijna Shastra can be classified as the philosophical branch of the Trika System of Kashmir Shaivism.

According to KA Subramanian's introductory note in *Isvara Pratyabhijna-Vimarsini*,[49] "Shaivism has not cut itself off from religion. In the Agmic literature on which the Shaiva Philosophy is based, there are generally four sections in each Agama — Vidya, Kriya, Yoga and Carya. The first deals with the categories and other purely philosophical matter. The second is occupied with various forms of spiritual initiation and the accompanying rituals. And because the self-realization is not possible without Yoga, therefore, the third discusses different types of Yoga. But the practice of Yoga is not possible without maintaining the highest ethical standard. The fourth, therefore, gives the rules of conduct. Shaivism is, thus, not concerned with pure speculative thought. It is a synthesis of religion, philosophy and ethics."

Eraknatha's Krama School

The Krama School was expounded by Erakanatha. According to Navjivan Rastogi,[50] "While all other systems including the Kula, Pratyabhijna and Trika of Kashmir Shaivism are Shiva-oriented, the Krama is Shakti–oriented. Krama system flourished in the beginning of 8th century." Krama denotes succession. It is a system that seeks to discover unity in the phenomenal duality — Bheda Abheda. Another difference between Pratyabhijna and Spanda Schools and Krama system is that the earlier two are more metaphysical and Krama is mystical."

Sumatinatha's Kula School

The Kula School of Kashmir was taught by Sumatinatha. Kula means family or extension. In the Kula system, the world is an extension of Shiva and it teaches how to live after realisation and attainment of universal consciousness. According to MG Chitkara,[51] "The difference between the Pratyabhijna System and the Kula System is only that the Pratyabhijna System teaches you how to realise your own nature in one place and exist there, reside there, while the Kula system teaches how you can rise from the lowest degree of your Self on the same level and state." The Kula tradition also has rituals associated with it. In Kashmir, some of the worshippers consume meat and wine and take part in ritual sex for the development of consciousness.

Lall Ded's Interpretation of Shaivism

Shiva philosophy can best be understood by only one Vaakh (poem) of 14th century poetess Lall Ded.

Guaran Vonnam Kuny Vachun
Neber Dopnam Ander Achun
So Goom Adi Vaakh Te Vachun
Tavay Hyut Lalli Nangay Nachun
The Guru taught me only one hymn
To recognise the inner self
That became the rhyme and cognition
The realisation culminated in a dance of ecstasy.

Contribution of Abhinavagupta

Abhinavagupta was one of the greatest philosophers, mystics and aestheticians. His work *Tantraloka* is an encyclopaedic treatise on Kashmir Shaivism. It is regarded as a synthesis of the Trika system of Kashmir. It contains the essence of all the scriptural works of Monistic Shaivism. The work also contains ritualistic and philosophic aspects. It includes ritualised sexual activity too. One of Abhinavagupta's important works is *Milinivijaya-vartika*. The work explains the ritualistic mysticism of Monistic Shaivism. Another work is *Isvarapratyabhijna-vimarsini*.

Buddhism in Kashmir during ancient times

Buddhism became an important part of the classical culture of Kashmir during the ancient period. *Nilamatapurana* also gives us a detailed account of how people celebrated the birthday of Buddha. Brahmin and Buddhist orthodoxy co-existed side by side and had respect for each other. As per *Nilamatapurana*,[52] "O Brahman, the god Vishnu, the lord of the world, shall be (born as) the preceptor of the world, Buddha name, at the time when Pusya is joined with the moon, in the month of Vaisaksha, in twenty eighth Kali Age." Buddha was considered as the incarnation of God Vishnu and thus worshipped by Hindus as any other God.

Buddhism increasingly became indistinguishable from Hinduism. It was ushered into the land of Kashmir without any turmoil. There was absolutely no forceful conversion, no bloodshed and no violence. People accepted the faith with open hearts, without any apprehensions or fear. The choice of acceptance or refusal was left to the will of the people. Curiously enough, people worshipped Hindu deities as well as held Buddhism in high esteem. For example, King Durlabhavardhana's queen Anangalekha built a Buddhist vihara. Lalitaditya built Rajavihara and made a colossal copper image of Buddha at Parihaspura. There are numerous examples where kings or their queens constructed Viharas to express their respect for Buddhism.

There were even some from the Naga community of Kashmir, (staunch believers of Shiva cult and snake worshippers) who embraced Buddhism voluntarily. Kashmir, in the ancient times, was indeed a celebrated centre of learning. Sharda (or Sarada) Peeth located in Sharda Desh (now in Pakistan-occupied-Kashmir) was famous for its temple of Saraswati in Northern Kashmir. It was the learning centre of great Sanskrit scholars and was also a famous centre of Buddhist learning.

Buddha perhaps understood the importance of Kashmir and that is why he had praised the land. According to *Yuan Chwang's Travel's In India* (Translation by Thomas Watters),[53] "When The Buddha and the Yaksha Vajrapani—not Ananda—were returning through air from the conquest and were conversing about Dragon of Udyana, Buddha drew Vajrapani's attention to the valley of Kashmir as they were flying over. Into these, the Buddha predicted, after my 'Pari-Nirvana', an Arhat named Madhyantika will introduce my religion…" Madhyantika is said to be the disciple of Ananda, and he introduced Buddhism to Kashmir. To recall Yuan Chwang's mention of the legend—Kashmir was originally a lake where a dragon lived and Madhyantika went to Kashmir with his 500 Arhats to rescue the valley from the dragon. He not only introduced Buddhism but brought many changes in the development of Kashmir. As per Yuan Chwang, Madhyantika is said to have introduced saffron cultivation in Kashmir.

Buddhism is believed to have become dominant in Kashmir during Asoka's period. Asoka, the grandson of Chandragupta and son of Bindusara, the great emperor of Mauryan Dynasty, ruled India in 269-232 BC. He sent Majjhantika along with monks to Kashmir to propagate Buddhism. He later helped settle these monks in Kashmir. According to Chinese sources, the legend goes that when Majjhantika reached Kashmir he found it was ruled by a Naga King. The king was very angry when he came to know about the activities of Majjhantika. He sent lightning and hurled rocks on him but all in vain as the latter, through his divine powers, remained unaffected. The king, therefore, was convinced of his great powers and he along with his men accepted Buddhism.

It is not known if both Madhyantika (disciple of Ananda) and

Majjhantika (believed to be Buddhist authority of Varanasi) are the same. According to Chinese sources, Buddhism spread in Kashmir just 50 years after the Mahapari-Nirvana of Tathagata (death of Buddha).

In his efforts to propagate Buddhism, Asoka built shrines, monasteries, viharas and inscribed Buddhist teachings on rocks and pillars in many places. According to M A Stein,[54] "The mention of Suskaletra and Vitastatra, in particular, as places where Asoka had erected viharas and stupas is significant as pointing to the survival in Kashmir of local traditions regarding him."

Asoka spread the tradition of Theravada Buddhism, (The school of the elders). Theravada was the oldest tradition among the 18 schools of Buddhism. The doctrine says that one should not have blind faith but try to find the truth practicing three things—investigation, reasoning and self experience. Asoka spread the same cult after convening the Third Buddhist Council at Patliputra. He is supposed to have visited Kashmir twice. According to Kalhana, Asoka laid the foundation of the town of Srinagari (Srinagar) near present village Pandrethan (known as Puranadhisthana in ancient times). He is said to have built 96,000 houses for the people. Asoka did not have aversion for other religions but respected them. He built the Shiva temples at Vijayeshvara and two temples known as Asokesvara at Vijayawada (modern Bijbihara).

Buddhism during Jalauka

Buddhism suffered a jolt just after the death of Asoka. His son Jalauka took over the reins of Kashmir. He was a pure and pious Shaivite and a staunch believer of the Shiva cult. He would worship at the temple of Vijayeshvara. King Jalauka was instructed by his Rajguru, (court priest), Sant Avadhuta, (described as the vanquisher of Buddhist cult) to spread the faith of Shaivism. So, initially, Jalauka was dead against Buddhism and even destroyed the viharas but later on, as per Kalhana, on account of some divine intervention, he started respecting Buddhist thoughts and reconstructed them.

Spread of Buddhism during Kanishka

The Kushan period saw a great resurgence of Buddhism in Kashmir. In fact, Buddhism entered its golden phase and reached its pinnacle under the patronage of King Kanishka. Kanishka, the greatest king of the

Kushan dynasty became a staunch follower of Buddhism. In his leisure time, the king would study Buddhism. It was during his rule that great luminaries such as Asvaghosa, a great philosopher, poet and author of *Buddha Charita*, Nagarjuna, the Buddhist philosopher, Vasumitra, the Buddhist scholar, Charaka, the great physician and Agisala, the famous engineer of his time adorned the royal court.

After Kashmir was conquered, Kanishka strengthened the roots of Buddhism in Kashmir. The main purpose of the council was to bridge the differences which had crept into Buddhism. It was during his reign that the Mahayana doctrine came into being. Kashmiri scholars contributed a lot in the emergence of this doctrine.

Fourth Buddhist Council (Sangha)

During Kanishka's period, the fourth Buddhist Council (Sangha) was convened at Kundala Vanvrhara (present day Harvan) in Kashmir. Kanishka gathered five hundred Bhiksus. The council was presided by Vasumitra to systematise the Sarvastivadin Adhidharma texts. There were other reasons behind Kanishka organising the council. He wanted to honour Asvaghosa, so he made him head of the council. He also wanted to recognise the Mahayana form of Buddhism so as to settle disputes between the different schools of Buddhist sects. The council was attended by the Buddhist celebrity Parshva.

According to Yuan Chwang,[55] "The council composed 1,00,000 stanzas of Upadesa Shastra explanatory of the canonical Sutras; 1,00,000 stanzas of Vinaya-vibhasha-sastras explanatory of the Vinaya; 1,00,000 stanzas of Abhidharma-Vibhasa Shastra explanatory of the Abhidharma." Kanishka collected all the texts, which were written in Sanskrit language, and took them away when he left Kashmir. In fact, two 'Fourth Buddhist Councils' took place. One in (Kundala Vanvrhara) near Srinagar around 100 BC and the other at Tambapanni, Sri Lanka, in the last century BC. Sri Lankan Buddhists refuse to accept the Kashmir council as an important Buddhist council.

Mahayana

Mahayana means 'the great vehicle' (Maha is great and yana is vehicle). Hinayana is known as the small vehicle (Hina is small and yana is vehicle). In Hinayana, the follower is to attain his own Nirvana as the faith is monistic, ie a man can help another person on the way. There both of them have to be enlightened. But Mahayana offers to everyone salvation by faith. Buddhism puts great emphasis on following the path of Bodhisattvayana, which means enlightenment. It refers to spiritual motivation. The Mahayanists did not see themselves as creating a new cult for Buddhism; rather they claimed to be reviving the original teachings of Buddha, handed down to them by him. According to A L Basham, [56] "The Bodhisattva doctrine, a logical development from the older Buddhism, thus peopled the heavens with mighty forces of goodness, and presented Buddhism with a new mythology. It was this which formed the hallmark of the Mahayana, The Great Vehicle."

Bodhisattvayana is one of the most important innovations of Mahayana Buddhism. The Mahayanists also developed a theology of Buddha called doctrine of The Three Bodies. They asserted that Buddha was not a human being as is preached by Theravada Buddhists. Mahayanists believe that Buddha is the manifestation of a universal spiritual being.

Mahayana Buddhism spread not only in Kashmir but also to other places.[57] The Kotan Kingdom, located in the Xinjiang Province in China, became a major centre of Buddhist teaching and rituals during the spread of the religion from India to China in the first and second centuries BC. But Kashmir became a vehicle for the spread of Mahayana in other places. It is, therefore, certain that Kashmir contributed to the spread of Buddhism in Afghanistan, Tibet and China.

Decline of Buddhism in Kashmir

The decline of Buddhism in Kashmir occurred for a variety of reasons. One of the reasons is that the Bhikshus started giving up their spiritual pursuit and devoted their time and energy towards material pursuits. Kalhana mentions in the *Rajatarangini*,[58] that "the Buddhist patron, Yukadevi, the queen of Meghavahana, constructed a vihara in which she placed those Bhikshu whose conduct conformed to the precepts in one half, and in the other half those who being in possession of wives, children, cattle and property, deserved blame for their life as householders." However, Buddhism continued to flourish in spite of the efforts made to annihilate the religion from the valley. According to PNK Bamzai,[59]

"Buddhism again suffered a reverse after the rule of the Kushan rulers and later in the fifth century AD, it was nearly wiped off from the Valley by the Hun ruler Mihirakula. Baka, Mihirakula's son, however, seems to have atoned for his predecessor's sin restoring the Caityas and Mathas." According to Sir Charles Eliot, "The Mahayanist Buddhism of Kotan was a separate stream and Yuan Chwang says that it came from Kashmir. Though Kashmir is not known as a centre of Mahayanism, yet it would be a natural route for men and ideas passing from any part of India to Kotan."

Impact of Buddhism in Kashmir

There has been enormous contribution of Buddhism in the life of Kashmiri Hindus. It brought many changes in the intellectual field. According to B N Kalla, [60] "Kashmir Shaivism, like Mahayana Buddhism has played a key role in the assimilation of different cultures in Central Asia, while adopting the logic of the Acharya; it refuted the fundamental concept of Shunyavad and looked upon the creation of absolute as real and as manifestation of the light of intelligence or universal consciousness."

Buddhism has had a great impact on the way of life and even Shaivism of Kashmir. Buddhism and Shaivism, in spite of their differences remained close to each other. The Buddhist Tantric rites are retained in Shaivism. According to R L Aima,[61] "One of the major results of this struggle between Hindus and Buddhists went in favour of Kashmiri Shaivism which was till then knowledge carried from teacher to disciple by word of mouth only. It was at this time that the first written document of this philosophy was born." He further writes that "Buddhism influences the religious rights of Kashmir Hindus. Even today during Yajna and Puja, Buddhist Trirattanas are propitiated."

There is a common belief that the Buddhist Tantra was developed from Hindu Tantra Cults. Both Buddhist Tantra and Hindu Tantra integrated thoroughly to produce sectarian forms. However, both are now barely related in spite of a surface resemblance. The Buddhist Tantra tells us that each one of us is a union of all universal energy. Everything that we need in order to be complete is within us right at this very moment. It is simply a matter of being able to recognise it. This is the tantric approach. There is a discernible resemblance to the cult of Shiva philosophy of Kashmir. According to P N K Bamzai,[62] "The philosophic literature of Mahayana therefore bears a deep impress of Kashmir Shaivism whose doctrines revolve round their fundamental conceptions of Shiva and Shakti." It is often claimed that Buddhist Tantra is a derivative from Tantric practice of Shaivism, but it is possible that the reverse will be true. According to Benoytosh Bhattacharyya,[63] "It is possible to declare, without fear of contradiction, that the Buddhists were first to introduce the Tantras into their religion, and that the Hindus borrowed them from the Buddhists in later times, and that it is idle to say that later Buddhism was an outcome of Shaivism." Buddhist scholars of Kashmir who participated in the 'Fourth Buddhist Council' at Kashmir were:

Acharya Vasumitra

A Kashmiri Brahmin, Acharya Vasumitra became the chairman of the Fourth Buddhist Council in Kashmir. His famous work is *Pancavastuka.* He also composed a commentary on the Abhidharmakosa and authored *Samaya-bheda-uparacana-cakra*, the main treatise containing eighteen sects.

Asvaghosa

Born in Saketa in northern India in 150 BC, Asvaghosa is one of the greatest Buddhist philosopher-poets and Sanskrit dramatists. He is said to be the author of *Mahayashraddhotpada Shastra* (Awakening of Mahayana Faith). He became a religious advisor of King Kanishka and was bestowed the chair of vice-presidentship of the Fourth Buddhist Council of Kanishka.

Vasubandhu

Born in a Hindu family at Gandhara in North-western India, Vasubandhu flourished in the fourth century. After initial studies in Buddhism, he went to Kashmir and started his higher studies with the leading teachers of Buddhism. His works are *Abhidharmakosa, Karmasiddhi Prakarana* and *Pancaskandhaka* among others.

Nagarjuna

Known to have born (150 – 250 BC) in southern India near the town of Nagarunakond, Nagarjuna belonged to a Brahmin family but later on accepted Buddhism. He founded the Madhyamaka school of Mahayana Buddhism. He wrote *Mulamadhyamaka-karika* (Fundamental Verses of the Middle Way), *Sunyatasaptati* (Seventy Verses on Emptiness), and *Vigrahavyavartani* (The End of Disputes).

Ravigupta

Ravigupta alias Suryagupta was a Kashmiri who flourished in the eighth century AD. He synthesised the doctrine of Nagarjuna and Asanga, which are identical in meaning. Ravigupta built twelve centres of Buddhism.

Legend goes that he had attained siddhi (salvation) of the Goddess Tara. When he contracted leprosy in his whole body, Goddess Tara approached him and asked him what he wished for. He said he wanted to get rid of the disease. His wish was granted except for a spot on his forehead. He asked the goddess the reason for not healing the spot; she told him that he was a hunter in his previous life and was re-born in hell. She then taught him a mantra for sadhana (renunciation) which was accompanied with stotra and told him that he would get nirvana from the cycle of rebirth.

Sarvajnamitra

Kalhana describes Sarvajnamitra as a great and famous Kashmir Buddhist monk. The legend goes that he was the illegitimate son of a king of Kashmir. As a baby , his mother left him for vultures but the birds took the baby to Mount Gondola in Nalanda, where some Brahmins looked after him. He learnt Buddhism from Ravigupta.

Sanghabuti

The first Kashmiri scholar to reach the Chinese capital in 381-48 AD, was Sanghabuti. He stayed there until his death. He translated several texts such as *Vinaya Pitaka* into Chinese language. He also translated *Abhidharmakosa* of Vasumitra into Chinese.

Dharmatrata

Dharmatrata, according to Yuan Chwang, is the author of *Tsa-abhidharmalun*. The work was completed by him while staying in a monastery.

Gautama Sanghdeva Dharmayasal

Gautama Sanghdeva Dharmayasal was a Kashmiri Buddhist who visited China and spread Buddhism there.

Kumarajiva

Born in 350 AD to an Indian father and a Kuchean (Chinese mother,) Kumarajiva became a Buddhist after the death of his parents. At the age of nine, he accompanied his mother to Kashmir where he started his studies in Buddhism—of Sarvastivadin doctrines. After three years, he converted to the Mahayana School of Buddhism at Kashgar, (Kashgar is an old city in the far western Chinese province of Xinjiang). Soon young Kumarajiva's wisdom and reputation as a translator spread to all corners. He translated 384 Buddhist texts including *Prajnaparamita, the Vimalakirti Nirdesa Sutra, Surangama Sutra, The Lotus Sutra*, etc.

Buddhabhadra

Born in Kashmir, Buddhabhadra went to China at the beginning of the fifth century to propagate Buddhism. His mastery over the concept of Vibhasa, earned him great respect in China. In 433 AD, he went to western China and translated 60 chapters of *Mhavibhasa-sastra.* He is said to have translated 13 works in 125 Volumes contributing greatly to the development of Chinese Buddhism. He also assisted Kumarajiva in the translation of Buddhist scriptures.

Gunavarman

A Buddhist, Gunavarman, was born in the fourth century in Kashmir. A Kashmiri Buddhist historian, Triloki Nath Dhar has given a lucid account of many Buddhist monks. About Gunavarman, he says that he was of royal blood but his grandfather was banished from Kashmir. Fate changed and at a certain point of time, Gunavarman was offered the post of the king of Kashmir. He declined the offer and instead went to Sri Lanka, Java and China to propagate Buddhism in 424 AD, which gave impetus to the growth of Buddhist culture in Java, Sumatra and other places.

Sanghabhadra

One of the famous and profound scholars of Vibhasa Shastra of the Sarvastivadin School, Sanghabhadra was born in Kashmir. He was naturally gifted. He was a disciple of the great scholar Skandhila, whose work *So-Kan-ti-lo* has been mentioned by Yuan Chwang. When he was young, he composed *Vibhasa Shastra* (Pi-po-sha-lun) of the Sarvastivadin School. He was the teacher of Vasubandhu. Sanghabhadra composed a treatise known as *Kosa-pao* or *Bud-hail* Sastra. According to Yuan Chwang,[64] "This Sanghabhadra was a native of Kashmir and a profound scholar in the Vibhasa Sastra of Sarvastivadin School." Sanghabhadra is said to have died in Matipur, central India. Vasubandu attributed to him the title of Lion King. Amongst his disciples were the famous Vasubandu and Vimalamitra.

Vimalamitra

Born in Kashmir, Vimalamitra was a disciple of Sanghabhadra and a follower of the Sarvastivadin School. He was known as the Sage of Kashmir. He travelled to China and became a disciple of Shri Singha there. After he came back from China he went to Tibet and spread Buddhism there. His famous work is *Vima Nyingthig* (Secret Heart Essence of Vimalamitra).

Dharmottaracharya

A great Buddhist logician of Kashmir, Dharmottaracharya flourished during the eighth century. He was the disciple of the great scholar Dhamakara Dutt. He wrote commentaries on two treatise of Dharmakirti. Triloki Nath Dhar says, (65) "Dharmottaracharya hailed during the eighth century." He further says that his famous works are *Pramanaviniscaya* and *Nyayabindhu*.

Fourteen
Beginning of Islamic Period

Sultan Shams-ud-Din 1339-1342 AD

A holy man's message to Shah Mir in his dream was that,[1] "he would succeed to the throne of Kashmir." According to Jonaraja, Goddess Mahadevi came in Shah Mir's dream and told him that he would become the king of Kashmir. But as per *Baharistan-i-Shahi,* Waqur Shah, the grandfather of Shah Mir, was a pious man who had undergone tremendous penance and he had declared,[2] "My son Tahir (Muqim-bin-Tahir) will have a son named Shah Mir, who will become the ruler of Kashmir and assume the title of Shams-ud-Din."

In 1312 AD, Shah Mir migrated to Kashmir along with his wife and children for employment. When King Suhadeva, who was ruling the country, came to know that Shah Mir was a religious person, he extended his hospitality by giving him a village Davar Kunail in the district of Baramulla to live in. In accordance with his own religious nature, King Suhadeva treated the guest as God's own man. Little did he realise the secret designs of the guest.

Taking advantage of the generosity and hospitality of their host,

Rinchan, also an outsider, and Shah Mir, both fugitives succeeded in their plans to usurp the throne of Kashmir. It was an epoch-making event in the history of Kashmir. A land that was ruled by Hindu kings for thousands of years became a Muslim state.

Shah Mir came from Swat and ascended the throne of Kashmir under the name of Sultan Shams-ud-Din and laid the foundation of the Sultan Dynasty. According to Muhammad Qasim Firishta,[3] the pedigree of Shah Mir is traced thus: "Shah Meer, (Persian) the son of Tahir, (an Arab), the son of Koorshasp, (a fire worshipper), the son of Neekodur (another fire worshiper), a descendant from Arjoon (Arjun of Pandava in Mahabharata) an infidel; an account of whom is to be found in the Mahabharut (Mahabharata), a work translated by order of Akbur Padshah (King Akbar)." This statement was in fact made by Jonaraja for Shah Mir. Other historians are critical of Firishta for this comment.

Under Shah Mir's rule, those belonging to Islam had an easy and comfortable life while the others suffered. It is true that he tried to conduct the affairs of the state wisely. He provided comfort to the people who had been facing miserable days on account of the invasions of Dulcha and Achala. Unlike his Hindu predecessors, who taxed the people to an extent that they were left only with a meagre subsistence, Shah Mir abolished the arbitrary taxes imposed by these unscrupulous kings. In its place, he fixed a quota of one-sixth as the revenue for the government. It was because he himself came from a humble background. He understood the long spell of sufferings the people had faced for centuries. He tried to protect them from exploiters so that they could earn their livelihood in peace. All this gave tremendous comfort to the people.

Shah Mir had two grandsons, Hshataka and Himda, whom he was very proud of. Both were active in running the administration. His son Jymsara was also very wise and active. He helped his father in running the administration smoothly.

With Shah Mir as king, Muslim rule was established in Kashmir. Says Jia Lal Kilam,[4] "Thus ended the Hindu rule not as a result of foreign aggression as in the case of neighbouring province of the Punjab, but as a result of a long chain of events..." Surprisingly, Shah Mir did not change the routine work of the government. As per PNK Bamzai,[5] "The official routine of the government was carried out in the Sanskrit language for at least one century after the accession of Shah Mir to the throne till under Zain-ul-Abidin when it was changed to Persian." Jia Lal Kilam has mentioned in his book that, [6] "Islam now was the court religion, but the administration continued in the hands of the traditional official class, the Brahmans. With them, the change of religion offered no advantages and the retention of the old creed no loss of status, and they continued to follow their old religion. Sanskrit was the official language and the people conducted their writing business in this language."

Having defeated the Lavanyas, Shah Mir subdued the Rajputs who were at Kashthavata. They were so frightened that they tried to flee the town. Shah Mir became the darling of the people. However, he did not live long. After five years of rule, he died in 1343 AD. He had five sons: Jamshid (Jymsara), Ali Sher, Shirsamaq, Siamook and Hindal. The eldest, Jamshid, became the king after his death.

Sultan Jamshid, 1342-1343 AD

Jamshid/Jymsara/Jumseed ascended the throne after the death of his father Shah Mir. Initially, Ali Sher, his younger brother was a great support to him. One could safely say that after the death of Shah Mir, Kashmir got two kings. The only difference between them that the former was known as the king, and the latter as prince. Ali Sher always helped his brother in conducting the affairs of the state. He also enjoyed all the powers of the King. Like a monarch, he would distribute presents and receive them too. Like the king, he would also award punishment to the guilty. Kashmir those days had plenty of mischief mongers and intriguers. However, the king did not quite like the actions of his brother. Soon, there arose some misunderstanding between the two. Ali Sher was instigated by his caucus to revolt against the king.

He also had the support of the Rajputs who had been defeated by Shah Mir. Taking advantage, the Rajputs sent a feeler to Ali Sher that they were prepared to fight for him. Ali Sher went to Avantipura to prepare for the fight.

The King and his efficient army went to Utpalapora (Kakapura) to face the revolt. However, as per Jonaraja, the king sent the following message to his younger brother,[7] "If you have not underestimated my affection by the instigation of wicked men, why do you not tremble in fear of the censure of the people? The wishes of the King who had gone to heaven (our father) to protect each other should be obeyed. Think of this and turn your affection again towards me."

The fight took the shape of a civil war and there was bloodshed everywhere. According to Jonaraja,[8] "The River Vitasta, the current of which was blocked up by dead bodies flowed backward." It was only through the intervention of a minister Siraji that both brothers agreed to end the hostilities for two months. Meanwhile, the king went to Kramarajya leaving behind the capital in the hands of Siraji. But Ali Sher cleverly corrupted the minister who betrayed the king and gave the kingdom away to Ali Sher. Tired of the civil war, King Jamshid fell ill and died.

King Jamshid had constructed a bridge across the river at Sujjapura. He had constructed water tanks near the resting places of travellers. He also introduced the laws of inheritance among Hindus as a result of which a widow could inherit the father's property.

Sultan Ala-ud-Din, 1343-1354 AD

Ali Sher became the king under the title of Sultan Ala-ud-Din. In order to make his position safe from any revolt or from his brothers, he offered lordship of Dvar to his third brother.

Sultan Ala-ud-Din ruled for eleven years. He understood the sufferings of the people and tried to heal the wounds inflicted on them on account of the invasion of Dulcha and Urdil. His rule also saw a devastating famine. Both the king and his son tried to give comfort to the people and to a great extent, their miseries were mitigated. He also made many changes in the legal system.

During his rule a great saint, scholar and philosopher was born. Her name was Lalleshwari, later known as Lall Ded. This Hindu saint and philosopher spoke her couplets in Kashmiri language. She was an exponent of the Kashmir Shaivism philosophy through her vaakh. In addition, her contribution to the Kashmiri language is tremendous.

King Ala-ud-Din also contributed to developmental work in the country. He constructed a sarai (rest house for travellers) for visitors to the country. Despite all his generosity and understanding, Jonaraja, who referred to King Ala-ud-Din as Alavadena [9], says that under the king's orders, a widow lacking character or without any children could not inherit the property of her husband. The King died in the year 1354 AD leaving behind two sons. The eldest succeeded to the throne as Sultan Shahab-ud-Din.

Sultan Shahab-ud-Din, 1354-1373 AD

By the time Shahab-ud-Din became king, law and order had been established and peace prevailed. People's memory of the invasions and famine had faded. They took care of their vocations and led simple lives. In short, they were happy.

Jonaraja in his *Rajatarangini*,[10] describes an early incident. Shahab-ud-Din, a prince then, went for hunting to the jungle with his friends Udayashri and Chandradamara, accompanied by their horse keeper. When they entered the forest Vakpusta, they saw some women saints who recognised the prince. The leader of the saints offered him a drink. The prince drank his fill and handed the rest to his friends. Both the friends shared the drink but the horse keeper did not drink any. The women saints then told the prince that he would rule the country and his two friends would share the prosperity. The yoginis said,[11] "Your kingdom will remain entire and Chandra will enjoy a part of your wealth, and Udayashri, as long as he lives will be blessed with undying prosperity; but the groom bereft of our favour will soon be left bereft of life." When the prince came back to his palace, to his utter amazement he was told that the horse keeper who had not shared the drink had died.

Although he was a Muslim, Shahab-ud-Din had faith in the predictions of the yoginis. Interestingly, this incident has been mentioned as a true story in the Persian chronicle *Baharistan-i-Shahi*. It says,[12] "During the reign of Ala-ud-Din, it so happened that his eldest son, Shihabu'd-Din, in the course of a hunting expedition, strayed into a jungle in the mountains along with his three companions Chandra, Udsheh Rawal and Ikhtuji. Their other followers were left far behind. Suddenly there appeared a woman from the woods; she had signs of austerity and righteousness stamped on her face." (Some people think that it was Lall Ded who had appeared there.)

With his domestic affairs under control and people happy and contented with life in general, King Shahab-ud-Din started looking at foreign invasions and started training the local army. He appointed two local Hindus, Chandra Dammara and Lula Dammara as their commanders-in-chief. Raising a well-trained infantry of 50,000 and

50,000 cavalry, they conquered Baltistan, Ladakh, Kishtwar and Jammu, one after the other. Encouraged by these conquests, Shahab-ud-Din then conquered the hilly areas of Poonch, Rajouri and Uri. Next was Sind. Like Lalitaditya, he went to conquer parts of northern India. He defeated the king of Udabhandapura (Ohind) and Porushpura (Peshawar), conquered Kashgar, Badakhshan and finally Kabul. Jonaraja says King Shahab-ud-Din had no other ambition.[13] "Deer-eyed women attracted not his mind, nor the pleasures of drinking nor the light of the moon. Only the march with his army occupied the king's attention." He seems to have been a born soldier. "Neither heat nor cold, nor evening nor night, neither hunger nor thirst obstructed his march. When this proud king was on the march he found no difficulty in crossing formidable rivers, inaccessible mountains and barren deserts."[14] writes Jonaraja.

He expanded and consolidated his kingdom. He reaffirmed the subjugation of the lords ruling in other Parganas (districts) under his sovereignty. The *Baharistan-i-Shahi* says,[15] "The first and foremost step which Shihabu'd-Din took after ascending the throne of his father was to coordinate civil administration of the Pargana in Kashmir. Within a short time, he welded the whole of Kashmir into a single unit. Some of the defiant chiefs and lords of Pargana were put to the sword and the others were brought under subjugation." It further says that Shahab-ud-Din attacked the king of Delhi, Feroz Shah, but no one won.

"Shihabu'd-Din with a huge army of 50,000 cavalry and 50,000 infantry reached the village of Sateh Lidar (Sutlej). Feroz Shah also arrived at the same place at the head of a large army. For some months, the two armies confronted each other and no one could overpower the other," says the Persian chronicle.

Pir Gulam Hassan in *Tarikh-i-Hassan Khuihami* has seconded the above statement.[16] "Truce was concluded on the initiative of Amir-e-Kabir, Mir Sayyid 'Ali Hamadani. The Amir proposed the marriage of the three daughters of Feroz Shah with the relatives of Sultan Shihabu'd-Din. The eldest daughter was married to Hassan Khan, the second one to Qutb-ud-Din brother of King Shahab-ud-Din, and the third one to Sayyid Hassan Bahadur." Hassan further says that the Amir came to Kashmir while Shihabu'd-Din was fighting with Feroz Shah. It can be gleaned from Hassan that Mir Sayyid 'Ali Hamadani first came to Kashmir and then went to Ferozpur to bring about conciliation between Shahab-ud-Din and Feroz Shah.

When it came to looking after his subjects, the king left no stone unturned. To provide employment to the people, he built a beautiful city near Hari Parbat and named it as Lakshmi Nagar after his Hindu wife Lakshmi. He constructed quarters for his army. He was tolerant and respected all religions as this incident narrated by Jonaraja [17]shows. The treasury was empty and the king told his minister Udayashri, a Buddhist by faith, about it. The minister came up with the idea to cut the image of God Vijayeshvara which was made of brass to turn it into coins. The king said that instead of melting the idol of Vijayeshvara they could melt the idol of Buddha. The king then lambasted the minister for his suggestion. He told him, "Past generations have set up images to obtain fame and earn merit and you propose to demolish them! Some have obtained renown by setting up images of Gods, others by worshipping them, some by duly maintaining them and some by demolishing them! How great is the enormity of such a deed."

During his period, the Hindus were in majority. To earn the goodwill of the people, he married a Hindu girl, Lakshmi, daughter of Avatar, a rich Hindu noble. In addition to having mutual respect for each other, both the king and the queen were attached to each other. The king would consult the queen on various decisions and respect her advice.

Queen Lakshmi had a sister, whose daughter Lassa was under her care. Lassa grew into a sensuous and beautiful woman. Suddenly, Shahab-ud-Din fell in love with her. For some time he did not express his feelings to anyone as he had great respect for the queen but then Lassa's attraction became irresistible and he decided to marry her. Offended, the self-respecting queen left the palace and went to her relative, the king of Sindhu. But the king brought her back to the palace. Eventually, the marriage with Lassa took place and the new queen started misbehaving with Queen Lakshmi. Fate was on the side of Lassa who managed to impress upon the king that the two sons of Queen Lakshmi be exiled. The King relented. The banishment of her two sons Hassan Khan and Ali Khan shocked Queen Lakshmi. She left Kashmir with her sons.

The king could not bear the separation of Queen Lakshmi and sent her a letter to return to the palace along with their two sons. The princes were angry and declined the offer. After a long dilemma, Queen Lakshmi decided to return to the king but by the time she reached Kashmir, the king had passed away. As per Firishta, he died in 1386 AD.

At the time of his death, Shahab-ud-Din's brother Hindal was present there and he seized the opportunity to ascend the throne under the name of Qutb-ud-Din.

Sultan Qutb- ud-Din, 1373-1389 AD

According to Firishta, Hindal after ascending the throne attained the title of Qutb-ud-Din. He ruled Kashmir for 16 years. Like his brother, Qutb-ud-Din, too, came as a man of peace. He invited his nephew Prince Hassan into his palace to live with him.

Prince Hassan, along with his brother and his mother, Queen Lakshmi, were looked after by Udayashri, a minister during Sultan Shahab-ud-Din's regime. Jonaraja has characterised Udayashri as clever and without any scruples. When Prince Hassan returned from exile, Qutb-ud-Din received him warmly. But soon, falling prey to palace intrigues, Udayashri defied the king and wanted Prince Hassan to become the king. He was defeated in this intrigue and both Prince Hassan and the minister escaped to Lohkot, where the host who was loyal to the king, caught and executed them.

During his initial days, the Lohara lord rose against the king of Kashmir, a rebellion which was quashed by Sultan Qutb-ud-Din sending Lolaka Dammara, his Commander-in-Chief, to subdue them. In this action Lolaka was killed.

The other trouble facing Kashmir during this time was famines. In India, a famine takes place due to failure of rains but in Kashmir, the famines were due to frequent floods. The King himself arranged relief for the starving people. He even performed a yajna (a ritual form of Hindu worship with holy fire). Says Jonaraja,[18] "The king saw that the people died of famine every year and he performed a Yajna (sacred fire) in the month of Bhadra, and distributed large gifts to priests and people."

Till the rule of Qutb-ud-Din, Hindus were in majority among the population, and performance of Hindu rituals, therefore, was very common even among the converts who were very poor. P N K Bamzai says,[19] "The performance of Yagna and the continuance of the Hindu dress, manners and customs among the converts of Islam shows the tolerant and humanistic teaching of the first preachers of the new faith in the Valley."

About his personal life, it is said that Sultan Qutb-ud-Din committed incest and kept his two sisters as his wives. This made Shah Hamadan, the famous Muslim preacher, very angry. He reprimanded the king and asked him to divorce them.

King Qutb-ud-Din, whom Jonaraja had named as King Kumbhadina, did not have any children. But, says Jonaraja,,[20] "At last there came a Yogi named Brahmanatha from Kashmira and through his favour the king obtained a son after a time." He was named Shringara alias Shankar who later on became the famous Sultan Sikandar. The birth of the child gave great joy to the king. "In the festivities which were held on the occasion, the king, out of the gladness of his heart, ordered the imprisoned to be released...."

Meanwhile, another son was born to Queen Haura. He was named Haivata/ Haibat Khan. Unfortunately, when the children were still infants, the king died. Queen Haura was left with all the responsibilities of rearing the children as well as running the administration. According to Firishta, Sultan Qutb-ud-Din died in 1396 AD.

Bibi Haura, as the regent and disciplinarian

Queen Haura was a highly respected woman in the kingdom. Gifted with sensibility and maturity, the ministers had praise and respect for her. When the king died and the eldest son Sikandar was crowned king, the ministers Uddaka (Rai Madari) and Sahaka, though rival to each other, lost no time in advising the queen to assume regency of the infant king.

The queen had to face many challenges to save the kingdom from the enemies. Though she was soft-hearted, she was stern when the occasion called for. Prem Nath Bazaz says,[21] "She had been reputed for her piety, kind-heartedness and benevolence previously but when the occasion demanded she displayed other amazing attributes of her character." Once, when she came to know that her own daughter and her son-in-law were conspiring against the infant King, she got them arrested and killed including their infant son.

It was during the reign of Qutb-ud-Din that Sheikh Noor-ud-Din alias Nunda Rishi, a great saint of Kashmir, was born. Nunda Rishi, was a Muslim saint who composed his verses in Kashmiri language to teach the tenets of Sufism. In the words of ML Kaul, "Nunda Rishi was no theologian. He called himself Nunda Sanz a fact that stands testified by his Shrukhs (Shloka couplets) and the elegy written by Shyama, an inmate of the Khanqah, in the wake of his death." Jonaraja in his *Rajatarangini* names him as Noor-ud-Din.

Sultan Qutb-ud-Din was a learned man who had a taste for the arts. He himself was a poet and a patron of learning. In his times, in 1379 AD. Sayyid Ali Hamadani paid a second visit to the country and baptised the king into mysteries of Sufism.

As per *Baharistan-i-Shahi* , (a Persian Chronicle Translated by Kashi Nath Pandita), "During his time and in the year AH 783 (AD 1381), though some say in AH 773 (AD 1371), His Holiness (Sayyid Ali Hamadani) arrived in Kashmir."

Sultan Sikandar, 1389-1413 AD

ML Gupta says,[22] "While Buddhism that took birth in India in 6th century BC was based on non-violence, Islam that took birth in 610 AD in Saudi Arabia was totally based on violence."

When Sultan Qutb-ud-Din died, his two children named Sikandar and Haibat were still young. But his prime minister Rai Magarey was in favour of making Sikandar the king. So, Sikandar was crowned as the king in 1389. In truth, it was the mother of Sikandar, Bibi Harun/ Bibi Haura who ruled the country by proxy. According to Firishta,[23] "Kootb-Ood-Deen was succeeded by his son Sugga, who assumed the title of Sikundur, and subsequently acquired the surname of Bootshikun, or the iconoclast. In consequence of his tender years, his mother, the Dowager-queen, whose name was Soorut Rany, exercised the supreme control for a considerable period."

Rai Magarey had assumed enormous powers in the lifetime of Sikandar's father. He wanted to prove his loyalty so he got the other brother Haibat killed thinking Sikandar would be pleased. On the contrary, Sikandar wanted to get rid of him and sent him to conquer Ladakh, which had seceded from Tibet. Rai Magarey conquered the place and declared himself an independent ruler. Sikandar went to conquer this new enemy and succeeded. Magarey was locked in prison where he committed suicide.

The annexation of Ladakh with the state gave tremendous fame to

Sikandar as a military strategist and a conqueror. As a result, he managed to conquer other neighbouring chiefs of Poonch, Rajouri, Jammu, and Gandhara which were the north western areas. He married Queen Shobha, daughter of the chief of north-western area.

So long as Rai Magarey was alive, the administration of the country was carried on traditionally. Sikandar was still young, having ascended the throne at the age of eight. The roles played by Magarey and Bibi Haura were very significant at this stage. During the rule of King Qutb-ud-Din, several troubles in the form of palace intrigues were born. But Bibi Haura's alertness quelled all threats of rebellion and plans of assassinating the king. Therefore, there can be no denying the fact that she played an important role in Sikandar's upbringing.

Her role as regent is amazing. The enemies had thought it easy to defeat this woman and to assassinate the minor king. Little did they know they would face a harsh, ruthless and even cruel administrator who could easily exterminate them. Bibi Haura was a lioness who defeated all those who wanted to exterminate Sikandar.

But when Sikandar acquired maturity he took the reins of the country in his own hands, writes Prem Nath Bazaz,[24] "His fanatical zeal for the spread of Islam seized him and he became tyrannical towards his Hindu subjects. He levied Jazia upon Hindus. Not satisfied with this he persecuted them by arresting them and then tortured them. Hindus were prohibited to perform any religious ceremony in temples or at their homes."

Not without reason, then Sultan Sikandar has been the most controversial ruler of Kashmir. His zeal for the spread of Islam and the subjugation of neighbouring areas led him to many countries. It was also a time when the Timurid Dynasty was persecuting Muslims in Persia. "Many Yavanas (Muslims) left for other sovereigns and took shelter under this king (Sikandar) who was renowned for charity,"[25] says Jonaraja. When they heard about Sikandar and his zeal for Islam, 700 Sayyids accompanied by Sayyid Muhammad Hamadani entered the valley.

Sikandar was still a boy when he became a disciple of Sayyid Ali Hamadani. The young king waited on Hamadani daily, like a humble servant, and obedient as a student he took his daily lessons from him. Encouraged by the presence of Sayyids and taught by Shah Hamadani,

Sikandar started persecution of Hindus and destruction of places of worship of Hindus. There was no city, no town and no village where the images of Gods were not broken.

Pir Hassan says,[26] "This country possessed from the times of Hindu Rajas many temples which were like the wonders of the world." Hassan has given details about how Sultan Sikandar destroyed Hindu temples such as Martanda near Matan, Maha Shri, and Tarapitha temples in Sikandarpora, Srinagar.

When the temples and idols were broken, the world trembled, but not the mind of the wicked king. In fact, Walter Lawrence in *Valley Of Kashmir* summarises the persecution of Hindus:[27] "It is generally accepted fact that up to about the beginning of the 14th century, the population of the Valley was Hindu, and about the middle and the end of this century the mass of the people was converted to Islam, through the efforts of Shah-e-Hamdan and his followers, and violent bigotry and persecution of King Sikandar, the iconoclast. The tradition affirms that the persecution of the Hindus was so keen that only eleven families of Hindus remained in the valley." He further writes,[28] "There was certain method in the mad zeal of Sikandar for he used the plinth and friezes of the old temples for the embankment of the city and for the foundation of the Jama Masjid. Having glutted his vengeance on Hindu temples, Sikandar turned his attention to the people who had worshipped in them and he offered them three choices: death, conversion or exile. Many fled, many were converted, many were killed, and it is said that this monarch burnt seven mounds of sacred thread of the murdered Brahmins. All the books of Hindu learning which he could lay his hands on were sunk in the Dal Lake and Sikandar flattered himself that he had extirpated Hinduism from the Valley." He considered Hindus as infidels and their persecution his religious duty.

While levelling of one of the temples was going on, says Firishta, [29] "The people were employed in digging the foundation, a copper-plate was discovered, on which was the following inscription: 'Raja Bulnat, having built this temple, was desirous of ascertaining from his astrologers how long it would last, and was informed by them, that after eleven hundred years, a king named Sikundur would destroy it, as well as the other temples in Kashmeer'. The King was surprised and vexed that a

Hindu prophet should have predicted the truth. He declared that if they had placed the plate against the wall, he would have preserved the temple to belie the prophet.

It was when fighting the king of Udabhandapura, that Sikandar saw the king's daughter Mera. He fell in love with her and married her. She gave birth to Zain-ul-Abidin, who would later on become a famous king. Queen Mera gave birth to another three princes namely: Noor Khan, Shaista Khan and Ali Khan.

King Sikandar had respect for learned people. Ladd Raja, the physician, Shankar and Suha Bhatta, were the councillors of the king and shared a close relationship with him.

Such was Suha Bhatta's loyalty to the king that he himself converted to Islam. He was baptised by Sayyid Mohammad Hamadani and assumed the name of Saif-ud-Din. He became the prime minister and was a more fanatical Muslim than the king himself. He killed the Hindus to show his master his faithfulness. He became fully engaged in making Kashmir a Hindu-less state. According to GMD Sufi,[30] "It is on record that Mir Muhammad Hamadani warned Suha Bhatta against such action and pointed out to him the well-known verse of Quran (II, 256) which runs:

'Let there be no compulsion in religion'.

It is true that Sikandar cannot be exonerated from his share of blame..."

Many Brahmins hanged themselves to death, some consumed poison and others drowned themselves in the Vitasta. Innumerable Brahmins jumped to their death from the mountains. The state was filled with gloom and hatred. The extent of this carnage is best described by Jonaraja,[31] "As the wind destroyed the trees, and the locusts the Shali crop, so did the Yavanas (religious fanatics) destroy the usages of Kashmir."

The fame of Sikandar's religious zeal spread to many countries and the fanatics belonging to Islam poured into the valley in hordes. Sikandar welcomed them with full Kashmiri hospitality. Adds Jonaraja,[32] "Attracted by the gifts and honours which the king bestowed on them and his kindness, the Mleechas entered Kashmir even as locusts enter a good field of corn." He destroyed the composite culture of the country evolved by Lall Ded and Noor-ud- Din, the great saints.

Agrees *Baharistan-i-Shahi*,[33] "Through sermonising and exhortations, he succeeded in enlightening the hearts of the people with the world-embellishing faith of the choicest among men—the faith of Islam." It further says,[34] "Through the blessings and support of Islam and the propagation of the commands of the Sharia, they were rewarded with victories wherever they led their armies confirming the saying that God helps those who help Muhammad's religion."

"....The world trembled but not so the mind of the wicked King. He forgot his kingly duties and took delight day and night in breaking images,"[35] says Jonaraja.

According to EF Knight,[36] "On all sides too are to be seen the remains of the ancient temples and palaces testifying to what a magnificent city Srinagur must have been before the iconoclastic Mahomedan invaders destroyed, so far they could, all the monuments of the idolaters."

Sikandar not only destroyed the temples of Kashmir but also used the material for construction. As per Assad Beg Qazvini , a historian in the court of Akbar,[37] "For instance, the tomb of his own Queen in Srinagur is built upon the foundation and with the materials of a Hindu temple; likewise the wall which surrounds the tomb of his son Zeinu-l Abidin was once the enclosure of a Hindu temple; and lastly the entrance of a Masjid in Nowa-Shehra of Srinagur, which, according to its inscription, was built during the reign of his son Zeinu-l Abidin, is formed of two fluted pillars of a Hindu peristyle. These instances prove that at least three different temples in the capital alone must have been overthrown either by Sikandar or one of his predecessors. But as the demolition of idol-temples is not attributed to any one of the earlier kings, we may safely ascribe the destruction of the three above mentioned to Sikandar himself."

Historian Sufi writes with a sort of admiration for Sikandar, and in an apologetic mood. "The Sultan was now fired with the zeal to change the character of his rule into an Islamic administration and a considerable advance was made in this direction. As his orders to this end were carried out either by recent coverts to Islam or other officials, it may be presumed that these converts and officials were not actuated only by zeal for the faith, many offences must have been committed which may have wounded the susceptibilities of Hindus."

His destructive inclination nonetheless, Sikandar introduced many social reforms. He forbade sale and distillation of wines, practice of sati, gambling, prostitution and even music.

Despite his religious fanaticism, Sikandar was married to a Hindu girl Shobha Mahadevi, daughter of his Prime Minister Rai Magarey. His commander-in-chief, Achaladeva, was also a Hindu. All of them were spineless except Rai Magarey who raised a revolt against him. He seized Ladakh and declared himself an independent ruler. But Sikandar defeated him and treated him mercilessly. He was put into prison where he died.

When the unquenchable thirst for the blood of Hindus did not abate, thousands of Hindus decided to leave the country for safety, knowing little what awaited them. They were caught near the border by the army deputed by the Muslim administration. At the behest of the King, the army stopped and killed the Hindus. Thousands of Hindus committed suicide and many perished during the exodus.

As per Narendra Sahagala,[38] "The state of Kashmir had become almost Hindu-less because of the massive and powerful campaign for religious conversion launched by Sikandar, the iconoclast, his son, cruel Ali Shah and anti-national Saif-ud-Din (Suha Bhatta) and the cruel Sayyids in their religious garb. Only a few Hindu families were living in Kashmir after paying taxes and after tolerating many difficulties and ignominies. The embers of the burnt libraries were still hot. The cries of the raped Hindu women were reverberating in Kashmir. The silence of the ruins of the temples was generating terror. The water of the Jhelum was still red with the blood of the Kashmiris. Amid this deep darkness there was refulgence from a lamp."

It was fearful and gruesome. The Hindus in Kashmir were in majority when Sikandar became the king in 1399 AD, but when he died what was left of them was a microscopic minority. Thus, to say that Islam came to Kashmir peacefully is a myth. Sikandar's rule is the blackest spot in the history of Kashmir.

Though, most of the Muslim historians, by and large, have condemned his actions, there are still some chroniclers who indulged in prevarication. They shamelessly defend the brutality of Sultan Sikandar. They justify the slaughter of Hindus; they justify the murders, rapes and pillage in the name of religion. In fact, *Baharistan-i-Shahi* gives a big pat to Sikandar.[39] "Despite the inexperience of youth, he (Sultan Sikandar) was gifted with remarkable piety and knowledge of sciences, esoteric as well as exoteric. *Sharh-e Shameh* is his work on logic. He also wrote a tract on mysticism in which he has clearly recorded that he was twenty-two years old at the time of writing that book." However, no other historian including Hassan has made any mention of this work. It further speaks of his benevolent nature and describes him as humane. "He also built a hospital, Daru'l-Shifa, in this land, where food, medicines and other requirements were provided for patients and the ailing. The physicians and medical practitioners of this land were given stipends and financial assistance to enable them to attend to the sick. They were required to pay daily visits to the hospital, diagnose diseases and prescribe treatments and cures."

Sultan Ali Shah 1413-1420 AD

Some historians and chroniclers such as *Baharistan-i-Shahi*, P N K Bamzai and Prem Nath Bazaz have tried in vain to remove the stigma of religious intolerance and persecution of Hindus from the face of Muslim kings as a whole, as it would be wrong to assume that all Muslims were zealots, because there existed people such as Mir Ali Hamadani, a Muslim priest, who was highly respected in the Muslim community and who also did not approve the religious persecution of King Sikandar. But, Hamadani was powerless and could not issue a fatwa against the king while disapproving his actions. It was the good luck of the remaining Hindus that Sikandar died.

After his death, his elder son Noor Khan (according to Firishta his name was Ameer Khan) who ruled under the title of Sultan Ali Shah succeeded to the throne. It is rightly said that a convert is more dangerous than an original Muslim although Ali Shah did not prove that dangerous for Hindus compared to Suha Bhatta, the prime minister of King Sikandar who converted to Islam and became Saif-ud-Din. He abetted the crimes perpetrated by King Sikandar upon Hindus. After the death of Sikandar, Suha Bhatta continued to hold the place of power. He continued to destroy the Hindu temples, an act objected to by Hamadani later on. To the good luck of Hindus, Suha Bhatta also died soon after.

As per Mohan Lal Kaul,[40] Sultan Ali Shah was advised by Mir Ali Hamadani, who has written in his book *Zakhira- Tul- Mulik* that Hindus be subjected to the following conditions:

- The Hindus will not construct any new places of worship or idol temples in the territory under the control of a Muslim ruler. They will not re-construct any existing place of worship or temple that may fall into ruin.
- They will not prevent Muslim travellers from staying in their places of worship or temples.
- They will receive any Muslim traveller into their houses and will provide him with hospitality for three days.
- They will not harbour any spies and will not act as spies themselves.
- If any of their relations shows any inclination to embrace Islam, they shall not prevent him from doing so.
- They will respect Muslims.
- If they are holding a meeting and a Muslim happens to come there, he will be received respectfully by them.
- They will not dress like Muslims.
- They will not adopt Muslim names.
- They will not ride a saddled horse.
- They will not carry swords or bows and arrows.
- They will not wear rings with diamonds.
- They will not openly sell or drink intoxicating liquor.
- They will not abandon their traditional dress so that they may be distinguished from Muslims.
- They will not openly practice their customs and usages among Muslims.
- They will not build their houses in the neighbourhood of Muslims.
- They will not cremate their dead.
- They will not mourn their dead loudly.
- They will not buy Muslim slaves.

The advice concludes with the note that if they (Hindus) infringe on any of the twenty conditions, they are not to be protected and Muslims may rightfully kill them and appropriate their property as if they were Kafir (idolaters) at war."

Ali Shah's regime was also not a stranger to conspiracies among the ministers. In fact, Suha Bhatta, the chief minister, Mohammad Khan and other ministers were not on good terms with each other. Their infighting created a lot of turmoil in the palace, which in turn had an adverse effect on the running of the administration. Suha Bhatta, who had attained a very powerful position, imprisoned Mohammad Khan and Margapati and put them in a fort at Bahurupa. However, Margapati escaped. Jonaraja says,[41] "The stones and the guard could not prevent his departure, while the noise of the waterfall drowned the clanking of the chain in his feet." Suha Bhatta then killed Margapati.

Meanwhile, Mohammad Khan joined hands with Piruja, the son of Sikandar, born to his wife Shobha Devi. Both of them attacked the king's forces but were defeated.

The Brahmins who had escaped the onslaught of Suha Bhatta had taken refuge with a Brahmin known as Ratnakara, who had developed close ties with Suha Bhatta. This closeness must have given them some relief and enabled them to come out of hiding. Unfortunately, a Muslim clergy known as Malan- ud-Din got Ratnakara arrested and imprisoned. The Brahmins could not consolidate their position. Meanwhile, Shahi Khan, the king's brother who was also a minister became jealous of Suha Bhatta. However, before he could do anything Suha fell ill and died. Shahi Khan gained popularity and he rose to power.

King Ali Shah was weak and un-ambitious as a King. After the death of Suha, he appointed Shahi Khan as his prime minister. Overcome by failure, Sultan Ali Shah expressed his desire to abdicate and go for Hajj to Mecca. On the way, when he reached Jammu, the King of Jammu, Raja Bhima Dev, who had given him his daughter in marriage, persuaded him to go back saying that going to Mecca would mean losing the throne. Raja Bhima Dev, along with his soldiers escorted Ali Shah back. On hearing the news of his brother's return, Shahi Khan, though happy, was concerned that he was heading back with a huge army. Says Jonaraja, [42] "Glad at the return of his brother, but angry at the approach of the army of the ally, the king of Madra (capital of Sagala, modern Sialkot now in Pakistan), Shahi Khan became sunk in joy and displeasure at the same time."

After arriving, Ali Shah practically drove Shahi Khan out of the country. He, however, turned to Jasrath, the lord of Khokhars(now in Pakistan) for help. Lord Jasrath helped him with men and material and he went to Kashmir to fight his elder brother. Says Srivara,[43] "Ever fortunate Jainollabnhadina having put to sword his enemies outside his country and repairing to his ancestral land donned the mantle of the Sultan like Rama."

With the help of Jasrath, Shahi Khan succeeded in not only defeating but also killing Ali Shah. A victorious Shahi Khan then became the king of Kashmir under the title of Zain-ul-Abidin.

"That Shahi Khan would have won an easy victory shows that Ali Shah, the rightful sovereign had lost the confidence of the people,"[44] writes Jia Lal Kilam.

Beginning of Srivara's Rajatarangini

Sultan Zain-ul-Abidin, 1420- 1470 AD

The rule of Zain-ul-Abidin, fondly known as Budshah, (King of Kings), is considered one of the most glorious reigns in Kashmir. Under his rule, Kashmir became the most powerful country. It had unparalleled prosperity with the economy and commerce flourishing. The social order was stable and national boundaries were thrown open to foreign countries. From the very beginning the king showed a humane nature. He stopped the genocide of Hindus.

Srivara says,[45] "After the (mis) rule of Ali Shah, his beneficent rule was experienced by everybody as an application of cooling sandal paste on a simmering desert at the end of the dog-days of scorching summer." Srivara describes his rule and justice as Dharma Raj like 'Yudhisthira's. Dharma Raj actually means rule of a righteous king. He was an upholder of virtue, justice, truth, human rights and fair play. [46]

Zain-ul-Abidin's religious tolerance: There was no Muslim ruler as tolerant as Budshah. Perhaps as a child he had heard the groans of aged Hindus when his father Sikandar and even his elder brother Ali Shah were slitting their throats. When he reached adolescence, he may also have witnessed horrifying shrieks of thousands of children and women whose houses were looted and burnt by soldiers, and they were forcefully converted to Islam. He may have considered all these to be against the cardinal principles of Islam.

Right from his childhood he had learnt that Allah is 'Rab-ul-Almeen' (God of the world), 'Rahmat-ul-Almeen' (merciful to the world), 'Rahman-ur-Rahim' (most gracious, most compassionate). He must have thought that God is preserver of the universe and benefactor of its people. He also must have realised that the persecution of Hindus by Sikandar and other kings had done more harm to Islam than good. He must have abhorred the killing of people feeling it was an un-Islamic act. The cardinal principles of Islam are a belief in the unity, mercy and supreme love of God's creations.

In respect of religious tolerance, PNK Bamzai writes,[47] "It is, however, for his high sense of toleration that Zain-ul-Abidin will always be known in history. Living in an age when religious persecution was the order of the day, his reign shines out as a bright gem amid the narrow-minded and short-sighted rulers of his time. He made Kashmir the real paradise in which men of all religions and nationalities mingled together and shared one another's joys and sorrows." By temperament, Hindus in the valley were peace-loving people. In return for his patronage and love, they offered Budshah their full cooperation. They vied with the Muslims in turning their homeland into a garden of peace and prosperity.

Confidence building measures: Budshah wanted to build confidence in Hindus by helpful measures so that the remaining Hindus would feel assured of a peaceful co-existence. He rebuilt temples that had been demolished by Sikandar and were lying in ruins. *Baharistan-i-Shahi* says,[48] "All those temples and idol-houses of the infidels which had been destroyed totally in the reign of Sultan Sikandar, May God bless his soul, were re-built and re-habilitated by him. Most of the unbelievers and polytheists, who had fled to the lands of Jammu and Kishtwar because of the overwhelming strength of Islam, were induced by him to return to Kashmir."

According to Jonaraja,[49] "Above the palace he built the two temples of Martanda and Amarnatha which illuminated the distant sky." He opened schools for students to study religious scriptures in Sanskrit. Scholarship was awarded to Hindu students going for higher studies to Banaras and Deccan. The most amazing thing he did was to call back Hindu migrants who had earlier been hounded by his father for not accepting Islam.

The King became the exponent of humanism, which ensures tolerance for other religions and patronage for all the people irrespective of different faiths. He appointed Tilakacharyya the Buddhist, Shiva

Bhatta and Rupyabhatta, the astrologers, to high positions. Jonaraja says,[50] "Shrimana Karpurabhatta, the preserver of lives, (physician), drew men of worth into the celebrated court of the king by his merit."

There is an incident showing the king's judicious nature and concerns. A person named Sadaulla came from Mecca. He claimed to be very knowledgeable and was jealous of the recluse with whose blessing the king had got a son. Sadaulla killed the recluse because he was close to the king and the queen. When the king came to know about it, he was appalled. He asked his religious guides, who were well-versed with the Islamic laws, the punishment for that murder. They informed him that Sadaulla be given the death sentence. But the king only got his head shaved and face blackened. Then he made him sit on a donkey, face towards the tail, had his body drenched with urine, and had him taken through the market places. People shouted, spat and jeered at him. Jonaraja says,[51] "The punishment was like death to him though he was alive; and pure flowers from heaven which perfumed all sides fell on the king as well as the blessing of the citizens, for this act of justice."

Zain-ul-Abidin's quest for learning: He loved to study Hindu scriptures and he was conversant with Sanskrit language. It is said that he loved reciting shlokas from Yoga Vasistha. Srivara, his courtier, was very often told to recite verses of these scriptures, which gave him lot of solace and moral strength especially at the time when his son revolted against him. Srivara says,[52] "Faithful application of the six schools of philosophy enriched his whole span of life like the seasons with their refreshing crops of flowers embellishing the pleasure garden of India." The six schools are: Samkhya, Yoga, Nyaya, Vaisesika, Mimamsa and Vedanta.

The books, which were destroyed by Sultan Sikandar, were prepared anew or purchased afresh for use of Muslim as well as Hindu scholars. The king himself started taking lessons on the *Ramayana* from Srivara. [53]"For learning how to achieve release from birth and death, the Sultan listened from my mouth recitations from the celebrated philosophy regarding transcendence, the Yoga Vasistha and what Valmiki had said (Ramayana)." Sultan got the *Mahabharata* and the *Rajatarangini* translated by his courtier Mullah Ahmed into Persian and the Persian and Arabic treatises were translated into Sanskrit. In fact, he revived the tradition of historiography. According to K Ayyappapanicker,[54]

"The Sultan was himself a great scholar, having command over several languages. There is a macaronic lyric in manuscript form ascribed to him, which contains one couplet in Kashmiri too:

'*The slender waist and delicate body are the passion's garden and pleasure's foliage,*

The simplicity of fancy; the majestic height is a pillar to the zenith and basis of the nadir.'

He further mentions that "Zainal Aabidin's (Zain-ul-Abidin) pen name was Qutb." During his rule, even Muslims studied Hindu scriptures. It is not as if he respected Hindu scriptures only—the fact is King Budshah was a devout Muslim and he did his best to spread Islam but not with violence, not by desecrating deities placed in Hindu temples, or by killing people who refused to be converted to Islam. He collected all the great Islamic scholars such as Hussein Quazi Rizwi, the Islamic theologian Maulana Kabir, and Quazi Jamal-ud-Din, a scholar of great merit. These notable personalities helped the spread of Islamic philosophy in the state. It was because of his efforts that Islam came to Ladakh.

Removal of taxes on Hindus : Budshah is considered a true scholar king of Kashmir. Once Shiva Bhatta, a physician, helped heal a boil the king was suffering from. When the king asked him what reward he wanted, Shiva Bhatta asked nothing for himself but requested that the Hindu community be allowed to live peacefully and the Jazia on the Brahmins be waived. He also requested the king that Hindus be allowed religious freedom, which the king gladly granted. Shiva Bhatta became the court physician and Afshar-ul-Ataba, head of the medical department. The Sultan also exempted the corpse tax on Hindus imposed by Sikandar. Hindus could now carry their dead to the cremation ground without any fear and without any payment of tax.

Believer of non-violence: The Sultan stopped killing of cows, birds and fish. He got trees planted on sides of the roads, and Chinar trees planted at various places. He constructed rest houses for travellers. According to Jia Lal Kilam,[55] "A free kitchen was established for Yogis and other Sanyasis (saints and religious preachers) and Pathshalas (schools) were established for the propagation of Sanskrit learning. Even now a mohalla of Srinagar is known as Jogi Lankar (Jogi is religious man) or Jogi Langar (kitchen for religious people)."

The sultan's popularity: Sultan Zain-ul-Abidin had gradually became famous not only in his country but in far off places too. The rulers of Marwar presented him with gifts; the Raja of Gwalior presented him music manuals; the ruler of Saurashtra sent him Bustard birds, the Sultan of Delhi sent him two King Swans, and the ruler of Khurasan gifted him mules and horses. His humane activities earned him the admiration and respect of other neighbouring rulers. According to Firishta,[56] "During his reign, the Raja of Thibet (Tibet) sent a pair of birds caught on the lake of Mansurowur (Mansarover). They were excessively beautiful, and were called the royal geese; they possessed the extraordinary faculty of separating particles of milk from water if they were mixed, after which they used to drink each separately."

Art and craft: During his reign, art and crafts flourished, writes Srivara. "Fifteenth century Kashmiri woollen clothes made of white Pashmina were made available through the courtesy of the Sultan.[57]"

Sultan Zain-ul-Abidin introduced the art of shawl embroidery, carpet making, handmade paper, silk weaving and papier-mâché in the state. According to GMD Sufi, [58] "Zain-ul-Abidin invited mechanics and craftsmen from Iran, Turan, Turkistan and Hindustan..." He was the only king who patronised learning and constructed institutions for imparting vocational training to people.

He was the king who gave a fillip to cottage industries. With wood available in abundance in Kashmir he wanted people to develop creativeness in woodcarving. Writes Omacanda Handa,[59] "Kashmir witnessed a golden age of renaissance of wooden architecture under its sagacious ruler Sultan Zain-ul-Abidin. He was the first exponent of secularism in Kashmir as understood in the modern terminology."

Music, singing and dance also got patronage. Srivara writes in his *Zaina Rajatarangini* that,[60] "the Sultan showered gold in the courtyard of the palace which was resounding with all the local melodies in vogue in Kashmir, the progeny of sages Kasyapa." A circular theatre hall was constructed at Bijbihara. Open air stages were improvised in the gardens and performances given. The Sultan would also invite rulers from adjoining places to these festivities of music and dances.

The most accomplished performing artists were Khuja, the disciple of Abdul Qadir, Mullah Zada the lute player, Mullah Jamal a vocalist,

Srivara the composer, and singers Jaffar and Srivara. A famous poet Yodha Bhatta penned a play *Zaina Prakasha* depicting in detail the life of the Sultan. Iranian musicians founded two schools of music in Kashmir during this period.

The Sultan had great respect for artists. Kashi Nath Dhar in his comments on Srivara's *Zaina Rajatarangini*, says,[61] "Actually the Sultan desired that people of merit in various fields should remain in Kashmir so that their talents could be indigenously exploited... These talented prodigies also became fans of the Sultan when they realised that he had praise for them and showered honour on them."

Law and order: Budshah provided food for low-caste unemployed people so that they would not resort to thieving. With the establishment of law and order and peace in the country, there was economic prosperity. During his reign, people felt safe and protected. Srivara mentions,[62] "Nobody could rob honest and well-behaved householders of even a single cowry under duress, not to speak of their dwelling or wife."

His defence preparedness: Budshah established a formidable army with which he conquered Tibet, Punjab, Ladakh, and other northern states. In addition to this, he sent his representatives to Delhi, Turkey, Khurasan, and Egypt. The introduction of cannons in the artillery became an auspicious day of celebration and jubilation. Mules carried the cannons. Srivara composed a poem on the occasion.[63]

The Sultan had to curb revolts from his own family— from people such as Mir Thakur who was the eldest amongst his own foster brothers. An expert in law, Mir Thakur belonged to the Thakur clan. The Sultan had given him a lot of freedom and Mir Thakur suddenly got power hungry. This angered the Sultan and Mir Thakur had to flee to Kishtwar. "He pampered the Said (Sayyid) there at Bhimber with undertaking menial jobs, so that the chieftain grants him asylum in his territory and does not arrest and hand him over to Sultan Budshah,"[64] says Kashi Nath in his comments on Srivara's *Zaina Rajatarangini*.

Savagery of nature-the famine: In 1460 AD, a violent storm with dust and rain and hail shattered Kashmir, destroying all vegetables and crops in the valley. This was followed by heavy snowfall. A severe famine broke out. The king immediately took steps to overcome the catastrophe and introduced rationing. Srivara has mentioned,[65] "Some accustomed to eat food in plates like gourmets to prescribed menu, and particular taste and flavour, now living on (a ration of) four masa (measure), did starve to death."

Again in 1462 AD, massive floods gripped the valley and washed away everything. There was another famine. Srivara, who perhaps was a witness, has given a grim picture.[66] "These floods, as horrifying as the pressure mounted by the unclean non-Aryans (Mleechas), swallowed the cattle, the kine, the human-being, the residential quarters and the grain, one and all, within their reach."

Zain-ul-Abidin the builder: Francis Younghusband has stated,[67] "He was the staunch friend of the cultivators, and built many bridges and constructed many canals." That apart, he introduced wooden buildings. It is said that his palace had twelve storeys with numerous rooms, verandas etc. He constructed another superb building named Zaina Dub. About this building, an anonymous poet has lauded it thus: [68]

Zaina Ladhey Sunaser Laray
Duba Tel Aftab Ghah Travan,

'the Sultan built a huge building of golden bricks as if the sun passed underneath its verandas.' But Chak rulers burned that building.

Public works: Aurel Stein has praised the peaceful reign of Zain-ul-Abidin during which he also undertook a lot of important irrigation works. Srivara and Jonaraja give a considerable list of canals constructed by the Sultan. Agriculture was Budshah's top priority. He was the only Muslim monarch who constructed many canals such as Kakapura canal, Chakdar canal, Martanda canal etc.

He paid great attention to irrigation and therefore constructed improvised canals at various places. He even built an artificial lake so that the water nuts could be grown there. Says Kashi Nath Dhar,[69] "We find the name of Dal Lake in any Sanskrit chronicle for the first time." The king was so fascinated by the lake that he would go floating in a houseboat for many days.

During the Sultan's reign, decorated houseboats were very common. "The houseboats of the Sultan fitted with weather-cock, draped in beautiful cloth with pinioned oars moving very fast presented a captivating sight like pretty-feathered flying birds in the company of fowler," says Srivara.[70] One could also witness the floating gardens, improved and made crop-yielding, during the Sultan's period. The two famous islands, Sona

Lank and Ropa Lank, were improved and became centres of attraction for visitors.

Zain-ul-Abidin, an environmentalist: The Sultan had a very intimate relationship with nature. He had great reverence for the rivers. He knew that Vitasta was the lifeline of the country. As per *Nilamatapurana*,[71] "Shiva at the request of Kasyapa, prevailed upon the goddess (Parvati) to show herself in the land in the shape of a river…." Thus, Vitasta came into being. Its birthday is celebrated on 13th of half of the month of Bhadrapada (Bhadoon which comes during August) every year by Hindus all over Kashmir. As an acknowledgement of the life sustaining qualities of Vitasta, Sultan Zain-ul-Abidin also joined the Hindus in celebrating the birth celebrations. Srivara mentions, [72] "While floating on the waters in a boat up and down he would lend ear to wise sayings, listen to music and also acknowledge the blessing of the city-dwellers."

Domestic problems: Zain-ul-Abidin had three wives. His sons, born from a queen, the daughter of the King of Madras were Adam Khan (Adamakhana), Hajji Khan (Hejyakhana), Jasrat Khan (Jassarathakhana) and Behram Khan (Baheramakhana) as per Jonaraja.[73] But Srivara has mentioned that the queen gave birth to only three children—Adam Khan the eldest, Hajji Khan the middle one and Behram khan the youngest.[74] All of them turned out to be spoilt brats. They went astray and turned rogues, indulged in violent activities, and behaved in a manner unbecoming of their status. Both Adam Khan and Hajji Khan used to fight on flimsy grounds and got into trouble for trivial reasons. Budshah tried his utmost to bring his sons to reason but did not succeed. In order to keep them apart so that they would not indulge in dangerous mischief, he sent the eldest to subdue Baltistan and the second to recover Lohara Kot who had revolted against the king. Hajji Khan who was at Rajouri wanted to come back to Kashmir to see for himself what was going on in the palace. The king of Rajouri promised him full support in case he revolted against his father. Hajji Khan was easily instigated and came back to the capital with his bodyguards to use them against his elder brother Adam Khan in the event of the death of his father. Writes Shyam Lal Sadhu,[75] "Zain-ul-Abidin created wonderful precedents in bringing the Hindus and Muslims emotionally together, but could not close the gulf between his own sons."

Though Firya Dammara and Taj Tantresa advised Hajji Khan not to revolt against his father, he went ahead supported by Rawats and Rawal from Rajouri. In the fight Hajji Khan was defeated. His life was spared by the king and he immediately left for Srinagar as advised, fleeing to Bhimber.

Adam Khan was, in fact, very dear to the Sultan and he was the real heir to the throne. The state had appointed him as the administrator of Kamraz district but instead of ruling the people with compassion he plundered them of their riches by use of force or deceiving them with false hopes. Then suddenly, he declared himself independent. It was during this period that the foundation of Zaina-Kadal (Third Bridge) was being laid. The Sultan decided to suppress the revolt by Adam Khan. He sent a personal letter to his second son Hajji Khan to come back to Srinagar along with his army. According to Pir Hassan,[76] "The Sultan sent a secret message to Hajji Khan to return along with his forces." Meanwhile Adam Khan reached Suyapura and the Sultan also reached there and decided to punish his eldest son by trying to put him to death, says Srivara in *Zaina Rajatarangini*.[77] Hajji Khan also returned and was received by his younger brother Behram Khan. Adam Khan was defeated. He fled to Gilgit and sought asylum from the ruler there.

Budshah was completely disappointed and exasperated by his son's misbehaviour. He became weak on account of his ailing health and his sons did not care for him. As happens among royal princes, his sons resorted to internecine warfare for the throne of Kashmir. Bitter disappointment was writ large on the face of the king and his sorrowful eyes were a mirror to his crushed heart. Unable to speak, he looked from his sick bed at people around him ruefully. Weak and heartbroken, King Zain-ul-Abidin while reciting the sacred verses of Kalima (religious recitation) on an auspicious Friday in the month of May expired in the year 1470 AD. Srivara who was present at the time of the Sultan's death says he looked bright and calm as if all his pain had vanished. Mohibbul Hasan in *Kashmir under the Sultans* says, [78] "His body was carried to the Mazar-i-Salatin (on the bank of Jhelum, near Zaina Kadal), and was buried there amidst the loud lamentations of his subjects." People, irrespective of their caste, creed or religion mourned his death. No family cooked food that day and even for the next few days. They felt the loss of not just a king but someone near and dear.

Sultan Zain-ul-Abidin died, yet he lives in the hearts of the people.

Heinrich Heine, a famous author has said that each tombstone conceals the history of a whole world, which cannot disappear without leaving a trace.

Sultan Zain-ul-Abidin was the noblest of kings who brought peace and prosperity to the country. His death was a great loss to the people of Kashmir. Constructing towns and buildings in his name, the people continue to remember him even today. Zaina Kot, Zainagir, Zaina Kadal, Zaindar Mohalla and Zainapur etc. are still named after him. As per Aurel Stein,[79] "Jayapura ...retained a certain importance for longer than Parihaspura and served occasionally as a royal residence even in late times. In it retired Queen Kota, the last of the Hindu rulers of Kashmir...Zain-ul-Abidin restored the town which had fallen into decay and built a new palace on the lakeshore. He also constructed a monastery for the Buddhists and an inn for the Hajjis."

Sultan Haider Shah, 1470-1472 AD

Strange are the ways of nature. It is not always true that a good father may give birth to good children as happened in the case of King Zain-ul-Abidin. When the king died, there was not a single soul who did not shed tears. Unfortunately, his children proved contemptible and were hated by the people. They took pleasure in the company of mean, vulgar people and engaged in pursuit of wild licentiousness and wickedness. Budshah had laid a high standard of administration by which the ordinary people benefitted. This great king was conscious that all his sons were incompetent to carry on the country's affairs efficiently. True enough, his son Hajji Khan who took over the kingdom became a cruel king. He put to death Jamshid and Mir, the trusted ministers of his father for having served him honestly.

He also took over the command of the country. He titled himself as Sultan Haider Shah. In the coronation rituals, Hassan Kosea (Kouchai) who was the in charge of the Royal Treasury, crowned the king. Just after taking over as king, he made his younger brother Behram Khan lord of Nagrama (Nagam) (a place presently on Srinagar Chrar-i-Sharif Road). He also appointed his son Hassan, the lord of Kamraz.

Kashi Nath Dhar, in his comments on *Zaina Rajatarangini*, states,[80] "Governorship of the district of Kamraz has always been earmarked for the heir-apparent." While he had revolted against his father Zain-ul-Abidin, two tribal chiefs namely Rawats and Rawal had helped the king.

These chiefs were given important positions. Mirza Hassan, the son of an important person Sayyid Nassir during Zain-ul-Abidin's rule was made administrator of Beeru. In fact, Sultan Haider Shah had his son married to the daughter of Mirza Hassan.

Initially, Sultan Haider Shah treated his subjects well including those who were against him. Srivara say,[81] "He (the Sultan) reciprocated with goodness even to those who had been against him. The lion salutes the hordes of elephants first and then kills them." The same way, the Sultan took revenge on them when he saw the time was ripe.

The assessment of Sultan Haider Shah's reign will not be complete without the role of a barber named Purna. King Haider took a fancy to this low and uneducated barber who at once was raised to a high position in the administration. Purna committed unbelievable atrocities upon the people. Purna alias Riktatara alias Loli Hajjam seems to have been suffering from acute sadism. Inflicting pain and killing people, whom he did not like, not by conventional methods but slow torture, gave him happiness. "The courtiers and the Thakurs who had worked with the king's father had their limbs cut off by the relentless and the sinful barber," says Srivara. He was such a sadist that once he impaled some people on the roadside. They shrieked for three days and three nights till they died. He mistook his elevation to high position as a license to permit administrative atrophy. According to Firishta,[82] "He (Sultan Haider Shah) gave himself up entirely to scandalous excesses, and permitted his ministers to exercise flagrant acts of injustice and oppression on his subjects. As an instance of which he formed a disreputable connection with a barber, (Purna) who, becoming the medium of communication between the King and the people, took from them large bribes for his pretended or real services."

To provoke the king against Hindus who resided within the vicinity of Khanqah of Sayyid, barber Purna damaged it and then blamed the Hindus. The infuriated king ordered persecution of the Hindus. Outwardly, Purna showed loyalty towards Hindus, but inwardly he betrayed them. The repression was so terrible that there broke out a revolt where Hindus burnt some mosques. The revolt was crushed with a heavy hand. During this period, such was the plight of the Brahmins that they gave up their Tilak and dress and exclaimed, 'I am not Bhatta

(Hindu), I am not Bhatta'[83]. Subsequently there were many temples where idols were broken and their wealth plundered. The lands of Hindus were confiscated and all other worshipping banned.

During Haider Shah's cruel and jungle rule, even Srivara was reprimanded and he had to beg for mercy. In fact, he had advocated the Hindu system of cremation and had deplored the Muslim burial. For this, he had to seek pardon, [84] "Muslims should excuse me for indulging in improper criticism in the context (of burying the dead), since the word of a poet knows no restraint."

Sultan Haider Shah was very addicted to liquor. Initially, he enjoyed wine made of grapes but then the grape wine proved ineffective and did not give him intoxication. As per the comments in *Zaina Rajatarangini* by Kashi Nath Dhar, [85] "The sultan used to drink so much that grape-wine or the sugarcane wine did not satisfy him. So the distillers now supplied him wine extracted from Guda, (the extract of the sugarcane dried after boiling) which of course was more potent…"

His death which fortunately came two years after he took over occurred because of drinking. He was sipping wine when suddenly his nose bled and he collapsed. A few days later he breathed his last. After the death of King Haider Shah, Purna was arrested and sent to jail where he died.

Sultan Haider Shah had a virtuous wife known as Gul Khatoon. As per Prem Nath Bazaz,[86] "This graceful lady was very popular among the Kashmiris because she walked in the footsteps of her father-in-law, the famous Budshah." He says that Gul Khatoon tried her best to dissuade the king from drinking but she failed. She had great interest in the education of girls and established a Madrasa at her own expense—an imposing, awe-inspiring and architecturally beautiful building. She was very tolerant towards Hindus.

According to William C Brice,[87] "The chronicles do not say whether Gul Khatoon belonged to a Muslim family of foreign origin or to a Kashmiri family. It is more than likely that she was the daughter of a Bayhaki Sayyid for the Kashmir rulers were always very eager to marry in the family of these descendents of the Prophet, and regarded such an alliance with pride. However, it is strange that unlike the royal ladies of foreign origin, Gul Khatoon favoured Hindu customs and ceremonies."

The Sultan was a great player of lute. He had mastered this art and used to teach others. In fact, he would invite Bahlol, the famous Rabab player and others and compose music. Srivara says that it was Bahlol who had invented the Rabab instrument. Kashi Nath Dhar says,[88] "Srivara has later on categorically stated that it was invented by one Bahlol, presumably a Kashmiri."

Like his father and uncle, King Haider Shah also built a bridge across the Jhelum in Srinagar and named it Noukadal.

Sultan Hassan Shah, 1472-1484 AD

As per the hierarchy, the throne after Haider Shah should have passed on to his younger brother Behram Khan, the youngest son of Zain-ul-Abidin due to the fact that Haider Shah's son was too young to become the king. Behram Khan had served his brother with devotion and honesty and was also tipped by some ministers to become the king when Haider Shah was struggling between life and death. But there arose a dispute regarding the successorship. Ahmed Yattu, who was an important figure in the administration, told Behram Khan to make Hassan Shah his heir apparent. Behram Khan did not like the idea. Among all the ministers, some were in favour of Behram Khan and others in favour of Hassan Shah. Finally, on account of Ahmed Yattu's efforts and canvassing, the supporters of Behram Khan also shifted their allegiance to Hassan Shah whose chances for kingship became bright. Meanwhile King Haider Shah died.

After his death, his son Hassan Shah was crowned the king of Kashmir. Yattu, who was given the title of Malik Hussein, supervised the coronation ceremony. The rituals were performed according to Islamic and Hindu traditions. Tilak ceremony (where Hindus use saffron paste to decorate the forehead) was also observed by the king. A holy fire yajna was also performed.

Sultan Hassan Shah was a very handsome and tolerant king. Srivara says, "Surprisingly, the lotus faces of the city-dwellers blossomed on having a look at the moon-face of this new Sultan.[89]"

Lover of art: On previous occasions, whenever there was any coronation the servants of the palace were presented cotton clothes but on Hassan's coronation even the servants were given silk garments such was the joy and gaiety on the occasion. According to Jonarajas[90] "The singers from

Karnata sat gracefully before the king as if they represented the six tunes —Kedara, Gauda, Gandhara, Bhangala and Malava." Dancing was also part of the celebrations.

Hyatt Khatoon, the seniormost queen of the Sultan was his most loved queen. When she gave birth to a beautiful son, Mohammad Khan, it was an occasion of great festivity too. As per Hassan in *Tarikh -i-Hassan*,[91] Sultan Hassan Shah had brought 1200 Qawaals from India. And Qawaalis were sung with the Sultan himself composing music and Sanskrit verses. He also sang songs which surprised the guests. The Sultan was well-versed with Bharat Muni's *Natyashastra*.Drama, comedy shows were put up. Mullah Hassan, the most celebrated instrument player played the Veena. Srivara himself translated a Persian song into Kashmiri. Three beautiful dancers, Ratnamala, Dipmamla and Rupmala performed a dance-drama on the occasion.

Hassan Shah's quest for learning: Sultan Hassan Shah was a generous king and had great love for learning. In addition to Islamic literature, he had a fascination for the philosophical lore of Hindus. Like his grandfather Zain-ul-Abidin, he also studied the six schools of philosophy. He granted freedom of worship to Hindus. He bestowed higher positions and jageer to Ahmed Yattu and Tazi Bhatt, who became his confidential adviser. Even the descendents of erstwhile poet Jonaraja were given liberal grants. He rehabilitated Magarey and Thakur who were holding important posts during the reign of his grandfather.

Hassan Shah's invasions: Meanwhile, the hurt Behram Khan who had fled the country, decided to invade Kashmir and usurp the throne. The Sultan sent Tazi Bhatt, his commander-in-chief, to fight the invader. Behram Khan on reaching Kamraz was disappointed at the absence of all those ministers who had instigated him to revolt against the king. He was defeated and then arrested along with his son. Both of them were kept captive in their own palace. A haughty minister of the Sultan known as Abhimanyu Padru gouged his eyes out piercing them with hot iron rods. Srivara has mentioned that Sultan Zain-ul-Abidin once in a fit of anger told Behram Khan that his eyes deserved to be gouged as he was not helping his father in the war against Hajji Khan [92]. After three years of struggle, Behram Khan died. Abhimanyu Padru was arrested in Bijbihara and put behind bars. His eyes were also gouged out.

Fath Khan, who later became king of Kashmir as Fath Shah, was the grandson of Zain-ul-Abidin. He had taken refuge with the Tatar Khan Lodhi, the governor of Punjab. When Fath Khan came to know about the civil war in Kashmir, he instigated Tatar Khan to attack the valley. The adjoining royalties of Kashmir such as Jammu, Poonch and Rajouri, though independent, were however interdependent on each other. Sensing the danger, these kings approached Sultan Hassan Shah. Tazi Bhatt was sent to lead the expedition against Tatar Khan, the uncle and governor of Sultan Bahlol Lodhi of Delhi. Malik Tazi Bhatt fought valiantly and as P N K Bamzai says,[93] "With the help of Jammu army, Tazi Bhatt marched to Sialkot and plundered." The joint efforts of all these kings defeated the powerful Tatar Khan Lodhi. Fath Khan fled from the scene."

The Sayyids ousted: During the reign of Sikandar, more than seven hundred Sayyids had come from Arabia. These Sayyids spread havoc in the country enforcing forceful conversion to Islam, and in the event of any resistance by non-Muslims they were killed. The Sayyids were foreigners and they considered Kashmiris as load carriers. In order to make themselves more important in the community, they managed to get Sultan Zain-ul-Abidin's daughter wedded to Sayyid Nassir, one of the leaders of the Sayyids, and the Sultan himself married another Sayyid girl. Hassan Shah married a Sayyid girl known as Hyatt Khatoon alias Mira Mukhat. The Sayyids developed relationships with the royals of Kashmir to ensure royal patronage for themselves.

Sayyids expectations: During Sikandar's period, the Sayyids succeeded in influencing the King to understand belief and unbelief, religious faith and idolatry, say Islamic fundamentalists. Sikandar indulged in making wholesale conversion of Hindus to Islam. The Sayyids expected that King Hassan Shah, too, would tread in the footsteps of King Sikandar. But Hassan Shah was not a Muslim religious bigot; he had characteristics of humanism in his blood. He patronised the liberalism of his grandfather Zain-ul-Abidin. He loved music, which is prohibited in Islam. He studied Hindu scriptures as well. Since his wife was a Sayyid, he also patronised the Sayyids.

Unfortunately, the Sayyids treated Kashmiris with disrespect and the local people were disgusted with them. They even offended Malik Hassan

Yattu the new prime minister, and Tazi Bhatt, the commander-in-chief, who brought it to the notice of the Sultan. The Sultan was angry and ordered the ouster of the Sayyids from the country. Hyatt Khatoon (the queen who belonged to the Sayyid clan) felt disgraced. She knew that the strong-willed king would not easily change his decision; therefore, she decided not to pressurise the king to revoke his decision. Gradually, she started taking interest in the administration and by her good work she was able to win the confidence of the Sultan.

The Sayyids had become nervous at the king's proclamation about their ouster from the country. They became angry with Tazi Bhatt and wanted to arrest him. But Tazi Bhatt was informed by his people about this. When he arrived with a party of police officers to arrest the Sayyids, strangely, the local population came out on the streets. The king was alarmed at this, and fearing a rebellion, he pacified the people and assured that no action would be taken against the Sayyids. In view of the changed scenario, the Sayyids were able to put Tazi Bhatt under house arrest.

Ultimately, with the help of some Dammaras, some Muslims like Magarey succeeded in killing the Sayyids. Alarmed at this, the Sayyids left the country to the great relief of the people of Kashmir.

Hassan Shah as builder: Sultan Hassan Shah constructed many buildings, mosques and even Hindu temples and Buddhist monasteries. A quadrangular building was constructed at Diddamatha. He also built a Khanqah in the name of his father. Royal buildings were constructed at Sopore and Anantnag. The queen mother Gul-Khatoon constructed a Madrasa. She and the Sultan inaugurated it.

The other queens and ministers also were gripped with construction fever. Queen Zulal built a Khanqah at Nowhatta. Queen Miriam Khatoon built a monastery; Ahmed Yattu built a mosque at Diddamatha. His wife constructed a hospital and so did his son. Tazi Bhatt also built a convent.

When the Queen mother Gul Khatoon, who was a restraining influence on the Sultan, died, everybody grieved and people lamented loudly. She was loved by both Muslims and Hindus.

The devastating fire: In 1479 AD, a fire broke out in the precincts of Pravaresapura, and spread in the whole city. Thousands of houses including the palace of Behram Khan, were burnt down. Even the houseboats turned into ashes. Jama Masjid, constructed by Sultan

Sikandar, was completely gutted. However, the mosque was rebuilt and the houses were reconstructed for people to live in.

Hassan Shah's administration: Malik Ahmed Yattu, the prime minister, was an efficient administrator and a patriot. Tazi Bhatt belonged to a very poor family, but he was a patriot and a brave soldier. Once while witnessing an archery competition as a spectator, he requested the king to permit him to join the competition. The king granted him permission and his arrow was dead on target while other famous archers, including the famous generals of the army, failed to achieve the goal. This was the turning point for Tazi Bhatt and he was appointed in the military force where he rose rapidly as a military commander and also a popular leader. He was so much loved by the people that Malik Ahmed Yattu adopted him as his own son. He had also adopted another boy named Jahangir Magarey.

Return of the Sayyids: Malik Ahmed Yattu and Tazi Bhatt were running the administration efficiently for a while when suddenly both fell apart. The queen (Hyatt Khatoon) sided with Malik Ahmed Yattu. In fact, she wanted to bring the Sayyids back to the valley. So, she took Malik Ahmed into confidence and told him to suggest to the Sultan to invite the Sayyids. Tazi Bhatt's popularity made Malik Ahmad and his son Navroz very jealous of him. They poisoned the ears of the king against him and asked him to recall the Sayyids. This was yet another unfortunate day for Kashmir. Later, Malik Ahmed realised his mistake but it was too late.

After reaching the valley, the Sayyids lost no time in consolidating their position. They succeeded in winning over the Sultan. Gradually, they eliminated powerful ministers like Tazi Bhatt. Then they got Malik Ahmed arrested. His wife and children were tortured and his property looted. Jahangir Magarey understood the game of the Sayyids and fled from Kashmir. Prem Nath Bazaz writes in *Daughters of Vitasta*,[94] "With the disappearance of Jahangir, the last of the nationalist-minded formidable nobles, the Sayyids were in full control of the administrative machinery. Mera Mukhat was their chief adviser; poor Hassan Shah was reduced to the position of a non-entity, a figurehead, a tool or an onlooker whose opinion was never sought, or, when voluntarily given, mostly ignored. He lost all interest in the government." The reality was, the Sayyids were ruling the country. Sayyid Hassan, the king's father-in-law was appointed as prime minister. New officers were appointed and they started taking bribes. The Sultan virtually became a prisoner in the hands of the Sayyids.

Taking control of the administration, they sent military expeditions to Baltistan and Ladakh. They annexed Baltistan but could not defeat the king of Ladakh. They attributed their failure to local Kashmiris whom they looked down upon—whether Hindus or Muslims.

Meanwhile, Sultan Hassan Shah fell ill with diarrhoea and then a snake bit him. His health started deteriorating and he was bedridden for a few months. Suddenly the king had a premonition and he called Queen Hyatt Khatoon and Sayyid Miya Hassan and told them not to enthrone his infant son Mohammad, but to crown Yusuf, the son of Behram Khan. The Sultan also told them to make Prince Mohammad the legal heir of the throne after Yusuf. He died and a seven days state mourning was announced.

With the king's death, the Sayyids were in complete control. They appointed their people on important positions. They mistreated the local people and taxed them heavily for anything and everything. Srivara says that accepting a bribe was considered by the officers of the state as a religious obligation, extortion their dexterity, oppressing the subjects was regarded as wisdom and addiction to women was regarded as happiness.[95] There was an internecine war for the throne between Yusuf, who was the king's choice, and Mohammad, choice of the Sayyids. As expected, the king's choice was not implemented and the Sayyids proved themselves masters and enthroned Mohammad. All the local ministers were either executed or they left the country as they felt the presence of the Sayyids had changed the tranquil atmosphere of Kashmir.

Sultan Mohammad Shah, 1484-1486 AD

Hassan Shah's last desire was to crown his brother Behram Khan's son Yusuf as the king. But the Sayyids did not honour his wish. On the other hand, in spite of state mourning in the country, they enthroned Prince Mohammad without the knowledge of the Queen Hyatt Khatoon.

By installing seven-year old Mohammad Shah as king, Sayyid Hassan became the regent of the ruler and by proxy the Sayyids began to rule over Kashmir. They did not allow even the ministers access to him. Gradually, they continued humiliating and harassing the people of Kashmir. They mocked those who were well versed in Sanskrit language.

Srivara says, "Jeering at the local and Sanskrit knowing litterateurs and scholars the Sayyids indulged in evil sports with women at their houses and with hawks (bird hunting) outside.[96] They also banned the playing of music and termed it un-Islamic."

Death of Prince Yusuf: Queen Hyatt Khatoon wanted to set Prince Yusuf free from prison. She wanted to bring peace to the country. She knew that with Yusuf as king, the ever growing powers of the Sayyids could be controlled. She was determined to fulfil the dying wish of her husband. Tazi Bhatt backed her. But unfortunately fate had something else in store for twenty-year-old Yusuf. The queen sent Idi Raina to the prison to set the Prince free but as soon as they came out of prison, the Sayyids came to know and Ali Shah Baihaqi, in connivance with other Sayyids, decided to kill the prince. They rushed to the gates of the prison and Sayyid Ali pounced on Prince Yusuf and killed him. Sultan Hassan Shah had imprisoned Prince Yusuf along with his father Behram Khan. The Queen was shattered by the news of Yusuf's death. She realised the evil designs of the Sayyids, but it was too late for her to do anything.

P N K Bamzai in *Cultural and Political History*,[97] has given a very grim picture of Yusuf's death. He says, on account of his being in prison, his mother Sobana Devi had not seen him for quite some time. When he was murdered, the dead body was handed over to his mother. "Sobana Devi, who had not seen him for many years, kept his dead body with her for three days and then had it buried." Srivara says,[98] "His mother Sobana Devi, already widowed, remained all her life in the cemetery living on barley." Yusuf was buried near his father's grave and Sobana Devi spent the last days of her life near the two graves.

Sayyids as regents: With young Mohammad Shah as king it was Sayyids such as Ali Shah Baihaqi and Prime Minster Sayyid Hassan who were almost ruling over Kashmir. The Sayyids considered themselves as belonging to the royal family. They committed atrocities on Kashmiris. In order to get rid of these arrogant, untamed Sayyids, Kashmiris continued their uprisings against them. The Kashmiri nobles, with the help of Purushuram, who was the head of Jammu army, attacked the palace and killed Sayyid Hassan, the prime minister and Miya Hassan the maternal grandfather of the king, as also many servants of the palace. One servant managed to escape and informed Sayyid Muhammad, the son of Sayyid

Hassan. He came, attacked the palace, and seized the treasure. However, the Sayyids were losing their battle and tried to bribe the local nobles. Saif-ud-din, a young and brave Kashmiri, crossed the river along with a strong army, and assisted Daud Magarey, son of Jahangir Magarey to attack the Sayyids.

Both the troops fought on the banks of the Vitasta. The Kashmiri forces tied the boats together, and tried to bridge the river so that the army could cross. Prisoners were set free to join the rebel army. The commander of the boatmen fought valiantly and killed many soldiers of the enemy. The defeat of the Sayyids was imminent. But they strengthened themselves by recruiting soldiers from Nandpora on the bank of Dal Lake. They dismantled the dyke wall on the river Vitasta and Navapur and the water surged into the city. The rebels who were advancing had to halt on account of the water. The Sayyids then dug a trench around the palace and filled it with water to protect the palace. They became ferocious and looted the local people of their belongings. They set their houses on fire. The houses of Jonaraja and Tazi Bhatt were also burnt. Although, the rebel soldiers gained victory over places around the city, the Sayyids still had control of the city.

Jahangir Magarey returned to the valley via Poonch. When the Sayyids learnt this, they tried to negotiate with him and offered him prime ministership under King Mohammad Shah. A seasoned diplomat, Magarey rejected the proposal and told them he could accept only on his conditions. They would firstly have to restore the treasury and secondly disarm themselves. This was not acceptable to the Sayyids. They launched an offensive once again. This time they met with some success. They captured the rebels and killed those who had infiltrated the city. Padma Bhatta of the Kashmir forces was killed. Ali Khan was in command of the Sayyid forces. The Sayyids killed Daud Magarey. Ahmed Pratiha died along with his platoon. Ultimately, the Sayyids were victorious and they killed many local people including a top physician, Yavanesvara. They celebrated the victory at Idgah. Temples were looted. Several heads were fixed on poles, which proved a deterrent for the rebel forces.

Kashmiri forces take control: All this did not dampen the courage of the Kashmiri forces. They got military help from Kishtwar and Gilgit, Hunza and Khovurpur. To subdue the rebellion, the Sayyids invited Tatar

Khan, the commander-in-chief of Delhi King Lodi's army in Punjab. The Kashmir army defeated the army of Tatar Khan in which about 2,000 Turk soldiers were killed. The Sayyids had to flee the country. Jahangir Magarey took over the administration in his own hands. Gradually, peace started returning to the country. Under the flag of Sultan Mohammad, Kashmiri nobles distributed the important posts of the government. The ministers confiscated all that had belonged to the Sayyids. Ali Khan was ousted. Purushuram, the leader of Jammu army got a handsome reward and he left for Jammu. The work of the resettlement of the country started. The Khanqah was rebuilt and repaired. Temples and shrines were restored. But the peace was very short-lived. Some of the disgruntled nobles of Kashmir sent secret messages to Fath Shah. Fath Shah (son of Adam Khan) invaded Kashmir twice and lost but the third time he won and took over Kashmir as Sultan. After his victory, Fath Shah got Mohammad Shah imprisoned. He was, of course, provided all the facilities that the ousted King deserved. Jahangir Magarey was wounded in the war and he became ineffective and insignificant.

Beginning of Prajyabhatta and Sukha's *Rajatarangini*

Sultan Fath Shah 1486-1493 AD

Fath Shah was enthroned as king of Kashmir. There were, however, two claimants to the throne then, Fath Shah and Mohammad Shah. The tussle for the throne of Kashmir remained between the two claimants for more than 32 years. Both of them became the king by turn. Mohammad Shah became Sultan of Kashmir five times and Fath Shah three times.

During the uncertain years of their reign, the political conditions of the country remained disturbed. Old nobles of Dammars and Tantrins and Lavanya were no longer powerful in the state. On the contrary, new types of families cropped up who wielded potential power and were known as king makers. Two families, the Magareys and Chaks reached the top in political power. The political, social and economical conditions prior to the enthronement of Fath Shah had deteriorated due to the high-handedness of the Sayyids. Fath Shah was a decent man. He wanted to bring peace to the country and prevent lawlessness.

Sudden rise of Chak Dynasty

Fath Shah appointed Saif-ud-Din Dar as prime minister. Saif-ud-Din had played an important role in getting the throne of Kashmir for him.

During the 14th century AD, when Suhadeva was the ruler of Kashmir, among some foreign migrants one person named Lankar Shah, also known as Lankar Chak, sought asylum from Suhadeva. The asylum was granted and Lankar Chak with his family settled at Trihgam, a place at Gagangir (modern Tangdar). He was a forerunner of the Chak dynasty destined to rule over Kashmir.

Lankar Shah won the favour of Shah Mir. Slowly, he brought many followers from his native place and settled them in the valley. These Chaks were very robust, strong and sturdy. Shamas Chak earned the goodwill of Malik Saif-u-Dar. During Malik-Saif-u-Dar's premiership, the country saw peace and tranquillity. According to Sukha,[99] "The subjects were happy in every way during his administration. They displayed the virtues of kindness and simplicity." According to Mohibbul Hasan,[100] "Since Fath Shah secured the throne through the efforts of Saifdar, he made him his prime minister. Soon, however, he became dissatisfied with him for keeping all power in his own hands and treating him (the king) only as a figurehead. He therefore secured the support of Nusrat Raina, Sarhan Raina, Musa Raina and Shamas Chak and decided to overthrow Saif-u-Dar."

According to Sukha,[101] "Fath Shah was not addicted to evil habits, regarding woman, dice or wine; and his chief minister was Somarajanaka (Shamas Chak) born of the Lunar dynasty (Lankar dynasty)." As the king was preparing to oust Saif-u-Dar, he got drowned in the Jhelum when the bridge he was crossing collapsed. Shamas Chak became the prime minister. But a misunderstanding crept up between the king and him. The king wanted to oust him. Before he could do so, Sayyid Mohammad Baihaqi managed to influence two important ministers, Ibrahim Magarey and Musa Raina, and with their help, he forced a war against Fath Shah, with the main purpose of placing Mohammad Shah on the throne. Shamas Chak ran away and took refuge elsewhere. Fath Shah also ran away to Nowshera where Shamas Chak joined him.

Sultan Mohammad Shah 1493–1505 AD

After defeating Fath Shah and Shamas Chak in the battle, Mohammad Shah with the help of Ibrahim Magarey became the king of Kashmir. With this, the restoration of Sayyid ascendency became a reality. The king wanted to destroy Shamas Chak and pursued the fugitive to Trihgam where he was residing. Not finding him there, he destroyed the houses belonging to the Chak clan and made Sopore his cantonment where he waited for his enemy. Shamas Chak, being the scheming and brave fellow that he was, took his small army and raided Mohammad Shah at night.

Taken aback, Mohammad Shah fled leaving behind all the baggage which fell into the hands of the enemy. But Musa Raina, who was siding with Mohammad Shah stood like a rock against Shamas Chak's onslaught. He sought the help of Kachi Chak and Idi Raina and inflicted a crushing defeat to him.

Meanwhile, Mohammad Shah's Prime Minister Sayyid Mohamed developed an aversion for Musa Raina, who had become very close to the second son of Mohammad Shah named Shamas-ud-Din. When Sayyid Mohamed advised Musa Raina to go to Skardu, Musa Raina did not like it. Not feeling secure in the company of Sayyid Mohamed, Musa shifted his loyalty and went to Fath Shah. He convinced Ibrahim Magarey and Hajji Padre, both in the cabinet of Mohammad Shah, that Sayyid Mohamed was managing to bring back the Sayyids in the country. So a war was declared against Sayyid Mohamed who was killed and Mohammad Shah ran away.

Mir Shamas-ud-Din Iraqi : During this period, an important event took place. Mir Shamas-ud-Din Iraqi, a Muslim of Shia faith, arrived in the valley. He was the founder of the Nurbakhshiyan order in Kashmir. The pandits had to face the religious conversion of Shia faith spread by Iraqi.

Fath Shah was ruling the country then. The exiled governor of Khurasan came to Kashmir to seek asylum. King Fath Shah gladly gave him asylum and also some confiscated land. This Shia preacher was able to convert one important noble, Hassan Chak, to Shia faith. Hassan Chak was a very influential noble and many Muslims as well as Hindus got converted to the Shia faith. Even King Fath Shah was sympathetic to this new Shia preacher. He helped him with more conversions, but later on, another noble, Ibrahim Magarey, opposed the spread of Shia faith in the kingdom.

Sultan Fath Shah restored 1505-1514AD

Musa Raina and Ibrahim Magarey, two important ministers in the court of Mohammad Shah who were supported by Sayyid Mohammad Baihaqi, were in fact hated by the people for their leaning towards the uncultured Sayyids who had ill-treated Kashmiris. Realising this, the two ministers resigned and joined the opposition headed by Shamas Chak. That brought an end to the rule of Mohammad Shah and also the death of Prime Minister Baihaqi and his others supporters.

After getting the throne for the second time, the first thing Fath Shah did was to appoint Shamas Chak as his prime minister. Shamas had not forgotten the destruction of his house and murder of his kin at Trihgam by Mohammad Shah and Sayyid Mohammad Baihaqi. He had nursed resentment against the Sayyids and decided to take revenge in the same brutal manner. He first razed the residence of Baihaqi to the ground. Next, he treated his three sons ruthlessly. Writes RK Parmu,[102] "Not feeling satisfied with the death of Sayyid Mohammad Baihaqi, Shames Chak became more drastic. Then his three sons, Saiyid Murtaza, Sayyid Ibrahim and Sayyid Yaqub were treated ruthlessly. Sayyid Murtaza was rolled down a hillock while fleeing for safety to Ladakh." Murtaza died and Ibrahim remained as a prisoner for two and half years with the Raja of Ladakh.

As already discussed, during Fath Shah's first rule, 1486 to 1493 AD, the arrival of a Muslim of Shia faith named Shamas-ud-Din in the valley had revolutionised the entire history of Kashmir. Shams-ud-Din Iraqi was a disciple of Sayyid Shah Qasim Anwar, the son of Sayyid Mohammad Nurbaksh of Khurasan, who had claimed himself as Khalifa. Shams-ud-Din had first come to Kashmir as an ambassador of Hussein Mirza, the governor of Khurasan. He could not take active part in the conversion of people into Shia faith as an ambassador. But Shamas Chak, the prime minister had made a promising inauguration for conversion to Shia faith accepting the faith along with his followers including the entire Chak clan. They were taught the Nurbakhshiyan faith.

Nurbaksh was born in Kohistan in 1392 AD. He became the disciple of Khwaja Ishaq of Kuttilan, who was himself the disciple of Sayyid Ali Hamadan, in whose name there is a Khanqah in Srinagar, However, it may be stated here that the Nurbakhshiyan doctrine was interpreted by Shamas-ud-Din Iraqi for Kashmiri Shia in his translation of the book *Fikh-i-Ahwat* (Comprehensive law). Mirza Haydar has noted in his book that,[103] "The people were (formerly) all Hanifi, but in the reign of Fath Shah, a man of the name of Shams came from 'Talish in Irak', who gave himself out as a Nurbaksh. He introduced a corrupt form of religion, giving it the name of Nurbaksh and practised many heresies. He wrote a book for these cowardly people called *Fikh-i-Ahwat* which does not conform to the teaching of any of the sects, whether Sunni or Shia."

In this connection, we may quote Mohibbul Hasan,[104] "*Tuhfatu'l-Ahbab,* written about the middle of the fifteenth century, is the life of Mir Shamsu'd-Din who introduced the Nurbakshia teaching into Kashmir. The author's name is not known but his father was an important disciple of Shamsu'd-Din and he himself was a fanatical Nurbakshia." Since then, Muslims in Kashmir were divided into two sects—Sunni and Shia—and they were perpetually against each other.

Musa Raina and Ibrahim Magarey, perhaps on account of jealousy and also Shamas Chak's inhuman activities against Baihaqi's children and religious antagonism, had turned against him. They convinced Fath Shah against Shamas Chak and he fell in with their plan. As a result, Shamas Chak was arrested and then imprisoned on the plea that he got Saif-ud-Dar killed. To get rid of him while he was in prison, Musa Raina employed Behram Dar and Dati Malik, perhaps kin of Saif-Dar, to kill him. Tradition confirms that though in chains Shamas Chak fought with his assassins heroically but ultimately succumbed to their arrows.

After the murder of Shamas Chak, the first thing Fath Shah did was to appoint Musa Raina in his place. Raina was a strong administrator. He recalled Shams-ud-Din Iraqi who came to live in Kashmir permanently. On his arrival, Shamas-ud-din proclaimed himself the representative of Sayyid Mohammad Nurbaksh. Raina, who was his admirer and religious mentor, began harassing Hindu infidels. They destroyed beautiful temples, the Hindu architectural wealth of Kashmir. They made random conversion of Hindus to Islam. According to Sukha, "Meera Shamas (Mir Shamas-ud-Din Iraqi) became Musa Chander's (Musa Raina) guru without giving him religious instructions. According to his advice Musa Chandra arrested men belonging to temples and confiscated lands of Brahmins."[105]

As always, jealousy was rife among the ministers of Fath Shah. Ibrahim Magarey, Jahangir Padru, Usman Dar and Kachi Chak started opposing Musa Raina citing his anti-Hindu policy. They finally declared war against him. Musa fled on horseback but he fell down while fleeing and died.

After his death, Fath Shah appointed Ibrahim Magarey as prime minister. But he remained prime minister for a very short period because Magarey chiefs who had helped him became angry with him. As a result, he was overthrown and he fled to Punjab.

The death of Musa Raina did not bring relief for Hindus. Their misfortune restarted when Mohammad Shah became the king again.

The four ministers who had opposed the activities of Musa began fighting with each other. As a result, there was no administration, no governance and people were fed up with the ministers. Some important men who had been forced to migrate to India were watching the conditions prevailing in Kashmir. Seeing that things had worsened, they organised themselves under the leadership of Ibrahim Magarey and other Chaks, to help Mohammad Shah get the Kashmir throne.

"A very sincere, daring, but grossly indiscreet Hindu leader shot himself into prominence as a sort of Shriya Bhatt, the famous minister of Sultan Zain-ul-Abidin. He undid the achievements of Shams-ud-Din Iraqi during the two years when the Muslim leaders were pre-occupied with their problems. He reconverted most of Hindus who had been forced to embrace Islam under pressure of Shams-ud-Din Iraqi during the preceding eight years (1506-1514)," [106] writes RK Parmu.

So, Mohammad Shah with the help of Ibrahim Magarey and Kachi Chak who had fallen out with his associates helped the attack against Fath Shah, who eventually surrendered. Mohammad Shah became the king for the third time.

Sultan Mohammad Shah, 1514–1515 AD

Mohammad Shah became the Sultan of Kashmir for the third time. Expectedly, he appointed Ibrahim Magarey as prime minister, say PNK Bamzai,[107] and Mohibbul Hasan.[108] However, RK Parmu writes that it was Kachi Chak who assumed the reins of the government. Coming to power, Kachi Chak had become an enthusiastic follower of Shamas-ud-Din Iraqi, who had given tremendous boost to Shia faith in Kashmir. Brahmins were driven forcefully to accept Shia faith. A Kashmiri Pandit, Nirmal Kantha, accepted Shia faith and became Kantha Bhatt. As per RK Parmu,[109] "And he (Kantha Bhatt) wanted to extirpate Hinduism, once for all. Accordingly, in 1518 AD, some eight hundred Hindu leaders were gruesomely massacred; and fear of death compelled their followers to walk into Muslim fold like dumb driven cattle." In support of this, RK Parmu has quoted *Baharistan-i-Shahi*'s description of this massacre: "The great task that Kachi Chak performed at the bidding of Mir Shamas-ud-Din Mohammad Iraqi was the massacre of the idolatry."

Meanwhile, Fath Shah, with the support of Chaks, who were his maternal relatives, raised a rebellion against Mohammad Shah, who without any resistance left for India. Fath Shah became king again.

Sultan Fath Shah, 1515–1517AD

Fath Shah became the king for the third time. This time, the monarch was only a figurehead. Continued ministerial jealousies played an important role in the dethroning of the monarch and instigated intrigues and counter-intrigues that destroyed the peaceful fabric of life. Fath Shah had very uneasy times with the nobles as he could not satisfy them. They raised a revolt against him. As a result, he fled to Punjab where he died in 1517 AD.

On hearing the news of his death, Mohammad Shah, who was also in exile, decided to come back to Kashmir. He proceeded towards the valley along with his personal 2000 combatants and aid from Sikandar Lodhi to capture the throne of Kashmir for the fourth time.

Sultan Mohmmad Shah, 1517–1528 AD

Mohammad Shah declared himself king of Kashmir for the fourth time in 1517 AD. He came to know that Kachi Chak was instrumental in throwing out Fath Shah and appreciated his role. Kachi Chak, therefore,was made the prime minister. Shah left Kashmir for Nowshera to bid farewell to the forces provided by Sikandar Lodhi, says Mohibbul Hasan[110]. He wanted to come back to Kashmir as early as possible but the winter season set in and there was heavy snowfall. The inclement weather made his return through the blocked roads impossible. He, therefore, had to stay outside Kashmir till springtime.

During his absence, the country was thrown into almost civil war-like conditions. The reason being that none of the nobles was honest, sincere or straightforward in his actions or activities. They were all self-serving opportunists and intriguers and had no human values. They had no consideration for the people who were suffering on account of frequent changes of monarchy.

By this time Mohammad Shah anticipated treachery from Shankar

Raina. On his arrival he got him imprisoned where he died. Rumours flew around that he was killed and his death in prison was unnatural.

Though Mohammad Shah occupied the Kashmir throne, some nobles such as Abdul Magarey, Lohar Magarey, Idi Raina and Jahangir Padru were engaged in a serious conspiracy to dethrone him and place Sikandar Khan, son of Fath Shah as king. When the news of Fath Shah's death in August 1517 came, the conspirators decided to act. They helped Sikandar Khan in getting the dead body of Fath Shah from Punjab to Srinagar and buried him near the grave of his father Adam Khan at Shayer, says Sukha,[111].

Fath Shah's death kindled the desire of Sikandar Khan's followers to declare him not as an aspirant to the throne of Kashmir but as the Sultan of Kashmir or rightful heir. They succeeded in occupying the fort of Nagam. But they had underestimated the strength of the king. Mohammad Shah sent his troops headed by Kachi Chak to subdue the revolt and they gave a crushing defeat.

Some nobles like Nusrat Raina resented the elevation of Kachi Chak to the prime minister's post and also the arrest of Shankar Raina. They sought the help of Lohar Magarey and started a revolt against the king. Kachi Chak, with the help of Jahangir Magarey, fought Nusrat Raina, who at once realised his weakness in fighting against the king. He therefore fled. In the war, Kachi Chak stood victorious.

Sikandar Khan, after being defeated by Kachi Chak, also fled from the valley. However, he did not sit quiet. He approached a Mughal ruler for military help. It was in 1525 AD that Sikandar came with a Mughal contingent to secure the throne. Tazi Chak was away from the capital. When he heard about the invasion by a Mughal army, his Kashmiri patriotism was stirred. All the Kashmiri nobles and Chak leaders such as Kachi, Tazi and Ghazi fought the Mughals, and forced them to retreat. Sikandar Khan was arrested and brought before Mohammad Shah who ordered his eyes be gouged out. He was imprisoned and later died. Thus, Mohammad Shah subdued his two opponents.

Jesus said, "No one serves two masters. Either he will hate one and love the other, or he will be devoted to one and despise the other." Strangely, Kashmiri nobles proved this absolutely wrong changing their loyalties so often. It was a strange paradox that these respected, elite nobles of Kashmir did not have consistency in their loyalty towards any one of the Sultans. The one thing that went to their credit was that whenever there was any outside attack, they forgot their mutual jealousies and collectively repelled the attackers.

Sultan Ibrahim Shah, 1528–1529 AD

By this time, Kachi Chak had become very powerful. For some time, a sense of selfishness engulfed him. Instead of helping Sultan Mohammad Shah or Sikandar Khan, he thought it best to capture the throne and install his own son Ibrahim Khan as the king of Kashmir.

In a bold move, he dethroned Mohammad Shah, arrested him in Lohkot, and declared Ibrahim Khan as the king with the title Ibrahim Shah I.[112] Of course, Ibrahim was a king only in name. Kachi Chak was ruling over the country.

Sultan Nazuk Shah, 1529-1530 AD

Important nobles such as Malik Ali Chadora, Ragi Chak and Abdul Magarey who were in exile conspired to defeat Kachi Chak who had imprisoned King Mohammad Shah and enthroned his son Ibrahim Khan as the king. Abdul Magarey approached Babur in Delhi and asked for military assistance to defeat Kachi Chak and his son.

Babur received these Kashmiri nobles courteously and provided them with well-trained cavalry under the leadership of his commanders Sheikh Ali Beg, Mahmud Khan and Mohammad Khan. The nobles made Nazuk Shah the king in 1529 AD. He was there only for a year as the majority of the nobles felt that he was unable to rule effectively. So they decided to bring back Mohammad Shah from prison to make him king for the fifth time in 1530 AD. Nazuk Shah was declared the heir apparent.[113]

During Nazuk Shah's period, a Suhrawardi saint Sayyid Ahmad Kirmani came to Kashmir. Sultan Nazuk Shah built a Khanqah in Srinagar, in his honour.

Sultan Mohammad Shah, 1530-1537 AD

With the defeat of Kachi Chak and Ibrahim Shah, Mohammad Shah, who was brought from the prison, became the king and provided an honourable place for Nazuk Shah as heir apparent. His rule continued from 1530 to 1537 AD. The Mughal army left for Punjab, but very reluctantly. Abdul Magarey was appointed as prime Minister of Kashmir. Though Kachi Chak had been very loyal to Mohammad Shah, it was he who had imprisoned

Shah, so it was natural that the king had no love for him.

Mirza Hayder Dughlat attacks Kashmir

Mirza Haydar was only in his teens when he left Babur. He held a prominent position in the Mongol empire and participated in Sultan Abu Said Khan's wars against Kurghiz, Uzbek and other tribes. He went to distant places and fought battles there. His success in fighting wars made him a hero. In 1931 AD, Haydar, along with Prince Sikandar Mirza, second son of Abu Said, and their forces fought valiantly in Ladakh. In Nubra, the chief fortified himself in the castle of Mutadar but the Mughal forces laid a siege and captured the fort. After Nubra, they proceeded to Maryul which was headed by Lata Jughdan and Tashi-kun and they gave up easily.

Winter had set in and it was difficult to remain in Ladakh. After his success in Ladakh and Tibet, Mirza Haydar decided to invade Kashmir with his huge army. At that point of time, he was informed that Abu Said Khan had fallen ill at Maryul. It was therefore decided that about one thousand soldiers would remain with Abu Said Khan and advance towards Balti, the rest 4000 men would accompany Mirza Haydar to Kashmir. With some difficulty, Mirza crossed Zojila Pass and first sent 400 of his best men under Tuman Bahadur Qabuchi to enter Srinagar. The next day, the whole army raided Srinagar. According to PNK Bamzai,[114] "In the course of a few days Dughlat's troops entered Srinagar, devastating with fire and sword the important towns on the way and frightening the inhabitants of Srinagar out of their homes."

However, the Kashmir army fought against the enemy and gave them a befitting reply. There are different versions of the fight which took place. When Mirza Haydar returned from Kashmir and reached Said Khan he had just recovered. Haydar gave his account of 'the victory' in Kashmir to him. Khan said, "For this mighty achievement, not only I (Said Khan), but all the Mughal Khakans owe you a debt of gratitude."[115] But according to PNK Bamzai,[116] "Regular guerrilla warfare ensued. Dughlat's forces hemmed in a small valley were drawn out of their dugouts into the open where they were given crushing defeat." The other version given by Prem Nath Bazaz in *Struggle for Freedom in Kashmir* is:[117] "The Mughals inflicted a crushing defeat on the Kashmiris. The vanquished forces were pursued captured and slain mercilessly." According to some chroniclers, it was a 'no win' situation for both sides and ultimately it was concluded that negotiations could end the stalemate. Thus writes Mohibbul Hasan,[118] "As a result of negotiations it was agreed that Khutba was to be read in the name of Said Khan, that Muhammad Shah's brother's daughter was to be given in marriage to Prince Sikandar Sultan, that presents were to be given for Said Khan."

Seeing the invaders directing their evil, inhuman, brutal force against the people, two rivals Kachi Chak and Abdul Magarey joined hands and fought the enemy forcing them to withdraw, as per Sukha.[119] This time also Kashmir gave a friendly send off to the Mughal army, says Sukha[120]. The Kashmir forces fought gallantly under the leadership of Kachi Chak and Abdul Magarey and routed the invader. The country faced great devastation on account of this battle. Mohammad Shah tried to save the situation by opening his treasury for the benefit of the people.

In 1533 AD, Abu Said Khan died and Mirza Haydar went back to Punjab. Kashmir enjoyed a brief spell of peace after which Mohammad Shah died in 1537 AD. The nobles divided Kashmir into five districts; each district was ruled by a noble.

Sultan Shams-ud-Din, 1537–1540 AD

Mohammad Shah's second son Shams Din succeeded him. Mohammad Shah was infected with an incurable disease before he died. His death shocked the people as also the nobles in the valley. According to Sukha, "When the king had ascended to heaven, the people lamented for him and said in their grief 'Whose protection should we now seek when thou hast gone to heaven'."[121] Like a rudderless boat, the people felt unsure of their lives. With the succession of Shams-ud-Din to the throne, the peace of the country got disturbed again due to the treachery and jealousy of the nobles.

Immediately after the king's death, a civil war broke out between Kachi Chak and Ragi Chak. Ragi Chak was forced out of Srinagar and his frightened followers hid themselves. According to Mohibbul Hasan,[122] "He (Kachi Chak) encamped at the village of Gaisu, and then proceeded to besiege the fort of Sopore, where Abdal Magarey, Lohar Magarey and the chiefs of Chadora had shut themselves in, as they did not think they were strong enough to fight Kaji (Kachi) in a pitched battle without the help of Ragi. When the siege was in progress, Ragi returned from Jammu." Ragi Chak's return did not help and the forces of Abdul Magarey and Ragi Chak were routed. Kachi Chak became the prime minister and was in fact de-facto ruler of Kashmir. After a brief interval, Shams-ud-Din passed away in 1540 AD.

Kachi Chak was a Shia by faith and had an authoritarian temperament. Abdul Magarey was Sunni by faith and was anti-Kachi. Abdul Magarey and Ragi Chak, both Sunnis, fled to Punjab and approached Mirza Haydar who was working in absence of Mirza Kamran. Mirza Haydar, a Sunni himself, received the two nobles of Kashmir warmly.

Sultan Islam Shah, 1540 AD

After Shams-ud-Din's death, his brother Ismail Shah was made the Sultan in 1540 AD. It was the time when Sultans of Kashmir were made rulers only in name. The de-facto rulers were their prime ministers. In the case of Ismail Shah, Kachi Chak was running the government. Ismail Shah was also the son-in-law of Kachi Chak, so his becoming the Sultan of Kashmir was no surprise. A very experienced warrior and an able administrator, Kachi Chak wanted to provide efficient administration to the people. He tried to keep his nobles satisfied by giving them sympathetic treatment. In many cases, he forgave even criminals attempting to assassinate him at the instigation of nobles.

However, peace in the country was illusory. Abdul Magarey and Ragi Chak, staunch enemies of Kachi Chak marched to the valley with the Mughal army under the command of Mirza Haydar. Being an excellent strategist, Mirza avoided a direct route as he knew Kachi Chak would have made all defence preparedness to safeguard the normal routes. Through hilly routes via Poonch, Haydar surprised Kachi Chak by reaching the valley. "Without a drop of blood on the ground and without his sword out of sheath, Mirza Haydar Duglat had succeeded in capturing Kashmir and surprisingly without much help from Humayun or Mirza Kamran."[123]

Abdul Magarey and Ragi Chak, with the help of Mirza Haydar Duglat, achieved a bloodless victory and forced Kachi Chak and Sultan Ismail to flee from the valley and take refuge in the mountains of Punjab.

Sultan Nazuk Shah, 1540 AD

After his ouster from Kashmir, Kachi Chak went to Sher Shah Suri for military help. Sher Shah provided him with five hundred cavalry soldiers. He invaded Kashmir to defeat Abdul Magarey but was defeated.

Nazuk Shah was proclaimed the Sultan of Kashmir in 1540 AD with the approval of Mirza Haydar. Abdul Magarey was made the prime minister. Both were under the tutelage of Mirza Haydar who was acting as governor of Kashmir on behalf of the Mughals. But soon he began interfering in the administration of the country. In the beginning, he was quite sympathetic and friendly with the nobles. In order to earn the confidence of Kashmiri nobles and the people, he consulted Abdul Magarey and Ragi Chak at every step in his bid to uplift the people and cultivate the land. This brought prosperity in the country. There was no danger of any other foreign invasion. Peaceful conditions in the country gave a fillip to trade and art and craft.

Kachi Chak along with his other followers was of Shia faith. Abdul Magarey, Ragi Chak and Mirza Haydar were devout Sunnis. Mirza Haydar wanted to be in the good books of Shias. But this was not to the liking of Abdul Magarey, Ragi Chak and other Sunnis who could not understand the strategic importance of Mirza's overtures to the Shias. Haydar visited Zadibal, the tomb of Mir Shams-ud-Din Iraqi to pay his respects.[124] This caused restlessness among Sunni nobles.

In 1543 AD, Ragi Chak began preparation for a revolt against Mirza, who got the information beforehand. Mirza attacked him and forced him to flee to Rajouri where he met Kachi Chak. Not finding Ragi Chak at Kamraz , Mirza got his house torched to the ground.

The next year, in 1544 AD, Kachi Chak and Ragi Chak, the two nobles of Kashmir but holding opposite religious beliefs, joined hands to oust the Mughal army and the Mughal governor. But Mirza, backed by both the Mughals and Kashmir army advanced against the Chaks and made an unexpected night attack. The Chaks were defeated and were forced to flee to Punjab. In September 1544 AD, Kachi Chak died outside the country at Thanna.

Mirza's orthodoxy, stemming from his Sunni faith, horrified every one because Kashmir had a composite culture, developed over centuries, wherein Hindus believed in the mystified metaphysical atheism, Sunnis in Wahabi faith, and orthodox Shias in Nurbakshia order. Also side by side, Sufism flourished harmoniously. Mirza Haydar's idea of one religion in the country was the result of his fallacious reasoning. The fanatic Sunni embarked on introducing one Sunni faith in the state. "He resorted to ruthlessness, brutality, torture and suppression (particularly of Shia followers). Many Shias were killed. Even in 1549-1550 AD, Daniyal, the son of Mir Shams-ud-Din Iraqi, was not spared and was executed."[125]

Such violent killing of people was against Kashmiri ethos, tradition and psyche. With the passage of time, Mirza became a religious bigot, so much so that he desecrated the tomb of Shams-ud-Din Iraqi at Zadibal (Rainawari).[126] "I hope and trust that through the intervention of God and by my own efforts, the land will gradually be entirely delivered of this (Shia Faith) misfortune."

The Chaks who were Shia by faith suffered more than anyone else. The two top leaders of Shia faith, Ghazi Chak and Kachi Chak, died, and Daulat Khan Chak fled the country to seek help of Shia followers from other parts of India.

Around this time, Islam Shah Suri, son of Sher Shah Suri, had developed suspicions about the sincerity of his father's nobles particularly of the governor of Punjab, Haibat Khan Niyazi. Haibat Khan and the Ghakhas chief were essentially friends of Emperor Humayun. The suspicion resulted in hostility between Islam Shah Suri and Haibat Khan. Haibat revolted and Islam Shah declared war on him and his allies and crushed them. He even chased him up to Bhimber in the Kashmir hills. Haibat fled from Punjab into the Sarong hills. Meanwhile, the Chak leaders wanted to take advantage of the differences between Islam Shah and Haibat Khan and they approached Haibat to seek his help to dislodge Mirza from Kashmir.

Mirza had kept a watch over the activities of the Kashmiri fugitive nobles. Mohibbul Hasan says,[127] Haibat Khan knew that Mirza Haydar was Humayun's man, therefore he rejected the proposal of Ghazi Chak and Daulat Chak. On the contrary, Haibat Khan sent a message to Mirza informing him about this conspiracy. In return, a pleased Mirza paid Haibat Khan a large amount of money.

Undeterred and driven by the zeal to oust Mirza, Ghazi Chak and Daulat Chak then approached Islam Shah Suri but Mirza had bribed him too with costly gifts such as Pashmina shawls and a reasonable quantity of saffron—rare items produced in Kashmir.

There is another version of this story. "Ghazi Chak", according to R K Parmu, "being the more unscrupulous and dauntless of the two, defected and joined Mirza Haydar." Thus, he left Daulat Khan alone. But, says Elliot Dawson,[128] "When Ghazi Chak joined Mirza Haydar, he informed him that Haibat Khan was moving towards the valley and had already encamped at Banihal with a huge Afghan army. In order to stop his forward movement to occupy the valley, he sent Kashmiri army under the command of Idi Raina and Yusuf Chak for the job. It is stated that Kashmir forces had complete victory against Haibat Khan who was killed in the fight."

R K Parmu however does not agree with both the above versions. He says,[129] "The correct position appears to be this: Islam Shah Suri, Haibat Khan Niyazi and Mirza Haydar had concluded a tripartite peace treaty."

Idi Raina, a Kashmiri noble, harboured resentment against Mirza Haydar for his intolerance of other faiths and particularly the killing of Daniyal, one of the most respected persons not only by the Shias but also all people. The Kashmiri nobles were also deprived of their jageers, and these were awarded to Mughals. From Poonch, Idi Raina sent a message to Daulat Chak who was loitering in Nowshera alone. He immediately joined him in a march to the valley. Most of villagers who were fed up with the oppressive rule of Mirza Haydar also joined Raina and Daulat. Mirza got worried and collected the Mughal military stationed in the valley, and with some Kashmiri soldiers went to take on Raina and Daulat. He marched towards Srinagar. Idi Raina and Daulat Chak along with their army were stationed at Khanpur.

Mirza Haydar was dismayed to learn that a successful revolt had broken out in Ladakh and Baltistan against Mullah Qasim, administrator of Ladakh and Mullah Baqi, administrator of Baltistan. In this revolt, Mullah Qasim was killed and his army fled. Mullah Baqi succeeded in escaping and proceeded towards Kashmir to meet Mirza Haydar near Anderkot. But the signs for Mirza Haydar were not good. The rebels defeated a rising in Pakhli. Another distressing news received was of the defeat of his cousin Qarae Bhadur, who undertook an expedition to Mankot on 12 October 1550 AD. Mirza had deputed Qarae Bahadur with an army comprising Mughal soldiers and untrained Kashmiri artisans. When they reached beyond the Baramulla mountain range, the Kashmiri troops defected to the enemy camp. Those who had revolted at Mankot were all Kashmiris, and so Qarae's army was outnumbered. In the ensuing battle fought on 25 October 1550 AD, the Mughals were defeated and Qarae was imprisoned.

The news of an all-round revolt made Mirza Haydar desperate. Against the advice of his military strategist, he undertook the invasion of the fort of Mankot with his 300 soldiers at night. As he went forward to fight, he was left with only a dozen soldiers at the end of the day. Like a foolhardy man, he tried to enter the fort when a poisonous arrow struck him. He died on the spot.

Kashmiris hated Mirza Haydar for his atrocities inflicted upon them when he invaded Kashmir with Kashgar forces in 1530–1533 AD. His forces indiscriminately massacred the people. It was a memory fresh in the minds of the people.

The life of Mirza Haydar Duglat

When one reads Mirza Haydar's life as a whole, one is likely to believe that miracles do take place. Mirza was born in 1499/1500 AD in Tashkent where his father was a governor. He was the second son of Mohammed Hussein Gurgan, who had earned the reputation of being cunning and deceitful. Because of his dreadful actions, he was murdered by the agents of Shaibani Khan, the chief of Uzbek clan in 1508. After the death of his father, young Mirza Haydar was moved to Bukhara where he remained with one of his relatives. In 1509 AD, he was shifted from Bukhara to Kabul where he lived with Babur.

He had the blood of Mongols from his father who belonged to the Chagatai clan of the Mongols, and from his mother's side he was closely related to Babur. He was a born fighter. In his two years' stay with Babur, Mirza accompanied him on his campaigns against several chiefs of neighbouring Uzbek. According to Henry Miers Elliot,[130] "The writer of this valuable work was the son of Muhammad Husain Mirza who was the eldest son of (Muhammad) Haydar, Amir of Kashgar. Muhammad Husain married the younger sister of Emperor Babar's mother. So our author, Haydar Mirza, was first cousin of Babar, and he seems to have inherited from his mother no small share of that ability and vigour which distinguished his more eminent relative."

It is not known if Mirza as a child had any regular schooling. Nevertheless, he turned out to be a chronicler and author of *Tarikh-i-Rashidi*. The chronicle was translated in English by Denison Ross and Sir Henry Haworth, the introduction to it given by N Elias.

Mirza Haydar's childhood in Kabul was spent with Zahiruddin

Muhammad Babur who was the son of Umar Sheikh Mirza, descendants of Timor, and his mother was a descendant of Changez Khan. He had the energy of the ferocious Mongols and also the courage of the Turks. This ambitious young man wanted to make conquests. He had accompanied Babur in his successful conquest of Samarqand and also took part in subduing the rebellion in Fergana, thus gaining the necessary expertise in military strategy.

After leaving Babur, Haydar undertook the service of Sultan Said Khan of Kashgar in 1514 AD. His know-how of military expeditions helped him when under the Sultan he invaded Baltistan and Ladakh and succeeded in conquering these places. This time, he had acquired an adventurous spirit. He then undertook the conquest of Kashmir.

Sultan Said Khan died in 1533 AD and his son Abdul Rashid Khan became the Sultan. According to Mohibbul Hasan,[131] "Meanwhile Sultan Said had died and had been succeeded by his son Rashid Sultan, who had begun his reign by putting to death all those whom he suspected of plotting in favour of his brother Sikandar." Therefore, Mirza Haydar had to flee to Lahore, where Mirza Kamran was the governor of Punjab. The governor had heard about Mirza's valour and received him very warmly. Luck favoured Mirza as Mirza Kamran had to go away from Punjab and he gave charge to Mirza Haydar. For one year, Mirza Haydar worked with zeal and earned the applause of Kamran who appointed him the tax collector. The amount he collected as taxes helped spread Islam faith and subdued small revolts.

Unlike his father, who had earned notoriety, Mirza Haydar developed the reputation of being trustworthy and gentleman-like. In 1537 AD, Kamran elevated him to the position of administrator of Punjab while he devoted his time to quell the revolt by his brother Hindal of Kandahar.

Mirza was always disturbed whenever he thought about the circumstances in which he had to leave Kashmir in 1532 AD. What took his mind back to Kashmir was the scenic beauty, the sweet drinking water, abundant fruits and fairy-like women. He craved to go back to Kashmir and was waiting for the right opportunity.

Meanwhile, in Kashmir, Kachi Chak had created a very difficult situation for other nobles. He, being of Shia faith, had created havoc for the Sunni nobles. So Abdul Magarey and Ragi Chak, who were of Sunni faith, were left with no alternative but to seek help from other quarters to oust him. Mirza Haydar was the best choice since he was also a Sunni. Both approached and requested him for help. In the meantime, Mirza Kamran who was away in Kandahar returned back in 1538 AD. The time was right and Mirza Haydar persuaded Mirza Kamran to undertake the invasion of Kashmir.

A strange development took place around the same time. Sher Shah Suri had strengthened his position in Bihar. In 1537 AD, he conquered Bengal. Taking notice of Sher Shah Suri's plans, Humayun, son of Babur, came with a huge army and encamped in Bijapur a place near Kannuaj. Sher Shah had already encamped on the other side of the Ganga opposite Kannuaj. Humayun asked Mirza Kamran for help. Kamran marched from his territories in the Punjab. Mirza Haydar advanced to Agra with 20,000 men to help Humayun. On 17 May 1540, the battle of Kanauji was fought at Chausa where Humayun was defeated. Mirza Haydar Duglat writes, [132] "Sher Khan gained a victory, and the Chagatai (Mughal) were defeated in this battle-field where not a man, either friend or foe, was wounded. Not even a gun was fired and chariots (Gardun) were useless."

In view of the above circumstances, Mirza Haydar could not proceed to Kashmir. Mirza Kamran, before starting for Agra, had instructed Baba Chuchak, one of his efficient generals, to wage a war against Kachi Chak and hand over the rule of Kashmir to Abdul Magarey. However, with the developments in India, Kamran decided not to proceed to Kashmir. Abdul Magarey and Ragi Chak had no use of Baba Chuchak as he was reluctant to accompany these two Kashmiri nobles. They had to wait till Mirza Haydar came back from Agra.

The yearning to go back to Kashmir was very strong in Mirza Haydar's mind. It was, in fact, this very desire, which prompted him to beseech Humayun to allow him to help Ragi Chak and Abdul Magarey, the two Kashmiri nobles, in defeating Kachi Chak. Mirza took only 400 soldiers with him and went to Kashmir. He had no difficulty in conquering Kashmir in 1540 AD. In fact, when Kachi Chak came to know about Mirza he went along with his troops to Rajouri to stop him, but Mirza had taken a different route via Poonch Pass. Kachi Chak was now sure that he would not succeed. He therefore abandoned his plans to fight Mirza and fled for his life. Mirza Haydar achieved a bloodless victory over Kashmir.

This time he made sure not to hurt the pride of the natives of Kashmir by becoming the king himself. He made Nazuk Shah the king. In order to earn the goodwill of Kashmiri nobles, he and Ragi Chak, both staunch Sunnis, extended their hand of friendship to the Shias and the Nurbakshia, by going to pay homage to their deceased spiritual leaders at Zadibal.

When he saw that everything in the country was under control, Mirza undertook military expeditions against the rulers of the territories that were part of Kashmir. In order to conquer Kishtwar, he invaded it but failed to subdue it. He diverted his efforts towards the development of agriculture. That gave enough food to the people and they were very happy with him.

Unfortunately, his religious bigotry overwhelmed his mind and he let loose all his evil against non-Sunnis inflicting them with death, destruction and devastation. To quote R K Parmu,[133] "He was intolerant of those who did not conform to the Sunni creed. He was excited to find Kashmir a land of orthodox and heterodoxy—Sunnis, Shias, Nurbakshia, Sufis, Shamasis and idolaters." He treated them ruthlessly. In 1548 AD, he desecrated the tomb of Mir Shams-ud-Din Iraqi at Zadibal. In 1549-50, he put to death his son Sheikh Daniyal and other leading Shias. In his own words, "no one dare openly profess this faith; all denied it because, they are aware of my severity towards them and know that if any one of the sect appears he will not escape the punishment of death."

His death is also a sign of his daredevilry and foolhardiness. The bulk of the Kashmiri population was hostile towards him. He displeased the Kashmiri military personnel by ignoring their sacrifice in the wars waged against neighbouring states. These actions created problems for him at the time of his expedition to Mankot on 12 Oct 1550 AD. His Kashmiri soldiers deserted him and joined Mankot defenders. Mirza was killed with a poisonous arrow.

Sultan Nazuk Shah, 1540 AD

Nazuk Shah continued to be the king of Kashmir. Idi Raina was the prime minister. All Mughal personnel were imprisoned. Truce between the Chak community and the Magareys had taken place mainly on account of the death of Kachi Chak who was hated by the Magareys and Idi Raina. But it was a fragile truce as the Magareys were hardcore Sunnis and Chaks, by and large, were Shias and were considered outsiders. Magareys were original natives of Kashmir.

With the death of Magarey, the Mughal paramountcy also got a serious setback. The Shah Mir clan lost its hold over the Kashmir throne and a new clan of Chaks came to power. Daulat Chak, Behram Chak, Ghazi Chak, Yusuf Chak and Bharam Chak were given jageers.

As expected, Idi Raina did not feel comfortable in the company of the Chaks. So he decided to use his powers as prime minister to clip the wings of Chaks by ordering the release of Mughal soldiers from prison. With them was released Mirza Qarae Bahadur, the leader of the Mughal forces. He then provided them with all the necessities to enable them to prepare for combat.

Daulat Chak, one of the most important nobles took the prime minister's action as hostile. As a result, civil war broke out between Idi Raina and Daulat Chak in Srinagar. Idi Raina sought the help of Mirza Qarae Bahadur.[134] But to avoid the use of foreign soldiers, they made peace between themselves. Meanwhile, in view of the prevailing situation in Kashmir, Mirza Haibat Khan, who was with the Ghakhas, decided to wage a war on Kashmir. But suddenly the nobles of Kashmir entered into a peace pact. This pact between Idi Raina, Daulat Chak and Husain Magarey helped in the defeat of Haibat Khan. According to Mohibbul Hassan,[135] "Afghans fought valiantly. Bibi Rabia, the wife of Mirza Haibat Khan, in particular, displayed great courage. But in the end, owing to their inferiority in number, the Afghans were routed. Haibat Khan, Bibi Rabia, Shahbaz Khan and many others were slain. The heads were sent by the Kashmiri nobles to Islam Shah." It must have gladdened Ismail Shah to see the heads of his enemies.

Though the Kashmiri nobles, irrespective of their faith, collectively defeated Mirza Haibat Khan, there still continued religious hostility between them. This hostility led to a civil war between the factions of Idi Raina, Magareys and Yusuf Chak against Daulat Chak. Daulat Chak and Idi Raina fought each other resulting in the defeat of Idi Raina despite help from Mughals. He fled to Punjab. He again tried to dislodge Daulat Chak but lost again only to be killed in the process. Says Mohibbul Hassan,[136], "Daulat forestalled their move himself by crossing the Jhelum in Srinagar and attacking them. Idi Raina was defeated and put to flight. But at Rawalpur, while in a hurried flight on horseback, his neck got entangled in a vine creeper and he was killed on the spot."

Daulat Chak was not averse to other religions as Mirza Haydar was. He allowed people to follow their own religion. He himself constructed three mausoleums.

The beginning of the rule of the Chak dynasty started with Daulat Chak. He became a very popular noble amongst Kashmiris. He rose to the position of prime minister and ultimately overthrew Nazuk Shah and installed Ibrahim Shah as the ruler, says PNK Bamzai[137]. Nazuk Shah, later on fled to Punjab.

Sultan Ibrahim Shah II, 1552–1555 AD

During Nazuk Shah's rule, Ibrahim Shah was sent to Ladakh to invade the ruler who had refused to send tributes to Kashmir. He defeated him and compelled him to pay the tributes. That is how Ibrahim Shah achieved prominence. Though he was made the king of Kashmir, he was like Nazuk Shah, only a titular head. It was, in fact, Daulat Chak who was the de-facto ruler armed with complete powers. As usual, jealousy among the nobles and the political conditions in the state made it unstable. Daulat Chak became arrogant. He married the widowed mother of Ghazi Chak.[138]

Infuriated that Daulat had married his mother, Ghazi Chak decided to overthrow him. He, along with his relatives, attacked Daulat while he was fishing in the Dal Lake. Daulat tried his best to save himself and ran to the hills surrounding the lake. However, a shepherd caught him and handed him over to Ghazi who imprisoned and blinded him. Thus, Ghazi took over as the prime minister of Kashmir.

Sultan Ismail Shah, 1555–1557 AD

After the defeat of Daulat, Ghazi Chak deposed Ibrahim Shah and installed Ismail Shah, brother of Ibrahim Shah, as the king of Kashmir and himself as administrator. Unfortunately, the Kashmiri nobles started intrigues against him. According to Mohibbul Hassan,[139] "In the spring of 1556, some chiefs headed by Nusrat Chak and Yusuf Chak, conspired to put Ghazi and his brother Husain Chak to death." The nobles were arrested. Meanwhile the Sultan died. Ismail Shah remained on the throne only for two years and died in 1557 AD.

Sultan Habib Shah, 1557–1561 AD

After the death of Ismail Shah, his brother Habib Shah was made the king of Kashmir and Ghazi Chak again became the administrator. During those years, there was no development as such in Kashmir. The nobles were engaged in their intrigues and mutual skirmishes. The king was there only in name. Ghazi Chak gradually became extremely arrogant. Some of his relatives then approached the Mughals to help them oust him.

Some of the Chak nobles too, such as Nusrat Chak and Yusuf Chak, conspired to overthrow Ghazi and his brother Hassan and put them to death. Ghazi came to know of this plot and called them. Believing their plan to be a secret, these two conspirators went to see the king. Ghazi imprisoned them at once. The news spread like wildfire and added to the seething anger in nobles such as Mohamed Magarey and Shamas Raina who felt that Ghazi did nothing to mitigate the feelings of hurt caused by the harsh rule of Mirza Haydar. Shamas Raina escaped to India to approach Emperor Humayun for help to invade Kashmir. When he reached there, Emperor Humayun had died. However, when Raina reached Lahore, he met Shah Abdul Mali who had escaped from the Mughal prison. He was close to Humayun but when Humayun died Akbar got Mali arrested. Both Abdul Mali and Shamas Raina collected nearly four to five thousand men and left to invade Kashmir. Ghazi Chak inflicted a crushing defeat on them at Hanjiwara in 1558 AD. "Many Yavanas (Mughal soldiers) perished in the battle and Yama (God of death) was pleased to receive the souls of men in the semblance of the stream of blood. The heads of the dead men were brought into the town from the field of battle, and the king hung them up in the buildings of the city," says Sukha[140].

After the death of Humayun, Akbar became the emperor of India in 1536. Akbar had thought his empire incomplete without Kashmir. Therefore, he dispatched Qarae Bhadur who had approached him for military help, with 7000 soldiers to invade Kashmir. Kashmiris, under the leadership of Ghazi Chak, remained united to fight Akbar's forces. The Mughal army was routed and Qarae Bhadur had to retreat. As a result of this defeat, the Mughal kings did not venture to invade Kashmir again for more than twenty-six years.

By faith, Ghazi Chak was a Shia but had belief in religious tolerance.

In fact, in 1561 AD, he ascended the throne of Kashmir in a dramatic way. According to R K Parmu,[141] "Inflated with pride and self-aggrandisement, he deposed Habib Shah, although he was also his nephew, because he did not find him even worthy of the name of a king. Immediately he proclaimed himself Sultan of Kashmir with the title of Nasir-ud-Din Mohammad Ghazi Shah, and founded the dynasty of the Chaks in succession to that of the Shahmiris (Shah Mir's)."

King Habib Shah was in the royal court where all the nobles had collected for government deliberations. Suddenly, Ali Chak, brother of Ghazi Chak, came near the king, took away his crown and placed it on the head of Ghazi Chak.

Fifteen
Rise and fall of Chak Dynasty

Sultan Ghazi Chak: 1561-1562 AD

There appears to be some differences among chroniclers about the dates of Ghazi Chak the king of Kashmir. As per RK Parmu, he ruled Kashmir from 1555 to 1562 AD.[1] But according to Mohibbul Hassan, Ghazi Chak ascended the throne in 1561 AD, which seems to be correct as per the chronological order.

The existing nobles did not object to the dramatic change of a ruler in Kashmir. On the contrary, they hailed Ghazi Chak as the monarch of the land. It is true that the last descendants of Shah Mir were useless. In the words of Sufi, "There appears to be no cause of lamentation over the displacement of the Shah Miri dynasty in Kashmir." Its rulers had become quite spineless. They displayed weakness of character and were not capable of leadership. As a matter of fact, they should have long been displaced to make room for kings of vigour and vitality.

Ghazi Chak was the son of Kajji Chak. At the age of eighteen, he worked as a soldier with his father. He became the first Sultan of Kashmir of the Chak clan. He ruled under the title of Nassir-ud-Din

Mohammad Ghazi Shah. "But with reference to the tyrannical oppression of his subjects (Riayyat) and the traditions he established about shedding blood, gouging out eyes, severing limbs and of killing blood-relations, no one knows whether a man so cruel has existed in any another epoch or not," says R K Parmu.[2]

Ghazi Chak as a king was very intelligent. He had a high sense of justice and awarded it with a strong hand. When the servant of his son plucked fruits from an orchard, his hands were cut off.[3] His son, who resented the punishment, was also put on trial for his arrogance. Yet, Ghazi Chak had many positive traits. He was a poet who respected the learned. He was very brave and just after taking over as the king of Kashmir, he re-conquered territories such as Skardu, Pakhli, Kishtwar and Gilgit.

But when it came to his religion, he was protective and vindictive. He wanted to avenge the atrocities inflicted upon Shias during the rule of Nazuk Shah. Some Sunnis under the leadership of Mullah Abdul, Ali Kokah and Doni Kokah had gone to the court of Akbar and requested him to intervene and to mitigate their woes. Akbar was, in fact, waiting for such an opportunity. But being a shrewd diplomat, he was very angry at the undiplomatic conduct of the envoys. He got all the three arrested and two Sunnis Mirza Muqim and Yaqub Mir executed.

By this time, Sultan Ghazi Chak's health began deteriorating rapidly. He was afflicted with a severe type of leprosy. The disease was of a very virulent type, says Sukha,[4] "Itching was caused by worms in his body, and pus and blood came out of it; and sights that are seen in hell appeared during his lifetime. Worms drank off his pus and blood and ate off his flesh, and he suffered pain during his lifetime greater than that of hell. Who was not grieved to hear him cry out 'O father? O friend! O son! My sufferings have come.'

Yet, in this state of health he went to subdue a revolt raised by the chief of Ladakh as his son Ahmed Khan had failed to do so. But the severity of his illness gave him great pain and compelled him to abandon the campaign. According to RK Parmu,[5] "He returned to Srinagar. But the arduous march and excessive cold had worsened the leprous state of his body so much that he lost his fingers as well as his sight which compelled him to abdicate in 1562 AD, in favour of his brother, Husain Khan Chak, whom he found master of the situation."

Sultan Husain Shah Chak, 1562-1570 AD

Husain Shah Chak was a very pious person. He was not a religious fanatic. He wanted to introduce liberalism in the state and founded an institution where all types of learned men could assemble. He loved the company of learned men. He wanted to introduce liberalism in state affairs too. It seems that he was fed up with the religious fanaticism of the rulers, whose actions and reactions had destroyed the peace and tranquillity of the country. Because of the religious feuds between Sunnis and Shias, many people had been killed and many rendered homeless.

King Husain Shah Chak was a liberal Shia and did not abstain from even drinking alcohol. According to Sukha,[6] "After having taken possession of the kingdom, the king relieved the subjects from misgovernment, just as the cloud in summer quenches the fire of the forest. He attained prosperity by always attending to the complaints of the people, and giving gifts to everyone who asked for it. His fame spread afar. The king drank new wine, sported with women, and enjoyed pleasures…"

But the King's rule was not free of rebellions. The first rebellion came from Shankar Chak while he was the governor of Rajouri. A loyal minister Muhammad Naji, and Ali Khan Chak, the king's younger brother went to fight Shankar Chak and defeated him. Shankar Chak, as per P N K Bamzai, was the brother of Husain Shah. Mohibbul Hassan also says Shankar Chak was the younger brother of Husain Shah but R K Parmu says he was Hussain Shah's son. After the revolt was averted, there was another revolt. One of his ministers Khwaja Baqqal and his son Khan-i-Zaman revolted with the help of Fath Chak and Shams Duni but other faithful ministers crushed the rebellion and killed Fath Chak and Shams Duni. Khan-i-Zaman was arrested and publicly hanged at Zaina Kadal Bridge.

In Delhi, King Akbar was keeping a regular watch over Kashmir. In spite of Qarae Bahadur's defeat at the hands of the Kashmiri people, Akbar's interest in the valley had not diminished. He had many reasons to annex the valley to his kingdom. The first reason was to make the 'Paradise on Earth' a part of his kingdom. Another reason was to avenge Qarae's defeat and punish Shias. He believed that Chak Sultans had misruled the country.

Husain Shah tried his best to make friends with the Mughals. But Akbar was not happy with the Chaks and hated them all the more as they were Shias. In 1568 AD, he sent two Shia envoys namely Mirza Muqim Isfahani and Mir Yaqub to Husain Shah to acknowledge his suzerainty. They were initially received with honour, but later on, there arose a religious dispute. They were charged with murder of a holy man. According to PNK Bamzai,[7] " The imperial envoy actively interfered in the Mandav affair and asked the governor of Srinagar, Ali Koka, to hand over the Qazi to the Shias who dragged them through the streets and executed two Qazis, Mulla Firus and Mulla Yusuf Almas." Husain Shah was disturbed by this episode. Being a peace loving king, he wanted to make peace with the Mughal emperor and went to the extent of sending his daughter with these envoys to the court of Akbar as a gift from him for his harem. Akbar refused to be moved by this offer. The girl came back to Kashmir. Sultan Husain smelt trouble.

His administration was excellent. According to Sukha,[8] "The king dispelled the fear from famine, from thieves, and from foreign potentate, and the people believed the kingdom of Kashmir to be equal to heaven." He was a liberal king with a secular outlook. He would also participate in the festivals of Hindus.

According to Sukha, the king suffered from epilepsy.[9] This was the real reason for his decision to abdicate in favour of his brother Ali Shah Chak. In 1569 AD, he appointed his brother Ali Shah as the king of Kashmir.

Sultan Ali Shah Chak, 1570-1579 AD

Ali Shah succeeded his elder brother Husain and titled himself as Ali Shah Chak. Like his brother, he was secular and peace loving. It was on account of his religious tolerance that he appointed a Sunni by the name of Mubarak Baihaqi as his prime minister. PNK Bamzai says,[10] "Ali Shah held the great Sunni saint Hamza Mukhdoom in great respect, as also the scholar-diplomat, Sheikh Yaqub Sarfi." He was also very tolerant towards Hindus.

In spite of his piousness, Ali Shah's period too was not free from intrigues. Nobles in Kashmir and also those who had been exiled tried to create trouble for him. Two noble—Shams Duni and Muhammad Maraj—raised a revolt. Ali Shah crushed the revolt with a firm hand. However, they were pardoned.

In another revolt, the sons of Nazuk Shah who were in exile entered into an alliance with the local nobles. However, this revolt was also crushed.

Meanwhile, Akbar sent a delegation consisting of Mullah Ashqi and Qazi Sadruddin in 1573 AD to ask Ali Shah to accept the Mughal suzerainty. Ali Shah readily accepted Akbar's supremacy as all the Chak rulers were very afraid of Mughal invasion and wanted to keep the emperor in good humour.

The year 1576 AD witnessed a devastating famine on account of heavy snowfall. This was followed by a fire. King Ali Shah rose to the occasion but the famine created havoc. All resources were exhausted. According to R K Parmu,[11] "The famine lasted for three years in all its horror and destructiveness. To make matters worse, the northern quarters of Srinagar were completely gutted by fire causing enormous loss of life and property." Meanwhile, Ali Shah died after he fell down from a horse.

Yusuf Shah Chak, 1579-1579 AD

When Ali Shah fell down from a horse, he was fatally wounded. Realising the seriousness of his injuries, he decided to abdicate the throne for his son Yusuf Shah Chak. But this did not turn out to be a smooth transition for Yusuf Shah's uncle, Abdal Chak, proved to be the first hurdle. Abdal Chak's claim to the throne was made even before the royal burial of Ali Shah.[12]

Those were the days when palace intrigues, jealousies of nobles and conspiracies against the legal claimants of the throne were the order of the day. Soon after Ali Shah's death, Abdal Chak sent a message to his nephew Yusuf telling him that the family tradition was that when a king died his brother took his place.[13] Yusuf Shah was not able to convince Abdal of his claim despite sending many important personalities such as Sayyid Mubarak to him. The more Yusuf tried to persuade Abdal Chak, the more the hostilities enhanced. Ultimately, Sayyid Mubarak told Yusuf Shah to attack his uncle. A fight broke out between the armies of the two. There are different versions as to where the two armies fought. According to Sukha,[14] "the battleground was Sikandarpora". Mohibbul Hassan and RK Parmu say it was Nowhatta. In the fight, Abdal Chak was injured by an arrow and subsequently died. His son who had joined him did not survive as well. Sukha satirically comments on Abdal's death: "He (Abdal Chak) fought with Yosobha Shaha (Yusuf Shah) at Sekandarapura (Sikandarpora), in which he destroyed the army of his enemy and then went to heaven, as if out of curiosity to see his brother."[15] After the fight, Yusuf Shah returned to the capital and buried his father Ali Shah's body, which was still waiting for burial, in true Shia tradition.

Abdal Chak's defeat at Nowhatta was a great relief to Yusuf Shah and this victory established his claim to the throne. He proclaimed himself as the king of Kashmir in 1579 AD and titled himself as Nassir-ud-Din Mohammad Yusuf Badshah Ghazi.[16]

Soon the king began spending his major time in romantic pursuits. "He was an accomplished scholar and a master of music," says PNK Bamzai.[17] He was hypnotised by the enchanting natural beauty of Kashmir. Before he became the king, he had married a commoner—a girl named Zoon who was later titled as Habba Khatoon. Together, they roamed different places in the valley. The discovery of the most beautiful scenic spot of Gulmarg , which subsequently became a tourist attraction, is credited to Yusuf Shah Chak.

After becoming the king, he continued to lead the life of a lovelorn romantic neglecting the duties of the state. His wife, who was also a very romantic poet, wanted to bring reason to the king so that he would abandon his merry-making with musicians and dancing girls and take the duties of the state seriously. But it was too late. By that time, the people had turned hostile to him. Even his nobles were disgruntled with the neglect of the administration and his way of life. Besides, there was no dearth of jealous enemies in the country and among the nobles.

So, barely two months later there was a revolt against Yusuf. The revolt was started by one Abdul Bhatt, who was expecting a berth in the state but was replaced by one Mohammad Bhatt. Abdul Bhatt considered himself as the kingmaker and started a serious revolt. He understood the pulse of the people and took upon himself to place Sayyid Mubarak Khan in place of Yusuf Shah. Sayyid Mubarak belonged to the Baihaqi Sayyid clan; Kashmiris had defeated the Baihaqi clan in 1484 AD during the reign of Mohammad Shah. In the revolt, Yusuf Shah was defeated and he fled from Kashmir.

Sayyid Mubarak Khan, 1579 AD

Sayyid Mubarak Baihaqi was a descendent of Baihaqi Sayyid, a powerful dynasty. He was highly respected by the people of Kashmir. He was a philanthropist by temperament. He doled out money to the needy and earned a good reputation among Kashmiris. His dream was to become the Sultan of Kashmir. And when the Kashmiri people and nobles revolted against Yusuf Shah, he became the natural choice for King. According to RK Parmu,[18] "After the death of Abdal Chak, Saiyid Mubarak Khan came out as the strongest and most influential leader."

After his defeat, Yusuf Shah was asked to leave the country and he went to Thana. Mubarak Khan's few months of rule were controversial. According to Mohibbul Hassan,[19] "Mubarak, who now replaced Yusuf Shah as Sultan led a very simple life, being averse to all pomp and show. He sold off the crown and the royal parasol (high umbrella) which was studded with precious stones. He was just and generous, and, though a good soldier, he was a man of peace." But according to RK Parmu,[20] "Sayyid Mubarak Baihaqi occupied the throne in 1579 AD. He proved to be worse than Yusuf Shah, which hastened his downfall. He acted very arrogantly and independently. He committed a great political blunder when he put in prison Ali Chak and Navroz Chak before he had consolidated his rule."

This way he had antagonised the Chak clan and Kashmiris hated his arrogance. They raised a revolt against him and compelled him to abdicate in favour of Lohar Chak. Mubarak ruled only for four months.[21]

Sultan Lohar Shah Chak, 1579–1580 AD

Lohar Shah Chak was the son of Shankar Chak and cousin of Yusuf Shah. His getting the throne of Kashmir was due to the efforts of Abdul Bhatt who compelled Mubarak to abdicate. For his role in the placement of Lohar Shah as sultan of Kashmir, he was made the administrator.

Abdal Bhatt sent a message to Yusuf Chak not to return to the valley. Lohar Shah ruled over the valley only for one year and his rule is remembered for economic prosperity. "He made food abundant and cheap. The prices of Shali (grains) fell so low that a Kharwar cost only a copper pica weighing 1x1/2 tolas."

All attempts by Yusuf Shah Chak to recapture the throne failed.[22] Frustrated, he knocked at the door of Emperor Akbar for military help. Yusuf committed a great blunder for which he had to suffer the rest of his life. It was the time when the Mughal emperor was yearning to annex Kashmir into his territory. So when Yusuf Shah Chak arrived at the court of Akbar, he was received very warmly. For Akbar it was a blessing in disguise and he agreed to provide military help to him. Akbar immediately ordered Raja Man Singh and Mirza Yusuf Khan to proceed to Kashmir. Sayyid Mubarak had introduced Yusuf to Akbar on 3 Jan 1580.

Though Man Singh was not in favour of undertaking the expedition to Kashmir, he reluctantly proceeded to Lahore accompanied by Yusuf Chak. At Lahore, the Mughal commander began rethinking about the wisdom of sending the Mughal army to invade the valley. The unprecedented holocaust as a result of previous Mughal invasions of Kashmir was lurking in the minds of the people. Mirza Haydar's invasion in 1533 AD, when the Mughals committed death, destruction and devastation was still fresh too. Meanwhile, the news spread like wildfire in the valley that Yusuf Shah was invading Kashmir accompanied by the Mughal Army. The Kashmiri nobles were shocked. They approached Yusuf secretly and offered him the throne of Kashmir on the condition that he would not bring the Mughal forces into Kashmir. It was a very awkward position for Yusuf Shah. He didn't know how to refuse the nobles and face Raja Man Singh and Mirza Yusuf Khan Rizwi at the same time. Another thing that bothered him was the thought of his country losing its independence should he bring the Mughals to Kashmir. He, therefore, decided to go to Kashmir without the Mughal army.

Sultan Yusuf Shah Chak, 1580-1586 AD

Leaving the Mughal forces at Sialkot, Yusuf Shah went to Lahore and with the help of Mohammad Bhatt, who was waiting for him along with 4000 armed men, left for Kashmir. This action angered the Mughal emperor. Yusuf Shah was proclaimed the Sultan of Kashmir for the second time in 1580 AD.

Akbar did not take kindly to the deceit by him. He sent Mirza Tahir and Saleh Aqil-with a Farman demanding personal attendance before him. Though Yusuf Shah kissed the emperor's letter and placed it on his head, he sent his youngest son Haider Khan to the court of Akbar. This did not pacify Akbar. He sent Sheikh Yaqub Khan Sarfi to Kashmir seeking Yusuf Shah's personal attendance at the Mughal court.

In the meantime, some Chak nobles raised a revolt. Haider Chak and Shamus Chak were leading the revolt. Yusuf Shah crushed the revolt.

Yusuf sent his elder son Yaqub with enormous wealth for the emperor. But even this did not pacify Akbar, who was blinded by his desire to annex Kashmir. With the Mughal threat hanging over his head, Yusuf Shah could not attend to the affairs of the country. This made him very unpopular.

Akbar then sent a contingent under the command of Raja Bhagwan Das to invade Kashmir. Raja Bhagwan Das left with a huge force along with the disgruntled Kashmiri nobles such as Haider Chak as the guide. When the Mughal army and Chak army were face to face at Baramulla, Bhagwan Das realised the futility of waging a war and once again decided to try a compromise. He sent a word to Yusuf Shah that he should meet him secretly. Yusuf Shah slipped out from his camp stealthily and went to the camp of Raja Bhagwan Dass at Buliyasa, to meet him. Both of them discussed the peace plan. It was also agreed that 'Khutba' would be read in the name of Emperor Akbar and coins minted in his name. Moreover, the departments such as mint, hunting, saffron and shawls would be imperial monopoly.

With this peace plan both of them presented themselves before the emperor. However, things took an ugly turn with Akbar not accepting the promise made by Raja Bhagwan Das to Yusuf Shah who was arrested and sent to prison at Patna.

As per William C Brice,[23] "Haydar Malik, Kashmiri soldier, scholar and engineer .....took up arms against the Mughal. He served Yusuf Khan Chak, son of Sultan Husain Shah (970-8/1563-70), for 24 years, and accompanied him in exile to Hindustan."

It is a paradox that a great emperor like Akbar resorted to violation of human rights and broke promises made by his trusted minister Bhagwan Dass to satisfy his ego. Bhagwan Dass, unable to bear the insult, committed suicide. Akbar was a Sunni and Yusuf Shah Chak was a Shia by faith. It is unfortunate that he did not even allow Yusuf Shah's love, Queen Habba Khatoon, to join her husband. According to R K Parmu,[24] "And so unbearable and disgusting was the question of separation for Habba Khatoon, the loving, doting and accomplished queen of Yusuf Shah, that she became a fakir (wanderer)."

Yusuf Shah was a tall, handsome and romantic person. He was a man of many accomplishments. An artist at heart, he loved poetry, music and dancing. His songs in Kashmiri and Persian were already popular with the masses. He was also a lover of nature. He once went into a small valley and saw it surrounded with snowy mountain peaks, lush greenery and blooming flowers and named it 'Gulmarg' (Meadow of Flowers). He also introduced another health resort in Kashmir and named it 'Sonamarg' (Meadow of Gold). Sultan Yusuf Shah was also a very learned person. He was a poet par excellence. He composed poetry in Hindustani and in Persian too.

Despite all these qualities, he lacked vision and committed many mistakes. Once he was installed as king, he ignored the work of the government. He found more solace in romancing Habba Khatoon. In spite of her insistence, he did not take up the work of the country seriously. Thus he had to leave the throne.

Sultan Yaqub Shah Chak, 1586 AD

After Yusuf Shah was jailed by Akbar, his son Yaqub Khan declared himself as the Sultan of Kashmir and titled himself as Nasir-ud-Din Mohammad Yaqub Badshah Ghazi. Unlike his father, Yaqub Shah was very brave and strong-willed. He gallantly fought the Mughals and they ultimately accepted him as the Sultan of Kashmir but under the command of Emperor Akbar. R K Parmu says that a peace agreement was accepted on 14 February, on the following terms, [25] "To proclaim Emperor Akbar sovereign of Kashmir and to recite the Khutba in his name; and to reserve the departments of mint, Shikaar (hunting), Saffron and shawl as imperial monopoly."

During Yaqub Shah's reign, there was greater unrest amongst the people of Kashmir. He became arrogant and pursued the policy of religious fanaticism. He also started misbehaving with the nobles of Kashmir, irrespective of their religious faith. Though Kashmiri nobles fought valiantly against the Mughal army, yet there arose an internecine war between the Sultan and the nobles. According to Sukha, [26] "Shamas Chakka became jealous of the king and constructed a fortification at Sadashivapur with the intention to fight. King Yakobha (Yaqub Shah Chak) then fought a great and tumultuous battle with him near Diddamatha in which Shamas Chakka took with him Alammashira and Malleka Alaka. It was on the advice of Malleka Alaka that Shamas Chakka then went to the village of Suyapura, situated in the midst of water, and occupied it. As the rising sun speedily destroys the darkness of night by its rays, even so Yakobha sent the soldiers of his enemy to Yama by arrows discharged with his own hand. Alammashira Khana fled after he had fought a while, and the king besieged Shamas Chakka within the town. Yakobha obtained the victory." The victory made him more arrogant. He then proclaimed himself as an independent king of Kashmir and abolished the treaty with the Mughals.

Yaqub Shah proved an unfit ruler. He got himself involved in the persecution of Sunnis, which made Akbar uncomfortable. In 1586 itself, a huge Mughal army under the leadership of Qasim Khan invaded Kashmir. So frustrated was the Kashmir army that the imperial army got no resistance. In other words, it seems that the people were happy to see the Mughal army coming into the valley, as if they had come to liberate the country. The Mughal army used the 'divide and rule' policy. Muslims were provoked against Hindus and Shias against Sunnis.

But some trusted nobles of Yaqub Shah such as Mahmud Bhatt, Shamus Doni, and Abdul Mali, continued the confrontation with the Mughal army. Sukha says,[27] "Yakobha saw his army broken and became uneasy with fear. He thus said to himself, "I believe my soldiers have been devoured by the Yavanas, even as the moon is devoured by Rahu." Yaqub Shah fled to Kishtwar and Kashmir, therefore, came under the imperial rule of Mughals in 1586 AD. This way the rule of Chak dynasty came to an end.

Sixteen
Kashmir under Mughals

Emperor Akbar, 1586–1605 AD

Abu'l-Fath Jalal ud-din Muhammad Akbar was born of Hamida Begum, the queen of Nassir ud-din Humayun, the second Mughal ruler after Babur.

Akbar was decidedly the greatest of all the Mughal emperors and one of the most renowned sovereigns of the world. At the time of his taking over the throne, he had only a few districts of Punjab under him and enemies all around. Of his reign, Beni Prasad writes in his book *History Of Jahangir*[1] "It symbolised the dawn of a new era in Indian politics; it gave the country a line of remarkable sovereigns; it secured to the four generations of Mughal emperors the services of some of the greatest captains and diplomats that medieval India produced." According to Pt Jawaharlal Nehru, Akbar was the 'Father of Indian Nationalism.'

It is true that Akbar stressed more on nationalism than religion, which is why his policy of secularism proved a boon for India. To please the Hindus he married a Hindu princess. He also employed Hindu ministers in his court. According to Stanley Lane-Poole,[2] "Akbar had not studied the history of India in vain. He had realised from its lessons that if his dynasty was to keep its hold on the country and withstand the onslaught of fresh hordes of invaders, it must rest on the loyalty of native Hindus."

Though Indian historians and chronologists have given the Mughal emperor accolades for his ability to become a remarkable sovereign there remains a blemish on his reputation. It is difficult to overlook his deceit with Yusuf Shah when he repudiated the treaty that had been negotiated with him by Raja Bhagwan Dass. Yusuf Shah remained in prison for more than two years till the emperor had consolidated his position in the valley.

The people of Kashmir were very unhappy with the Mughal occupation of their land. Fresh in their memory was Mirza Haydar's reign of death, destruction and religious persecution. Trust in Mughals was not easy to come by and this kept alive the nationalist spirit among Kashmiris. The fight for independence continued engaging them in sporadic skirmishes and in guerrilla warfare against the Mughal army.

But the Mughal army had come to stay. Akbar was not at all inclined to grant any independence to the Kashmiris. Apart from basking in the cool climate and natural beauty of Kashmir, he realised its strategic importance due to its proximity to many countries such as Russia and Afghanistan.

According to Abdul Majid Mattoo,[3] "The successors of Sultan Zain-ul-Abidin were not able to administer the kingdom efficiently. This situation sapped the vitality and strength of opposition to foreign aggression."

To subdue the state completely, Akbar deputed the first governor of the Mughal Empire, Qasim Khan, who entered Srinagar with a huge army on 16 October 1586. Akbar was publicly proclaimed the emperor of Kashmir. A khutba was read in the name of Akbar-e Azam and a coin minted in his name. "Such a mass of dust was raised by the marching army as to strike terror to the sun in the sky, even as from Rahu. Their Infantry, their cavalry, and their elephants could not be numbered."[4]

Governors under the reign of Akbar:

Qasim Khan Mir Bahar 1586-1587 AD

Mohammed Qasim Khan Mir Bahar was the son of Mirza Dost's sister, an old servant of the Timurids. He reached Srinagar on 18th June 1586. In order to win over the sympathy of nobles, he warned his army not to give suffering to the people.

Yaqub Khan Shah, the eldest son of Yusuf Khan, had in fact declared himself as the Sultan of Kashmir. On account of the Mughal invasion, Yaqub Shah had fled to Kishtwar. The Kashmiri army under Shamus Chak and Ibrahim Khan resorted to guerrilla warfare. They called back Yaqub Shah and under his leadership attacked the Mughal forces in Srinagar on November 19 1586 along the slopes of Shankaracharya/ Takht-i-Suleiman hillock. Says *Baharistan-i-Shahi*,[5] "Yaqub Shah moved from Ghasu and appeared on the Suleiman mountain." Mubarak Khan and Sheikh Daulat, at the head of a large Mughal army, fought the Kashmiri rebels but none succeeded. Poet Sukha says,[6] "Thus the war continued between King Yakobha (Yaqub Shah) and Keshma Khana (Qasim Khan), and for a month none of them was either victorious or defeated." Though Kashmiri soldiers were at an advantageous position on the hills, unfortunately there came a storm followed by rain. Says Sukha,[7] "And when the battle was about to be commenced, the mountains became covered with clouds which brought in a storm..." The rebel forces suffered defeat. The Kashmiri soldiers laid down their arms and fled wherever they could. Yaqub Shah also fled to Kishtwar once again.

According to facts compiled by Henry M Elliot in *The History of India*,[8] "Mohamed Kasim Khan Mir-Bahar was sent with a large force to affect the conquest of Kashmir. After seven marches, they entered the mountains. When they reached the pass of Kartal, Yaqub, the son of Yusuf Khan, considering himself ruler of Kashmir, came with a considerable force to oppose them. He closed the pass, and the stone of dissension was cast among the Kashmiris. The chiefs of Kashmir were distressed with the rule of Yaqub and several deserted him and joined Kasim Khan."

Qasim Khan tried his best to improve the condition of the state but to no avail. Initially, he governed with good intentions and then became arrogant and haughty. He taxed the people who were already stressed and frustrated. This proved counterproductive for him as it increased the unrest among the people. Just after winter, the people approached Yaqub Shah and the son of Mir Yadgar, the brother of Yusuf Shah and instigated them to revolt again. According to *Baharistan-i-Shahi*,[9] "In the course of the assault, his opponents had taken a firm resolve to see him killed. Therefore, they did not appear at their appointed places. The reason was that all of them were unhappy with his rule."

Yaqub Shah and Shamus Chak fought against the Mughal forces but were again repulsed. The attack by Kashmiri rebels was repulsed five times. They still persisted, and on the sixth occasion inflicted disaster on the Mughals who did not completely lose the battle but they were frustrated. Abul Fazal in his *Akbarnama* has named Yaqub Shah and Shamus Chak as "two scoundrels."[10] Unfortunately, Yaqub Shah was deserted by his supporters. He had to flee to Kishtwar. Raja Bahadur Singh was the ruler of Kishtwar. He had married his daughter to Yaqub Shah. But when Yaqub Shah reached Kishtwar, the king chided him and told him to go back.

As per Mohibbul Hassan, [11] "Raja Bhadur Singh of Kishtwar, who was his father-in-law, also criticised him for his cowardice in having ran away without fighting the Mughals. Yaqub Shah returned to the Valley with a small following." With his 8000 horses, he, along with Shamus Chak who had 3000 horses and 7000 foot soldiers, started guerrilla warfare.

It was out of sheer frustration that Governor Mohammed Qasim sent his resignation to Akbar. As per Abdul Majid Mattoo,[12] Akbar did not accept his resignation. R K Parmu does not mention this and instead says that Mirza Yusuf Khan Rizwi succeeded Qasim Khan as governor of Kashmir.[13]

Mirza Yusuf Khan Rizwi, 1587-1593 AD

The son of Mir Ahmed Rizwi, Yusuf Khan Rizwi was earlier appointed by Akbar as mansabdar of Bihar but was later sent to Kashmir to replace Governor Qasim Khan.

When he reached with additional Mughal forces to fight the Kashmiri forces headed by Yaqub Shah and Shamus Chak, he managed to win and the Kashmiri forces had to flee. Ibrahim Chak and Ismail Naik surrendered whereas Yaqub Shah fled to Kishtwar and Shamus Chak to Kamraz. The other nobles surrendered to the Mughal forces.

Shamus Chak, later on, presented himself before Akbar. Sayyid Bhauddin played an important role in his pardon. Akbar not only treated Shamus Chak well but granted him a mansab and got married to his daughter. Writes Abul Fazal,[14] "Also on this day the daughter of Shamus Chak entered the harem. He had long cherished this wish. On this occasion it was gratified."

After defeating the Kashmiri forces, Yusuf Khan Rizwi tried to bring peace in the valley. The economy was in shambles as the atrocities inflicted upon the people had aggravated the chaotic situation. Akbar sought a report from him. According to Poet Sukha,[15] "The creator has created

Kashmir like a second heaven; and even the king of the serpents with his two thousand tongues cannot describe the glories of the country." Having heard all the great praise, Akbar decided to visit Kashmir personally.

Akbar's first visit to Kashmir, 1589 AD

All Mughal kings were fascinated by the enchanting beauty of Kashmir. Akbar, Jahangir, Shah Jahan and Aurangzeb visited the valley and were mesmerised by its beauty. Francis Younghusband, in his forward in the *Ancient Monuments of Kashmir* by RC Kak says, "To the dwellers in the heated plains of India, it (Kashmir) has therefore ever been a paradise of bliss." During Humayun's period, Mirza Haydar Duglat made two attempts to invade Kashmir. He failed in 1533 AD, but in 1540 AD he succeeded. The khutba was recited and coins minted in the name of Humayun.

Akbarnama [16] says that Akbar was also very keen to annex Kashmir, which he ultimately did. Writes Abul Fazal. "He (Akbar) said that God, the author of desires, had implanted in him an irresistible wish, and that Jinnat Ashiyani (Humayun) had had the same longing. Our going thither is, apparently, the fulfilling of his honoured desires." *Akbarnama* also states that Akbar selected the Bhimber route.[17] "Three thousand stone cutters and mountain-miners and two thousand beldars (coolies) were sent in advance for levelling the route."

Abul Fazal says that when the retinue reached Kashmir, "They halted at Khanpur.[18] A remarkable thing there is a tree called Hal Tal (the place has been authenticated by M A Stein also) on the roadside, which is a wonder for beholders. It has a strong trunk, many branches, and numerous leaves. If a twig of it is set in motion, the whole tree begins to shake. There are plenty of trees of this species, but they do not behave like this one."

It was on 27 April 1589 AD that Akbar visited the valley, says R K Parmu.[19] Abdul Majid Mattoo too writes,[20] that Akbar decided to visit Kashmir in 1589. But as per Mohibbul Hassan,[21] Akbar arrived in Kashmir in June 1588 AD. *Baharistan-i-Shahi* gives us the date of Akbar's arrival in Kashmir as 1587 AD.

Abul Fazal says,[22] "The next day he marched 1 3/4 Kos (a measurement of distance) and reposed near Thana. This village is at the foot of the defile of Rattan Pantsal. At this place, the Kashmiri language begins." Akbar's arrival in Kashmir was a momentous event for Kashmiris who brought numerous presents for him. Writes Abul Fazal,[23] "Though the cavalier of fortune's plain was unattended, the Divine glory was radiating from his august forehead, and wherever he went, crowds of men and women offered up thousands of supplications. Every one of them brought vows of long standing before him, and reaped eternal bliss."

Says Poet Sukha,[24] "After the people of Kashmir had seen the sovereign, a continuous festivity was held in every house." It was a great day for the people of Kashmir. They collected in strength to cheer the Emperor of India. Men, women and children thronged the route from where the great king was to pass to catch a glimpse of him. He had come to heal the wounds of the people of Kashmir. However, those who were against Mughal rule became nervous.

The important people accompanying Akbar were Prince Jahangir and Todar Mal. According to Walter Lawrence,[25] "Akbar apparently visited Kashmir three times. In 1587, he brought with him his revenue minister Todar Mal, who, with more speed than precision settled the revenue arrangements of the valley from his camp at Pattan."

Seeing economic deterioration, failure of administration and great suffering of the people, Akbar immediately began streamlining the administration and redressing the grievances of the people.

"The most important event that occurred during his presence was the submission tendered by Yaqub Shah Chak," says R K Parmu.[26] In fact, Yaqub Shah had no choice but to surrender as another important person Shamus Chak had surrendered and even given his daughter in marriage to Akbar. All this dampened Yaqub's spirits and he surrendered. Akbar accepted his apology and sent him to Bihar like his father where he died in October 1593. He was laid in a grave by the side of his father Yusuf Shah.[27]

Another important step introduced by Akbar in the state was paying cash to defence forces instead of distributing them land.[28]

Akbar introduced a number of reforms which helped in the economic recovery of the country. He brought peace to Kashmir, showed religious tolerance and allowed Hindus to practice their religion. He abolished the Jazia too. According to Henry Miers Elliot,[29] "From the Arabic (Jaza in Urdu) subjugation; conquest; compensation. A capitation tax levied by Mohammedans on their subjects of another faith. The correct word is

Jazya." Akbar also abolished Begaar (forced labour).

Akbar had a great association with Abul Fazal and it was Fazal who influenced the formulation of his new tolerant religious policy. In addition, two Shia sons of Sheikh Mubarak exerted a powerful influence upon the emperor's mind leading him away from orthodox Islam. The emperor also issued an order according to which forcible conversion to any religion was prohibited. Even the prisoners of war could not be forced to abandon their religion and adopt a new one.

Akbar also treated Brahmins with compassion and affection. As per Jia Lal Kilam,[30] "During his stay in Kashmir, Akbar participated in the national festivals of the Pandits. On the 13th day of Bhadoon, which is celebrated by the Pandits as the birthday of Vitasta (River Jhelum), he ordered illuminations all over the city. He personally participated in the festivities. All this was a great and a decisive step taken towards recognising their distinct social existence. As a group, they again came into prominence."

"For this work," says Narendra Sahagala,[31] "one influential Hindu, Aditya Pandit, was appointed head of the ministry specially established for it. Some villages were made protected zones for the Pandits only. They were given land free of cost."

But Akbar's real contribution to Kashmir is the revenue administration, says R K Parmu. He deputed Sheikh Faizi, Mir Sharif Amuli, Khwaja Muhammad Husain, Shams-ud-din Khafi and Kunwar Man Singh who assessed the land revenue and measurement of land.[32] Qazi Ali Baghdadi was appointed Settlement Office of Kashmir.[33] The Mughals divided the country into 41 Parganas by which revenue, cash and kind were assessed. These measures improved the condition of the Valley. Qazi Ali's measures deprived the other officers of their bribe money. Poet Sukha says,[34] "The Kaji gave nothing to any one, nor enjoyed anything himself, but collected a large quantity of gold by robbing others, even as mice collect paddy." Jia Lal Kilam says,[35] "Pandit Tota Ram who later acted as the Peshkar to the first Mogul Governor Mirza Yusuf Khan Rizwi was appointed to assist Qazi Nurullah and Qazi Ali. Together they produced a report, which became the basis of land settlement."

Earlier, Yusuf Khan Rizwi, the governor, was misappropriating the revenue of the state. When his own Peshkar, Tota Ram, exposed the corruption, the governor decided to punish Tota Ram who approached Akbar and filed a complaint. It was then that Akbar deputed Qazi Ali to go to Kashmir to investigate and check the frauds.

Mirza Yadgar, 1592 AD (Proclaims himself ruler of Kashmir)

Qazi Ali stopped the corrupt practices of embezzlement of government funds, a move that infuriated officers including the governor. They hampered investigations. For instance, when Yusuf Khan Rizwi was to attend court, he made Mirza Yadgar, his cousin and one of the officers, in-charge of the subah (province). Akbar sent Husain Beg Sheikh Umari to assist Qazi Ali in his investigations. Meanwhile, a servant of Husain Beg raped the wife of a soldier of Yusuf Khan Rizwi. The rebel forces took the opportunity to attack Husain Beg and Qazi Ali. Husain Beg fled to Rajouri and Qazi Ali was killed. *Akbarnama* mentions that Qazi Ali was killed in 1592 AD but poet Sukha says,[36]"The Kaji fought several times with him and then fled. His horse perished in ascending a hill, and he also went to heaven."

In that turmoil, Mirza Yadgar proclaimed himself the king of Kashmir and the khutba was read in his name. At that time, Akbar was preparing for his second visit to the Valley, and Mirza Yusuf Khan Rizwi was at Lahore with him. An infuriated Akbar ordered the arrest of Yusuf Khan and Zain Khan Kokah was asked to proceed immediately to Kashmir via Swat. Sadiq Khan also headed for Kashmir with a large army via Poonch.

The proclamation by Yadgar Mirza was problematic but the Mughal officers managed to nip the problem in the bud. Commanders Shahbaz Afghan, Ibrahim Khan Kakar and Saran Beg Turkaman attacked him in his compound. The beheaded head of Mirza Yadgar was shown to Akbar.

It was at Prince Salim's request that Yusuf Khan Rizwi was brought before Akbar and he explained his position. Akbar pardoned him and sent him to Kashmir again.

Akbar's second visit to the valley, 1592 AD

It was during Governor Yusuf Khan Rizwi's tenure that Akbar paid a second visit to Kashmir in the first week of October 1592. He stayed in the Valley for nearly three weeks. On his arrival, there was great jubilation. Houses, palaces and roads were illuminated.

Akbar was a cool-headed diplomatic emperor. A part of his endeavour was to make peace with rebels and bring peace to the country. To achieve this, he introduced matrimonial diplomacy to thaw the hostility of the local people. Some of the Mughal nobles offered to marry the daughters of Kashmiri nobles and this cemented ties to a great extent. Akbar himself accepted the daughter of Shamus Chak as his wife. The daughter of Mubarak Khan and Husain Chak also married Prince Salim. Akbar's second visit also marked the construction of Nagar Nagar Fort (Hari Parvat Fort). He visited various health resorts and enjoyed the Saffron blossom at Pampore. He also went to Baramulla in a boat and visited Wular Lake. He left in the last week of October 1592.

Asaf Khan, 1593–1597 AD

In 1593, Yusuf Khan Rizwi was transferred from the Valley and Asaf Khan was made the governor. He was the son of Badi-uz-Zaman Qazwini of Persia. His rule was short but important as he continued with the assessment and reorganisation of land and land revenue. He distributed the land into 38 Parganas and fixed the revenue, less than what his predecessors had fixed, (Qazi Ali had earlier distributed Kashmir into 41 Parganas). By and large, the peasants and the people were happy during his tenure. In 1593 AD, Asaf Khan had to go back and Muhammad Quli Khan was deputed the governor of Kashmir.

Muhammad Quli Khan, 1597-1598 AD

After Asaf Khan, Emperor Akbar deputed Muhammad Quli Khan as the governor of Kashmir, as per R K Parmu.[37] However, P N K Bamzai and Abdul Majid Mattoo have stated that Quli Khan succeeded Yusuf Khan Rizwi and not Asaf Khan.

By then the Chak dynasty was still trying to reclaim the Kashmir throne. But Muhammad Quli Khan dealt ruthlessly with the rebels, thus bringing under control all terrorist activities of the rebels.

Akbar's third visit to the valley, 1597 AD

On 6 April 1597, Akbar paid his third and last visit to Kashmir.[38] Father Jerome Xavier and Benedict Gomez, who were the earliest known European visitors to Kashmir, accompanied him.[39]

It was a time when the people of Kashmir were facing atrocities from both men and nature. Akbar himself was witness to a terrible famine during his visit which devastated people in every way. The poor went to the extent of selling their children for a morsel of food. Emperor Akbar immediately ordered grains to be brought from outside the valley. This brought some comfort.

Tradition says that the emperor who wanted to mitigate the suffering of people started construction of a huge fort at the top of Hari Parbat to provide employment and income to the people. But the emperor ordered a township be built for the Mughal army so that they did not mix with civilians.[40] "Under the orders of King Akavara (Emperor Akbar) a fort was built with the inappropriate name of Nagar Nagar."

Says Sukha,[41] "Now all of a sudden, the old town built by Alabhadina (Ala-u-Din), with its two thousand houses, was in flames, as if in sorrow for its separation from the Moguls whom it saw depart in order to live in the new town."

Akbar's inscription on the fort states,[42] "The foundation of the fort of Nagar-Nagar was laid in the reign of the just sovereign, the king of kings, Akbar, unparalleled among the kings of the world, past or future. He sent one Crore and ten Lakh rupees from his treasury and two hundred Indian master-builders, all his servants. No one was forced to work without remuneration. All obtained their wages from his treasury."

Quli Khan was given charge of supervising the Nagar Nagar Fort.[43] In fact, it was Yusuf Khan Rizwi who had constructed barracks for the soldiers as they were forbidden to stay in the city. When Akbar came and saw the construction of the barracks he ordered that a strong fortified fort be constructed instead. He thought that it could serve two purposes—give employment to the people and give the soldiers a magnificent fortified place of their own. As per Walter Lawrence[44], "It is said that the fort and the Hari-Parbat hill were commenced with the view of attracting the Kashmiris back to Kashmir, whence they had fled in the troubled times of Chaks." He further says, "High wages were given to men and women…"

When Akbar visited Kashmir for the third time, he had Ladakh and Baltistan under his subjugation. After spending three months, he left just before winter set in. Quli Khan was an able governor and he had brought peace to the subah. After 11 years of service, Akbar called him back and a new governor Mirza Ali Akbar was given the charge of Kashmir.

Mirza Ali Akbar, 1598–1609 AD

There is confusion about the date when Mirza Ali Akbar took charge as governor. According to P NK Bamzai,[45] "He was the Mughal governor when Jahangir took over the throne of India. But according to RK Parmu's[46], "Jahangir appointed him governor of Kashmir. He died in 1616 AD."

Ali Akbar's tenure was also not free of famine and other epidemics. Says PNK Bamzai,[47] "The Valley was devastated by famines and floods which occurred frequently. The emperor, however, sent supplies of grain from Lahore and Sialkot which mitigated their severity."

Akbar had tried to win over his enemies diplomatically. He would send ambassadors to the chiefs of various neighbouring countries and ask them to accept the sovereignty of the king. He sent a saintly person Talib Isfahan and Mehtar Yari to Little Tibet (Baltistan). Talib Isfahan had come from Isfahan as an ascetic during the period of Yusuf Shah Chak. He was a puritan and experienced in political matters. He impressed Ali Rai, the chief of little Tibet so much that Ali Rai presented his daughter to Prince Salim (Jahangir).

This mighty emperor, Akbar the Great, breathed his last in 1605 AD. After his death, his son Jahangir took over the throne of India.

Emperor Jahangir, 1605-1627 AD

Emperor Jahangir was born on 31 August 1569 from a Rajput queen named Maryam-uz-Zamani with the blessings of the saint Sheikh Salim Chisti. It was on October 24, 1605 that Jahangir, 36 years old, ascended the throne at Agra amidst great rejoicings.

Prince Jahangir had accompanied Emperor Akbar on his first visit to the valley of Kashmir. Tradition says that as soon as he entered the Valley, so mesmerised was he with the panoramic view in front of him that he uttered the words "Ya Allah" (Oh My God), and then started his never-ending visits to the Valley. His numerous visits to Kashmir[48] "were marked by the construction of lovely pleasure gardens like Shalimar and Chesham-e Shahi and he set a fashion which was followed by his nobles,"says Walter Lawrence.

Jahangir had extreme aesthetic sense and deep appreciation of beauty. In his crusade to improve the beauty of the place, his wife, Empress Noor Jahan, also joined him. She assisted him in the construction of pleasure gardens. Empress Noor Jahan, daughter of Mirza Ghiyas Beg, was the eighteenth and last wife of Jahangir. It is said she was born in a moving caravan while travelling from Tehran to India in 1577 AD.

There is a general belief in Kashmir that Noor Jahan belonged to Kashmir and was born to Malik of Chadora, which is not true. The fact is that the people of Kashmir were so impressed by her that they created a myth that she belonged to Kashmir. However, Firishta has given the correct place of her birth—present-day Kandahar, Afghanistan.

Known as Mehr-un-Nissa, she was first married to Sher Afghan alias Ali Quli Beg Istajlu. After the death of Sher Afghan she was sent to the court of Jahangir, who entrusted her to the care of his stepmother Ruqayya Sultana Begum. But fate had something different in store for her. One day during the New Year celebrations, her captivating appearance caught the king's eye. She was brought to his special harem and day by day Jahangir's infatuation for her grew. She was titled Noor Mahal or "Light of the Palace", but upon her marriage to Jahangir in 1611 AD, she was conferred the title Noor Jahan "Light of the Universe." Noor Jahan became the chief queen. She was also titled Malika-i-Jahan (Empress of the universe). She had an extraordinary influence upon Emperor Jahangir.

It was during Jahangir's rule that the seeds of British rule in India were sowed. He permitted the British to trade in India. This was a monumental mistake, and for this small mistake, India had to suffer slavery for about two hundred years. However, both Jahangir and Noor Jahan visited the valley very frequently.

Writes L N Dhar,[49] "The great emperor visited the state thirteen times. The Mughal rulers never came alone, but were always accompanied by hundreds of Nobles, Amir and Umara, princes and army generals."

Jahangir was essentially a lover of nature, art and education. He was a good writer and recorded detailed descriptions of wildlife in his autobiography *Tuzuk-e-Jahangiri*. He admired paintings and collected many of them in his palace. Many of them are still found in museums around the world. True to his words, he left the governance in the hands of Noor Jahan. He stated in *Tuzuk-e-Jahangiri*, "I have bestowed sovereignty on Noor Jahan, who is wise enough to conduct the affairs of the state. I require nothing beyond a bottle of wine, a piece of meat to keep myself merry." But it was not only Noor Jahan who enjoyed the power. Her father, Mirza Ghiyas Beg and her brother Asaf Khan also enjoyed limitless power.

Jahangir was very impressed by the scenic beauty of Kashmir with its snowy mountain peaks, small brooks, singing rivulets and charming waterfalls cascading down from the mountain peaks. The massive lakes in the heart of the city of Srinagar are one of the greatest treats for the people living around them. Against the mountain backdrop, these lakes are nearly 7 km long and about 2.5 km broad. In the centre of two lakes, Zain-ul-Abidin had constructed two tiny islands now called Char Chinar. It is said that Emperor Jahangir would spend nights on these islands, Sona Lank and Rupa Lank, in the company of Noor Jahan. He was a pleasure-loving monarch. He once said that even if he lost all his empire but had only Kashmir, he would not mind. In 1606 AD, he got the sides of Verinag Spring fixed with marble stones. A beautiful garden was also laid around the spring.

Jahangir's love for Kashmir was very intense. According to Stephen Meredyth Edwardes and Herbert Leonard Offley Garrett,[50] "One remembers how Babur in his memoirs, mentions the scent of a melon which reminded him of his country; in the same way we find Jahangir so moved by ecstasy at the sight of the flowers and the meadows of Kashmir that he burst into song. His love for Kashmir was so intense that he journeyed thither thirteen times..."

Jahangir was famous for his justice "Adle Jahangiri" to the people. William Wilson Hunter writes,[51] "Jahangir tried to work wisely for his empire. A chain hung down from the citadel to the ground and communicated with a cluster of golden bells in his chamber, so that every suitor might apprise the emperor of his demands for justice without the intervention of the courtiers."

Like his father, he too had religious tolerance. Jahangir noticed and appreciated the Hindu contribution to the sciences, the arts and overall additions to the Mughal culture. Many Hindus held prominent government positions.

Dr Ishwari Prasad says,[52] "There is much in his character that deserves to be condemned but there is a great deal that entitles him to be placed among the fascinating personalities of Indian history."

Jahangir's love-hate relationship with Shah Jahan gave rise to many speculations. Though Shah Jahan was not present at the time of his death, it is believed that he connived to hasten Jahangir's death. Writes CH Linsay-Forbes,[53] "In 1627 Jahangir died suddenly, not without strong suspicion of having been poisoned at the instigation of his son, Shah Jahan."

It is said that when he was asked his last wish at the time of his death, he expressed his desire to be buried in Kashmir. However, that did not happen. SL Sadhu has written that Jahangir actually died in Kashmir at Verinag.[54] "The news of his death was kept confidential for reasons of State and, under the orders of Noor Jahan..." However, SR Bakshi has given a vivid account of the emperor's last hours,[55] "At a place midway between Rajouri and Bhimber, Jahangir asked for a cup of his favourite wine Aab-i-Hyatt, raised it to his lips, and then fell back in a coma.... The end came in the early hours of 28th October, 1627." He further writes, "Sobs and tears broke out when Maulana Hassam-ud-Din recited Kalima and prayed for peace for the soul of the departed monarch. Noor Jahan moaned in pain; she neither wailed nor uttered a cry. "Death," she seemed to say, "be proud of thy possession."

Sir Francis Younghusband has showered lavish praises upon Jahangir and his wife Noor Jahan for their efforts to beautify Kashmir "...Be it Shalimar Bagh, or royal garden, the favourite resort of the Mughal Emperor Jahangir and his wife, the famous Nurmahal, for whom the Taj at Agra was built as a tomb."[56] It is strange a person of Younghusband's calibre did not know who built Taj Mahal. The famous Taj was in fact built by Shah Jahan for his beloved wife Mumtaz Mahal.

Governors under the reign of Jahangir:
Mirza Ali Akbar, 1598-1609 AD

Mirza Ali Akbar ruled the Valley and focused on oppressive measures to weed out the anti-Mughal elements. He expected complete submission from the people and from Kashmiri nobles. Any sign of disloyalty was suppressed ruthlessly. According to R K Parmu,[57] "Mirza Ali Akbar, the governor of Kashmir behaved diplomatically. He assumed a conciliatory attitude towards the rebels. He employed trickery, chicanery and deceit and himself feigned sympathy with their cause."

According to *Baharistan-i-Shahi*, there was effective opposition from Zaffar Khan and his followers. The governor, with the help of Qazi Saleh, convinced the opposition that they would be handsomely rewarded if they had faith in the Mughal administration. Believing that, Zaffar Khan agreed to attend the court of the governor, but when he and his followers reached there, all of them were arrested and sent to prison, where they were killed. The remaining Chaks were hunted down and this was how the Chak clan was annihilated.

Writes Narendra Sahagala,[58] "During the time of Jahangir, there was one Meru Pandit, an army officer and a Sardar posted at a fort in the south. Jahangir appointed him chief of the security guards of Queen Noor Jahan. One day, Jahangir was surrounded by Mohabat Khan, a rebel, and his soldiers on the bank of the Jhelum. But Meru Pandit along with the security guards brought down Mohabat Khan. Jahangir gifted him estates in Kashmir and appointed him chief in charge of security of all fortresses in Kashmir."

Hasham Khan, 1609–1612 AD

Hasham Khan followed Mirza Ali Akbar as governor of Kashmir. His period was free of any incident. Emperor Jahangir used to visit the Valley almost every year. According to Henry Miers Elliot,[59] "Emperor Jahangir long entertained the design of conquering Tibet, and in the course of his reign Hasham Khan, governor of Kashmir, under the orders of the Emperor, invaded the country with a large force of horse and foot and local Zamindars. But although he entered the country, and did his best, he met with no success and was obliged to retreat with great loss and with much difficulty." He further says, "The imperial order was now given that Zaffar Khan, governor of Kashmir, should assemble the forces under his command and effect the conquest of that country."

This clearly indicates that Zaffar Khan took over the governorship during the period of Jahangir. However, many chroniclers have not mentioned his name.

Sardar Khan, 1612-1615 AD

Sardar Khan was a sensible governor. He worked for the betterment of the people who were, by and large, happy. But during his period a great epidemic of plague spread in the valley killing hundreds of people. The disease continued till the new governor Ahmed Beg Khan took over in 1618. Writes Shyam Lal Sadhu,[60] "Dead bodies of the victims were thrown naked into the river and people abstained from taking fish for a long time…The rivers were the only source from where people fetched water for drinking and other needs and one can well imagine the horror that they felt, especially the women, when they saw dead bodies float down while they filled their pitchers."

Such was the savagery of nature that devastated the Valley. The government could not cope with the situation and throwing the bodies in the flowing river was seen as an easy option. Soon the governor was shifted and Ahmed Beg Khan took over.

Ahmed Beg Khan, 1615-1618 AD

Ahmed Beg Khan, who superseded Sardar Khan, was well versed with the local conditions. According to R K Parmu,[61] "He was appointed on the clear understanding that he would subdue Kishtwar. Ahmed Beg was able to crush the Chaks, who had joined Kishtwaris in their fight against Mughals, but he could not defeat Kishtwar."

The devastation caused by the plague continued and people were dying like flies. It did gradually subside on its own but another catastrophe befell the country. A great fire engulfed Kashmir and did not spare even the Jama Masjid of Srinagar.[62] Unfortunately, the Sunnis suspected Shia chief Haider Malik and his father of burning Jama Masjid in retaliation for Mirza Haider burning Shamus-ud-Din Iraqi. The suspicion was based on mistrust between Ahmed Beg and Haider Malik.

The history of enmity between Sunnis and Shias goes back to the medieval period. Haider Malik, an orthodox Shia, and Governor Ahmed Beg, a staunch Sunni could not live comfortably in the presence of each other, particularly when Haider Malik was in the good books of Jahangir and Noor Jahan.

The accusation against Haider Malik that he had conspired to get Jama Masjid burnt is not true. However, according to RK Parmu,[63] "The emperor ordered that Haider Malik and his father should rebuild the mosque at their own expense."

Jama Masjid was originally built by Sikandar. It got burnt and the Sanctum Sanctorum was rebuilt by Sultan Hassan Shah.

Dilawar Khan, 1620-1621 AD

Ahmed Beg Khan was called back from Kashmir and Dilawar Khan was placed as the governor. High on the agenda of Mughal rulers was the conquest of Kishtwar, a place on the north side of the Kashmir Valley. It is a small state enclosed by tall hills adjacent to the Bhaderwah valley. The Chenab River which flows through it is its lifeline.

Kishtwar is one of the important towns of Jammu and Kashmir. It has played a very important role in the history of Kashmir right from the time of Kota Rani, who ruled over Kashmir in the late 14th and early 15th century. Kota Rani's husband sought refuge in Kishtwar when Achala invaded the valley. Similarly, Kishtwar was a refuge for rebels and freedom fighters of the Valley. The Mughal rulers who had vowed to destroy the Chak clan were followers of the Nurbakshia sect of Shias. The Chaks, to avoid Mughal persecution, also took also refuge in Kishtwar. Yaqub Chak even married the daughter of the king of Kishtwar.

According to SR Bakshi,[64] "The district of Kishtwar had been able to maintain its independence in spite of the conquest of Kashmir. Efforts had been made in the time of Akbar to conquer it, but those were not crowned with success. Dilawar Khan, the governor of Kashmir, brought the Raja of Kishtwar to Jahangir in 1920."

It was a determined Dilawar Khan leading a huge army comprising 10,000 horses and foot soldiers who conquered Kishtwar. Says Sukhdev Singh Charak,[65] "A little after, in 1620 AD, Raja Sangram Dev rendered distinguished services to Jahangir assisting his officers in Kashmir in their expedition against Kishtwar." He further says, "Pratap Singh alias Bhup Singh, Raja of Kishtwar, was son-in-law of Sangram Dev."

Iradat Khan Mir Saman, 1621-1622 AD

Iradat Khan's appointment as governor of Kashmir was made on account of a rebellion raised by Kishtwar against Mughal occupation. Earlier, Kishtwar had succeeded in revolting against the Mughal army chief Nazr Ullah Arab, who led a small contingent of Mughal forces against Kishtwar. It ended with the death of Nazr Ullah Arab. This time Jahangir ordered Iradat Khan to suppress the revolt. He was able to suppress the rebellion and restore law and order. As per *Tuzuk-e-Jahangiri*,[66] "As it was reported that the Zamindars of Kishtwar had again raised their heads in disobedience and sin, and engaged in sedition and disturbance, Iradat Khan was ordered to proceed hotfoot, before they had time to establish themselves firmly, and inflict punishment on them to tear up the root of sedition." Iradat Khan was able to restore law and order in Kishtwar. He then posted the Mughal army at strategic points to immediately suppress any future rebellion.

Itiqad Khan, 1622-1627 AD

Itiqad Khan was the last governor during Jahangir's tenure. Jahangir had presented him with one of his special swords called 'Sar-andaz'. He replaced Iradat Khan and was known for his cruelty and tyranny. Devoid of human values, he passed orders which were unjust and unwarranted. For instance, he prohibited people from using forests, fruit gardens and saffron fields and reserved them for government use. This deprived the common farmer of his earnings. According to *Tuzuk-e-Jahangiri*,[67] "Itiqad is the father of Mumtaz-Mahal, the wife of Shah Jahan."

Emperor Jahangir's Achievements

It is true that the Mughal rulers never wanted to show that they were foreign rulers in Kashmir. It is also true that Mughal governors ruled like they were conquerors of the land. But when complaints came to the notice of the Mughal monarchs, they set things right according to the wishes of the people. According to the Memoirs of Jahangir, once a plague broke out in the valley and people died like flies.[68] "Things had come to such a pass that from fear of death fathers would not approach their children and children would not go near their fathers. A strange thing happened in the wards in which the disease began. A fire broke out and nearly 3000 houses were burnt." And with that, the plague was also wiped out.

The personality of Jahangir is fully revealed in his memoirs. He loved nature and possessed a remarkable power of observing it. His frequent visits to Kashmir are ample proof of this. His broad-mindedness was reflected in his religious policy. His sense of justice made no distinction between rich or poor. He was a great builder. He established inns and hospitals. He also gave liberal grants to saints and scholars. He was efficient in his duties towards the country.

With Kashmir coming under the domain of Mughal monarchy, planned and systematic administration was established. The monarchs heard the grievances of the people and they were redressed immediately.

Jahangir's Reforms

Jahangir also brought in some reforms. He put a ban on sati which was prevalent among the Hindus. The custom was also prevalent among Muslims in some remote parts of Kashmir. Jahangir repealed all those laws which he thought were against the interest of the common people. He prohibited the strangulation of the girl child at the time of her birth, an inhuman custom among Hindus. He also repealed all those laws which prohibited Hindus from studying their scriptures and performing their religious rituals.

Perhaps Jahangir's greatest disservice to the people of Kashmir was that he prohibited inter-marriages. According to PNK Bamzai,[69] "It was reported to him that in some hilly parts there existed the custom of inter-marriages between Hindus and Muslims. A Hindu could marry a Muslim girl and vice versa. Jahangir did not approve of it; he prohibited the marriage of a Muslim girl to a Hindu."

Mughal Expansion

Kishtwar and some parts of Tibet had become the asylum for defeated kings and other disgruntled nobles. They had become a great headache for the Mughal administrators of Kashmir. The Mughal armies helped in the annexation of Kishtwar, Poonch near Tibet and far Tibet. According to *Akbarnama*, Akbar sent Mirza Beg to subdue Tibet.

During the reign of Jahangir, old canals were repaired to store floodwaters and prevent floods in the valley. The Mughal rule saw a boost in saffron cultivation and the rearing of silk cocoons by planting of mulberry trees.

The land revenue departments consisting of Muqadam, Patwari, Qanungo and Chowdhury were responsible for maintaining the land records and the land produce, which determined the collection of land revenue.

Emperor Shah Jahan, 1627-1658 AD

Shahbuddin Mohammed Shah Jahan was born on January 5, 1592 to Jahangir's second Rajput queen. He was the ruler of the Mughal Empire in the Indian subcontinent from 1627 until 1658. The name Shah Jahan comes from Persia, meaning 'King of the World.' He was the fifth Mughal ruler after Babur, Humayun, Akbar and Jahangir.

Shah Jahan was one of the most glorious emperors of the Mughal dynasty. It was during his reign that the empire touched the heights of affluence, prosperity and opulence and his reign came to be known as the 'Golden Period of Indian History.' During his long reign, the empire, however, witnessed many important events.

The death of Jahangir was followed by a war of succession. His youngest son Sharyar, who was wedded to Ladli Begum, the daughter of Noor Jahan from Sher Afghan, proclaimed himself the new king at Lahore. This was done at the behest of Noor Jahan. However, Shah Jahan was helped by his father-in-law Asaf Khan, who was also the brother of Noor Jahan. After placing Noor Jahan under house arrest, Asaf Khan immediately sent a messenger to Deccan where Shah Jahan was and informed him about the developments.

Shah Jahan had a passion for architecture and gems. Jahangir was fond of paintings and Akbar loved poetry. True to his passion, he built a tomb for his wife Mumtaz Mahal in Agra—the legendary Taj Mahal. A 'Teardrop on Eternity', or in Rabindranath Tagore's words 'one tear-drop... upon the cheek of time.' In addition to the Taj Mahal, the Red Forts in Delhi and Agra, the Jama Masjid in Delhi, the Shalimar Gardens of Lahore, sections of the Lahore Fort and his father's mausoleum are the surviving legacies of his great architecture. Shah Jahan was a lover of ornamental architecture. During his rule, he built numerous artistic buildings and beautiful gardens in India and Kashmir.

As a child, Prince Khurram (as he was known then), was very dear to Akbar. He acquired a reasonable education. In 1610 AD, he was married to the daughter of Mirza Muzaffar Husain. Then in 1612 AD, he married Arjumand Banu Begum, daughter of Asaf Khan. Arjumand Banu Begum later came to be known as Mumtaz Mahal. She was also titled as Malika-i-Jahan (Queen of the World). It was in her honour that Shah Jahan built a unique mausoleum—the Taj Mahal at Agra, one of the wonders of the world.

There are conflicting reports about Shah Jahan's rule. Vincent Arthur Smith writes, "Shah Jahan failed both as a man and as a ruler. The dazzling splendour of his court and the remarkable beauty of his buildings, especially of the Taj Mahal misled the world into thinking that his reign was a golden period in Mughal history." However, some of the chroniclers say that during his period, the country progressed by leaps and bounds. According to F Ward Deny,[70] "Under Shah Jahan, the Mughal Empire reached its greatest strength and magnificence. Shah Jahan's land revenues amounted to more than $120,000,000, including Kashmir and five provinces in Afghanistan."

Amongst his children, Emperor Shah Jahan was very fond of Dara Shikoh, also known as Padshahzada-i-Buzurg Martaba. The other sons were Shah Shuja, Aurangzeb and Murad Baksh. He wanted Dara Shikoh to be the heir to the throne. According to Henry Mires Elliot,[71] "In the eyes of his father the emperor, Prince Dara Shikoh was superior to his brothers in both merit and age. When other sons departed to their respective governments, the emperor, from excessive love and partiality, would not allow Dara Shikoh to go away from him."

Shah Jahan had a very strange life in his old age. He suddenly fell ill in 1757 AD and stopped attending any public function. Immediately, a rumour spread that the Emperor was dead. The sons of this great monarch started fighting for succession. Shah Shuja declared himself king of Bengal, Murad Baksh in Gujarat allied with Aurangzeb in the battle of succession. Dara Shikoh also declared himself emperor of India. Murad Baksh fell prey to Aurangzeb's sweet-talks.

The first war of succession started on 15 April 1658 at Dharmat and Dara Shikoh lost the battle. He then collected a large army and faced Aurangzeb and Murad at Samugarh near Agra. Though Dara was initially wining, his elephant got injured and he shifted to a horse, with the result that his forces could not see him and there was commotion and disarray on the battlefield. Dara Shikoh had to flee from the battlefield and the victorious brother Aurangzeb went to Agra and put Emperor Shah Jahan under house arrest on 8 June 1658. Shah Jahan remained in captivity for eight years and in 1666, the 'King of the World' left for his heavenly abode while reciting the Kalma and verses from the Holy *Quran*.

Governors under the reign of Shah Jahan

Itiqad Khan, 1627-1633 AD

Unlike his father, Shah Jahan was a disciplinarian and deputed provincial governors who were loyal to him. He reshuffled the governors. Before Zaffar Khan took over as the governor of Kashmir, Itiqad Khan, the governor during Jahangir's rule continued for six years. But Itiqad Khan's misdeeds and oppressive rule came to the notice of Shah Jahan who immediately dismissed him and placed Zaffar Khan in his place.

Zaffar Khan, 1633-1635AD

Zaffar Khan Ashan was a distinguished poet, author and a seasoned governor. He was a brave soldier too. He was the son of Khwaja Abdul Hassan, the governor of Kabul. Zaffar Khan earned the reputation of being very efficient and a humanist by temperament and deeds. He had no religious fanaticism. He mitigated the hardships of the people caused by the previous governor. Shah Jahan revoked all the unjust laws and returned the saffron fields and fruit gardens to their owners. As per R K Parmu,[72] "He (Shah Jahan) would not tolerate incompetence or abuse in the provincial administration, and lost no time to remove even his favourite officers from their charge if their conduct was found unsatisfactory or complaints against them reached the court." Shah

Jahan's commands (*Farman*) were engraved on the stones and these stones were visible near the Jama Masjid mosque and other places. Parmu further says,[73] "The *Farman* has tremendous historical importance. It enumerates the various cruel and oppressive taxes and perquisites by which unsympathetic, greedy, unscrupulous and parochial governors of Kashmir like Itiqad Khan collected from the population there causing them much distress and poverty."

When Zaffar Khan was ordered by Shah Jahan to conquer Tibet, which was governed by Abdel, the son of Ali Ray, who was the chief during Akbar's rule, he was able to defeat Abdel. Abdel, having lost the battle was compelled to read Khutba in the name of Emperor Shah Jahan. According to HM Elliot,[74] "Zaffar Khan was apprehensive that the snow would fall and close the passes, and that, at the instigation of Abdel, he might be attacked from the side of Kashmir. Therefore, without making any settlement of the country, and without searching after Abdel's property, he set out on his return, taking with him Abdel, his family, and some of the leading men of the enemy. He left Muhammad Mural in charge of the country." In 1635 AD, the country witnessed violent scenes of conflict between Shias and Sunnis. However, Zaffar Khan dealt with the situation with a heavy hand and restored peace in the Valley. He did not forgive the Sunnis and deported some Sunni leaders to Agra.

Zaffar Khan also had good aesthetic taste. He laid down many gardens in the valley.

Prince Murad Baksh, 1635-1636 AD

Prince Murad Baksh, the younger son of Shah Jahan, replaced Zaffar Khan as the governor of Kashmir. During his tenure, the administration of Kashmir was neglected as he was busy with other pastimes. As per PNK Bamzai,[75] "He (Prince Murad Baksh) had earlier married the daughter of the Maliks, nobles of the Southern district of the Valley. Taking undue advantage of their relations with the Prince, they ravaged the land by loot and undue exaction from farmers." The suffering of the people increased manifold during Murad Baksh's rule. According to Sham Lal Sadhu, [76] "The Prince appointed many favourites from his wife's clan on high posts and the latter exploited their powers. People were put to suffering, and their protest was expressed in the well-known doggerel: "Kaava Yeni Vol, Muradun Mol…" (The world is shortlived even as the wedding festival of crows….)"

The Prince remained as governor for one year only. He was called back and Ali Mardan Khan was given the charge.

Ali Mardan Khan, 1636–1637AD

Ali Mardan Khan had come from Iran and joined Shah Jahan's government. A very popular man, he was very tolerant towards all faiths and was a liberal governor. He was very learned and had human values. He was very competent in both political and financial matters. He abolished all the burdensome taxes on poor people imposed by Itiqad Khan. It so happened that a famine broke out during Ali Mardan period. He approached Emperor Shah Jahan who immediately sent grain from outside Kashmir that was distributed free among the people.

It was a time when Shah Jahan had waged wars against the Portuguese (1631-1632), Ahmednagar, Bijapur and Golconda in 1636. These things kept him busy in India and therefore his visits to Kashmir were not frequent.

Ali Mardan established his credibility as soon as he took over the administration of Kashmir. According to Henry Miers Elliot, [77] "Adam Khan now wrote to Ali Mardan Khan, the new governor of Kashmir, informing him that Sangi Bamkhal, the holder of Great Tibet, had seized upon Burag in Little Tibet, and meditated further aggression. Alí Mardan Khan sent a force against him under the command of Husain Beg. On the meeting of the two forces, Sangi's men were put to flight. He then asked for forgiveness, and offered to pay tribute."

Ali Mardan Khan was a great builder. According to PNK Bamzai, [78] "To him goes the credit of laying out a number of gardens, the chief among them is that of Cheshma Shahi near Srinagar." He also constructed many roads. Says RK Parmu,[79] "Ali Mardan Khan, his (Shah Jahan's) noted builder, architect and statesman, got the imperial high-road connecting Kashmir with West Punjab widened and dressed to suit heavy traffic."

He was a God-fearing and efficient administrator. He was also secular and treated Shias, Sunnis and Hindus alike. Narendra Sahagala in *Memorial Of Mistakes* says,[80] "Ali Mardan, had appointed one Hindu leader, Pandit Mahadeva, as his chief advisor and entrusted all powers of the state to him. Muslims belonging to the upper class started getting jealous of him because of his calibre, wisdom and capacity for work."

As per Jia Lal Kilam,[81] "In the civil administration, the Pandits held very high places. Pandit Mahadeva was the Peshkar (chief minister) of the Mogul Subedar, Ali Mardan Khan (1650-1657 AD.) It was during the period when he was Peshkar that the imperial highway from Srinagar to Gurjara was constructed."

Ali Mardan Khan died of old age just before the announcement of Aurangzeb as the successor to the throne of India. His sensible wife, known as Begum Amir Khan, kept the news hidden and announced it after Aurangzeb was coronated. When Aurangzeb came to know this, she was highly honoured by the king.

Tarbiyat Khan, 1637–1641 AD

Tarbiyat Khan belonged to Turan and he came to India during the period of Jahangir. Impressed with his services, Shah Jahan gradually elevated his position. In 1637 AD, he was sent as the governor of Kashmir but when a great famine took place he was unfortunately not able to cope with it. Hence he was replaced by Zaffar Khan. There was another reason for his being ousted as governor of Kashmir. According to RK Parmu,[82] "He died as a result of heart failure consequent on the displeasure of the emperor because he and Mullah Fazil Kabuli had dissuaded him from entering upon the conquest of Balakh and Badakhshan."

Zaffar Khan, 1641–1657 AD

Zaffar Khan succeeded Tarbiyat Khan and became governor of Kashmir for the second time. The famine had shattered the very spirit of the Kashmiri people. They heaved a sigh of relief when Zaffar Khan took over. The new governor gradually tried to improve the situation and when he left the country there were no problems left for the people. According to RK Parmu,[83] "The emperor (Shah Jahan) provided an additional sum of 20,000 rupees for relief work. Zaffar Khan fought the crisis satisfactorily."

It was during his period that Shah Jahan paid another visit to the Valley in 1651 AD.

Lashkar Khan, 1657–1659 AD

It is said of Lashkar Khan that he was essentially a good man who had feelings for the poor. According to PNK Bamzai,[84] 'It was only during the time of Shah Jahan's last governor, Lashkar Khan (1657-59) that a measure of prosperity and happiness returned to the Valley."

Emperor Aurangzeb, 1658-1707 AD

Aurangzeb was born on November 3, 1618 at Dohad near Ujjain. He was the third son born to Emperor Shah Jahan and Mumtaz Mahal. Due to the revolt of Shah Jahan against Noor Jahan favouring her son-in-law Sharyar Khan to succeed the throne, Aurangzeb and his brother Dara Shikoh were sent to Lahore as hostages in 1662 AD. But as soon as he was released, Mir Mohammad Hasham, a well-known scholar was deputed for educating Prince Aurangzeb. The young prince was known for his valour, strength, and courage. He once tamed an infuriated elephant single-handedly.

Aurangzeb was married to Dilras Banu Begum alias Rabia-ud-durrani and Begum Nawab Bai

In 1658 AD, Aurangzeb raised the flag of revolt for succession against his father and brothers. He managed to influence Murad, his younger brother and kept him by his side. Aurangzeb fought his brother Dara's forces at Dharmat and Samugarh. He defeated and killed him and his son too. Then he imprisoned Shah Jahan, his own father. Aurangzeb's actual succession to the throne took place on June 5, 1659. "On the 26th of May, 1659, he had formally ascended the throne in state," says Stanley Lane-Pool in *Rulers of India*,[85] "He assumed the title of Abul-Muzaffar Mohammad Muhi-ud-Din Aurangzeb Bahadur Alamgir Padshah-i-Ghazi."

In the history of the Mughal dynastic rule over India, Aurangzeb's personality and his role as an emperor of India is very important. The Mughal Empire was founded by Babur after the first Battle of Panipat in 1526 AD. Akbar consolidated his grandfather's victories and contributed greatly to the expansion of the Mughal Empire. The empire was at its zenith during Jahangir's rule. But Shah Jahan, though a magnificent builder took certain religious measures which gave a clear indication of its downward trend. Aurangzeb's measures of religious intolerance against Hindus resulted in further disintegrating the Mughal Empire.

Tradition believes that it was Mir Mohammad Hasham, a theologian teacher of Aurangzeb who taught him the *Quran* and *Hadith*. This made Aurangzeb a staunch and die-hard Sunni Muslim. His teachers, perhaps, taught him to make India a land of orthodox Islam (Dar-ul-Islam) and free the country from infidels. After this, Aurangzeb's personal life was, in the words of Muhammad Hashim Khafi Khan authored *Muntakhabu-L-Lubab*, "Of all the sovereigns of the House of Timur-nay all the sovereigns of Delhi no one, since Sikandar Lodi has ever been apparently so distinguished for devotion, austerity and justice. In courage, long-suffering and sound judgment, he was unrivalled." He further says, "He often passed his nights in vigil and devotion and denied himself many pleasures naturally belonging to humanity."

Having earned such laurels from Khafi Khan who declared him as a saint, it is difficult to understand Aurangzeb's role at the time of the war of succession. He got his elder brother Dara Shikoh killed. Dara's son, who had hidden himself, was also killed ruthlessly.

Aurangzeb's most inhuman act was imprisoning his ailing father, who perished in prison. Thus Khafi Khan's praises of Aurangzeb do not fit very well.

In his mad zeal to make India Dar-ul-Islam, Aurangzeb left no stone unturned to banish and annihilate infidels. Temples such as the famous temple of Kesava Rai in Mathura, Vishwanath in Benaras and Somnath in Kathiawar were demolished. Imposition of Jazia tax was reintroduced. Sir HM Elliot says in *The History of India*,[86] "His aim was to curb the infidels and to distinguish the land of faithful from an infidel land." But there are some chroniclers who do not believe that Aurangzeb unleashed communal frenzy. Writes Alexander Hamilton, a British historian who toured India towards the end of Aurangzeb's fifty-year reign and observed that everyone was free to serve and worship God in his own way, "During the fifty years of his reign, not a single Hindu was forced to embrace Islam. He did not interfere with any Hindu religious activities."

Some scholars such as Romila Thapar and MN Roy have gone even beyond that and argued that Aurangzeb was a benevolent ruler, very tolerant towards other religions. Romila Thapar has even attempted to dismiss "local legends" of Aurangzeb's cruelty as "mere rumours." However, Francois Bernier has stated that Dara was condemned as a heretic (Kafir) which carried a sentence of death. Religion has often been used to undermine or eliminate political rivals be it in the East or the West. In February 1663, Aurangzeb sent Khidmatgar Khan to build roads so that he was able to go to Kashmir. He started his tour of Kashmir on 23 April 1663.

Aurangzeb had five daughters and five sons. Zeb-un-Nissa Begum (born 15 February 1638 from Dilras Banu Begum) was the first daughter. Some Indian historians have mentioned the name of Hafiza Maryam as the teacher of Aurangzeb's daughter. Prem Nath Bazaz also mentions in the *Daughters of Vitasta* that,[87] "For her attainments, she was held in reverence at the Mughal court."

Hafiza Maryam was the wife of Mirza Shakur Ullah of Kashmir. She had received a good and liberal education. Her reputation had reached the Mughal courts, particularly Aurangzeb, who had visited Kashmir on health grounds.

Zeb-un-Nissa had accompanied him on his visit to Kashmir. Aurangzeb was so impressed by the literary taste and erudition of Hafiza Maryam that he reposed confidence in the nobility of her character and placed his beloved daughter Zeb-un-Nissa under her care. Through her efforts, Zeb-un-Nissa memorised the *Quran* in three years.

As per Henry Miers Elliot,[88] "Zeb-un-Nissa Begum was born on 5th February 1639. Owing to the King's teaching, she became thoroughly proficient in knowledge of the Holy *Quran*, and received as a reward the sum of 30,000 ashrafis. Her learning extended to Arabic and Persian, to the various modes of writing, and to prose and poetry."

Dewan-i-Makhfi of Zeb-un-Nissa states,[89] "She collected a fine library and employed skilled calligraphers to copy rare and valuable books for her; and, as Kashmir paper and Kashmir scribes were famous for their excellence, she had a scriptorium also in that province, where work went on constantly."

Zeb-un-Nissa (Jewel among women) was devoted to poetry and gave herself the pen name Makhfi. PremNath Bazaz in *Daughters of Vitasta*, says,[90] "The Princess owed her education to the Kashmiri lady and as is clear from certain preserved letters of Zeb-un-Nissa, she remained indebted to Hafiza Maryam throughout her life."

Some of the governors during Aurangzeb's period tried to be more loyal than the king himself. They tried to impose Islamic rules on non-Muslims. With the result, the non-Muslims became desperate and helpless. Tradition affirms that some respectable Hindus went to meet Hafiza Maryam and begged her to help them in their distress on account of the reign of terror let loose by Mughal governors such as Iftikhar Khan, (1671-75), Muzaffar Khan (1690-92) etc. Hafiza wrote a letter to Emperor Aurangzeb informing him that the atrocities and misrule done by the governors against Hindus was not a good sign of Mughal administration and was un-Islamic. It is said that Aurangzeb after reading the letter said, "If Hafiza Maryam has written about the governors it must be true." He forthwith removed these governors and sent better and moderate governors to the relief of the Hindus.

Governors under the reign of Aurangzeb

Itimad Khan, 1659-1662 AD

After assuming the crown as emperor of India, Aurangzeb sent Itimad Khan as the governor of Kashmir, He replaced Lashkar Khan, the last governor sent by Shah Jahan. Itimad Khan is said to have been a learned man. He administered the country very justly. People were happy with his rule.

Ibrahim Khan, 1662-1664 AD

Ibrahim Khan replaced Itimad Khan in 1662. He was the son of Ali Mardan Khan. He remained governor for two years. During his period, the relations between Shias and Sunnis became very bad. Ibrahim Khan, being of Shia faith, tried to help Shias who took undue advantage during his governorship. When reports reached Aurangzeb, Ibrahim Khan was recalled and in his place Islam Khan was appointed governor.

Islam Khan, 1664-1665 AD

Islam Khan was an able administrator. He was very well read and dabbled in poetry too. He was a devout Muslim. In addition to his normal administrative duties, he tried to spread Islam wherever he was given any assignment. People were, by and large, happy and Emperor Aurangzeb visited the valley during his tenure.

Emperor Aurangzeb's visit to Kashmir

Aurangzeb had recovered from an acute bout of sickness and was feeling very weak. It was his desire to visit Kashmir to improve his health. He did so accompanied by his daughter Zeb-un-Nissa and Francois Bernier, who was a physician by profession and has written memoirs of Aurangzeb's rule and the places he visited with Aurangzeb in *Travel in the Mogul Empire*.

According to Francois Bernier's memoirs, [91] "So large a retinue has given rise to a suspicion that instead of visiting Kachemire, we are destined to lay siege to the important city of Kandahar, which is situated equally on the frontiers of Persia, Hindoustan and Usbec. It is the capital of a fine and productive country, yielding very considerable revenue; and the possession of it has consequently been at all times warmly contested between the Monarchs of Persia and India."

While coming to Kashmir, Emperor Aurangzeb faced a lot of hardship on the way. P N K Bamzai writes,[92] "The journey was rendered hazardous and troublesome by the precipitous mountain passes which lead to Kashmir. Several persons, along with the animals they rode on, were killed on the way and many injured." He further states, "Aurangzeb considered a visit to Kashmir sheer luxury and the cause of great hardship to the poor Kashmiris who had to supply labour for the transport of baggage and supplies for the emperor and his large retinue." As per Bernier, 30,000 porters were employed to carry the luggage of the camp from Bhimber to Kashmir.

"While crossing the terrible Pir Pantsal Pass, a frightened elephant turned back from the front and stampeded towards Bhimber like a sudden calamity or a whirlwind; a terrible confusion befell the men and animals in the narrow pass. Some elephants and some porters of the government fell into the pit of destruction and were so thoroughly crushed by the attack of the moving mountain that not to speak of the men, not a bone of the elephants could be seen," writes Muhammad Saqi Mustad Khan in *Maasir-i-Alamgiri.*[93] He further says, "On the occurrence of this terrible accident, the heart of the humble-cherishing emperor was greatly grieved, and from that very time he resolved never again to visit Kashmir."

Bernier also relates a story that when they reached the top of Pir Pantsal they met an old man. He states,[94] "The old man was also very angry with those who made a noise. After I had entered his cave, and softened his countenance by means of half a roupie, which I humbly put in his hand, he informed me that noise made there stirred up the most furious tempests imaginable. It was wise in Aureng-Zebe, he added, to be guided by his advice, and to order the army to pass with stillness. His father, Chah-Jehan, always acted with the same prudence; but Jehan-Guyre having upon one occasion derided his counsel, and, notwithstanding his earnest remonstrance, having ordered the cymbals to be beaten and the trumpets to be sounded, narrowly escaped destruction."

However, Aurangzeb stayed for three months in the valley and visited various pleasure spots such as Dal Lake, the saffron fields etc. R K Parmu mentions[95] "In Srinagar, he stayed in the palace on the slope of the Hari Parbat hillock, overlooking the Dal Lake."

Bernier says,[96] "The King left this city on the sixth of December, at three o'clock in the afternoon ; a day and hour which, according to the astrologers of Delhi, cannot fail to prove propitious to long journeys."

It is said that Aurangzeb came to Kashmir when Islam Khan was governor. But Islam Khan was governor in 1664 AD, while many chroniclers, including Elliot, say that Aurangzeb was in Kashmir from 1st May to 29th September 1663.

Saif Khan, 1665-1667 AD

On arrival in Kashmir as governor, Saif Khan was appalled by the rampant corruption. A strict man of iron will, he tried to eradicate it as far as he could. To wipe out the corruption, he even lashed some people to death.

During his tenure as governor, he was asked to send two important men—Rishi Pir Pandit Padshah and Mullah Tahir Ghani—to the court of Aurangzeb. Mullah Tahir Ghani was the greatest Persian scholar and poet of Kashmir. He was the pupil of Mohsin Fani (Fani authored the famous Persian work *Debistan-e-Mazahib*). His fame had even reached Persia. RK Parmu says,[97] "In the case of Ghani, when the governor approached him with the imperial command, the latter offered all possible excuses. When nothing appeared to help, he suddenly turned mad, tore his garments to shreds and shortly after passed away." He further writes, "The early sudden death of the greatest Kashmiri Persian poet of his generation will ever remain a blot on the character of Aurangzeb."

Rishi Pir Pandit Padshah was a Hindu ascetic. As per Walter R Lawrence,[98] "A legend goes that a messenger was sent citing the Rishi to appear before the emperor at his court in India. The Rishi travelled in one night through the air to India, and appeared in a terrible form, mounted on a lion, as the emperor lay asleep. Aurangzeb, in his fear, agreed to the Rishi's retaining his title of Padshah." It is said that Aurangzeb became so terrified at the awe inspiring sight of a man mounted on a lion that he started trembling and with a choked voice begged Rishi pir for forgiveness.

Saif Khan introduced Islam in Tibet. The chief of Tibet, Dalia Mahamuni, accepted Islam and his name was changed to Daldal Muhammad. He read the Khutba in the name of the emperor and a coin was also issued in the name of Aurangzeb. A mosque was also built in Tibet. Saif Khan, who had managed his role well in the spread of Islam, was awarded a royal robe and a promotion. Murad Khan of Tibet, who had helped him in this campaign, was also awarded the robe of honour. After being alleviated in his post Saif Khan was assisted by Mumtaz Khan as Subedar of Kashmir.

Mubariz Khan, 1667-1669 AD

Mubariz Khan succeeded Saif Khan as governor of Kashmir. Although a very noble and God-fearing Muslim, he was a weak governor. During his governorship, there was no development as such. It will not be an exaggeration to say that Mubariz Khan was only biding his time. "He used to walk barefoot up to the Jama Masjid to offer his prayers," says R K Parmu,[99] "This cannot be said of the Uzbek soldiers who were his bodyguards. They committed all sorts of lawless acts and tortured the people."

Saif Khan, 1669-1671 AD

Saif Khan became governor of Kashmir in 1669 again. Writes PNK Bamzai,[100] "As usual they (Mughals) laid out gardens, built mosques and inns. Saif Khan, for instance, built Safa Kadal (the seventh Bridge in Srinagar). His advisor, Chowdhary Mahesh, laid out a vast garden with numerous terraces, fountains and cascades on the slopes of the hill at Ishabar." Many villagers were settled there, which gave a tremendous boost to agriculture.

Jia Lal Kilam concedes that Saif Khan was himself a great builder. "But so much was the beauty and grandeur of the Chowdhary garden that the Viceroy could not hide his feelings when he used to remark bitterly:

Chowdhary Mahesh bag na kard
Dar Dili Saif Khan dag kard

(Chowdhary Mahesh did not lay a garden. He simply created a scar in the heart of Saif Khan).[101]

During this period, the Mughals had full control over Kangra and Chamba hills. Saif Khan was in direct touch with Delhi. The Kangra fort had great importance and it was believed that "he who holds the fort holds the hills."

Iftikhar Khan, 1671-1676 AD

Iftikhar Khan remained as governor of Kashmir for three years. He earned the reputation of being a very good administrator. But his period saw a very great inferno, which destroyed almost the whole of Srinagar including the Jama Masjid. Under Aurangzeb's orders, the Masjid was rebuilt.

According to Bamzai,[102] "Iftikhar Khan tyrannised over the Brahmins to such as extent that they approached Guru Tegh Bhadur, the ninth Sikh Guru at Anantpur in Punjab and solicited his personal intervention with the emperor. This ultimately led to the Guru's martyrdom and the conversion of the Sikh community into the fighting Khalsa force under his son, Guru Gobind Singh." A delegation led by Pandit Kirpa Ram went to Punjab and explained to Guru Tegh Bhadur about forceful conversion of Hindus to Islam by Aurangzeb. While pondering over the situation, Guru Tegh Bhadur said to his disciple, "The world is grieved by oppression of the Turks. No brave man is to be found. He, who is willing to sacrifice his life, shall free the earth from the burden of the Mohammedans." His son, Guru Gobind Singh, then only nine-years old, said, "For that purpose who is more worthy than you who is at once generous, holy and brave." It was then that Guru Tegh Bhadur decided to protect the Hindus by sacrificing himself. As per D N Kundra,[103] Guru Tegh Bhadur sacrificed himself on 11 November 1675. His sacrifice proved a great factor in the downfall of the Mughal Empire. Hari Ram Gupta, eminent teacher and historian of Sikh history states, "A great storm arose at the martyrdom of the Guru and that storm carried off the empire of Aurangzeb as if it were a dead leaf lying on the road."

Qawamuddin Khan, 1676-1677 AD

Like his predecessors, Qawamuddin Khan was noble and aristocratic. His rule saw no extraordinary development but he made sure that law and order prevailed in the country.

Ibrahim Khan, 1677-1683 AD

Ibrahim Khan was reappointed as the governor of Kashmir. His first appointment was in 1662. "Although he lived a luxurious life with very easy going habits, he found time to establish law and order in the country,"[104] says RK Parmu. His reign also saw Shia-Sunni riots in which Shias were punished and suffered a lot.

Hafiz Ullah , 1685-1689 AD

Hafiz Ullah Khan faced the important task of maintaining law and order in the country. In addition, he had to supress the revolts by some rulers of adjoining areas.

Muzaffar Khan, 1689-1692 AD

Muzaffar Khan nursed resentment against the Hindus for a murderous attack made by Shivaji Maratha against his father Shaista Khan. His opportunity to avenge this came when he, as governor, taxed Kashmiris, particularly Hindus, so much that they had to seek the help of Hafiza Maryam.

Abu Nasr Khan, 1692-1697 AD

Abu Nasr Khan was the brother of Muzaffar Khan. He, like his brother, amassed wealth by hook or crook. Six years of his rule saw unrestricted taxes upon people.

Fazil Khan, 1697-1700 AD

The people of Kashmir had already suffered on account of heavy taxation imposed by Muzaffar Khan and Abu Nasr Khan. Then came a natural calamity in the form of heavy floods, and with that there was an epidemic. A religious Fazil Khan became really distressed and sad while dealing with the miserable grievances of the people. It was during his governorship, in 1700 AD, that a Kashmiri trader named Khawaja Noor-ud-Din Ishbari had taken *Moi Mubarak,* the sacred hair of the Prophet Mohammad, from Sayyid Hameed, a descendant of the Prophet, and brought it into the valley, along with the heist of Noor-ud-Ishbari. This holy relic is placed in the Hazratbal Mosque on the banks of Dal Lake.

Ibrahim Khan, 1700-1707 AD

Ibrahim Khan was governor of Kashmir three times. Fortunately, in his third term he managed the administration of the country in a mature manner. The people were happy and the valley became prosperous.

Nawazish Khan Rumi, 1707 AD

Nawazish Khan Rumi's appointment as governor of Kashmir came in 1707 AD. He was on his way to Srinagar when news of Aurangzeb's death reached him. Therefore he had to make a hasty retreat to reach Delhi.

"Of all the sovereigns of the house of Timor – nay all the sovereigns of Delhi – no one, since Sikandar, has ever been apparently so distinguished, of devotion, austerity and justice," writes Mohammad Hashim Khafi Khan, a 17th century historian in *Muntakhabu-i-Lubab.* "After his success in the war of succession, Aurangzeb ascended the throne in July 1658 and ruled India and Kashmir up to February-March 1707. During this period, he moulded the very character and basis of the empire and ultimately became responsible for his and Mughal dynasty's downfall."

Emperor Bahadur Shah, 1707-1712 AD

Aurangzeb died in 1707. As usual, the war of succession began among his five sons—Prince Mohammad Sultan, Prince Muazzam, Prince Azam

Shah, Prince Akbar and Prince Kaam Bakhsh. All the sons were holding the posts of governors/administrators in different parts of India. According to MTh Houtsma in *Encyclopaedia of Islam*,[105] "Muhammad Muazzam was the second son of Emperor Aurangzeb Alamgir by Rahmat al-Nissa, Nawab Bai, the daughter of Radja (King) Tajuddin Khan of Radjauri (Rajouri) in Kashmir."

Padshah Muazzam Bahadur Shah Alam was married to the daughter of Raja Roop Singh and also to Rahmat Banu, the daughter of the king of Assam. When Aurangzeb died, Muazzam was governor in-charge of North-West territories of India. On hearing of the death of his father, he declared himself as the emperor of India from Lahore and titled himself as Bahadur Shah. Aurangzeb's third son Azam also declared himself as the monarch from Ahmednagar, Deccan. In the battle against his brother, Azam was killed. Then his youngest brother Kaam Bakhsh rose in revolt against Bahadur Shah. On 16 July 1709, Kaam Bakhsh's small army was routed and this made Bahadur Shah free from succession disputes.

Aurangzeb had imposed Sharia law within his kingdom with harsh enforcement of strict edicts. This led to increased militancy from many constituencies including the Marathas, the Sikhs and the Rajputs. Thus, rebellion was rife at the time of Aurangzeb's death and Bahadur Shah inherited a very unstable polity. A more moderate man than his father, he sought to improve relations with the militant constituencies of the rapidly crumbling kingdom. However, he could do little to mitigate the damage already done by his father. Indeed, Bahadur Shah's shortcomings—his lack of military skills and leadership qualities—added to the problems of the empire. In the words of J N Sarkar, "All seemed to have been gained by Aurangzeb but in reality all was lost. It was the beginning of his end, not only his end but the very end of the Mughal rule in India."

Aurangzeb's religious policy, which was based on religious intolerance, became a major cause for the downfall of the Mughal Empire. His religious policy had antagonised all Hindus who were subject to persecution, discrimination and above all hatred from the emperor as well as from the Muslim administration. His policy of making India 'Dar-ul-Islam' did not succeed but evoked hostility to such an extent that his successors had to suffer.

Although Bahadur Shah-I had no rival for succession as king, the Mughal rule in Delhi was in the process of disintegration and that had an effect on the administration of Kashmir. Bahadur Shah had to fight the Rajputs who had raised their heads. The Sikhs under the leadership of Banda Bhadur, also revolted. According to PNK Bamzai,[106] "Banda Bairagi mustered a strong force of 40,000 armed Sikhs around him, sacked the town of Sadhaura (near Ambala) and gained his crowning victory by defeating and slaying Wazir Khan, the commandant of Sirhind, and plundering his camp." Banda Bairagi resolved to attack Lahore but was defeated and he fled to Jammu.

"After the campaign against Banda, Bahadur Shah moved to Lahore. He was planning a visit to Kashmir, but with declining health he fell ill and passed away on 27 February 1712,"[107] says PNK Bamzai.

Governors under the reign of Bahadur Shah.

Jaffar Khan, 1707–1709 AD

Jaffar Khan's reign as the governor of Kashmir was unjust and cruel. He indulged in excesses, became alcoholic and neglected the administration. He was assisted by his deputy Abdullah Khan Dehbedi, who eventually joined him in his licentiousness.

Arif Khan, 1709–1709 AD

Arif Khan took over from Jaffar Khan but only for a short period. There was not much done during his tenure. However, according to PNK Bamzai,[108] "It was in his reign that Qazi Haider known as Qazi Khan, a learned Kashmiri, who rose to be the Supreme Judge at Aurangzeb's court, died in Agra. His dead body was brought to Kashmir."

Ibrahim Khan, 1709–1709 AD

Ibrahim Khan was very popular during Aurangzeb's rule. He was once again deputed as the governor of Kashmir. But as soon as he reached Srinagar, he fell ill and died. His fifth term lasted only three months.

Nawazish Khan, 1709–1711 AD

After the death of Ibrahim Khan, Arif Khan was the acting governor. He made many changes to improve the conditions of Kashmir. Nawazish Khan did not come to Kashmir and he allowed Arif Khan to work there. Kashmir witnessed floods followed by fire during this period.

Inayat Ullah Khan, 1711–1712 AD

Inayat Ullah Khan was a Kashmiri by birth and was married to the famous Hafiza Maryam, the teacher of Zeb-un-Nissa. He was assisted by Amanat Khan who had earned admiration as a gentle person. However,

Amanat Khan died during Inayat Ullah Khan's tenure.

Emperor Jahandar Shah, 1712–1713 AD

Mui'zz-ud-Din Jahandar Shah Bhadur was born on May 9, 1661. After the death of Bahadur Shah-I on 27 February 1712, the war of succession among his sons—Azim-ush-Shan, Rafi-ud Daula, Khujista Akhtar Jahan Shah, Buland Akhtar—began as usual. Azim-ush-Shan fought for succession but lost and Jahandar Shah became the king.

Jahandar Shah was born to Queen Nizam Bai. He was married to a dancing girl known as Lal Kunwar who took over the position of prime queen from Anup Bai. Soon the king became a puppet in her hands. In fact, she became the de-facto Sultan of India. This became one of the causes of rebellion. Jahandar Shah's nephew Farrukh Siyar, and his brother Azim-ush-Shan joined hands and dethroned him. He was captured and a professional strangler was brought to behead him. His head was brought before Farrukh Siyar, who had taken over the reins of the country.

Governors under the reign of Emperor Jahandar Shah

Inayat Ullah Khan, 1712–1713 AD

Inayat Ullah Khan continued to be the governor of Kashmir. It was during this period that a Bombas leader known as Muzaffar Khan raised a rebellion. Inayat Ullah went to subdue the rebellion. According to PNK Bamzai,[109] "While Inayat Ullah was engaged in the campaign, Jahandar Shah lost his throne and his successor, Farrukh-Siyar, recalled him to Agra."

Emperor Farrukh Siyar, 1713-1719 AD

Farrukh Siyar was born to Sahiba Nizwan, daughter of Mir Muhammad Taqi, a Kashmiri noble, at Aurangabad in the Deccan on August 20, 1685. He was the second son of Azim-ush-Shan and grandson of Bahadur Shah-I. In September 1715, Farrukh Siyar married Indra Kunwar, daughter of Maharaja Ajit Singh of Jodhpur. He was also married to at least two other women, namely Fakhar-un-Nissa and Bhup Devi, daughter of Raja Jaya Singh of Kishtwar. Jahandar Shah was defeated at the second battle of Samugarh near Agra. Thus his rule ended within months and Farrukh Siyar replaced him. In fact, it was the powerful Sayyids, who had come to India with the patronage of Muslim kings who helped Farrukh Siyar attain his throne. In return, the king made

Sayyid Abdullah a minister and Sayyid Hussein Ali the finance minister. However, a Muslim, Mir Jumla, who was very close to the King succeeded in creating differences between the Sayyids and the king. Banda Bairagi, who was later on executed by Abdul Samad Khan, the governor of Lahore, engaged Farrukh Siyar in various problems like rebellions in Punjab. Then came the Jat uprising. So the king recalled Inayat Ullah and sent him as governor to Kashmir. By 1719, the conditions in Delhi had deteriorated so much that Hussein Ali, who had come from the Deccan with a huge army captured Farrukh Siyar. He was blinded and finally killed.

Under these conditions, far off places in Kashmir, which were not administered by the elected governor, were practically ruled by their agents who misruled the valley and were not answerable to anyone. During these years of misrule, the Hindus of Kashmir witnessed the worst type of religious persecution by the Muslim rulers. Mughal officers instigated the Muslims to loot and plunder the property of Hindus.

Governors under the reign of Emperor Farrukh Siyar

Sadat Khan, 1713–1717 AD

Sadat Khan never visited Kashmir. His assistants Ali Muhammad Khan, Azam Khan and Ehtram Khan executed the work of administration one after the other. During his reign, the rebellion of Bombas leader, Muzaffar Khan was crushed. According to R K Parmu,[110] "Muzaffar Khan was forced to come to terms and Haibat Khan was taken to Srinagar as a security." Meanwhile, the King of Poonch also raised a revolt but the rebellion was put down with a firm hand.

Inayat Ullah Khan, 1717–1720 AD

Earlier, the cruel governor Inayat Ullah Khan was recalled as a punishment. Later, when he had earned the confidence of the king, he was once again made the governor of Kashmir. But he made his deputy Mir Ahmed Khan look after the affairs of the country.

Emperor Rafi-ud-Darajat, 1719 AD

Rafi-ud-Darajat, the son of Nurunisa Begum, became the 10th Mughal emperor. He succeeded Farrukh Siyar in 1719, being proclaimed Badshah by the Sayyid brothers. He was a controversial figure and was deposed shortly afterwards. He was killed at the behest of the Sayyid Brothers in 1719 AD in Delhi because one of the Sayyids fell in love with his wife.

Inayat Ullah Khan, 1717 – 1720 AD

Inayat Ullah Khan continued to be the governor of Kashmir.

Emperor Shah Jahan-II, 1719 AD

Shah Jahan-II was born to Nurunisa Begum. The Sayyids, after killing his brother Rafi-ud-Darjat, installed him as the King. But they would not allow him to move out of the Red Fort.

Emperor Nekusiyar/ Nikusiyar Mohammed, 1719 AD

Nekusiyar Mohammed was the 12th Mughal emperor. He took the throne in 1719 AD at the age of 40. He was the grandson of Aurangzeb and was brought up in a harem in Agra. A local minister Birbal (not the Birbal of Akbar's fame) used him as puppet and proclaimed him emperor. As a prince, he had spent his life inside the harem and talked like a catamite. He was laughingly ignored. He was put in jail by the Sayyid brothers. He died around 1743 AD at the age of 63. Inayat Ullah Khan continued to be the governor of Kashmir.

Emperor Mohammed Ibrahim, 1720 AD

Mohammed Ibrahim was the 13th Mughal emperor. He was born to Nurunisa Begum. He took the throne in 1720, after a war of succession. He was also the claimant of the throne at the behest of Sayyids after Muhammad Shah joined the Nizam's camp. He fought with Mohammad Shah at Hasanpur and was defeated.

Inayat Ullah Khan continued as governor of Kashmir

In view of the prevailing conditions in Delhi, there was no interference in the working of the governor Inayat Ullah Khan. He had assumed more or less the powers of a ruler. But he did not declare himself as the King of Kashmir as he was dedicated to Mughal rulers.

Emperor Mohammad Shah 1720-1748 AD

Mohammad Shah, son of Khujista Akhtar Jahan Shah and Qudsiya Begum, became the emperor of India. Mohammad Shah took over the reins of the country when the Mughal dynasty was on the wane. He is always referred to as Mohammad Shah Rangeela—the word rangeela meaning a man who is given to worldly pleasures. He was married to Malika Uzzamani. After assuming the kingship, he dismissed Governor Inayat Ullah and appointed Abdul Samad Khan as governor. This governor restored the restrictions on Hindus and even Shias.

Inayat Ullah, who was initially appointed as the governor of Kashmir, had left a legacy of being an absentee governor who appointed deputies to administer the country. Similarly, Abdul Samad Khan also appointed his subedar, Abdul Barkat Khan, as his deputy. This way dozens of governors were appointed who employed their deputies in turn. This made the Kashmiris miserable. Added to this, natural calamities such as acute famines befell the valley. The hapless people did not get any substantial help from the centre.

Meanwhile, a new star was rising in the firmament of Persia, namely Nadir Shah, who had captured the throne of Persia in 1736. He easily captured Gazni too. Then in 1739, Nadir Shah invaded India. Mohammad Shah, the emperor, was said to be busy in his enjoyments. According to Reginald Massey in *The Music of India*,[111] "When Nadir Shah the Persian conqueror was advancing on Delhi in 1737, the emperor was watching a musical drama and no one dared to interrupt his enjoyment of it. The producer, therefore, did some quick improvisation. He forced one of the performers, acting a comic part, to sing the news on the stage as part of the play." Though Mohammad Shah understood, it was too late. Two days after reaching Delhi, Nadir Shah ordered a general massacre and thousands of men and women were killed and dead bodies lay scattered in the streets of Delhi. After the victory, Nadir Shah made Mohammad Shah his prisoner. The economic deterioration of the country plus the degenerating political conditions and the weak kings were enough temptations for any adventurer to come and try his fate. Nadir Shah decided to try his. Only those who could pay heavily were spared. Thus, Nadir Shah collected an enormous booty from India and went away to Persia.

He was also keen to take the famous 'Koh-i-Noor', the "Mountain of Light" from Mohammad Shah. The diamond was with the Mughals from the time of Babur. He searched for the jewel which was nowhere to be found, though a desperate Nadir continued the search. As per Monisha Bhardwaj,[112] "Many frustrated days later, a harem woman secretly informed him (Nadir Shah) that the emperor always stored it in the pleated folds of his turban. On hearing this, Nadir Shah devised an elaborate plan by which he could obtain the bewitching gem. He invited

Mohammed Shah to a feast, and between luscious courses, proposed an exchange of turbans in a ceremony of friendship and goodwill. Mohammad Shah was rendered speechless, but unable to refuse this courtesy, he gracefully handed over the turban." This way, the Koh-i-Noor went to Persia. The jewel travelled back to India and became the possession of Maharaja Ranjit Singh. After Maharaja Ranjit Singh's death, the Koh-i-Noor was passed on to British Royalty, and since then, this diamond is in the crown of British Royalty.

Governors under the reign of Mohammad Shah:

Inayat Ullah Khan, 1720-1721 AD

As usual, Inayat Ullah Khan's deputy Mir Ahmed Khan governed Kashmir, followed by other deputies—Abdullah Khan Dehbedi and Abdul Samad Khan. During this period, there were Shia-Sunni communal riots in the valley. The riots later on flared into Hindu-Muslim conflicts.

Abdul Samad Khan, 1721-1723 AD

Abdul Samad Khan was a strong governor of Kashmir. He worked for peace. He had five assistants. It was during his period that Kashmir witnessed one of the worst famines. However in 1723 AD, he was dismissed and a new governor, Azim Khan, was appointed.

Azim Khan, 1723-1724 AD

Azim Khan tried to diminish the aftermath of the famine. The prices of commodities shot up and people died of hunger.

Inayat Ullah Khan, 1724-1725 AD

Inayat Ullah Khan once again ruled Kashmir as governor. But he could not bring many reforms. By this time he had become old and mostly remained ill. He died in 1725 AD.

Aqidat Khan, 1725-1727 AD

Aqidat Khan invited Abu Barkat Khan to assist him. Both the governor and his assistant created hell for the people of Kashmir leading to resentment among the masses. According to RK Parmu,[113] "With notorious Abu Barkat Khan as deputy, law and order came to a standstill, both high and low suffered the consequences."

Asghar Khan, 1727-1729 AD

Replacement of governor Aqidat Khan by Asghar Khan did not give any relief to the people of Kashmir. He also depended on Abu Barkat Khan, who tyrannised the people. Ultimately, he was ousted and sent out of the valley.

In view of the people's revolt, the king appointed Amir Khan as governor.

Amir Khan, 1729-1736 AD

Amir Khan did not change his deputy Abu Barkat Khan. But after two years, he got fed up of him and dismissed him from the post of deputy governor. In his place was appointed Ehtram Khan, who proved to be most inefficient, incompetent and ineffective. Amir Khan had no choice but to bring Abu Barkat Khan back as his deputy.

Dil Diler Khan, 1736-1737 AD

Amir Khan was replaced by Dil Diler Khan. But he did not visit the valley and also continued to depend on Abu Barkat Khan as his deputy. When a devastating flood gripped the valley, there was complete destruction all around. The Bombas tribe again raised their head. According to PNK Bamzai,[114] "To add to the miseries of people, Haibat Khan again raided the northern district of the Valley. But now Abdul Barkat despatched a strong force under a powerful Kashmiri noble Mir Jaffar Kanth—who not only defeated Haibat but brought the Bombas tribe under complete subjugation."

Fakhar-Ud-Daulah, 1737-1738 AD

Fakhar-ud-Daulah remained governor only for one year. He was assisted by Qazi khan. During this period, Mir Jaffar Kanth raised a rebellion. The governor and his assistant failed to suppress the disgruntled elements (as per RK Parmu).[115] They were therefore replaced by Inayat Ullah Khan Kashmiri.

Inayat Ullah Khan II, 1738-1740 AD

Inayat Ullah Khan appointed Hassam-ud-din Khan as his assistant. The previous governor Fakhar-ud-Daulah had sought help from Nadir Shah. He got a royal *Farman* from Nadir Shah and imprisoned the deputy, Hassam-ud-din Khan, who was essentially a weak man. But the Kashmiri nobles fought against Fakhar-ud-Daulah and he was forced to leave the valley. Inayat Ullah Khan consolidated his position and personally looked after the administration of Kashmir. Just then Abu Barkat appeared on the scene and murdered him. Thus Asad Ullah Khan became the governor.

Asad Ullah Khan, 1740-1744 AD

Asad Ullah Khan could not change deputy Abu Barkat Khan, who had by this time gained lots of power and popularity. He was also supported by the Gujjars. But soon both of them fell out. Meanwhile, a trusted noble raised a rebellion. He joined hands with the Shias and attacked Srinagar. Abu Barkat Khan had grown old and he could not fight the rebellion. This move was the last nail in his coffin. According to PNK Bamzai,[116] "The rebel leader, Bir Ullah Beg, won over most of the troops of Abu Barkat Khan and thus succeeded in controlling the whole Valley. Abu Barkat Khan was arrested and thrown into prison." With this, there was a civil war in the Valley. Mohammad Shah appointed Abu Mansur Khan Safdar Jung as the next governor.

Abu Mansur Khan, 1745– 1748 AD

Abu Mansur Khan was an intelligent man. He too did not go to Kashmir and made Jang Nisar Khan his deputy. Nisar Khan acted tactfully. He sent Abu Barkat Khan to Delhi. He also crushed the rebellion and appointed Bir Ullah to a high post. Jang Nisar improved the conditions in the valley within a short span. But the development was followed by a severe famine. According to RK Parmu,[117] "Kashmir suffered devastating effects of famine and civil strife caused by the followers of Mahtavi Khan in 1748." The famine had shattered the Valley. Meanwhile Abu Mansur Khan replaced Nisar Khan and made Afrasiyab Khan his deputy. Mahtavi Khan was a local leader who ignited civil strife.

Emperor Ahmed Shah, 1748-1753 AD

After the death of Mohammad Shah, his son Ahmed Shah Bhadur was proclaimed the emperor of India on 29 April 1748. Ahmed Shah was only 21 years old when he was called upon to shoulder the responsibilities of an emperor. Born to Qudsiya Begum, he was married to Gauhar Banu Begum. Being a young and inexperienced monarch he proved an utter failure. It is also alleged that he was pusillanimous, vicious, dissipated and perfidious. Such a person could not cope with a formidable opposition from alienated Hindus, Rajputs, Marathas and Sikhs.

Meanwhile, on 2 June 1747, Nadir Shah was assassinated. Among his chief commanders was Ahmed Shah Abdali, an Afghan who had risen to a high rank. Abdali collected the members of his tribe, established himself at Herat, and captured Kandahar. He also dismissed the governors appointed by Nadir Shah. This way he captured the whole of Afghanistan. The next thing he did was to attack Punjab in 1749 AD and he retired after getting a large bounty.

Because of a weak Mughal emperor, the political conditions in Kashmir deteriorated. On account of misrule of Mughal governors and their agents, the people of Kashmir longed for a change. But events show that while wanting a change they approached the brute Afghans in the person of Ahmed Shah Abdali to invade Kashmir. Mir Muqim Kanth and Khwaja Zahir Diddamari, the most influential Muslims of Kashmir, went and invited him to invade which he gladly accepted. In 1753 AD, Abdali sent a strong force under Abdullah Khan Ishak Aqasi. A war took place at Shupiyan and ultimately Ishak Khan defeated the Mughal forces and this way Kashmir came under Afghans.

Bahadur Shah Zaffar was the last of the Mughal emperors in India. He was born on October 24, 1775, and was the son of Akbar Shah II from his Hindu wife Lalbai. He became the Mughal emperor upon his father's death on September 28, 1838.

Abu Mansur Khan 1748–1758 AD

Abu Mansur Khan continued to be the governor of Kashmir. The civil war continued and his deputy Afrasiyab Khan could not subdue it. Instead, he was assassinated. Abu Mansur Khan then appointed Ahmed Khan, son of Afrasiyab Khan, as his deputy. Ahmed Khan remained as deputy only for a short time and was replaced by Malik Hassan Irani. It seems the deputies could not handle the situation arising out of the unfortunate famine which had left a trail of devastation and poverty. Sensing the gravity of the situation, Abu Mansur Khan replaced Ahmed Shah and appointed Quli Khan as the governor of Kashmir.

Quli Khan, 1751–1751 AD

After his appointment as governor, Quli Khan sent a Kashmiri noble known as Mir Muqim Kanth as deputy governor. According to R K Parmu,[118] "For the first time a leading Kashmiri noble, Mir Muqim Kanth, was appointed deputy governor. Meanwhile, there was a rebellion of the soldiery under Abdul Qasim Khan, the son of Abu Barkat Khan. As soon as Mir Muqim Kanth took over, he reduced their Jageer and also reduced their allowance. Mir Muqim Kanth's house was put aflame. This shocked him and he resigned from the post of deputy governor."

This was the turning moment in the history of Kashmir— when Mir Muqim Kanth along with Khwaja Zahir went to Ahmed Shah Abdali and asked him to take over the reins of Kashmir.

Salient features of Mughal rule over Kashmir

"Hindustan is a place of little charm. There is no beauty in its people, no graceful social intercourse, no poetic talent or understanding, etiquette, or manliness. The arts and crafts have no harmony or symmetry. There are no good horses, grapes, melons or other fruits. There is no ice, cold water, good food or bread in the markets. There are no baths and no Madrasas. There are no candles, torches or candlesticks." This was stated by Shehenshah Babur, founder of Mughal Empire in the *Baburnama*,[119]. It is strange how Babur framed this opinion about a country which had a magnificent and glorious past and splendid cultural heritage. Perhaps Babur did not visit Kashmir, hence this statement.

Mughal monarchs, therefore, felt that their kingdom was incomplete without annexing Kashmir to it. Even with a large army, Babur failed to invade Kashmir. Kashmir nationalism was so intense then that the Mughal forces had to withdraw. After the death of Babur, Humayun got involved in a war with Sher Shah Suri. Humayun was defeated and therefore decided to proceed to Kashmir. However, later, he did not go but sent Mirza Haydar Duglat at the invitation of Abdul Magarey and Ragi Chak. Again Kashmir nationalism prevailed as people joined hands to fight the enemy. They sent back the Mughal forces. It was only during Akbar's rule that the Mughals succeeded in capturing the throne of Kashmir.

During the early years of Mughal rule, the governors allotted lavish jageers to their own people and these new jageerdars fleeced the peasantry. Akbar, Jahangir, Shah Jahan and even Aurangzeb made land revenue reforms that benefitted the peasants.

Position of women during Mughal period

The Mughals produced a galaxy of great women. Women had much say in the administration of the country. Women like Noor Jahan, Begum Hamida, Akbar's mother, Mumtaz Mahal, Jahanara, Zeb-un-Nissa were de-facto rulers of India. However, a famous Mughal governor and foster brother of Akbar, Mirza Aziz Koka's satire on Mughals is, "Every man should have four wives; a Persian, with whom he can converse; a woman from Khurasan for the housework; a Hindu woman to raise the children, and one from Transoxiana, whom he can beat as a warning to the others."

Crops and pulses, vegetables and fruits

During the Mughal period, there was not much change in the crops that were grown. Rice, pulses, wheat were already being grown and some canals were built for irrigation. According to Abdul Majid Mattoo,[120] "During the reign of Akbar, Yusuf Khan Rizwi built a canal connecting a stream known as Nullah Sind with Baghi-ilahi. Under Jahangir, some old canals like Lachama Kul were repaired under the supervision of Malik Haydar, and Harvan canal was laid out for watering Nur Afza Bagh."

The rice and pulses from the valley were of inferior quality. The pulses and rice of Rajouri, Poonch and Kishtwar were much superior. Even today, people appreciate the Rajmah (kidney beans) from Kishtwar. Even saffron from Kishtwar was much superior to that from other parts of the valley. Saffron was given great importance during the Mughal rule. According to *Tuzuk-e-Jahangiri*,[121] "In Kishtwar, there is produced much wheat, barley, lentils, millet, and pulse. Differing from Kashmir, it produces little rice. Its saffron is finer than that of Kashmir." As regards vegetables, they were always in abundance in the valley. The floating gardens would produce many vegetables and they were exported to other places.

Though Kashmir is full of fruits, its quality can vary. According to *Tuzuk-e-Jahangiri*,[122] "There are pears of the best kind, better than those of Kabul or Badakhshan, and nearly equal to those of Samarkand. The apples of Kashmir are celebrated for their goodness. The guavas are middling. Grapes are plentiful, but most of them are harsh and inferior, and the pomegranates are not worth much. Watermelons of the best kind can be obtained. There are no Shah-Tut but there are other mulberries everywhere....In fact, the mulberries of Kashmir are not fit to eat, with the exception of some on trees grown in gardens, but the leaves are used to feed the silkworm."

There are a few varieties of cherries. Says a *Tuzuk-e-Jahangiri*,[123] "Before my father's time there were no Shah-Alu (cherries). Muhammad Quli Afshar brought them from Kabul and planted them, and there are now ten or fifteen fruitbearing trees."

Land revenue arrangements

According to William Wilson Hunter,[124] "Akbar's revenue system was based on the ancient Hindu customs, and survives to this day. He first executed a survey to measure the land. His officers then found out the produce of each acre of land and settled the government share, amounting to one-third of the gross produce. Finally, they fixed the rates at which this share of the crop might be commuted into money payment." The Mughals had, to a great extent, organised law enforcement agencies, revenue assessment and collection system. The officers were:

- Patwari — who kept record of the land owners
- Tahsildar — the one who would collect the produce as taxes
- Amil or Karori — to expedite the collection of revenue
- Fotedar or Khazinadar — the treasurer in each Pargana
- Amin or Munsif — appointed as assessment officer
- Qanungo — to decode the rules and traditional practices
- Chowdhury — In charge of one or two Parganas
- Dewan — the chief revenue and finance officer
- Subedar — or the governor

Judiciary

- Qazi — occupied third place after Subedar and Dewan
- Mufti — The Qazi would seek his advice in legal matters

Police

- Thanedar — the in-charge of one small Thana
- Kotwal — police officer, just one or two in a Subah
- Muhtasib — looked after the public morale.
- Bakshi — the chief of the police next to Subedar

In the words of Sir Francis Younghusband, who termed the Mughals as "Splendid Mughals", they had an obsession for art, architecture and laying beautiful gardens. Their aesthetic tastes were superb. For instance, the beautiful Baradari such as the one at Shalimar Gardens with beautiful paintings on the roof is one example. In fact, one Baradari at Shalimar garden has walls of polished black stone, which shines even today. Around this Baradari, there are tanks that are full of fountains. There is also the Hari Parbat fort constructed by Akbar.

The Mughal passion for erecting gardens is well known. The Shalimar garden was constructed by Jahangir, and Prince Khurram supervised the construction of a canal that passes through the garden. The Nishat Garden, which also came up during Jahangir's rule, was constructed by Asaf Khan. This garden has become more popular than Shalimar. It is erected at one end of the Dal Lake.

Dara Shikoh, son of Shah Jahan, built Pari Mahal on the ruins of a Buddhist monastery. Dara was a follower of Qadiri order of Sufi Islam.

Nasim Bagh, Cheshma Shahi, Achbal and Verinag are some of the other famous gardens constructed by the Mughals.

After the death of Aurangzeb, there was a decline in the Mughal rule in Kashmir. The rule of his successors was marked by local riots and internecine struggles. There were great famines in the valley. Curiously, in other parts of India, the famines were due to insufficient monsoons but in Kashmir they were due to heavy snowfall or rainfall. Constant rainfall swelled rivers and canals which caused floods.

The Mughal rule in Kashmir was both good and bad. While on one hand, the kings tried to improve the conditions of the country, some of their governors created havoc. However, when the black clouds of darkness hovered over the waning Mughal supremacy, the valley woke up to the dawn of the Afghan rule.

Seventeen
Kashmir under Afghans

The Mughal Empire in Delhi was in a state of disintegration due to weak emperors who ruled over India after the death of Aurangzeb. Due to the crusading Islamic idealism of Aurangzeb, bitterness crept among the people. The treatment of the majority of Hindus was so harsh that it planted the seeds of revolt and disenchantment against the Mughal administration and the Mughal monarchy.

In Kashmiri language, there is a phrase — *Kuali Khote Kual Sardie*, which means 'a man, while wandering in search of a hot stream, finds only a cold stream'. He proceeds further in the hope of finding a warm stream only to find the next one colder than the one he left. The people of Kashmir thought that with the ushering in of the Afghan rule, their problems would be over but the new rule brought more miseries.

The Afghan rule in Kashmir was unbearably harsh and ruthless. Not only Hindus but Muslims also became the target of Afghan rulers. Writes Zahid G Muhammad in *Press and Freedom Struggle in Jammu and Kashmir* (Article),[1] "After Mughals it was Afghans that ruthlessly trampled down the people of the state. The Afghan governors proved to be ferocious bigots, tyrants and barbarians. The women, both Hindu and Muslim, were targets of the lustful eyes of some lascivious Afghan soldiers. Many beautiful damsels were put in their harems. Many Kashmiris, both male and female, were captured and sent as presents to their masters, friends or kinsmen at Kabul."

On the Indian front, the decline of the Mughal Empire had led to territorial gains for the Maratha confederacy. The Peshwa from Maharashtra had become a very potent force to reckon with. Peshwa Baji Rao-I wanted to conquer Punjab. He thought that if he struck at the trunk of the withering tree (of Mughals) the branches would fall themselves. He subjugated Gujarat, Malwa and Bundelkhand. In 1737 AD, he appeared at the gate of Delhi and could have ended the Mughal Empire in one stroke, but retreated. He was not content with the kingdom of the south. He wanted to establish dominion in the North too. Ahmed Shah Abdali was equally ambitious to gain control over Northern India.

The Sikhs, inhabitants of Punjab, also wanted to establish their independent rule in their own mother country. From 1755 to 1765 AD, the Sikhs, under the leadership of Jassa Singh Ramgharia, Jassa Singh Ahluwalia and also Ala Singh Jat had opposed Ahmed Shah Abdali but later on accepted his sovereignty. Kashmir could not have been an exception. Quli Khan, Mughal governor in Kashmir, had appointed a very influential Muslim, Mir Muqim, as his deputy but he was forced to retire soon. The Mughal army posted in the valley started harassing people. As per tradition, Mir Muqim and other influential Muslims such as Khwaja Zahir-ud-din Diddamari approached Ahmed Shah Abdali to invade Kashmir, which Ahmed Shah very much wished. "He dispatched Abdulla Khan Ishak Aqasi, one of his trusted generals, at the head of an Afghan army 15,000 strong to conquer Kashmir."[2]

In this battle, the Mughal army, under the leadership of Abdul Qasim, fought heroically but weakened against the onslaught of the Afghan army. Abdul Qasim was defeated and Kashmir came under the rule of Afghans. The Afghan military leader Abdulla Khan unfurled the Afghan flag on Hari Parbat fort and he was declared the first Afghan governor of Kashmir. The Afghans ruled over Kashmir for a period of 66 years.

The topography of Afghanistan on the north-west side of India is mountainous and rugged. There is a vast stretch of land locked by different countries in Central Asia. It is bound by Russia to the north, Pakistan to the east-south, China to the east, and Iran to the west. Originally, it was known as Arianna or Bactria. It later became famous as Khurasan (the land of rising sun.) Earlier, Afghanistan had served as a passage for traders, tourists and invaders such as Persians, Turks and Mughals to India. This was the ideal passage for ancient civilizations such as Aryans and Greeks, and invaders like Alexander, Mohammed Gazni and Mohammed Gore.

Accepting of Islam by Afghanistan is not an extraordinary event. In fact, in the first quarter of the seventh century AD, Prophet Mohammed laid the foundation of Islam and within a short period of eighty years after his death, the new religion spread to many countries of the world including Persia, Syria, Western Turkistan, Sind, Egypt and Afghanistan. Before Afghanistan came under Islam, the people used to follow Buddhism. During the reign of Kanishka, Buddhism prevailed in Afghanistan. King Samanid of Persia had paramountcy over Afghanistan. One of King Samanid's main slaves named Alaptgin had impressed his master so much by his intelligence and his valour that the king appointed him as the governor of Khurasan. Soon Alaptgin declared himself as an independent king of Khurasan but he died in the year 962 AD. His slave Subuktgin got the kingdom of Gazni and Afghanistan. Subuktgin was a great warrior and a military general who organised the youth in Afghanistan into a compact body of fighters. With them he started conquering other places and his kingdom extended from Sirhind to Lamghan and Multan.

King Ahmed Shah Abdali, 1723–1772 AD

Born in 1723 AD, Ahmed Shah Abdali was the first king (Ameer-e-Afghan) and founder of Afghanistan. His father, Mohammed Zaman Khan, was a descendant of the Sadozai dynasty belonging to the Popalzai clan of the Abdali tribe. After becoming king, he titled himself as Durr-i-Durrani, meaning 'the pearl of pearls'. He was known as Durrani, and so was his successor.

Ahmed Shah alias Ahmed Khan, was a brave and fearless fighter. In his twenties, he was one of the most trusted and important soldiers of Nadir Shah, who had collected enormous wealth by looting other countries. Nadir Shah also took the 'Koh-i-Noor' from India. In spite of his fondness for Ahmed Shah, he always kept a watchful eye over him, but the officers of all ranks in the army treated him, in private, with great respect. When Nadir Shah was assassinated in 1747 AD, Ahmed Shah was left with Nadir Shah's treasury and became commander of his 15,000 troops, who gladly accepted him as their leader.

It was in October 1747 that the assembly of Pashtu chiefs held a 'Loya Jirga' (Assembly of Heads of Cities, Towns and Villages) which after nine days of deliberation elected Ahmad Khan as their Shah, the king of Afghanistan. He came to be known as Ahmed Shah Abdali. Immediately after taking over as king, he began to consolidate and enlarge his kingdom. He seized Gazni and then Kabul. He wrested from the Mughals their territories west of the Indus. The Pashtu tribesmen rallied under his banner, and Ahmed Shah led them on nine campaigns into India in search of booty and territorial conquests.

His campaign against India started in the year 1747. In 1751 AD, he razed the famous Amritsar temple, along with its sacred tank, to the ground, in which thousands of Sikhs were killed. George Forster says,[3] "Pyramids were erected, and covered with the heads of slaughtered Sicques (Sikhs) and it is mentioned that Ahmad Shah caused the wall of the principal mosques, which had been polluted by the Sicques (Sikhs) to be washed with their blood, that contamination might be removed, and ignominy offered to the religion of Mahomet (Mohammad), expiated."

Ahmed Shah added Kashmir, Sind, and western Punjab to his domains and founded an empire which extended from eastern Persia to northern India and from the Amu Darya (Amu river) to the Indian Ocean. In 1761, after the battle of Panipat against the Marathas, he established his supremacy in India. Once in Delhi, he took off with as much wealth as possible, thereby enriching his treasury.

With the decline of the Mughal Empire, the Marathas, under the command of Sadashiva Rao Bhau, attacked Delhi to oust the Mughals. However, Ahmed Shah Abdali marched with his huge forces and thus was fought the famous Battle of Panipat.

Afghan Emperor Durrani deputed 29 governors to Kashmir. By and large, all these governors resorted to loot, repression and persecution of Hindus. When the Kashmiris invited Ahmed Shah Abdali to invade Kashmir in the hope of being saved from the clutches of oppressive Mughal governors, they soon realised, in the words of Sir Francis

Younghusband, the difference between "brute Pathans" and "splendid Mughals". The Pathan rule proved ruthless and fearful for Kashmiris. Shah Abdali died in 1772 AD at Murghah in Afghanistan. Some of the chroniclers have placed his date of death as 1773 AD.

Governors under the reign of Ahmed Shah Abdali

Abdullah Khan Ishak Aqasi, 1753 AD

"It was not, therefore, anything surprising or unprecedented that the Kashmir nobles sought assistance of Ahmed Shah Durrani in this misfortune, in the hope that the Afghans would prove to be the friends of Kashmiris in the days of their need. But no sooner had Durrani annexed the valley to his Afghan kingdom then the Kashmiris realised that they were thrown from the frying pan into the fire. The very first Afghan governor Abdullah Khan Ishak Aqasi, who ruled the valley for only six months, proved to be a ferocious bigot, a tyrant and barbarian",[4] says Prem Nath Bazaz.

Abdullah Khan's assistant Mir Muqim Kanth, says Anand Kaul,[5] "Was an extreme figure of terror to the Pandits and many Pandit families fled away to other countries in his time." Abdul Aqasi ruled Kashmir only for six months. As per R K Parmu,[6] "He laid the foundations of the government with the blood and tears of Kashmiris. He tyrannised them and killed many in order to extract all the money they possessed." He made businessmen his target. The traders had to shut shop and the economy of the country was in shambles. This gave rise to rebellion and he was forced to quit the country and post his deputy, Khwaja Abdullah Khan, as the governor of Kashmir. But soon, Abdul Aqasi's adviser Punjabi Khetri, Sukhjewanmal turned the tables.

Raja Sukhjewanmal, 1753-1762 AD (Declares himself king)

Raja Sukhjewanmal was the first Hindu, a Punjabi Khetri of Bhera (West Punjab) to become the governor of Kashmir. In fact, he, with the help of Abdul Hassan Khan Bandy, a Kashmiri noble, killed Khwaja Abdullah Khan and his two sons and proclaimed himself the governor. Raja Sukhjewanmal ruled Kashmir for eight years. During his rule, he had to face the ire of Ahmad Shah Abdali. Though he ratified him as the governor of Kashmir, yet he sent his own trusted man Khwaja Kijak as deputy governor to keep an eye on him. Abdali forced Sukhjewanmal to pay heavy tributes, which he could not do. According to R K Parmu,[7] "The demand itself was so preposterous that Sukhjewanmal found it impossible to satisfy, particularly when Kashmir had only recently been drained of its wealth by Abdali's governor, Abdullah Khan Ishak Aqasi."

Because of non-payment of tributes, there was a fight between Kashmiri nobles and the Afghan nobles loyal to Ahmed Shah Abdali. Sukhjewanmal, with the help of Kashmir nobles, attacked Abdali's trusted officers and killed Khwaja Kijak, Malik Hassan Irani and Azam Khan at Baramulla. Narendra Sahagala writes,[8] "King Sukhjewanmal declared himself independent soon after assuming power in Kashmir. He snapped all ties with Ahmed Shah Abdali, who declared open war for eliminating this Hindu king of Kashmir. He launched an armed campaign on Kashmir but was defeated. During the reign of Sukhjewanmal, both the Hindus and the Muslims lived a life of peace. Different relief operations were carried out and Hindus were given back their land. Trade and agriculture were encouraged and Sukhjewanmal appointed Abul Hassan as his Prime Minister. The two worked together and contributed to the development of Kashmir without any discrimination."

It was during Sukhjewanmal's tenure that Sikhs from Punjab came and settled in various parts of Kashmir but mostly in a place known as modern Traal. According to TG Vigne,[9] "Trahul (modern Traal) is the principal residence of Kashmirian Sikhs; that is, Sikhs whose ancestors first came to Kashmir in the services of Rajah Suk Juwan, a Hindu of Shikarpur, and who was sent to the valley as governor by Timur Shah of Kabul." With the appointment of Abul Hassan Khan Bandy as the prime minister, there was peace all around and the country started progressing economically too. When a famine broke out in the valley, he introduced rationing and this brought relief to the people to a great extent.

The defeated Ahmed Shah Abdali, meanwhile, tried another plan to regain Kashmir. He released a Kashmiri noble Mir Muqim Kanth, who was previously a deputy governor, to act as his secret agent. Mir Muqim tried to create a rift between Raja Sukhjewanmal and Abul Bandy. "But all was not to go well with Kashmir," Jia Lal Kilam writes,[10] "Mir Muqim, who was all these years biding time at Kabul, having learnt of the Afghan discomfiture at the hands of Sukhjewanmal, thought it useless to wait any longer at Kabul, and started for Kashmir. On arrival there, he found no scope to regain the lost power. He could trust nothing better than his favourite weapon of intrigue. In a short while, he succeeded in bringing about a rupture in the harmonious relations that existed till then between Sukhjewanmal and his prime minister Abul Hassan Bandy. The result was that Abul Hassan was sent to prison and Mir Muqim was appointed in his stead in the year 1757 AD. But Mir Muqim could not maintain his position for more than a year."

Abul Hassan Bandy was prime minister again. The continuous hostility between him and Mir Muqim Kanth so disturbed Raja Sukhjewanmal that he stripped them of every responsibility and appointed Pandit Mahanand Dhar, a Kashmiri Pandit as his prime minister. Dhar was a devout Hindu who immediately banned Azan and cow slaughter by Kashmiri Muslims. This move gave birth to many enemies within the Muslim community.

In June 1762, after his victory over the Maratha confederacy at the third battle of Panipat, Ahmed Shah Abdali sent his general Nur-ud-Din Khan Bamzai with a huge force to attack Raja Sukhjewanmal. Maharaja Ranjit Dev of Jammu also helped Abdali by sending his eldest son Brij Dev with a large contingent of forces. Brij Dev started in June and when he reached the Banihal pass he found that Sukhjewanmal had closed the passes. However, the whole contingent under the charge of Nur-ud-Din entered the Valley. Writes Sukhdev Singh Charak,[11] "He (Sukhjewanmal) had fortified the mountain passes. But in spite of this, the combined army of three-four thousand Afghans and about the same number of Dogras marched into Kashmir through the Tosamaidan pass." Sukhjewanmal fought valiantly but was defeated and captured. "He was blinded and taken to Lahore before Ahmad Shah Abdali in a wretched condition. The latter ordered him to be trampled to death by an elephant,"[12] says R K Parmu.

Nur-Ud-Din Khan Bamzai, 1763 AD

After the death of Raja Sukhjewanmal, Nur-ud-Din Bamzai took over the reins of the country. As governor, he restored law and order within three months and left for Kabul leaving behind Buland Khan Bamzai as his successor and governor of Kashmir.

Buland Khan Bamzai, 1763-1765 AD

Buland Khan Bamzai remained as governor of Kashmir for two years. He neglected the work of the government. Added to this, a Shia-Sunni conflict marred the peace and tranquillity of the country. When the report of the conflict reached Kabul, He was recalled and Nur-ud-Din was installed as governor for the second time.

Nur-ud-Din Khan, 1765-1766 AD

As soon as he took over as governor, Nur-ud-Din appointed Mir Muqim Kanth and Pandit Kailas Dhar as *Madarulmiham* (chief minister) and *Sahibkar* (prime minister). Both the nobles did not see eye to eye. Meanwhile, Nur-ud-Din fell for a Kashmiri girl and put her in his harem. This action of his created great resentment in the minds of the people, writes Jia Lal Kilam,[13] "They went to Mir Muqim's house and asked him to intercede on their behalf with Nur-ud-din Khan and get the girl set free. Nur-ud-Din had expected Mir Muqim to side with him, and he became greatly resentful to find that Mir Muqim not only sided with the people, but even fanned the flames of agitation." So, he got him killed but he manoeuvred the murder in such a way that the suspicion fell on Kailas Dhar. In fact, Nur-ud-Din called Mir Qanungo and gave him a pistol on which the name of Kailas Dhar was inscribed. He was told to shoot Mir Muqim dead and leave the pistol there.

Kailas Dhar was upset at the news that Mir Muqim was murdered by Mir Qanungo, his arch enemy. When the governor came to know about the murder, he tried to exploit Kailas Dhar instead of punishing him by amassing as much wealth as he could. Kailas Dar then went to Lahore to meet Ahmed Shah Abdali and apprised him of what was going on in Kashmir. As a result, Abdali summoned Nur-ud-Din, who left for Kabul leaving behind Jan Muhammad Khan to look after the country.

Lal Khan Khatak, 1766 AD

Jan Mohammad was not formally appointed as the governor of Kashmir. When he took over from Nur-ud-Din Bamzai, there was, at that time, a trusted Khatak chief of Nur-ud-Din by the name of Lal Khan who was stationed at Biru where he had constructed a strong fort. As soon as Nur-ud-Din left for Kabul, Lal Khan wasted no time in attacking Jan Mohammad and the Kashmiri army. He defeated him and began to rule

Kashmir. Though timid, he was a tyrant and looted people in the valley. He was ruthless towards the Hindus. When Ahmed Shah Abdali heard of Lal Khan's reputation, he appointed Khurram Khan as the governor of Kashmir. Lal Khan Khatak fled from the valley the moment he heard Khurram was coming with a large army.

Khurram Khan, 1766-1767 AD

When Abdali appointed Khurram Khan as the governor of Kashmir, he also appointed Pandit Kailas Dhar as the revenue collector. Khurram as per R K Parmu, was secular. Though a bit superstitious, he was an easy-going person.

All these years, Mir Muqim's son, Mir Fazil Kanth, believed that Pandit Kailas Dhar was his father's murderer. To avenge his father's death, he sought the help of Mohammad Khan, a Bombas chief, attacked Khurram Khan's forces and took possession of Sopore town. Fazil was also joined by Lal Mohammad. Collecting a force, Khurram Khan and Kailas Dhar started for Sopore to fight the enemy but on reaching Pattan, Khurram Khan had a change of mind and taking Kailas Dhar along with him, headed towards Kabul. The city was left at the mercy of Mir Faqirulla, Lal Mohammad and their supporters. "Having found no body to withstand him, Fazil Kanth himself assumed the reins of the country's rule in the year 1767 AD," says Jia Lal Kilam,[14] "He started his rule with an announcement of allegiance towards Abdali, and began to rule in his name."

Mir Fazil Kanth, 1767-1768 AD

The rule of Fazil Kanth was shortlived. He took over as the governor of Kashmir solely with the intention of avenging the death of his father. Believing that Pandit Kailas Dhar had killed his father, he began to work for the destruction of Pandits in a well-planned manner. He appointed a large number of Bombas from the neighbouring hilly districts. The Bombas treated Kashmiri Pandits miserably. As per R K Parmu,[15] "Many were killed and some two thousand were compelled to embrace Islam."

Ahmed Shah Abdali came to know about these atrocities and sent Nur-ud-Din Khan Bamzai at the head of large army against Fazil Kanth. Ultimately, Kanth fled and took shelter with the Khakas Chief in Karana and died there. Nur-ud-Din became the governor of Kashmir for the third time

Nur-Ud-Din Khan Bamzai, 1768-1769 AD

Nur-ud-Din Khan's first priority was establishing law and order. But no sooner had he taken over as governor than Ahmed Shah Abdali appointed Khazanchi as the governor of Kashmir. As soon as Muhammad Khazanchi came from Kabul to take over the administration, there was a fight between them. Khazanchi was defeated in Muzaffarabad and he fled to Kabul to report the matter to Ahmad Shah Abdali.

Abdali was furious and he sent Pandit Kailas Dhar and Khurram Khan with an army of 20,000 to subdue Nur-ud-Din. On learning about this, Nur-ud-Din left Srinagar, leaving the country in the hands of Lal Khan Khatak. PMK Bamzai writes,[16] "Nur-ud-Din left Lal Khan Khatak in charge of the operations and himself went to Jammu to watch the course that the subsequent events would take." Without much resistance, Khurram Khan entered the city and took over as the governor of Kashmir. Lal Khan fled from the valley.

Khurram Khan, 1770 AD

Khurram Khan tried to restore peace in the valley. But Lal Khan Khatak gave restless nights to him even though he was in hiding. Khurram deputed his commander Amir Khan Jawansher to bring Lal Khan to book. But PNK Bamzai says,[17] "Khurram Khan was feeble and could not act with determination against Lal Khan. Amir Khan Jawansher reported this to Ahmed Shah Abdali following which Khurram Khan had to resign and Amir Khan Jawansher became the governor of Kashmir."

Amir Khan Jawansher 1770–1772 AD

Amir Khan Jawansher was a Shia by faith. As soon as he took over the reins, he launched a massive attack against Lal Khan and defeated him. Lal Khan had to flee to Ghari where he died. Amir Khan then appointed as chief minister Mir Fazil Kanth, the son of Mir Muqim Kanth who was murdered at the behest of Pandit Kailas Dhar. Kanth had not allowed his painful lurking memory to die down. Therefore, he avenged his father's death by arresting Pandit Dhar and beheading him in open court. This spread a wave of terror. As per R K Parmu,[18] "He (Mir Fazil Kanth) extended his vengeance to the entire Pandit community. They were molested, tortured and taxed beyond their endurance. And the governor, Amir Khan Jawansher, did not lift a finger. On the other hand, he abandoned himself to a life of luxury, drinking and debauchery."

Jawansher's ill-conceived policy revived the Shia-Sunni controversy. He was cruel to both Hindus and Muslims. His rule was a notorious one marked by oppression and high-handedness. Jawansher was also bewitched by the scenic beauty of Kashmir. He was fascinated by the beauty of the women. "One morning while basking in the sun, his eyes fell on a beautiful Hanji (Boatman's) girl whom he later married and made his queen," writes PN Bamzai.[19] He constructed a fort at Shergarhi and reconstructed the wooden bridge, which came to be known as Amira Kadal (Amir's Bridge). He built a summerhouse in the middle of Dal Lake (now known as Sona Lank). During this time, Ahmed Shah Abdali died in Afghanistan and his eldest son Timur Shah took over his father's empire. Timur Shah also confirmed the governorship of Amir Khan.

King Timur Shah Durrani 1772-1793 AD

At the time of Ahmed Shah Abdali's death, Timur, his eldest son, was at Herat. On hearing the news, he at once proceeded towards Kandahar, the capital of Afghanistan. But, one of the ministers, Shah Wali Khan, wanted his son-in-law Suleiman, the second son of Abdali, as the king of Afghanistan. However, Timur reached the capital just in time, killed Wali Khan and saved Afghanistan from civil strife. Timur Shah Durrani succeeded to throne of Khurasan on October 16, 1772 AD. At the time of his accession, there were several uprisings in India. Vary noticeable was the deterioration in the character of Mughal emperors and their indulgence in worldly pleasures. According to J N Sarkar, "Monarchical type of government in itself is a great weakness; a day is bound to come when strong kings would be followed by weak kings."

After four years, Timur Shah thought of invading Kashmir and killed Amir Khan, who had declared himself as the King of Kashmir. The royal force under the leadership of Hajji Karimdad marched to Kashmir and Jawansher was defeated.

Governors under the reign of Timur Shah Durrani

Amir Khan Jawansher 1772–1776 AD (Declares himself king)

Amir Khan Jawansher continued to be the governor of Kashmir when Timur Shah became the king. Amir Khan sent his tributes to Timur Shah the moment he took over as king. Shah was happy and he conferred upon him the title of 'Diller Jung'. This was the turning point for Amir Khan. He declared himself as independent king of Kashmir and let loose a reign of terror against both Hindus and Sunnis. This inflamed passions and some of the nobles went to Timur Shah seeking his intervention.

At this, Timur Shah despatched a strong force to Kashmir under the leadership of Hajji Karimdad Khan. Says PNK Bamzai[20] "This time Amir Khan acted diplomatically. Knowing well that he had no chance against the Haji's forces he entered into correspondence with influential nobles at Timur's court to intercede on his behalf. The trick succeeded and Hajji Karimdad Khan's expedition was recalled and governorship confirmed in the name of Amir Khan Jawansher."

Later on, Timur Shah again sent Karimdad Khan to invade Kashmir. This time Amir Khan was defeated and arrested. Says PNK Bamzai, [21] "Amir Khan, defeated and deserted, fled to the Pir Pantsal where he was ultimately captured and sent to Kabul. He passed several years in captivity but in the end Timur forgave him and set him free." Timur Shah deputed Hajji Karimdad Khan as governor of Kashmir.

Hajji Karimdad Khan 1776-1783 AD

Just after the arrest of Jawansher, Hajji Karimdad Khan took over the governorship of Kashmir. He turned out to be more ruthless than his predecessor. According to George Forster, [22] "The Kashmirians exclaimed with bitterness at the administration of Hajji Kareemdad, who was notorious for his wanton cruelties and insatiable avarice; often for trivial offences, throwing the inhabitants, tied by the back in pairs, into the river, plundering their property, and forcing their women of every description."

Immediately after taking over as governor, Hajji Karimdad appointed Abdur Rahim as chief Qazi and Pandit Dila Ram Quli as chief secretary. He started campaigns against some neighbouring chiefs such as chief of Skardu and Raja Murad Khan. The latter was defeated and had to pay heavy tributes to him. On the home front, distressed Kashmiri nobles secretly sent a message to Ranjit Dev, the ruler of Jammu, to attack Kashmir. They also assured him of all help. With Karimdad Khan busy with Skardu, Raja Ranjit Dev took the opportunity to attack the Kashmir Valley. According to Sukhdev Singh Charak, [23] "Towards the close of his career, Ranjit Dev had acquired sufficient power to consider seriously the conquest of Kashmir valley for himself. The tyrannical rule of the autonomous Afghan governor, Hajji Karimdad Khan, goaded the people of the valley to seek aid from whichever quarter it could be procured to overthrow the tyrant." Unfortunately, the strong forces of Ranjit Dev were routed and they had to face severe losses. "The thirst for blood and money induced Hajji Karimdad Khan to commit the basest act on the Kashmiri people," says PNK Bamzai.[24] "Without considerations of caste or creed he levied numerous unjust and killing taxes which resulted in complete impoverishment of the people."This merciless tyrant levied taxes on people without even thinking whether they would be able to bear their burden. Some of these taxes were: *Zari niaz* (Presentation Tax), *Zari ashkhas* (Property Tax on middle class gentry), *Zari hubbub* (Grain Tax on Cultivators), *Zari dudah* (Religious Tax on the Pundits), *Dadhsh* (Mercantile Tax).

The people of Kashmir had to bear the atrocities of Hajji Karimdad Khan for seven years. He died in 1783 AD. After his death, his son Azad Khan took over as the governor of Kashmir.

Azad Khan, 1783-1785 AD (Declared himself king)

When Azad Khan took over as governor of Kashmir, he was only eighteen. Pandit Dila Ram continued as his prime minister. Narendra Sahagala writes,[25] "In the presence of Dila Ram in the court, Subedar Azad Khan would feel easy in handling the court activities. Dila Ram was not only a political leader and the prime minister for implementing the orders of the Subedar, he was also a clever diplomat. Through his clever manipulation, he prevented the Subedar from issuing orders for merciless killings. It was through him that many public welfare schemes were launched. He also succeeded in keeping under check the demonic instincts of the Subedar." In spite of checks and balances by Dila Ram, Azad Khan turned out to be another tyrant and continued the policy of persecution of people. In fact, "Azad Khan had, in the first three months of his government, become an object of such terror to the Kashmiris, that the casual mention of his name produced an instant horror and an involuntary supplication of the aid of their prophet," according to George Forster.[26]

Azad Khan was unpredictable, impulsive, yet very brave. RK Parmu says,[27] "Azad Khan was a very funny and idiotic planner. For example, once he decided to convert the Maisuma area into a lake. He built a weir at Athwajan, but the water could not reach Maisuma, and the plan proved a failure."

Amongst his expeditions for conquest in 1783 AD, he defeated the Raja of Kishtwar and forced him to offer heavy tributes. He also succeeded in annexing Poonch and Rajouri. The chiefs of these places accepted his sovereignty and also paid rich tributes to him. He succeeded in establishing his supremacy in many strategic places in Muzaffarabad Valley. These victories made him haughty and so he declared himself as independent ruler of Kashmir and titled himself as 'Nadir Shah the Second'.

This news reached Timur Shah when he was returning home after having been defeated by Sikhs in Punjab. However, he waited for one year and then sent Murtaza Khan, the brother of Azad Khan, with a force of 15,000. Murtaza fought valiantly. Many times Azad Khan was at the brink of defeat but he routed the royal forces and came back to Srinagar triumphant.

Timur Shah again sent Madad Khan Ishkzai to overthrow Azad Khan. "Madad Khan came with fifty thousand horse and foot by way of Muzaffarabad in 1785," says R K Parmu.[28] A terrible battle took place near Khushi Pura village, which culminated in a victory for Madad Khan who seemed to be a very good strategist. Azad Khan lost this time and he escaped to Poonch where he committed suicide. With this came to an end the tyrannical rule of Azad Khan. As per R K Parmu,[29] "In short, during the regime of Azad Khan the population was oppressed in incalculable ways. For small faults he inflicted capital punishment which caused bitterness, hatred and animosity against him."

It was during Azad Khan's tenure that the famous traveller George Forster visited Kashmir and his account is mentioned in his book *A Journey From Bengal To England: Through Northern Part Of India*."

Madad Khan Ishkzai, 1785-1786 AD

After gaining victory over Azad Khan, Madad Khan became the governor of Kashmir for nine months only during which time he tried to ease the sufferings of the people. Unfortunately, he changed and stopped caring for his subjects anymore. Some of the nobles then started scheming and plotting against him.

"This enraged him and he let loose an orgy of repression and cruelty on his enemies, their relations and friends, and, in certain instances, outdid Karimdad Khan and his son Azad Khan in cruelty and oppression," writes PNK Bamzai,[30]. However, later, he stopped the repressive measures to the extent that he abolished the Jazia and other taxes on Hindus.

But he was called back, and while leaving Kashmir, he handed over the reins of the government to Mirdad Khan.

Mirdad Khan, 1786-1788 AD

Since Afghan rulers were deeply preoccupied with their campaigns against India and Iran, they could not concentrate on the development of the valley which would have made the people happy. The appointment of governors was so quick, and their tenures so short, that none could rule effectively. So the governors ended up only filling their purses and enjoying the beauty of Kashmir.

Mirdad Khan selected Mullah Ghaffar Khan as deputy governor, Mullah Habib as Qazi, Mullah Qawamuddin as chief justice and Pandit Dila Ram Quli as Dewan. Everything functioned smoothly initially but there arose a rift between the governor and the deputy. When this news reached Timur Shah, says PNK Bamzai.[31] "Timur deputed Murtaza Quli Khan as his personal representative to Kashmir. Subsequently, there were riots against the governor especially against Dila Ram Quli, the Dewan who was blamed for having ignited Shia–Sunni sectarian disputes."

According to Jia Lal Kilam,[32] "After listening to the mischievous harangues of certain persons, in whose breasts the enmity against Dila Ram lay hidden, they closed the doors of both the mosques as a protest and went to meet the Pandit. An attack was made upon Dila Ram who was seriously wounded. He would have met with his death had not the Subedar arrived on the spot, and pacified the mob." Pandit Dila Ram survived the attack and continued his loyalty to the governor.

In his book *The Kashmiri Pandit,* Anand Kaul has related an interesting story about Dila Ram.[33] He says that Dila Ram was from Rainawari and belonged to a poor family. Once he was asked whether he would like to become the governor or brother of the governor's wife, at which, Dila Ram, thinking it to be a joke, replied that he would like to be the governor's brother-in-law.

Then one day when the governor was holding office, says Anand Kaul, "Tar Khan, the brother-in-law of the governor, was reading out to him a petition written in poetry by someone who was burning in his heart at the atrocities committed by the governor and each verse ended with 'Sag Shavi, Sag Shavi' (thou shall become a dog, thou shall become a dog). The governor got offended at this and as he looked around he saw Dila Ram. He summoned him and told him to read out the petition. Dila Ram read it out changing the ending of each verse into 'Sag Shavam, Sag Shavam' (I shall become a dog, I shall become a dog). The governor asked him why it he was reading it differently than his brother-in-law. Dila Ram said that it was indecent to read like that before a governor. The governor was pleased with him and appointed him as his Dewan in place of his brother-in-law." Mirdad Khan fell ill and died on 22 April 1788 after being governor for only two years.

Mullah Ghaffar Khan, 1788 AD

Mullah Ghaffar Khan took over the reins of Kashmir as governor after the death of Mirdad Khan. He ruled for less than four months. It seems that he was appointed on an adhoc basis till the monarch at Kabul appointed Jumma Khan Alkozai as regular governor.

Jumma Khan Alkozai, 1788-1793 AD

As soon as Jumma Khan took over the administration of Kashmir, he tried to bring peace to the valley. As per RK Parmu,[34] "Very soon he called his three sons, Abdullah Khan, Rahmatullah Khan and Muhabbat Khan from Kabul to assist him in running the administration." The efforts of Jumma Khan and his sons brought considerable income to the state which started progressing financially. People were happy under his leadership.

It was during his period that Arnimaal, the famous poet of Kashmir and wife of Bhavani Dass Kachru, made a special contribution to poetry in Kashmiri language. Pandit Bhavani Dass Kachru also composed Persian poetry. His celebrated poetical work *Bahar-i-Tawil,* written in the same meter, became a landmark in the realms of Persian poetry.

According to Prem Nath Bazaz,[35] "Jumma Khan, who functioned as the Afghan governor of Kashmir for a period of four years from 1788 to 1792 AD, was no less harsh than other Pathan Subedars in treating the Kashmiris and exploiting the country, but the severity of his bleak rule was relieved by a silver lining. He patronised learning and respected scholars and savants."

However, he was summoned by Timur Shah to Kabul and asked to pay tributes. He went to Peshawar along with Pandit Dila Ram Quli to explain to the king the reasons for not being able to pay tributes. Before leaving, he deputed his son Muhabbat Khan to look after the administration. But just after he left, the valley was engulfed in sectarian violence between

Shia and Sunnis. The Bombas too raised a rebellion. Jumma Khan had to return from Peshawar to pacify both Shias and Sunnis. He also crushed the rebellion of the Bombas. Unfortunately, he died on 18 May 1793 AD. After his death, Rahmatullah Khan took over.

Rahmatullah Khan, 1793 AD

Rahmatullah Khan remained in power for three months as Timur Shah did not accept his appointment as governor. He sent Mirza Hazar Khan as governor in 1793.

Mirza Hazar Khan/Mir Hazar Khan, 1793 AD

Mirza Hazar Khan had just started his job as governor of Kashmir, when news of Timur Shah's death and Zaman Shah taking over as the king of Afghanistan reached him.

King Zaman Shah Durrani, 1793-1801 AD

In Afghanistan, the death of Timur Shah on 18 May 1793 disturbed the political scenario. Timur Shah had declared Zaman Shah, his fifth son out of twenty one children, as his heir apparent. After his death, there was a 'Loya Jirga' who decided to install Zaman Shah as the king of Afghanistan.

At the time of his death, Timur Shah was survived by his twenty-one sons. Naturally, there followed an internecine war of succession. It was with the support of a very powerful chief of Barakzai clan, Payanda Khan, that Zaman Shah was declared the king at the age of 23. His brothers, as well as his nephew, raised the banner of revolt, but he defeated all his opponents and even forgave them for their treason.

Zaman Shah tried to invade India but he came into conflict with the British and the Shah of Persia. Their attacks thwarted his plans and he was forced to protect his own land.

Governors under the reign of Zaman Shah

Mirza Khan/Mir Hazar Khan 1793-1794 AD

(Declared himself king)

Timur Shah had replaced Rahmatullah Khan with Mir Hazar Khan. When news of the death of Timur Shah was received, Hazar Khan continued to remain governor. Zaman Shah endorsed the orders of his father and confirmed his appointment as the governor. But looking at the uncertain condition of Afghanistan and the war of succession there, Hazar Khan did not comply with the order to pay the revenue of Kashmir and thought it best to declare himself independent.

Afghan governors, by and large, always tried to antagonise the local people of Kashmir. Hazar Khan was no exception. After he declared himself independent, he became ruthless towards the people and expected them to be on his side despite his high-handedness. During his governorship, Pandits suffered the most. They were persecuted with a vengeance. Pandit Dila Ram was beheaded at Khanyar and others were subjected to Jazia. Hazar Khan proved to be a heartless and treacherous ruler for Shias and Pandits.

Different writers endorse the fact that Pandits suffered the most at the hands of Hazar Khan. Writes Jia Lal Kilam,[36] "...The next Subedar created a record of his own perhaps unbeaten in the annals of Kashmir by the most merciless and brutal treatment that he meted out to the Kashmiri Pandits." Pir Gulam Hassan in *Tarikh-i-Hasan* has also stated that Pandits were the worst sufferers[37]. PNK Bamzai writes,[38] "Hazar Khan, however, began his independent rule badly. He put Dila Ram Quli to death and let loose a reign of terror against the usual targets, Shia and Hindus. Thousands of innocent Hindus tied up back to back in pairs were drowned in the Dal Lake..."

It is unfortunate that having lived under the Buddhist beliefs of non-violence for centuries, the Afghan rulers learnt nothing about humanitarianism and respect for fellow human beings. They were not concerned with the development of the people of the valley. Writes R K Parmu,[39] "To debar them from any public office of profit in future, Hazar Khan planned to close down the revenue and settlement department, and forbade them to study Persian in order to turn them into hewers of wood and drawers of water only."

Zaman Shah sent Hazar Khan's father to advise his son and make him accept the sovereignty of the Afghan rule. But Hazar Khan arrested his own father and put him in jail. An infuriated Zaman Shah then sent Ahmad Khan Shahinakbashi and Rahmatullah Khan with a large army to Kashmir. Hazar Khan was defeated at Baramulla. He sought refuge in disguise at the Khanqah Mosque in Srinagar but the Afghan army, without caring for the sanctity of the sanctum-sanctorum, went inside, dragged him out and arrested him.

Rahmatullah Khan was declared the governor of Kashmir. Both he and Ahmad Khan Shahinakbashi governed the state.

Rahmatullah Khan, 1794-1794 AD

Rahmatullah Khan's stay in Kashmir was very short. Initially, he and Shahinakbashi governed the valley with great care, affection and compassion. But soon they fell out. The atmosphere of Kashmir was affected by the animosity between the two. Zaman Shah summoned both of them back to Kabul.

Rahmatullah Khan took with him Pandit Nand Ram Tikku who was appointed as an officer under King Zaman Shah. Nand Ram was placed under the supervision of Wafadar Khan. But due to his intelligence and dedicated work, he soon rose to the position of a minister in Kabul. His keen knowledge of financial management enabled him to handle money matters well. Once, facing very scarce money supply, Nand Ram stuck coins in his own name, with the inscription of *sim az m'sbud u zarb az nand ram*, meaning "Silver from god and coinage by Nand Ram," says Anand Kaul.[40] Nevertheless, things did not improve for the Pandits in Kashmir. Then Kifayatullah Khan came to replace Rahmatullah Khan as governor of Kashmir.

Kifayatullah Khan, 1794-1795 AD

Kifayatullah Khan was a peace loving man and genuinely tried to bring comfort to the people of Kashmir. When, after three months, he went to Kabul to apprise King Zaman Shah about the developments in Kashmir, he requested that Kashmir be exempt from paying tributes till the situation improved. While leaving Kashmir, he made Mirza Badr-ud-Din in charge. Unfortunately, riots broke out between Shias and Sunnis. "It so happened that Aga Rahim, who was the chief merchant (Malik-ut-Tujar) in Srinagar, caused the death of Khwaja Isa, a Sunni noble, in order to avenge the murder of one Muhammad Taqi, a Shia," says RK Parmu,[41] "Although by itself it was a solitary instance, it infuriated the Sunnis to such an extent that they set fire to the house of Aga Rahim and razed it to the ground. Then they inflicted tyrannies upon the Shias."

Given the turmoil in the valley, Kifayatullah Khan rushed back and took charge. The Bombas once more took to guerrilla warfare. Failing to quell the situation, Kifayatullah Khan was dislodged and Zaman Shah deputed Arsalan Khan as the governor of Kashmir. Arsalan Khan instead appointed his deputy, Muhammad Khan Jawansher, to look after the affairs of Kashmir.

Muhammad Khan Jawansher, 1795-1796 AD

Muhammad Khan Jawansher's efforts to bring peace to strife-torn Kashmir were hampered by ex-governor Kifayatullah Khan, who was still in Srinagar and created problems. So Muhammad Khan arrested him and sent him to Kabul. But, in a turn of events, commanders Miyan Baluch and Khudadad Khan of the Kashmir army hatched a coup and arrested the governor. They declared themselves independent. There was turmoil everywhere. Nobody knew who the king was. People were frustrated and perturbed.

Once again, Zaman Khan sent his army led by Mukhtar-ud-Duala and assisted by Abdullah Khan Alkozai, son of Jumma Khan. They restored the sovereignty of the state. Abdullah Alkozai was appointed as the governor of Kashmir. The fact is, Afghan rulers did not know the technique of administrating Kashmir successfully. These governors were only sword-wielding people lacking administrative acumen. The other drawback was that the governors were deputed in quick succession, most of them being uncultured, incorrigible fanatics with no administrative expertise.

Abdullah Khan Alkozai/Rahmatullah Khan, 1796-1800 AD

On assuming charge of Kashmir, Abdullah Khan appointed his brother Rahmatullah Khan to look after the affairs of the country. He also appointed Pandit Sahaj Ram as the revenue collector. Entrusting the function of the government to the two of them, he left for Kabul.

Knowing that the governor was not in the country, the Bombas raised a rebellion. Both the armies fought bravely and suffered heavy losses. The news reached King Zaman Khan who sent Abdullah Khan to resume charge. Once he took over the administration of Kashmir, Abdullah Khan replaced the top officers of the government. According to R K Parmu,[42] "He dismissed almost all the old hands from their office, expelling many of them from the country also."

The Bombas were a source of perpetual nuisance for the administration. Abdullah Khan decided to end the menace and therefore collected a large army and led a strong expedition to crush them. PNK Bamzai writes,[43]"He succeeded in forcing their leaders to submission. Subsequently he married the daughter of the Bombas chief, Fatah Khan, and gave him a principality in Jageer."

He was a kind ruler. Adds Jia Lal Kilam.[44] "He was a man of great courage and organising skill and possessed a keen eye for singling out individuals to carry on his administration. He appointed in preference to other Muslim notables, Pandit Sahaj Ram Dar, as his Sahib Kar and delegated to him all the administrative functions as were necessary to bring about a rehabilitation of the country."

Pandit Sahaj Ram appointed Pandit Hardas Tikku as his assistant. Hardas Tikku was the brother of Nand Ram Tikku who was Dewan under Wafadar Khan, the prime minister of Zaman Shah. Hardas, therefore, kept Zaman Shah apprised of every development. But Abdullah Khan and Pandit Hardas fell out and the former left for Kabul leaving behind his brother Atta Mohamed Khan Alkozai in 1800 AD as the governor of Kashmir. On reaching Kabul, Zaman Khan imprisoned Abdulla for his misrule over Hindus.

RK Parmu notes, "I am inclined to identify this Sahaj Ram with Sahaj Ram Sapru, the Pandit grandfather of Sir Muhammad Iqbal, the great poet and philosopher." He further says, "According to this document one Sahaj Ram Sapru who was in-charge of the revenue of Kashmir expended the money in marriages etc in his family. When the report went to the governor, he summoned him. Sahaj Ram admitted his guilt like a brave man. He was young and charming. The governor was moved and offered him death or Islam as a penalty. The Pandit accepted Islam and at the same time requested that as a Muslim he would not like to live in Kashmir. He was allowed to settle in Sialkot."

Atta Mohamed Khan Alkozai, 1800–1806 AD (Declared himself king)

When Abdullah Khan left for Kabul he handed over the governorship to his brother, Atta Mohamed Khan. The Prime Minister of Afghanistan Wafadar Khan did not accept him as governor of Kashmir as he wanted his brother Vakil Khan, who was already in Srinagar, to be the governor. So, he sent Mullah Ahmad Khan with a large army to assist Vakil Khan in running the administration. When Atta Mohamed came to know about this he killed Vakil Khan and then raised a revolt against Mullah Ahmad Khan when he was still at Muzaffarabad en-route to Srinagar. Mullah Ahmed's army suffered defeat and Atta Mohamed Khan declared himself as the king of Kashmir. During his reign, the Shia-Sunni feud aggravated. The Sunnis believed that Pandit Hardas aggravated the sectarian feud.

Meanwhile, Atta Mohamed became notorious for raping women. People shaved the heads of their women to make them look ugly. "Atta Mohammed Khan had developed a diseased mind which turned him into a ferocious libertine," says R K Parmu.[45] "He began to molest girls of noble families, nay any handsome girl in order to satisfy his carnal madness." Writes Walter Lawrence,[46] "Atta Mohamed Khan was a ferocious libertine, and his agent, an old woman named Koshib, was the terror of Brahmin parents, who rather than allow the degradation of their daughter destroyed their beauty by shaving their heads or cutting their noses."

It was also a time when Afghanistan was caught in a civil strife. The war between the brothers Zaman Shah and Mahmud Shah, to capture the throne of Afghanistan, had destabilised the governance of the country. Mahmud Shah deposed Zaman Shah who was arrested and put in prison.

King Shah Mahmud Durrani, 1801-1803 AD

Zaman Shah was deposed and blinded by his brother Shah Mahmud Durrani in 1801 AD. When Shah Mahmud, the son of Timur Shah and half brother of Zaman Shah, ascended the throne of Kabul, riots between Shias and Sunnis broke out in Afghanistan. The Sunnis, who were a majority, were in favour of Shah Shuja becoming the King of Afghanistan. Thus, backed by Sunni nobles, Shah Shuja dethroned Shah Mahmud in 1803.

King Shah Shuja, 1803-1809 AD

Zaman Khan did not accept the inhuman treatment he suffered at the hands of Shah Mahmud, who not only removed him from the Kabul throne but also blinded him. After collecting sufficient forces, he succeeded in dethroning Shah Mahmud in 1803 AD. But before he could sit on the Kabul throne again, Shah Shuja who was supported by the majority Sunnis, captured the throne and proclaimed himself as the king in 1803 AD. Shah Shuja was the governor of Herat and Peshawar from 1798 to 1801.

After assuming the kingship of Afghanistan, Shah Shuja wanted to punish Atta Mohamed. He sent Sher Mohamed Khan Mukhtar-ul-Duala at the head of a large army against Atta Mohamed who was defeated in the military engagement in February 1806. He was arrested and died in 1806. Shah Shuja assumed the reign of Kashmir.

On the international front, Napoleon had allied with Russia and

Britain was gaining ground in India. Britain was worried that Napoleon and Russia could attack India, so it sent feelers to Shah Shuja to join hands against the forces of Napoleon and Russia which Shah Shuja gladly did. He allied Afghanistan with the United Kingdom in 1809 AD.

Meanwhile, the succession war between brothers Shah Shuja and Shah Mahmud continued for a long time. Shah Mahmud ultimately succeeded and he took over the reins of the country once again.

On the other hand, Maharaja Ranjit Singh, who ruled Punjab, wanted to annex Kashmir to his kingdom. It was in 1813 AD, when Atta Muhammad Khan Barakzai was ruling Kashmir as an independent ruler that Maharaja Ranjit Singh sent Dewan Mohkam Chand to attack Kashmir. Fateh Khan, commander of Shah Mahmud Durrani, agreed to make a joint attack on Kashmir. The Afghans were to have two-thirds of the territory, while the Sikhs agreed to take one third. After reaching Pir Paschal range, Fateh Khan left Mohkam Chand behind and proceeded further himself. He defeated Atta Khan at Shergadi and captured the whole of Kashmir. With it, Fateh Khan broke his word as well. He did not give one-third of the territory to the Sikhs but handed it over to Shah Shuja. Maharaja Ranjit Singh extorted the *Koh-i-Noor* from him. According to Joseph Davey Cunningham,[47] "Runjeet Singh was equally desirous of detaining Shah Shuja in Lahore, and of securing the great diamond which had adorned the throne of the Mughals. The king evaded compliance with demands for time, and rejected even the actual offer of a moderate sum of money; but at last the Maharaja visited the Shah in person, mutual friendship was declared, an exchange of turbans took place, the diamond was surrendered, and Shah Shuja received the assignment of a Jageer in Punjab for his maintenance and a promise of aid in recovering Caubul (Kabul)."

Shah Shuja's wife Wafa Begum carried the diamond as they took shelter in Punjab. According to Kartar Singh Duggal,[48] Wafa Begum had promised Maharaja Ranjit Singh the diamond in exchange for the release of her husband.

Atta Muhammad Khan Barakzai, 1806-1813 AD (Declared himself king)

With Atta Mohamed Alkozai out of the way, Sher Mohamed Khan placed his son Atta Muhammad Khan Barakzai as the governor of Kashmir in 1806 AD. As per R K Parmu,[49] "Sher Muhammad Khan was a scholar, a generous man and a strong ruler."

Shah Shuja committed a diplomatic blunder when he dismissed him. It helped Prince Qaiser, son of Zaman Shah, to proclaim himself king in Kabul. Shah Shuja was compelled to proceed at the head of his army to Peshawar. A bitter war ensued. Sher Mohamed Khan and others were killed and Shah Shuja was victorious.

The death of his father Sher Mohamed Khan at the hands of Shah Shuja infuriated Atta Mohamed Khan Barakzai and he retaliated by declaring himself an independent ruler of Kashmir. Though Shah Shuja sent his army under Akram Khan to punish him, he did not succeed in his mission. Barakzai kept an eye on the developments in Kabul. He learnt about the defeat of Shah Shuja at the hands of Fateh Khan and Shah Mahmud Durrani. Tactfully, he offered asylum to Shah Shuja in Kashmir. Unsuspecting foul play, Shah Shuja accepted the offer. On reaching Srinagar, he was kept in Hari Parbat fort as royal prisoner.

Barakzai was a shrewd strategist. He was wary of Fateh Khan attacking Kashmir anytime. On the other hand, Fateh Khan knew that he alone could not defeat Barakzai. So, he sought Maharaja Ranjit Singh's help for the second time. Ranjit Singh obliged at once as he had already set his sights on Kashmir as the next state to be annexed to his kingdom. Atta Khan Barakzai had already reached Tosamaidan, the route the enemy had taken to invade Kashmir. He had the support of Shah Shuja in this war but both leaders were appalled when they saw their own army defecting and joining the enemy forces. They made an important decision on the spot—to contact Sikh leaders with an offer of the Koh-hi-Noor and eight Lakh rupees. It was their only way to win the war.

By this truce with the Sikhs, Barakzai and Shah Shuja changed the whole situation. Peace was simultaneously signed between General Mohkam Chand and Fateh Khan on one side and Shah Shuja and Atta Mohamed Khan Barakzai on the other. General Mohkam received the money and returned to Punjab with Shah Shuja and Barakzai. Fateh Khan was declared governor of Kashmir.

King Mahmud Durrani, 1809-1818 AD (Second Term)

The peace treaty signed between the Sikh Army and Fateh Khan on one hand and Atta Khan Barakzai and Shah Shuja on the other at Shergadi in 1803 AD contained decisions which banished Barakzai and Shah Shuja. Fateh Khan was appointed as the governor of Kashmir under the paramountcy of Shah Mahmud Durrani.

Governors under the reign of Shah Mahmud Durrani

Fateh Mohamed Khan, 1813 AD

Fateh Khan became the governor of Kashmir in 1813. There was complete lawlessness in the valley due to the wars and indifference of Pathan governors to the abject condition of the people. He began trying to enforce law and order but decided to go back to Kabul. He left his brother Azim Khan as deputy governor in the year 1813 itself.

Maharaja Ranjit Singh was very annoyed with Fateh Khan for breaking his promise. He decided to capture the fort of Attok, which was held by Jahandad Khan. In a diplomatic move, Ranjit Singh offered Jahandad Khan a jageer and Jahandad offered the fort of Attok to the Maharaja. This way Attok came into the domain of Ranjit Singh. Fateh Khan tried to capture Attok from the Sikhs but was defeated by Ranjit Singh at Hazro on July 12, 1813 AD.

Azim Khan, 1813-1819 AD

Azim Khan was made the governor of Kashmir in 1813 AD. There is difference of opinion among some chroniclers with regard to the humane rule administered him. According to PNK Bamzai,[50] "Muhammad Azim Khan began his administration well. He appointed experienced and influential nobles like Sahaj Ram Dhar and Dewan Har Das Tikku in high administrative posts and organised his fiscal and judicial administration on more humane lines." However, another chronicler Prem Nath Bazaz says,[51] "Azim Khan has been hateful for his acts of cruelty from the very start of his career."

According to Narendra Sahagala,[52] "The trend of religious conversion, which started with the reign of Shamir continued without any interruption for 500 years till the rule of the last Afghan ruler, Azim Khan." In view of this, some Hindu nobles tried to approach Maharaja Ranjit Singh to instigate him to invade Kashmir.

As per the Shergadi truce, the Maharaja had to recover rupees eight Lakh as tribute from the Kashmir governor but this did not happen.

First Sikh invasion of Kashmir

Therefore in 1814, Ranjit Singh sent an army to invade Kashmir. When the Sikh army reached Pir Paschal, nature came to the help of Azim Khan. There were several cloudbursts which caused severe cold weather making many from the Sikh army run away from the battlefield. According to Joseph Davey Cunningham,[53] "The more advanced division surmounted the lofty barrier, a detachment of the Afghan force was repulsed, and the town of Shupiyan was attacked; but the assault failed, and the Sikhs retired to the mountain passes. Azim Khan, the governor, then fell on the main body of Ranjit Singh, which had been long in view on the outkirts of the valley and compelled the Maharaja to retreat with precipitation. The rainy season had fairly set in, the army became disorganised, a brave chief Mitha Singh Behrania was slain and Ranjit Singh reached his capital almost alone about the middle of August."

Azim Khan becomes ruthless

Devoid of talent or knowledge, Azim Khan, under the intoxication of his success against the Sikh army, became more intolerable to Pandits and Hindus. He used the pretext that Hindus, in connivance with some Muslim nobles, brought the Sikh army to Kashmir. According to Anand Kaul,[54] "He suspected that the Sikh army had been sent by Maharaja Ranjit Singh at the secret instigation of the Hindus of Kashmir..." To avenge his anger ,he got Dewan Har Das Tikku killed. Then he persecuted Kashmiri Hindus. He was harsh and ruthless towards Hindu revenue collectors.

This was the time when Kashmiris were experiencing distressing times. Agricultural production was lean on account of repressive measures taken by the governor. Thus the exorbitant taxes imposed by Azim Khan yielded low revenue collection. In order to raise the revenue collection, Azim Khan appointed influential, intellectual and resourceful Hindus such as Birbal Dhar, Mirza Pandit and Sukh Ram Safaya as revenue collectors.

Given the abject economic condition of Kashmir peasantry, it was impossible for Birbal to collect the required amount, and one year his collection fell short one Lakh rupees. But Azim Khan did not want to listen to any excuses and wanted the required amount by any means. How Kashmiris were finally compelled to invite the Sikh army to liberate them from the tyrannical rule of the Afghans has been vividly described by Anand Kaul. [54] "Owing to failure of crops, one Lakh rupees remained as outstanding against the Zamindars of Pandit Birbal Dhar's district.

Azim Khan deputed 100 soldiers to recover the arrears from Pandit Birbal Dhar. Birbal Dhar, knowing clearly that Azim Khan would unleash his evil ways to recover the money, undertook the most dangerous adventure to free Kashmir from the clutches of heartless Pathan rule."

Birbal Dhar seeks help from Maharaja Ranjit Singh

Pandit Birbal Dhar and his uncle Mirza Pandit Dhar decided that to free the country from the yoke of the Mohammedans no time should be lost in inducing Maharaja Ranjit Singh to take Kashmir.

Birbal, along with his son Raja Kak, left the same night leaving behind his wife and daughter-in-law whom he hid in the home of a Muslim, Qudus Gojawari, with the help of Pandit Wasa Kak Harkarabashi. Both father and son fled on horseback to Devasar the same night. After a few days, they reached Lahore where Maharaja Ranjit Singh was. Raja Dyane Singh of Jammu, who was Maharaja Ranjit Singh's prime minister, introduced Pandit Birbal Dhar to Maharaja Ranjit Singh. It is difficult to imagine how much hardship Pandit Birbal and his son must have suffered in riding over the plains.

Azim Khan came to know about the escape of Birbal Dhar. What followed was wanton savagery on the part of the governor of Kashmir. Azim Khan's treatment of Kudmaal the wife of Birbal, and his daughter-in-law was so degrading that people have dramatised it to show how tyrannical a ruler can be.

Vindictive Azim Khan

Azim Khan let loose his vindictive actions against Kashmiri Pandits and all those Muslims also who had helped Birbal to escape. His wife and daughter-in-law had escaped and taken refuge in the house of their milkman at Gojawari. According to Prem Nath Bazaz, [55] "Azim was furious and issued instructions for a thorough search of all possible hiding places. Some people knew the secret but refused to divulge it. For days, the governor whimpered and shouted and swore but in vain." Unfortunately, Birbal Dhar's own son-in-law Munshi Trilok Chand informed Azim Khan of the hiding place of those two women. Azim Khan was merciless towards the women. Tradition says that Kudmaal told Azim Khan that her husband Birbal had gone to bring the Sikh Army and as such his days in Kashmir were numbered. She then took a strong dose of poison and committed suicide in the presence of Azim Khan. As per Prem Nath

Bazaz,[56] "While being carried in a boat towards Shergarhi, the governor's palace, she gulped a piece of alms (precious stone) which adorned her gold ring to commit suicide." The daughter-in-law was sent to Kabul. The refuge giver, a Muslim milkman called Qudus Gojawari was brutally killed and his house was put to flames. Luckily, Mirza Pandit was not killed nor was he punished.

Prophesy of Kudmaal

Writes Prem Nath Bazaz,[57] "Rebuked and accosted in fearless tones a Kashmiri woman who was known for her docility and submissiveness, Azim Khan was crestfallen. His wounded pride and inflamed rage would have invented the cruellest method of torture to deal with Kudmaal but, to his chagrin, convulsions shook the noble lady from head to foot; she fell down senseless and died soon after." Tradition says that the dying brave daughter of Kashmir, Kudmaal, had made a prophesy that it was the end of Afghan Rule in Kashmir. True enough, soon Kashmir was free of Afghan rule. With it also came the end of Muslim rule which had continued in the valley for about 500 years.

Birbal Dhar approached Maharaja Ranjit Singh and requested him to take Kashmir under his domain and save the Kashmiri Hindus. The Maharaja was initially reluctant because of his defeat in the last invasion at the hands of Azim Khan in 1814 AD, which was fresh in his memory, but Birbal assured him that the whole of Kashmir including the Muslim population were against Afghan rule.

Before Ranjit Singh's army came to invade Kashmir, Azim Khan had to go back to Kabul. The political conditions in Kabul were not stable on account of Shah Mahmud recapturing the Afghan throne with the help of Fateh Khan. Now both of them decided to evict Hajji Feroz Mahmud's brother from Herat where he was ruling. Soon Fateh Khan succeeded in capturing Herat. Intoxicated by this success, Fateh Khan's youngest brother, Dost Mohammed, insulted the daughter-in-law of Feroz. Stung with anger, Feroz injured Fateh Khan's eyes with a dagger. This resulted in a civil war in Afghanistan.

Fateh Khan asked his brother Azim Khan to come back to Afghanistan. According to R K Parmu,[58] "Azim Khan was seized with alarm when he came to know that Birbal Dhar had succeeded in his mission. To avoid the approaching doom at the hands of the Sikhs, he hurriedly renounced Kashmir in 1819 AD, leaving his family and a huge treasure of one crore in cash and kind in the custody of Pandit Sahaz Ram Sapru, to follow him, and the country in charge of his brother, Jabbar Khan." However, Joseph Davey Cunningham has a different story to tell. [59] "Azim Khan hastened from Kashmir, which he left in charge of Jabbar Khan, one of his many brothers. He at first thought of reinstating Shah Shuja but proclaimed Shah Ayub as king, and in a few months he was master of Peshawar, Gazni, Kabul and Kandahar."

Jabbar Khan, 1819 AD

Tradition says that Jabbar Khan was a good and reasonable man. He would have ameliorated the abject conditions of the people but for the uncertain conditions in Afghanistan. Also with Ranjit Singh's invasion of Kashmir, he could not do anything.

Most Afghan governors had a low understanding of the complexities of Hindu philosophy. They did not believe that sometimes even miracles can take place. Anand Kaul in *The Kashmiri Pandits*[60] says, "Jabbar Khan was once told by someone that it was a common notion among the Pandits that snow falls invariably on the Shivratri night (13th night of the dark fortnight of Phalguna). To test this, he ordered that the Pandits not be allowed to observe the festival in Phalguna (February-March) but in Har (June-July). Accordingly, it had to be observed on the corresponding night in the later month. It so happened that even on this night flakes of snow and hailstones fell preceded by a heavy rainfall. " The bards then mocking at him sang:-

"*Wuchten ye Jabbar Jandah, Hardas tih Karan wandah.*"

"Look at Jabbar, the wretch. Even Har (summer) he turned into winter."

Birbal was not only a political adventurer but also a seasoned diplomat. He was successful in convincing Ranjit Singh of the support both from Muslims and Hindus of Kashmir. He also kept his son Raja Kak as a guarantee with the Maharaja.

The Sikh Army under generals Sardar Hari Singh Nalwa, Sardar Jawala Singh and Raja Gulab Singh proceeded towards Kashmir with Birbal as their guide. Jabbar Khan, the governor of Kashmir, came with his army to face the Sikh forces. Thirty thousand armed Sikhs invaded Kashmir. A fierce battle took place near the Pir Paschal where Afghan forces got a crushing defeat. Jabbar Khan went himself to fight the Sikh army at Shupiyan where he was injured and his army ran away. According to Joseph Davey Cunningham, [61] "The passes were scaled on 5th July 1819, but Jabbar Khan was there to receive them. The Afghans repulsed the invaders, and mastered two guns; but they did not improve their success, and the Sikhs rallied again and attacked them, winning an almost bloodless victory."

The victory of the Sikh army in Kashmir was celebrated by illuminating Lahore, and Raja Kak Dhar was offered a royal robe. This marked the end of the Muslim rule in Kashmir and the beginning of Sikh rule. Writes Sir Walter Lawrence,[62] "It must have been an intense relief to all classes in Kashmir to see the downfall of the evil rule of the Pathans."

Eighteen
Highlights of Medieval Era

Sayyid Bulbul Shah

Islam in Kashmir did not come suddenly; it was a gradual process. Muslims from outside had settled in Kashmir long before the Shah Mir dynasty usurped Kashmir by intrigue and brutality. Muhammad Alafia, an Arab mercenary who had come from Turkistan, sought refuge in Kashmir. At that time Chandrapida was ruling the country. He who bestowed on Alafia the territory of Shakalbar. However, as per GMD Sufi, a Syrian known as Hamim, son of Sama, was the first Muslim to enter Kashmir. He founded a masjid in Shakalha.

During that time there was hardly any systematic conversion. However, the fourteenth century saw a radical change in the spread of Islam when Rinchan took over the reins of Kashmir and got converted to Islam. Sayyid Sheriff Abdul Rahman Sharifu'd Din Suhrawardi, titled Sayyid Bilal, came to be popularly known as Bulbul Shah. He entered Kashmir during Suhadeva's period (1301-20 AD). There are different versions about the native town of Bulbul Shah. Some say that he came from Iran and others say he came from Turkistan.

Bulbul Shah, the first Suhrawardi Sufi had led a life of self-abnegation. He was the disciple of Shah Nemat-Ullah Farisi Shirazi. In addition to converting Rinchan to Islam as Sultan Sadr-ud-Din, he also converted his brother-in-law, Ravan Chander. His pervasive teaching of Islam helped in baptising as many as ten thousand Kashmiris in the valley. Many legends are attributed to this legendry saint. It is said that once during extreme winter the lakes and the river Jhelum froze. Drinking water became scarce. Even this revered saint was searching for water. He himself went to the river to get water and tried to break the frozen snow. He found it hard to do so. Tradition says that he then looked up and prayed to god for the Sun to appear in the clouded sky. Suddenly the sun appeared and the frozen snow started melting.

Bulbul Shah died in 1325 AD and is buried in his own Khanqah in Bulbul Lankar, which was built by Rinchan. In the memory of his service to Islam, a town was named after him as Bulbul Lanker, which is still there in Srinagar city.

Shah-e-Hamadan/Hamdan 1314-1384 AD

Shah Hamdan was known by the name of Sayyid Mir Ali Hamadan. His father's name was Sayyid Shahab-ud-Din and mother was Fatimah. He was born in 1314 AD. He belonged to an educated Sayyid family. In his early years he had read the holy *Quran*. His first teacher was his own uncle Hazrat Alal-ud-Din and later on Sheikh Mahmud Mizdiqani, a renowned saint of his time, imparted spiritual guidance to him. Shah Hamdan belonged to the philosophical school of Kibroya of the Suhrawardi Order.

It is said that there was a difference of opinion between Shah Hamdan and Timur in the method of conversion of people to Islam. The ostensible reason for this seems to be that Timur wanted forcible conversion, something Shah Hamdan may not have approved of. Timur's nobles thought it futile to invade countries like India. However, Timur told them,[1] "My object to the invasion of Hindustan is to lead an expedition against the infidels, according to the law of Mohammad, to purify the land from the defilement of misbelieve and polytheism, and to overthrow the temples and idols, where we shall be champions and soldiers of the faith before God." Shah Hamdan also wanted to spread Islam but by compassion and affection. Tradition says that he converted approximately forty thousand people to the Islamic Order.

He came to Kashmir in 1375 AD. At that time Sultan Shahab-ud-Din was abroad. His brother received the Muslim saint with great warmth and respect. Shah Hamdan stayed in the valley for four months and went back only to return in 1379 AD when he stayed for almost two-and-a-half years. Nearly 700 Sayyid followers had accompanied him. In fact, he had decided to come to Kashmir to spread Islam by persuasion and love. His compassion and kindness attracted people to him and the faith he taught. He was not only converting people but was also trying to help them settle in their life by encouraging them to learn various trades. He left Kashmir for the second time and returned in the year 1383 AD. According to Hamid Naseem Rafiabadi,[2] "He, Shah-e-Hamdan, paid the third visit in 1383, stayed in Kashmir for a short period, and then left Kashmir on account of ill health. He then stayed at Pakhli (a district of Mughal Punjab) for ten days at the request of the ruler of that place whose name was Sultan Muhammad. However, *Baharistan-i-Shahi* does not mention Hamadan's third visit." There are different versions about his death. It is said he breathed his last in 1384 AD and he was buried in Kolab in Khatlani.

Tradition says that Shah Hamdan was against religious persecution. He wanted people to accept Islam after understanding its merits. He was a great scholar who explained to people the nobility of Islam. During the rule of Sikandar, his prime minister, a convert, Suha Bhatta was desecrating deities and idols in temples. Writes historian GMD Sufi[3], "But it must be remembered that this sort of religious zeal is deplored by Islam which positively prohibits it. It is on record that Mir Hamadan warned Suha Bhatta against such actions and pointed out to him the well known verse of the Quran (II-256) which runs, 'Let there be no compulsion in religion'." Eulogising Shah Hamdan's human values, Mohammad Ishaq Khan writes,[4] "The essence of Sayyid's admonitions to rulers—inadequately brought home in the modern assessment of his work, is his concern for rendering equitable justice, irrespective of religious differences."

According to Jia Lal Kilam,[5] "Bulbul Shah was followed by Sayid Jalal-ud-Din of Bukhara and Sayyid Taj-ud-Din, the cousin of Mir Sayyid Ali Hamadan. Sayid Taj-ud Din was accompanied by his two disciples, Sayid Masud and Sayid Yusuf. There also came Sayid Hussein Simnani, the younger brother of Sayid Taj-ud Din. It is said that Taj-ud Din and Sayid Hussein came to Kashmir under instructions from Ali Hamadan to find if the country could give them protection against the attacks of Timur who was suspected of contemplating a wholesale massacre of the Sayyids."

Shah Hamdan was mentioned by many titles such as Qutb-e-Zaman, Sheikh-e-Salikan-e-Jahan, Qutb-ul-Aktab, Moih-ul-Ambiya-o-ul-Mursaleen, and Afzal-ul-Muhaq-e-qeen-o-Akmal-ul-Mudaq-e-qeen.

In addition to his being a religious preacher, he was also a social reformer. When he visited the valley for the second time, the converted Muslims still observed Hindu beliefs. He stressed the need to stop Sati, which was prevalent among the Hindus. In some parts of Kashmir even the Muslim women were buried with their dead husbands. He emphasised character building among the people. When he learnt that Sultan Qutb-ud-Din had kept his two sisters as his wives, he reprimanded him and asked him to divorce them. It is said that his followers were renowned artisans. He popularised shawl making, weaving, pottery and calligraphy.

Sultan Sikandar built a mosque to commemorate the visit of Shah Hamdan in 1395 AD. The mosque is one of the best wooden style Muslim architectural marvels of Kashmir. Ravaged by fire in 1480 AD, it was reconstructed and expanded by Sultan Hassan Shah. In 1493, it was demolished again and rebuilt as a two-storey structure. Again in 1731, a fire destroyed the mosque. Abul Barkat Khan, a Muslim officer reconstructed it. Every year the people celebrate Urs here on the last lunar month. On this day thousands of people assemble and recite verses from the holy *Quran*.

Lall Ded-Lall Moj-Lall Arifa, 1320-1390 AD

Common people call her Lall Ded, but this great Kashmiri woman is called reverently by many names, such as Lalla the hermit, Lalleshwari, Lall Moj (Mother Lalla) and Lall Arifa.

It is surprising how the chroniclers of that period forgot to write about Lall Ded. Khwaja Azam Dyadmari was the first historian, who, in his famous book *Tawarikh-e-Kashmir* (History of Kashmir), talked about Lall Ded.

The history of Kashmir would be incomplete without the name of Lall Ded and her Vaakhs or sayings. Her Vaakhs in Kashmiri dialect have become synonymous with the art, culture and heritage of Kashmir. She is a symbol and source of inspiration for Kashmiri women. Her philosophical approach and the desire to embrace the whole world found brilliant expression in her Vaakhs. According to R K Parmu,[6] "Lall Ded was destined to be a great reformer of the Brahminical religion of Kashmir. She turned out to be the Kashmiri off-shoot of that mighty reformation movement of the fourteenth century whose leaders were Ramananda, (pioneer of Bhakti movement during 15th Century), Kabir, the mystic poet of 13th Century, and Guru Nanak, the first Guru and preacher of Sikhism, and others."

Lall Ded regulated the mechanism of individual assimilation of spiritual experience—in other words one's duty as a social being was to upgrade social consciousness. She crystallised the experience of man, his intrinsic development, cosmic realisation and the vision of the infinite. She became the source of most sublime spiritual experiences—aesthetic delight, transforming the old system of knowledge into a new one, where there is no divide, no segregation, no confusion, no conflict and no darkness. Yet, she was a simple woman who also faced problems like any other Indian woman.There are many legends about her life.

According to PN Kachru,[7] "Almost all the earlier chronicles starting from Jonaraja's *Rajatarangini* down to mid-17th century, have remained silent about Lall Ded. It was first in *Asrar-ul Abrar*,in 1654 AD, that Baba Dawood Mishkati replaces the name of the 'Nayika' of the forest with the name of Lall Ded." Baba Dawood Mishkati has mentioned a group of three Yoginis (women saints) in the episode of Prince Shahab-ud-Din and the chief was the Nayika. However, KN Dhar says that towards the close of the 19th century these Vaakhs were collected and translated through the efforts of Sir Aurel Stein and Sir George Grierson, and Dr Barnett rendered them into English verse.

The introductory note of the *Lallvakyani* is interesting.[8] "The present collection of verses was recorded under very similar conditions (similar means the way Sir Aurel Stein tried to collect the folk tales of Kashmir). In the year 1914, Sir George Grierson asked his friend and former assistant Mahamahopadhyaya Pandit Mukunanda Rama Shastri, to obtain for him a good copy of *Lallvakyani*, as these verses of Lalla's are commonly recited by Pandits. After much search, he was unable to find a satisfactory manuscript. But finally, he came in touch with a very old Brahmin named Dharma Dass Darwesh of the village Gush. Just as this professional storyteller recited folk tales, so he made it his business, for the benefit of the pious, to recite Lalla's songs as he had received them by family tradition."

According to B N Parimoo,[9] "She became famous in every quarter of the Valley and acted as a soothing balm for people in distress. But before attaining that exalted position, she had to suffer immensely." Lall Ded was born to a middle-class Brahmin family in a village of Pandrethan formerly known as Puranadhisthana. According to PNK Bamzai, Lall Ded was born during Sultan Alau-ud-Din's period ie 1343 to 1354 AD. However, according to some of the writers such as Prem Nath Bazaz and T N Dhar, Lall Ded was born in 1335 AD, when Udyanadeva was on the throne of Kashmir. No historian, not even Jonaraja, has given the correct date of her birth. However, this great soul appeared on the horizon of Kashmir.

The mysterious smile on her face evoked pleasure and joy. As she entered adolescence, she ran the family errands according to the wishes of her parents. She remained above materialistic desires, and was always engrossed in her transcendental bliss. Says Prem Nath Bazaz,[10] "From the early years of her childhood it became manifest that she was an intellectual prodigy but times were so out of joint that nobody took any particular notice of her uncommon talents which were allowed to remain undeveloped till she entered her teens."

Indian women, or for that matter women the world over, have faced enormous multiple discriminations and have been subjected to social and gender bias. Lall Ded was no exception. As per tradition, she was married off at the early age of twelve.

Unfortunately, she was married to an illiterate Brahmin, Sona Pandit, at a village in Pampore. Just after the marriage Lalleshwari's name was changed to Padmavati by her in-laws. Her dull husband lacked the capacity to appreciate her nobility and divine spark. According to Prof Neerja Mattoo,[11] "The marriage, as is the case with most where the woman dares to follow an independent course, was doomed from the very beginning. The couple was ill-matched. The husband had none of the sensitivity or subtlety of mind to appreciate Lall Ded's deeper expectations from life." She remained ill-treated and ill-fed despite having an affectionate father-in-law.

Most of the chroniclers have suggested that her mother-in-law was cruel and cunning. It was the prevailing tradition of the day for mothers-in-law to keep their daughters-in-law under pressure and strain, often cursed, often thrashed, and often unfed, because it was felt that they would become disobedient. The birth of a son was treated as a boon—a fall back in their old age in terms of physical and financial help.

Lalleshwari's mother-in-law made her do all household chores from morning till late night. She was starved and the starvation continued for a long time.

It so happened that there was a feast in the house and each family member was busy with the preparation since morning. Suddenly Padmavati was asked to get water from the river. When she went to fetch water, she met other girls of the locality there and joined in their laughter and giggles. Suddenly one of the friends teased her about the feast and how much she was going to enjoy the food. The laughter was gone, the giggle vanished and Lalla thus replied:

"*Hond Mairitan Ya Kath*
Lalli Nilavath Chali Na Zahn"
"Let them slaughter ram, lamb or goat,
the feast for Lalla is only shingle for her meal."

The story goes that Lalla's father-in-law who was passing that way overheard this conversation between her and her friends. Shocked, he wanted to ascertain the facts. As per Arjan Nath Kaul,[12] "...In order to satisfy himself, he snatched the thali from Lalla's hand when the evening meal was served to the members of the family and lo! the stone was there. He fell at Padmavati's feet in adoration and reverence. He entreated this apostle of patience to forgive him for all that she had been enduring in his home for such a long time."

The angry father-in-law scolded and rebuked his wife and told her to be considerate in future. This aggravated the situation. The mother-in-law could not bear the insult and she tried to instigate her son. She managed to poison his ears and succeeded in creating suspicion about Lalla's infidelity. Day in and day out, she was maltreated, rebuked and cursed at every step. Prem Nath Bazaz writes,[13] "Lalla's husband was not only totally indifferent to the trials that she had to undergo; he often sided with his mother to the exasperation of the young and virtuous wife."

To quote Yuri Borev,[14] "Tragedy is a stern word... (yet) tragedy is always optimistic: even death serves life. The tragic then shows global metaphysical problems of existence and the social meaning of human life." And this applied to Lalleshwari. One fine morning the brave woman shed her shackles and left the house and went on to become immortal as Lall Ded.

Almost all the Hindu chroniclers have stated that Lalla left her husband's house and went to her first guru Sidh Srikant. However, there are some Muslim writers who refute this. According to Mohammad Ishaq Khan,[15] "Mula Ali Raina, who was the first to mention her, says that she was a chosen disciple of Sayid Husain of Simnani. It was at the latter's command that Lalla took spiritual charge of Nuruddin just after his birth." This assertion is controversial. As a daughter-in-law in that household, it was unlikely that she would become the disciple of Sayyid Husain of Simnani.

Many myths, legends and miracles are woven around her name, which indicate the reverence in which Hindus and Muslims held her alike. It is said that once she brought water from the river in a pitcher at which her mother-in-law shouted at her saying the water was not sufficient. She was ordered to fill all the pitchers. It is with her pitcher that she filled all the other pitchers and yet there was water still left in it. She threw the water on the ground and it became a spring known as Lalltrag.

A legend about Lall Ded is that when she saw Sayyid Ali Hamadan she cried "I have seen a man." Then she jumped into the oven of the baker's shop. She emerged out of the oven clad in a green dress. While stating this story Sir George Grierson says,[16] "The above story will give some idea of the legends that cluster around the name of Lalla. All that we can affirm with some assurance is that she certainly existed, and that she probably lived in the fourteenth century of our era, being a contemporary of Sayyid Ali Hamadan at the time of his visit to Kashmir."

Kashmir Shaivism is inherently monistic in substance. It does not deny the existence of a personal god or of gods. But emphasis is on meditation by the devotee under the guidance of a guru. And that is how Lalla started her meditation under the guidance of her guru Sidh Mol, a Shaivite scholar of that time. Soon she started translating her thoughts into *Vaakh* (couplets). Shyam Lal Sadhu says,[17] "Lall Ded was ushered into this atmosphere. Her delicate heart broke against the harsh treatment she received at the hands of her in-laws." He further says, "Before long she became a recluse and passing through various phases of discipline, she realized the unity of all creation."

She became a staunch devotee of Kashmir Shaivism. According to K Ayyappapanicker,[18] "Lall Dyad (Lall Ded) had a strong affinity with the Pratyabhijna of Trika which originated in Kashmir and was expounded by various philosophers in various ages, like Somananda, (9th Century), Utpaladeva, (10th Century), and Abhinavagupta, (11th Century)." Though the esoteric philosophy of Shaivism embraces both knowledge and devotion, yet to assimilate it was beyond the common man. It is this saint who translated this terse subject into the common man's dialect. According to PNK Bamzai, [19] "The greatness of Lalla lies in giving the essence of her experiences in the course of her yoga practices through the language of the common man."As per Neerja Mattoo,[20] "The most significant contribution of Lall Ded is that she brought the difficult Shaiva Philosophy out from the closest of the Sanskrit scholars to the wide open space of the Kashmiri speaking common people."

According to Richard Carnac Temple,[21] "It is not to be assumed that Lall Ded was thoroughly acquainted with the whole Yoga theory or that she necessarily thoroughly understood it, but that she had studied under learned exponents of Trika Philosophy and was well acquainted with the general teaching and phraseology they employed is quite evident from the *Lall-vakyani*. Such an exposition as has been given of Shaivism and Yoga is necessary for a comprehension of her word."

According to Shashi Shekher Toshkhani,[22] "Eventually, Lalla reaches a stage where she acquires an uninterrupted and unmediated awareness of the ultimate reality."

Writes P N Razdan /Mahanori,[23] "Lalleshwari seems to have delved deep into the realms of her self-consciousness guided by sparkling rays of the inner, master Sun, which reveals the ultimate Truth, gifts one with the right choice of inspiring words of wisdom that kill all evil and pain, of every kind, cool and compose the soul and delight the mind with intuitive foresight and divine discrimination and discernment."

Tradition says that after some time, Lall Ded's husband realised her qualities and he went to seek her pardon. As soon as he reached her place, a discussion was taking place between the guru Sidh Mol and disciple Lalla. The husband also decided to participate in it. The debate was to investigate the brightest light, sacred pilgrimage, the best friend and the best happiness. Some of the writers have mentioned that the discussion took place between Lall Ded, her husband and Sidh Mol, while some say the discussion was held between her, Nund Rishi and Nund Rishi's disciple Baba Nasru-ud-Din. The discussion went as follows:

Speaker one:

No light to match that of the moonlight
No pilgrimage as holy as Ganges
No relation like that of a brother
No contentment and glee without a wife.

Second speaker:

No Light like that of the eyes
No Pilgrimage as holy as knees
No relation better than one's pocket
No ease than that of a blanket

Lalleshwari:

No light better than the spiritual nectar
No pilgrimage holier than that of knowledge
No relation as personal as God
No pleasantness without the fear of Almighty

Listening to the reasoning given by Lalla, it is said that Guru Sidh Mol at once accepted his defeat and exclaimed, *Gav Tcsath Gauras Khasithay*, meaning "The knowledge of the disciple has surpassed that of the Guru." According to Chitralekha Zutshi,[24] "Scholars and lay persons alike recognise Lalla Arifa—or Lall Ded as she is commonly known—as the first mystic poet of the Kashmir Valley. She is credited with having introduced and given substance to the idea of Kashmiriyat through her verses, which have formed the cultural repertoire of generations of Kashmiris."

Lalleshwari expressed her thoughts in the form of couplets. Her life and teachings revolve around one God and that is Shiva. Her struggle was to get rid of the bondage of the soul and achieve the 'Nature of Shiva, to merge with Shiva.' Shaivites achieve this through ascetic practices and penances, with an emphasis on yoga and renunciation. Many Shaivites become wandering Sadhus. As per PNK Bamzai,[25] "She pursued yoga under Sidh Srikant until she succeeded in reaching the Abode Of Nectar."

Lalla must have been conscious of the social and religious degradation. The intellectual climate was overcast with the clouds of fanaticism of both Hindus and Muslims. The clash had reached a point of no return. According to Prem Nath Bazaz,[26] "The warfare of ideas and ideals in which the people of Kashmir were involved in the fourteenth century was no ordinary one; it was a gigantic clash of two great cultures of the world." It is, therefore, clear that Islam was taking root in the country and the Brahmins were losing their authority in the administration of Kashmir. As per Shyam Lal Sadhu,[27] "The Hindu society in Kashmir suffered irretrievable demoralisation and corruption for several generations preceding her birth and it failed to protect itself against aggression from without and decay from within. As a consequence, not only did the populace suffer but what had a great impact on the history of Kashmir, the Hindus lost the ability to rule their country and had to yield place to Muslims." Narendra Sahagala writes,[28] "History gives an account of some of the fights and small battles between the two sides. Since these Muslim Pundits had the support of the Sayyids and the Government, it resulted in the destruction of the basic society."

According to J N Ganhar,[29] "There is a striking resemblance between the spiritual experiences of Lalla and the Buddha. Like him she wandered far and wide in search of the truth, made visits to shrines and pilgrimages, and sought salvation in the company of holy men, but mostly in vain. Ultimately she suddenly found it in her own soul."

Lall Ded's renunciation started developing into spiritual emancipation. Her spirit could no longer be contained. She went forth to satisfy the spiritual cravings of the people and apply balm to their wounds. According to Sir George Grierson,[30] "There are few countries in which so many wise sayings are current as in Kashmir, and none of these have greater repute than those attributed by universal consent to Lal Ded."

Vaakh
Khyan Khyan Manusho kun no vatak
Na khyan gachkho ahankari
Somi asakh somi rozakh
Somi yenay muchrane barnyan tuer
Greed plunges you in gluttonism, you are nowhere
And acute austerity makes you haughty
Choose moderation and the golden middle path
Latches, doors get unlocked
vistas agog with light, open up..
Vaakh
Zanam pravith vaibhav na chondum
Lubhan bhugun bhrum na pray
Somi ahaar syatha zonum
Choolum dukh-bhav polum dye
I cherished the human form but not the desires
Never was I greedy for enjoyment and pleasure
I ate little and found it abundantly satisfying
The pain I bore patiently yet I nourished Him inside me

Lall Ded emphasised that discipline, moderation and sincerity could open doors of success for man. "Self-abnegation, purity of thought, consistency in word and deed, absence of greed, avarice and egoism in general, and non-attachment, are the essence of Lall Ded's teachings,[31] says Prem Nath Bazaz.

Lall Ded was a rebel. She minced no words in putting across her views against the customary and traditional ways of worship or offering sacrifice to the deities and idols, and she upheld the torch of rebellion until her death. According to Mohammad Ishaq Khan,[32] "By declaring Lall Ded, a Shaivite Yogini of the fourteenth century Kashmir as an avatar of Kashmiris, Nuruddin immortalized her name as a rebel against the Brahminical supremacy." She rebelled against idol-worship, animal sacrifice, pilgrimages and recitation of scriptures without knowing their meaning. Yet she knew that Kashmir had a great culture and tradition. She said:

Since aeon we emerged into being
And we shall hold tomorrow too
Look Shiva is creator and destroyer
The celestial delight of Sun does not die

Writes Chitralekha Zutshi,[33] "Lall Ded was undoubtedly against organised religion, particularly as represented by Brahmanism, and probably laid the ground work for the propagation of Islam among the Kashmir populace."

Her guru, her mentor and preceptor or her God was Shiva—Shiva the formless, timeless and spaceless Supreme God. Adi Shankaracharya interpreted the name Shiva as meaning, "one who purifies everyone by the utterance of his name", or "the pure one". As such, the name Shiva is considered the holiest of holy names. For Lall Ded, Shiva is universal consciousness.

In one *Vaakh* she says:

Time and again I craved to know
Oh mentor tell me the name of the nameless
Exhausted and helpless I resigned to solitude
Suddenly something was born out of nothingness.

Mohammad Ishaq Khan,[34] writes, "According to tradition, quoted in several hagiological works, for three days after his birth, Nuruddin, did not take milk from his mother. But then, Lall Ded visited the house of Satar Ghanai, the father of the newly-born, and addressed the baby :

'Thou were not ashamed of being born; why then art thou ashamed of sucking.' The baby started taking milk."

Mohammad Ishaq Khan says,[35] "As Nuruddin remarks in one of his popular verses:

"*Tas Padman purchi Lalay*
Yam Gallay Amrit chawu...

That Lalla of Padampora
Who had drunk to her fill the nectar.
She was an avatar of ours
O God, grant me the same sacred power;

He further says, "Undoubtedly, Lalla gave unique orientation to the evolution of a new cultural pattern in Kashmir. The influence of her

Vaakhs was deep on Nuruddin during the formative state of his mystical career; likewise, the impact of her revolt against social and religious discrimination was tremendous on the folks, for whom, even from the point of view of Hindu scriptures, she was the saviour in their hour of calamity and enslavement."

She became a poet of class. Her verses are faultless and flawless. According to BN Parimoo in *Lalleshwari*,[36] "Her sublime experiences, and her inspired poetry flowed out spontaneously, as water gushes out of natural springs. The water flows through channels, the depressions and gorges already present, so also it true of a poet's inspiration." In her Vaakhs she speaks of the common man—about the boat and boatman, potter, the voyun (grocery merchant), gardener, Kaandur (the baker). In short, she simplified the mystified philosophy. According to Neerja Mattoo,[37] "There is no elitist, Brahminical choice of word, phrase or metaphor—these are drawn from a woman's world of domesticity, though she walked out of marriage and home. Her poetry is a woman's work and in the process, gives a voice to women. So Lall Ded gave voice to women of Kashmir."

Not that the young kids were deprived of the flavour of her *Vaakh*. Tradition says that she wrote for them also the play-way rhyme to understand the subtle meaning of god:

"*hu kus, bo kus, telivan tche kus*
mohuk baat lodum degi
shwas khich khich vae mano
boo madhya heri poni sorum
boo madhya venis tekhis tekha chiye"

In this Vaakh she has made a playful lingo and with that she imparted to the children her divine message.

Writes K Ayyappapanicker, [38] "Although Lalla's poetry is perfectly in consonance with Pratyabhijna system of Kashmir Shaivism, it is essentially the personal experience of an individual in spiritual journey."

Lalla's mystical poetry successfully blends monistic philosophy of Shaivism and dualism of Islam. She manages to address her message to the common, ignorant and uneducated people, whether Hindus or Muslims in the countryside through their own simple Kashmiri dialect. The Muslims titled her Maryam-i-Makani, Arifa Majzuba, and Majnun-i-Aquila etc. The fact is that her sayings are meant neither for Hindus nor for Muslims. They are addressed to human beings without caste, creed and religion.

Lall's approach to religion was primarily humanistic.It is said that Kashmir is a paradise on earth. But in this paradise there have been religious communities who have been antagonistic to each other. Through their verses, Lall Ded and Nund Rishi inspired the people to live homogeneously.

Sheikh-Nur-ud-Din, 1378-438 AD

Hazrat Sheikh Nur-ud-Din Wali Noorani, reverentially known as Sheikh-ul-Alam, Alamdar-e-Kashmir, Sarkhel-e-Rishiya, and affectionately called Nund Rishi by the local folks, was a most venerated Muslim saint of Kashmir. He was also named Nund Sahaz by his Hindu followers. He was born in 1377 AD at village Qaimoh, which is on the BC Road near Bijbihara.

Originally, his father Sheikh Salat alias Salat Sanz had migrated to the Valley from Kishtwar where his ancestors belonged. Salat Sanz was the first Hindu who got converted to Islam through Sayyid Husain Simnani, who with Sayyid Tajuddin had come to Kashmir to help in conversion of Hindus to Islam. According to Mohammad Ishaq Khan, [39] "From his family name of Nanda it seems he became Nund Rishi after accepting the Rishi cult." Kashmir was ruled by Sultan Shahab-ud-Din, when the two Sufis came. They were deputed by Sayyid Hamadan to take care of Islamic movement in Kashmir. Nur-ud-Din was only 12 years old when Sayyid Simnani died in Kashmir. After his father's conversion to Islam, the young Nund Rishi remained in the company of Kubrawiya Sufis. His association with them seems to have greatly influenced him towards Sufism. Then there was also his association with Lall Ded. According to Mohammad Ishaq Khan,[40] "There is yet another important element among the sources of Nuruddin. While the influence of Lall Ded on him can hardly be denied, the association of the Yogini with Hussein Simnani must have induced him to seek inspiration from both." Thus Sheikh Nur-ud-Din's Rishi cult was also a blend of Lalla's Shaiva philosophy and Islamic Sufism.

Among Hindus, the Rishi order was not an organised movement. This name of Rishi was given to any person who talked and practiced about divine powers. But Muslims made Rishihood a cult in which many of them participated. Nur-ud-Din who accepted this Rishi Order made it a popular cult. Tradition says that the word rishi is derived from Persian word 'Raish or Rish' which means the wings of a bird.

Sheikh Nur-ud-Din was influenced and impressed by Hindu Rishis who had discarded the pleasures of life and were in pursuit of spiritual advancement—the realisation of the ultimate reality. In Rishihood they adopted various phases of Bhakti by singing in praise of the Almighty. Some of these rishis adopted mysticism as a method to achieve spiritual advancement.

According to Mohammad Ishaq Khan,[41] "It signifies a movement of indigenous, mysticism within the fold of Islam." But the fact was that the Rishi movement was an off-shoot of the Bhakti movement and Kashmiri converts to Islam had no inhibitions about practising it. The Rishi Cult was a composite blend of Hinduism and moderate Islam.

After the death of his father Nuruddin was sent to the carpet weaving centre, but the weaving technique did not inspire him. He then renounced the world and went to live in a cave for twelve years. That took a toll on his health. But his undertaking penance attracted huge followers, irrespective of caste, creed and religion.

"One instrument holds my rapt attention
The other teaches me to renounce the world;
The paddle points down to the grave;
This is the craft to which my parents have apprenticed me."

Sheikh Nur-ud-Din's sayings in Kashmiri language are not only interesting but seem to have been conjured up by some divine blessings. According to Chitralekha Zutshi,[42] "Nooruddin was able to create a framework for regional culture through his use of the Kashmiri language to propagate a devotional religion, which was significantly, outside the purview of the state. In fact, the reigning Sultan of Kashmir, Ali Shah (1413 – 20), ordered him arrested for preaching rebellious ideas to the people."

Describing the hollowness of human life in the world, Nur-ud-Din said:
(Translations by Mohammed Ishaq Khan)

"This life is a hollow bubble;
We are just a drop in the vast ocean,
An ass like me is unable to bear its brunt,

Having deserted home, why should I care to live?"

Envying the attainment of salvation by the Janaka Rishi of Dandakvan, Nund Rishi was longing for similar spiritual progress and he says:

(Translation by P N Razdan/Manohri)

Janaka Rishi of Dandakvan.
Living on herbs, wild fruit, was
A perfect Bhakta, a pearl among devotees!
Grant me that boon, O Deva.
He is beside me and
I'm beside him,
Blissful I feel with him,
In vain, I went seeking Him
In strange lands, for
My Friend Himself graced me
In my own house!

Nur-ud-Din's life was simple. During his lifetime he witnessed cultural and religious transformation of the people of Kashmir. He produced a determined philosophy of composite culture. In his *Shrukhs* (verses) and poetry he writes:

"What qualities hast thou found in the world?
To allow thy body a free, loose rope?
The Musalman and Hindu sail in the same boat
Have thy play and let's go home."

In another stanza he writes:

"Among the brothers of the same parents
Why did you create a barrier?
Muslims and Hindus are one.
When will God be kind to His servants?"

After the death of Sheikh Nur-ud-Din a huge Khanqah was built at Chrar village in South Kashmir. The famous shrine stands on the land which belonged to Sangram Dar. In accordance with historical findings, the Tomb of Sheikh Noor-ud-din-Noorani was built by Zain-ul-Abidin after his death.

Like Lall Ded, Noor-ud-din's message gave a unique shape to a new culture, which got the name of 'composite culture'. It was through this composite culture that various ethnic communities, who could not see eye to eye among themselves, lived harmoniously till 1988 AD when Pakistan sponsored religious fanatics came to Kashmir and destroyed the centuries old culture. These fanatics also torched even the sanctum sanctorum, of Hazrat Noor-ud-din-Noorani at Chrar-e-Sharif in 1995, wherein the mortal remains of the saint were placed.

Habba Khatoon

Habba Khatoon was the last Kashmiri Muslim Queen. She was born in a poor Muslim peasant's house. She had a natural gift of composing and reciting poetry in Kashmiri language. Her melodious voice mesmerised listeners. Her lyrics were considered flawless in technique and in imagery.

She was named as Zoon (The moon). Her father, Abdul Rather, and mother Janam were residents of Chandrahar Village near Pampore, eight miles to the south-east of Srinagar. It is difficult to say whether her parents appreciated her talent. They did sent her to a madrasa where she studied the *Quran*. She also read a few books particularly *Gulistan Bostan* of Sheikh Saadi.

Her talents surfaced in childhood when she composed high quality poetry and was declared a poet. Throwing away the traditional way of life of a common highland lass, Zoon spent time in composing poetry and singing the verses while walking, talking and roaming about. It is said that she had a golden voice and people loved to hear her songs. Her fame as a poetess and musician travelled far and wide.

As was the practice then, Zoon was married to a peasant boy Aziz Lone, a traditional Muslim whose routine was to go to the fields with the plough and return home in the evening. The condition Zoon's in-laws made before accepting her as their daughter-in-law was that she would not sing or compose poetry but would live like other common village girls. The marriage was performed but Zoon did not give up her singing. Her husband, as well as her in-laws, felt ashamed when they heard her singing and people admiring her. The marriage proved a failure. Perhaps stress at the in-laws place resulted in her poems of distress. In fact, there is one such poem that has become synonymous with every woman of Kashmir:

Kashmiri
Vareeviyan seet var chas no
Char kar myon malinyo ho
Look I am in discord with the in-laws
Listen, to me, your offspring,
Do resolve my distress

Yusuf Shah Chak, the Sultan of Kashmir, was once passing the fields where Zoon was deeply absorbed in her singing. The heir-apparent to the Kashmir throne was enchanted by her melodious voice as also her beauty when he saw her. Ultimately, he succeeded in marrying her.

The Sultan made her his Regent Queen and she was titled Habba Khatoon. For fourteen years, she enjoyed royal life and they were her most productive years, composing and reciting poetry. However, writes KN Dhar, [43] "She was forced to live with her parents. Habba, at such a tender and impressionable age could not recover from the rebuff she received at the very threshold of her conjugal life. Her despondency flowed out in the form of poetry pulsating with a natural fusion of sound and sense. Her fame reached the amorous ears of Yusuf Shah, who admitted her to his harem as a 'Keep', and did not allow her the status of a queen. Both the chroniclers, Birbal Kachru and Hassan Khohyami are punctilious about using the phrase 'sharing the same bed,' about her."

Habba Khatoon's marriage to Sultan Yusuf Shah Chak is also not confirmed by the historians. Writes William Charles Brice,[44] "Birbal Kachru in his *Majau'at-ut Twariksi*, which he wrote in the middle of the 19th century says that being a good singer and possessed of a melodious voice, she captivated the heart of Yusuf Shah Chak, who married her. But this account appears to be apocryphal, for it is not supported by any earlier authority. Neither the historian Haydar Malik nor the author of the *Baharistan-i-Shahi*, who were contemporaries of Yusuf Shah refer to her, although they mention all the prominent queens of the mediaeval period."

According to K N Dhar,[45] "Unfortunately, for us, we are actually at sea about the life of this Nightingale of Kashmir. No authoritative contemporary record has been unearthed so far to test the veracity of the popular tradition which associates Habba with Yusuf Shah Chak."

Yusuf Shah was tall and handsome and a romantic person. He was a man of many accomplishments. An artist at heart, he loved poetry, music and dancing. His songs in Kashmiri and Persian were already popular with the masses. Apart from being in great love with Habba Khatoon, he also loved nature. Therefore, it is not hard to imagine that once he found an artist in a rustic woman Zoon, he would have fallen for her. On her part she also wanted admiration of her art of composing lyrics, music and singing. She found all those things in the Sultan.

She composed a poem for the Sultan.

Meha Karmy Tchay Kit Posh Das Waanay
Chav Main Daanay Daanay Posh
I weave the joy for you
The wedding wreath of flowers
Come enjoy the exotic pleasure of happiness and ecstasy

In this poem, she humbles herself and puts her beloved on a pedestal. She says, "I am the earth and you are the limitless sky." This shows the amount of love she had for the king.

Soon, great misfortune befell the royal couple. Akbar, the Emperor of India, wanted to annex Kashmir to his empire. He sent Raja Bhagwan Das with a large force to invade Kashmir. But the peace-loving Sultan decided to submit to Akbar. Without telling his ministers he went into the tent of Raja Bhagwan Das who knew that the war could destroy both Mughals as well as the forces of Sultan Yusuf Shah. He thought it best to have an agreement with him and promised him safety of his life and also the Sultanate of Kashmir but under the Mughal supremacy. But Akbar imprisoned Yusuf Shah and sent him to Bihar.

The situation was bad and contained nothing but endless despair, desperation, and hopelessness. Yusuf Shah was yearning to return to his country and to Habba Khatoon. Tradition says that after some time she started singing while roaming in the valley. Interestingly, in between huge and gigantic mountains, full of pines at Gurez, Baramulla side, there is a small hillock on the bank of Kishenganga. The hillock is named Habba Baal (Hill of Habba Khatoon). Tradition says that while she became a wanderer, she reached Gurez and went to the top of the hillock. Nobody knows what happened to her afterwards. There is another view that she finally settled in Paanta Chhouk (Panta Chowk), near a mosque and died there.

The rhyme and the rhythm of her songs will continue to reverberate not only through the length and breadth of the Valley but also in the hearts of the people of Kashmir.

Verse

Tche Kamu Souni Miyani Brham Dith Niyunakho
Tche Kihozi Gaya Miyan Diee

Translation

Hey! who taketh you in a hypnotic spell
Leaveth me in lurch why do you despise me

According to William C Brice,[46] "In the first place, there is a strong tradition, which is impossible to ignore, in Kashmir, that Habba Khatoon lived in the second half of the 10th/16th century; and in the second, there is a large body of her songs and poems in Kashmiri which are attributed to her and to no one else. What seems more probable is that she was a mistress of Yusuf Shah.....She continued to live quietly in a cottage close to the mosque, both of which she had built, and died at the age of about 55 years."

Habba Khatoon inspired the women of Kashmir to read and write. She also taught the women artistic use of Kashmiri language. Irrespective of their caste and creed, women sing her songs and enjoy the romance of ache and pleasure which her works provide. Writes KN Dhar,[47] "Habba's songs are musical in essence and pathetic in spirit. She has also been acclaimed as a melody-queen of Kashmiri poetry. Her popularity is also due to the fact that her songs are not only a replica of Kashmiri sentiments but also a potent vehicle of Kashmiri music. Her originality in this sphere is undisputed."

Strangely, chroniclers of that time have not recorded anything about her. It is, in fact, Birbal Kachru and Hassan Khohyami, who have first mentioned her.

Says Tariq Ali, in his book *The Clash of Fundamentalism*[48] "Habba Khatoon gave the Kashmiri language a literary form and encouraged a synthesis of Persian and Indian Musical style. She gave women the freedom to decorate themselves as they wished and revived the old Circassia tradition of tattooing the face and hands with special dyes and powders. The clerics were furious. They saw in her the work of Iblis, or Satan, in league with the blaspheming, licentious Sufis. While

Yusuf Shah remained on throne and Habba Khatoon was untouchable, she mocked the pretensions of the Clergy, defended the mystic strain within Islam and compared herself to a flower that flourishes in fertile soil and cannot be uprooted."

Habba Khatoon, the songstress of Kashmir, through her delightful songs revealed aesthetically her emotional experience—of love and tragedy, and irreplaceable loss, a blend of sweetness and pathos.

Rupa Bhavani 1621 – 1721 AD

Rupa Bhavani is among the most venerated women in the history of Kashmir. Also known as Alakeshvari, Rupa was born to Pandit Madho Joo Dhar, great grandson of Mer Pandit Dhar. Madho Dhar, who lived in Mohalla Khanqah Sokhta near present Safa Kadal, was a devout follower of Goddess Sharika. He visited Sharika Parbat (Hari Parbat) regularly to meditate. A legend says that Pandit Madho Dhar believed that he was bestowed with a daughter, Rupa Bhavani who was the Goddess Sharika herself. Her angelic features convinced him that she was an incarnation of the Goddess herself . According to Shyam Lal Sadhu, [49] "As the little girl sat on her knees, he worshipped her with flowers and put into her mouth fruit which he used as an offering every morning, as is the usual practice. The divine form desired him to ask for a boon. 'Would that you come to us in this very form,' was his reply. 'Let it be so'!"

It was in 1621 AD that a baby was born in his house. It was the auspicious day of Jethpoornamashi and she was named Rupa. When young, she accompanied her father to places of worship. She also joined him in his discourses with other saints. Thus began her spiritual voyages.

Rupa was married at a very tender age to Hiranand Sapru of Habba Kadal. And then began a saga of pain and sufferings as her mother-in-law started treating her badly. According to Shyam Lal Sadhu,[50] "Her mother-in-law appears to have had a motiveless aversion towards Rupa. She looked at her with suspicion and infected her son with the same." The discomfort reached a point where Rupa had to leave the house to return to her father's place. Encouraged by her father, Rupa started her meditation in earnest. Like Lall Ded she started renunciation and meditation. However, she left her father's house and built her hut on the outskirts of Srinagar. After spending twelve years in meditation she left the place and went to Manigam near Kangan. Towards the end of her life she returned to Srinagar and lived in Safa Kadal. The mystic poet had many legends woven around her life including her birth, her renunciation, and even her death. She entered the Maha-nirvana in 1721 AD. The day is commemorated in Kashmir as Sahibi-Saptami. Tradition goes that the devotees, including Muslims, took her body for cremation and found only a few hairs and some flowers under the coffin cloth.

Rupa Bhavani became the incarnation of Goddess Sharika for Kashmiri Brahmins. The poetry she wrote is in *vaakh* form like Lall Ded's. Like Lall Ded she also believed in human beings irrespective of their caste, creed and religion. In her *vaakhs* one can find the influence of Trika Philosophy and also Islamic Sufism. She was, in fact, a mystic poet. Her *vaakhs* are terse and subtle. Her philosophy was simple. She believed that the path to realisation was shunning of the ego and disassociation from all material objects.

Rupa Bhavani composed verses much in the manner of Lall Ded whom she has referred to in most reverential terms.

Verse : (Translations by Dr Krishana Raina)

I dashed down into the nether regions and brought the vital breath up;
I got its clue out of earth and stones;
Then my Kundalini woke up with nada;
I drank wine by the mouth,
I got the vital breath and gathered it within myself.

Verse :

Selflessness is the sign of the selfless;
Bow down at the door of the selfless.
The selfless are of the highest authority,
The kings of the time and the wearers of the crest and crown.

Verse:

I did not come on this earth as a seed,
To fall in the circle of births,
I am not the elements
Earth, water, fire, air and ether
I am beyond the primordial universal self and the individual self,
I am the Supreme Consciousness

Srikantha Acharya

Srikantha Acharya is the one of the finest and earliest known scholars who wrote in Kashmiri language. He flourished in the 13th century.

His work *Mahanay-Prakasha* is a mystical work. Though he wrote in Kashmiri, yet he used Sanskrit words in plenty. The verses can be seen to have been written against the backdrop of Kashmir's Shaiva Tantric Philosophy. They are also nearer to Yoga Shastra.

Bhattavar

Bhattavar was a minister in the court of Zain-ul-Abidin, in the 14th century. His famous works are *Katha-Bansaur*, a narrative poem in Kashmiri language, describing the romance of Usha-Aniruddha which has been taken from *Harivamsha* (A Purana depicting the pastime of Krishna that took place after the battle of Kurukshetra). It also describes the slaying of the demon Bana by Lord Krishna.

Narayan Kaul Ajiz

Narayan Kaul Ajiz was a Kashmiri Brahmin. He flourished during the period of Jahangir. He was a great scholar of Persian language. In fact, he was the first Kashmiri Brahmin who excelled in Persian language. His famous work is *Tarikh-i-Kashmir*.

Sahib Kaul, 1658-1707 AD

Sahib Kaul alias Anandanatha was a celebrated poet who flourished during the period of Shah Jahan and Aurangzeb. He was a thinker, seer and a great Sanskrit scholar of his time. His famous work is *Krishnavtar Charit* (The Life of Lord Krishna) in Kashmiri language. Sahib Kaul was a great Shiva philosopher. He was an authority on Kula Shastra of Trika philosophy. He also translated *Ram Avatar* into Kashmiri language. Though being a staunch believer of Shiva philosophy, he was also a believer of Vedanta philosophy.

Arnimaal

"Arni Rang Guom Shravun Yeehay, Karoo Yeehay Darshoon Deehay"

"The turbulence in my life lost my shine too. I crave for some warmness, When shall the beloved come, I long to have glimpse of him."

That is the couplet one can hear in every house of a Hindu family in Kashmir. It is composed by the famous poetess of Kashmir known as Arnimaal. She was born during the period when the Hindus in Kashmir were being harassed by the Afghan rulers. Says Shashi Shekher Toshkhani, "When barbaric Afghan invaders were trampling the Kashmir Valley in 18th Century, this poetess was composing komal (delicate) poems." It was the time when Kashmir was ruled by the Pathans (Durrani Dynasty from Afghanistan).

Since childhood, Arnimaal was refined and sophisticated in her manners and very talented in the art of poetry. She was born in the Palhalan village of Baramulla. As was the tradition, she was married in her childhood. Her husband Bhawani Dass Kachru of Rainawari was a respected person in the court of Jumma Khan who was the governor of Kashmir (1788 – 1793 AD). Bhawani Dass was a renowned scholar of Persian literature.

The marriage made Arnimaal happy. However, it was shortlived. Being an important member of the court, Bhawani could not attend to his wife. Tradition says that he was a very handsome man with a striking personality and he felt that Arnimaal was not up to his expectations. Thus he neglected her. A heartbroken Arnimaal converted all the feelings of dejection into couplets. Love, sorrow, agony, dejection, pathos is quite evident in her poetry. The poetry tells us how much in love she was with her husband.

Ultimately, her husband's indifference made her return to her parents, who tried their best to look after her but they could not bring back her cheerfulness. She carried on with her lifeless existence. Time passed and she realised she had grown into an old woman. It was then that she started composing her love lore, still hoping against hope that her husband would come back.

And then one day, out of the blue, Bhawani Dass Kachru remembered his wife. Filled with remorse and regret he left all his engagements and rushed back to her but it was too late. Arnimaal was no more. Her lyrics in Kashmiri are excellent. The words are selectively used and touch the depths of are heart. The charm of her songs shall remain a treasure in the hearts of Kashmiris and in the annals of art in Kashmir.

Munshi Bhawani Dass Kachru

Munshi Bhawani Dass Kachru, a Kashmiri Brahmin from Rainawari Srinagar, was a respected scholar in the court of Governor Jumma Khan (1788 – 1793). He was a Persian poet of class having acquired mastery in Persian language. His masterpiece is *Behar-e-Tavil*, which he wrote under the pen name of Neku. *Behar-e-Tavil* is considered a great contribution towards the Persian language. Most of the Persian writers would envy him but they appreciated his command over the language, his calibre and erudition.

Parmananda, 1791-1879 AD

Parmananda is considered the greatest poet of Krishna Bhakti. He was born in a village called Seer near Matan. His father's name was Krishna Pandit and mother was Saraswati Devi. He studied Persian language up to elementary level. It was the time when Pathans were ruling Kashmir and Timur Shah Durrani had appointed Jumma Khan Alkozai as the governor of Kashmir. The Persian language had replaced Sanskrit. Parmananda started writing poetry in Persian during his youth. He was married to Maalded, a woman older to him. His father was a Patwari of the village. However, after the death of his father, he succeeded him as the Patwari.

Parmananda wrote many narrative poems such as *Radhaswaymvara*, *Sudamacharita* (The story of Sudama) and *Shiv Lagan* (The marriage of Shiva). All these are based on Sanskrit Puranas. *Shiva Lagan* gives us the fascinating story of Shiva's wedding with Parvati. The poem also tells us about the snow Linga at Amarnath cave. His poetry in Kashmiri language was set to musical tunes, which became popular among Kashmiri Hindus. Parmananda's Kashmiri language is an amalgam of Kashmiri and Sanskrit. The poems are mystical with puns and rhyming jingles, yet have deep spiritual meaning.

He Wrote: *Sar Korum Samsar Naduri Drav*

'I searched the world but found it mortal'

Pandit Saheb Ram Kaul

Pandit Saheb Ram Kaul was a great literary luminary who flourished during Maharaja Ranbir Singh's period. He was the son of Pandit Dila Ram, the Revenue Officer in Maharaja Gulab Singh's service. Pandit Dila Ram died when Saheb was only seven years old. Saheb Ram got married to a religious minded woman known as Poshmal Ded.

He initially learnt Sanskrit from his maternal uncle and later on at a Sanskrit pathshala. Soon he mastered Vyakarna and Alankara (Rhetoric). He also mastered two schools of Indian Philosophy—Vedanta and Mimamsa. His famous work is *Niti Kalpalata* describing the basics of good polity. His other works are *Sahayek Vivarnam*, *Gita Vyakhya Sahibi*, *Rajatarangini Sangraha*, and *Tirtha Sangraha*. George Buhler praised his work *Tirtha Sangraha,* about the ancient shrines of Kashmir. The work proved a great help to Sir Aurel Stein in locating the places easily.

Baba Dawud Khaki, 1313 AD

Baba Dawud Khaki was a Sufi saint. Born in 1313 AD, he received his early education from Mulla Bashir and Mulla Raziu'd Din, but he was the chief disciple of Hazrat Sheikh Hamza Makhdoom Sahib. He was also the chief Qazi of Kashmir and a scholar. A mosque in his name is at Anantnag town in Rishi Bazaar of Mohalla Khaki. The mosque is more than 600 years old. It is said that Shah-e-Hamadan visited the town and offered prayers where the mosque now stands. The ground floor of the mosque was completed by Mir Mohammad Hamdani, the son of Shah Hamdan and the second floor was constructed by Dawud Khaki. His important works are *Risala-I Ghusliya*, *Rishi-Nama*, and *Wirdu'l Muridin*. Baba Dawud died in 1586 AD.

Mulla Mohammad Tahir Ghani

Mulla Mohammad Tahir Ghani is considered one of the greatest poets of Persian language. He is said to have flourished during the 17th century. He was popularly known as Ghani Kashmiri. His poetry was not only appreciated in Kashmir and in India but by the great litterateurs of Iran and other countries. Ghani's work has universal connotations. Persia's most famous poet was so impressed by his works that he came to Kashmir just to meet him.

In an interview to *Greater Kashmir,* on August 2004, Sayyid Taffazul Hussain said, "In the process I discovered dozens of verses of Ghani's Dewan which had been Translated by Galib without acknowledging Ghani's name." He also says "Apart from aesthetic expressions the poetry of these two great poets, Tahir and Galib, is an exercise in philosophy also." Mulla Tahir was a Sufi poet. He has tried to deal with complex problems of human beings.

As per PNK Bamzai, Ghani was born in Kashmir during the Mughal period in the early part of Shah Jahan's reign. He lived in a small house at Rizvar Kadal. Some of the historians have placed his birth in 1630 AD. He was the pupil of Mohsin Fani. When Aurangzeb heard about Ghani Kashmiri he directed his governor Saif Khan to send him to court. Tradition says that when Saif Khan approached Ghani and told him about Aurangzeb's orders, he replied:

"Tell the emperor that Ghani has become insane."

"How can I lie to the emperor," Saif Khan said.

Ghani got up and tore his clothes.

According to R K Parmu,[51]"When the Governor approached him with the imperial command, the latter offered all possible excuses. When nothing appeared to help, he suddenly turned mad, tore his garments to shreds and shortly after passed away."

Tahir Ghani had his education in Kashmir. It is surprising that a poet of his calibre could learn the language totally and dominate the literary scene not only in Kashmir but in Iran too. He wrote about one Lakh verses but never in praise of any king. He transformed Kashmir into a contributor to the Islamic and Indo-Persian Culture. The famous poet Iqbal honoured Ghani with the title of 'Nightingale of poetry'. Ghani was also the founder of Sabak-e Hindi School of Persian poetry.

Mahmud Gami, 1765-1855 AD

Mahmud Gami was also a celebrated poet of Kashmir. He made Kashmiri language richer by his Vatsun (couplets) and Masnavi. His major contribution to Kashmiri literature is that he introduced the Persian Masnavi and Ghazal. His works are *Yusuf Zulaikha*, *Laila-Majnu* and *Shirin-Khusro* in Kashmiri language. His lyrics are beautiful and have a variety of themes. He had also composed an astounding number of Ghazals. *Yusuf Zulaikha* has 700 verses. Yusuf is the God of Love and Zulaikha his wife. His works are considered as lyrics of great excellence. Mahmud Gami died at the age of 90.

✦ ✦ ✦

References

Chapter- 1

1. *Travels in Kashmir, Ladakh Iskardo*: Godfery Thomas Vigne Vol II p 44
2. Ibid p 45
3. Ibid p 43
4. Ibid p 47
5. *Nilamatapurana*: Translation Ved Kumari Ghai, Shlokas, 45,46,80,82,83,48,53,54,72
6. *Kalhana's Rajatarangini*: Translation MA Stein Introduction p 22
7. *Baharistan-i-Shahi*: Translation Kashi Nath Pandita (Chapter 1)
8. *Kalhana's Rajatarangini*: Translation MA Stein Introduction p9 Para 4/ I.
9. *Nilamatapurana*: Translation Ved Kumari Ghai, Vol 1 p15
10. *Ain-I-Akbari*: Abul Fazal Translation H Blochmann Vol II p 355
11. *Position of Women in Ancient Kashmir*: [Article] Ved Kumari Ghai
12. Ibid (Article)

13. *Indian Epigraphy*: DC Sircar p 14
14. *Encyclopaedic Dictionary of Pali Literature*: B Barauh p 1181-2
15. *Srivara's Zaina Rajatarangini*: Translation Kashi Nath Dhar [Introduction]
16. *A Textbook Of Historiography*, 500 BC to AD 2000: E Sreedharan p 330 -338
17. Ibid p 338
18. *The Saga of the Kings of Kashmir*: Translation *Rajatarangini* Ranjit Sitaram Pandit (Forward) Jawaharlal Nehru
19. Ibid (Translator's note)
20. *History of Ancient India*: Rama Shankar Tripathi p 4
21. *Ancient India*: A K Warder and Ramesh Chandra Majumdar p 4
22 *The Wonder That Was India*: A L Basham p 45
23. *History of Indian Literature*: Moriz Winternitz p 96
24. *Students Britannica India*: Dale Hoiberg and Indu Ramchandani p 254
25. *Programming Language Pragmatics*: Michael Lee Scott p 4
26. *Kalhana - The Chronicler* Article K N Dhar
27. *Kalhana's Rajatarangini*: Translation M A Stein Comments Vol 1, p 6
28. *A Textbook of Historiography, 500 BC to AD 2000*: E Sreedharan p 333
29. *History of Indian Literature*: Moriz Winternitz p 96
30. *Cultural and Political History of Kashmir*: P N K Bamzai p 35
31. *Rajatarangini of Jonaraja*: Translation J C Dutt, p 1
32. Ibid p 3
33. Srivara's *Zaina Rajatarangini*: Translation Kashi Nath Dhar I/I SL-3
34. Ibid SL-8

Chapter- 2

1. *Companion to Tantra*: S C Banerji p 39
2. Ibid
3. *The Tarikh- i-Rashidi*: Mirza Haydar Duglat p 424
4. *Kashmir*: Francis Younghusband

5. *Al-Hind: The Making of Indo-Islamic World*: Andre Wink p 237
6. *Travels In the Mogul Empire*: Francois Bernier
7. *Tuzuk-i-Jahangiri*: Translation Alexander Rogers p 136
8. *Where Three Empire Meet*: E F Knight p 23
9. *The Happy Valley*: W Wakefield p 2-3
10. *A Short History of Jammu Raj*: Sukhdev Singh Charak p 8
11. *Dogra Legends of Art & Culture*: Ashok Jeratha p 13
12. *On Roads*: Bhumesh Sharma p 8
13. *Glimpses of History Jammu & Kashmir*: Jyoteeshwar Pathik p 62
14. *A Short History of Jammu Raj*: Sukhdev Singh Charak p 35
15. *Duggar Ka Itihas*: (Hindi) Shiv Dutt Nimohi p 46
16. *A short History of Jammu Raj*: Sukhdev Singh Charak p 291
17. Ibid p 30
18. *Kalhana's Rajatarangini*: Translation MA Stein Comments Vol-1I p 433
19. *Kashmir under the Mughals*: Abdul Majid Mattoo p 31
20. *Tuzuk-i-Jahangiri*: Translation Alexander Rogers p 296
21. *Ladakh*: Sir Alexander Cunningham 356
22. *The Valley of Kashmir*: Walter Roper Lawrence p 23
23. *Kashmir: History And People*: S R Bakshi p 73
24. *Cultural and Political History of Kashmir*: P N K Bamzai at p 62
25. *Kalhana's Rajatarangini*: Translation MA Stein Comments Book-I SL-37
26. *Nilamatapurana*: Translation Ved Kumari Ghai SL 100
27. Ibid SL 73
28. Ibid SL 80
29. *Travels in Kashmir and Panjab*: Charles Hugel Baron p 172
30. *On Yuan Chwang's Travels in India*: Translation Thomas Watters Vol-I p 256
31. *A Journey from Bengal to England*: George Forster p 11
32. *Travels in Kashmir Ladakh, Iskardo*: Godfrey Thomas Vigne p 43
33. *Travels in the Mogul Empire AD 1656 -1668*: Francois Bernier p 430

34. *Indian Serpent Lore or the Nagas in Hindu Legend and Art*: J Ph Vogel p 223
35. *Kalhana's Rajatarangini*: Translation M A Stein (Introduction) Vol-1 p 29 Para 27
36. *Tree and Serpent Worship*: J Fergusson p 45
37. *Rupa Bhavani*: S L Sadhu p 13
38. *The Valley Of Kashmir*: Walter Roper Lawrence p 191

Chapter- 3

1. *Glimpsis Of History Of Jammu & Kashmir*: Jyoteeshwar Pathik p 19
2. *Nilamatapurana* Translation Ved Kumari Ghai SL 909 -911
3. *The Saga Of The Kings Of Kashmir* Translation *Rajatarangini* Ranjit Sitaram Pandit SL 63/ I
4. *Nilamatapurana* Translation Ved Kumari Ghai SL 6-7
5. *Daughter Of Vitasta* Prem Nath Bazaz p 24
6. *Nilamatapurana* Translation Ved Kumari Ghai SL 8-9
7. *Glimpsis Of History Of Jammu & Kashmir* Jyoteeshwar Pathik p 19
8. *Kalhana's Rajatarangini* Translation M A Stein Book-I SL 83
9. T*he Saga Of The Kings Of Kashmir* Translation *Rajatarangini* R S Pandit SL 85/ I
10. *Kalhana's Rajatarangini* Translation M A Stein Comments Book - I SL-101
11. Ibid SL-107
12. *Tree And Serpent Worship* J Fergusson p 47
13. *On Yuan Chwang's Travels* Translation Thomas Watters Vol-I p 267
14. Ibid Vol-I p 269
15. *Kalhana's Rajatarangini* Translation M A Stein Book-I SL 107
16. Ibid SL 131/ 1
17. *Daughter's Of Vitasta* Prem Nath Bazaz p 60
18. *Kalhana's Rajatarangini* Translation M A Stein Book –I SL 151
19. *History Of India* Vincent A Smith p 176
20. *Tree And Serpent Worship* J Fergusson p 45
21. *Kalhana's Rajatarangini*Translation M A Stein Comments p 29

Vol-1/1
22. *Kashmir Through the Ages* Ram Bakshi p 53
23. *Kalhana's Rajatarangini* Translation M A Stein Comments SL 168 Vol - 1/1
24. *The Doctrine Of Vibration* Mark S G Dyczkowski p 1
25. *On Yuan Chwang's Travels In India* Translation Thomas Watters Vol-I p 271
26. *Kalhana's Rajatarangini* Translation M A Stein Comments Vol - 1/ SL 176

Chapter- 4

1. *Kalhana's Rajatarangini* Translation MA Stein Vol-1/1- SL 187
2. *Programming Language Pragmatics* Michael Lee Scott p 73
3. *Encyclopaedia Of Kashmir* Suresh K Sharma Vol-5 p 115
4. *Tales From Rajatarangini* Shyam Lal Sadhu p 10 – 11
5. *The Saga Of The Kings Of Kashmir* Translation *Rajatarangini* Ranjit Sitaram Pandit SL 269/ I
6. *Kalhana's Rajatarangini* Translation M A Stein Vol-1/1 SL 276
7. Ibid Comments Vol-1/1 SL 287
8. Ibid Vol-1/1-287
9. Ibid Vol-1/1-289
10. *On Yuan Chwang's Travels In India* Translation Thomas Watters Vol-I p 289
11. Ibid Vol-I p 289-290
12. Ibid Vol-I p 288
13. *Kalhana's Rajatarangini* Comments MA Stein Vol 1/I - SL/ 341
14. *Tarikh-e-Hassan* Pirzada Gulam Hassan Vol-3/74
15. *Kalhana's Rajatarangini* Translation M A Stein Vol1/1 SL 354 -355

Chapter- 5

1. *Encyclopaedia of Kashmir - Cultural Heritage*: [Article] G L Kaul p 147
2. *Kalhana's Rajatarangini*: Translation MA Stein Vol-1/1 SL/ 20
3. Ibid Vol 1/1 SL/ 48

4. *Daughters of Vitasta*: Prem Nath Bazaz p 63
5. *Kalhana's Rajatarangini*: Translation M A Stein Vol I/ II SL/80
6. Ibid SL/109
7. Ibid SL/118
8. Ibid SL/128
9. Ibid SL/144

Chapter- 6

1. *Kalhana's Rajatarangini*: Translation M A Stein Vol-1 Book-III SL 16
2. Ibid SL 7
3. Ibid SL 9
4. Ibid SL 73
5. Ibid SL 97
6. Ibid SL 131
7. Ibid SL 305-306
8. *Imperial Gazetteer of India, Provincial Series*: Kashmir, p 23
9. *Studies in the Buddhist Culture of India*: Lal Muni Joshi p 17
10. *Kashmir History and People*: S R Bakshi p 63
11. *History of Indian Literature*: Maurice Winternitz Vol-III, p 97
12. *Cultural and Political History of Kashmir*: P N K Bamzai Vol-I p 115
13. *Baharistan-i-Shahi*: *A Persian Chronicle* Translation Kashi Nath Pandita Chapter-1
14. *Kalhana's Rajatarangini*: Translation M A Stein Vol-1 Book-III SL 480
15. Ibid Vol-1 Book-III SL 482
16. Ibid SL 490
17. *Daughters of Vitasta*: Prem Nath Bazaz p 65

Chapter- 7

1. *History of Ancient India*: Ram Shankar Tripathi p 344
2. *The Doctrine of Vibration*: Mark S G Dyczkowski p 2-3
3. *Encyclopaedia of Religion and Ethics*: James Hasting Part 6 p 554
4. *The Kashmiri Pandit*: Anand Kaul p 3

5. *Yuan Chwang's Travels in India*: Translation Thomas Watters Vol-I p 258-259
6. Ibid Vol-I p 283-284
7. *Al-Hind*: Andre Wink p 252
8. *Kalhana's Rajatarangini*: Comments M A Stein Vol-I/IV SL/10
9. Ibid Vol I/IV-SL/ 29
10. *Ancient Indian History and Civilization*: Sailendra Nath Sen p 293-294
11. *Kalhana's Rajatarangini*: Translation M A Stein Vol-1/IV S 62, 63
12. *History of Ancient India*: Ram Shankar Tripathi p 345
13. *Kalhana's Rajatarangini*: Translation M A Stein Vol-1/IV SL- 78
14. Ibid Comments Vol 1/IV SL 126
15. Ibid Vol 1/IV SL 126
16. *Alberuni's India*: Alberuni Vol-II p 178
17. *The Wonder That Was India*: A L Basham p 71
18. *History of Ancient India*: R C Majumdar p 261
19. *Kalhana's Rajatarangini*: Translation M A Stein Vol-1/IV SL129 /130
20. *Ancient India*: R C Majumdar p 267
21. *Reynaud's Memoirs* p 189
22. *Travels in Kashmir and the Punjab*: Baron Charles Hugel p 159
23. *Kashmir*: Francis Younghusband p 135
24. *Kalhana's Rajatarangini*: Translation M A Stein Book-4 SL-478
25. *Nepal*: Perceval Landon p 31
26. *Kalhana's Rajatarangini*: Translation M A Stein Comments Vol-1/IV SL/531
27. *The Dhyanyaloka of Anandavardhana*: Jeffrey Moussaieff Masson, M V Patwardhan p 5
28. *A History of Kashmiri Pandits*: Jia Lal Kilam p 12
29. *India as Seen in the Kuttani-mata of Damodaragupta*: A M Shastri p 220
30. *Early History and Culture of Kashmir*: [Article] Sunil Chandra Ray
31. *Kalhana's Rajatarangini* Translation M A Stein Vol-1/IV SL/622
32. Ibid Vol 1/IV SL/647
33. Ibid Vol 1/IV SL/649
34. *Daughters Of Vitasta*: Prem Nath Bazaz p 99
35. *Kalhana's Rajatarangini*: M A Stein Comments Vol-1/IV SL/686

36. Ibid SL/713
37. Ibid SL/710
38. *Nilamatapurana*: Translation Ved Kumari Ghai SL 217-218

Chapter- 8

1. *Kalhana's Rajatarangini*: M A Stein Comments Vol-1/V SL 24
2. *A History of Kashmiri Pandits*: Jia Lal Kilam p 13
3. *The Saga of the Kings of Kashmir*: Translation *Rajatarangini* Ranjit Sitaram Pandit Vol-1/V SL/17
4. *Kalhana's Rajatarangini*: M A Stein Comments Vol-1/V SL 44-45
5. *Ancient Monuments of Kashmir*: R C Kak p 125.
6. *Memorial of Mistakes Converted Kashmir*: Narendra Sahagala p 78
7. *Ancient India*: R C Majumdar and A K Warder p 356
8. *A History of Kashmiri Pandits*: Jia Lal Kilam p 13-14
9. *Imperial Gazetteer of India Provincial Series*: *Kashmir And Jammu*: p 23
10. *The Saga of the Kings of Kashmir*: Translation *Rajatarangini* Ranjit Sitaram Pandit Book V SL/182
11. Ibid SL 184
12. Ibid SL 160
13. *Jammu Kashmir and Ladakh*: Desh Bandhu p 40
14. *A History of Kashmiri Pandits*: Jia Lal Kilam p 15
15. *Kalhana's Rajatarangini*: M A Stein Comments Vol 1/V SL/225
16. *Daughters of Vitasta*: Prem Nath Bazaz p 26
17. Ibid
18. *Ancient India: History and Archaeology* Dilip Kumar Ganguly p 183
19. *Kalhana's Rajatarangini*: Translation M A Stein Comments Vol-1/V SL/248
20. *Daughters of Vitasta*: Prem Nath Bazaz p 29-30
21. *The Saga of the Kings of Kashmir:* Translation *Rajatarangini* Ranjit Sitaram Pandit Book V SL/257
22. *Kalhana's Rajatarangini*: Translation M A Stein Comments Vol-1/V- SL/301
23. *The Saga of the Kings of Kashmi*r: Translation *Rajatarangini* Ranjit Sitaram Pandit Book V- SL/349

24. *Ancient India*: R C Majumdar p 358
25. *Kalhana's Rajatarangini*: Translation M A Stein Book V SL/441
26. Ibid V- SL/444

Chapter- 9

1. *Kalhana's Rajatarangini*: Translation M A Stein Vol-1/VI SL/7
2. Ibid SL /15
3. Ibid SL /51
4. Ibid SL/117
5. Ibid SL/132
6. Ibid SL/156
7. Ibid SL/159
8. *Ancient India*: R C Majumdar p 301
9. *Daughters of Vitasta*: Prem Nath Bazaz, p 30
10. *The Saga of the Kings of Kashmir*: Translation *Rajatarangini* Ranjit Sitaram Pandit VI-SL/194
11. *Daughters of Vitasta*: Prem Nath Bazaz, p 35
12. *Kalhana's Rajatarangini*: Translation M A Stein Vol 1/VI SL/289
13. Ibid SL/310
14. Ibid SL/312
15. *The Saga of the Kings of Kashmir*: Translation *Rajatarangini* Ranjit Sitaram Pandit SL/313
16. *The Wonder That Was India*: A L Basham p 92
17. *Kalhana the Chronicler*: K N Dhar Article for Sri Parmananda Research Institute.

Chapter- 10

1. *The Saga of the Kings of Kashmir*: Translation *Rajatarangini* Ranjit Sitaram Pandit Book p 261
2. *Kalhana's Rajatarangini*: Translation M A Stein Vol 1/VII SL/5
3. Ibid SL/13
4. *The Saga of the Kings of Kashmir*: Translation *Rajatarangini* Ranjit Sitaram Pandit Book VII SL 15/16
5. Ibid SL 35
6. *Kalhana's Rajatarangini*: Translation M A Stein Vol-1/VII SL/38
7. *History of Ancient India*: Ram Shankar Tripathi P 348/ 349

8. *Alberuni's India*: Alberuni Vol-II p 13
9. *History of Ancient India*: Ram Shankar Tripathi p 349
10. *Kalhana's Rajatarangini*: Translation M A Stein Vol-1/VII SL/90
11. Ibid SL 99
12. *The Saga of the Kings of Kashmir*: Translation *Rajatarangini* Ranjit Sitaram Pandit Book VII SL 120
13. *Kalhana's Rajatarangini*: Translation M A Stein Vol-1/VII SL/153
14. Ibid SL/164
15. *The Saga of the Kings of Kashmir*: Translation *Rajatarangini* Ranjit Sitaram Pandit SL 200/ VII
16. *Daughters of Vitasta*: Prem Nath Bazaz p 71
17. *Ancient Monuments Of Kashmir*: Ram Chandra Kak p 139
18. *Bilhana*: Prabhakar Narayan Kawthekar P 22
19. *History of Indian Theatre* M L Varadpande p 274
20. *Kalhana's Rajatarangini*: Translation M A Stein Vol-1/VII SL/235
21. Ibid Vol-I Book VII - SL/237
22. *The Saga of the Kings of Kashmir*: Translation *Rajatarangini* Ranjit Sitaram Pandit Book VII-SL 435-441
23. Ibid Vol-I Book VII - SL/444
24. *Kalhana's Rajatarangini*: Translation M A Stein Book VII SL/322
25. *The Saga of the Kings of Kashmir*: Translation *Rajatarangini* Ranjit Sitaram Pandit Book VII SL/395
26. Ibid SL/460
27. *Kalhana's Rajatarangini*: Translation M A Stein Book VII SL/475
28. Ibid SL/558-590
29. Ibid SL-588
30. *Gazette of the Chamba State*: Rose Hutchison p 80
31. *The Saga of the Kings of Kashmir*: Translation *Rajatarangini* Ranjit Sitaram Pandit Book VII SL/716
32. Ibid (Comments) Book VII – SL/703
33. *Valley Of Kashmir*: Walter Roper Lawrence p 338
34. *History of Ancient India*: Ram Shankar Tripathi p 349
35. *Kalhana's Rajatarangini*: Translation M A Stein Vol-1/VII SL 879-880
36. Ibid SL 869-873
37. Ibid SL 874

38. *A History of Kashmiri Pandits*: Jia Lal Kilam p 18
39. *Kashmir: A Wailing Valley*: M L Gupta p 20
40. *Harsa of Kashmir and the Iconoclast Ascetics*: [Article] A L Basham
41. *Kalhana's Rajatarangini*: Translation M A Stein VII - SL 1093-1094-1095
42. *Ancient Indian History and Civilization*: Sailendra Nath Singh
43. *Kashmir Problem Has Origin In Fall Of Buddhism*: (Article) K Jamnadas
44. *Early India: from Origin To AD 1300*: Romila Thapar p 428
45. *Tales from Rajatarangini*: S L Sadhu p 110
46. *Kalhana's Rajatarangini*: Translation M A Stein VII SL 961-962
47. Ibid – VII SL 1147-1148
48. Ibid VII SL 1730

Chapter- 11

1. *Daughters of Vitasta*: Prem Nath Bazaz p 83
2. *Kalhana's Rajatarangini*: Translation M A Stein Vol-1/VIII SL 133
3. Ibid SL-VIII/368
4. *Daughters of Vitasta*: Prem Nath Bazaz p 84
5. *Kalhana's Rajatarangini*: Translation M A Stein VIII-174
6. Ibid SL-VIII SL 297
7. Ibid SL-VIII SL 368
8. *Culture and Political History of Kashmi*r: P N K Bamzai Vol-I p 162
9. *Kalhana's Rajatarangini*: Translation M A Stein Vol 1/VIII SL/ 375-376
10. Ibid VIII-SL 378
11. Ibid VIII SL- 443-444
12. Ibid (Introduction) p 16
13. Ibid VIII SL 923
14. Ibid VIII SL 927
15. *A Short History of Jammu Raj*: Sukhdev Singh Charak p 60
16. *Kalhana's Rajatarangini*: Translation M A Stein Vol-1/VIII SL 947-953
17. Ibid SL 1171-1172
18. Ibid SL 1206 -1207

19. Ibid SL-1273
20. *History of the Panjab Hill States*: J P Vogel Vol-1 p 294
21. *Rajatarangini Jonaraja*: English Translation J C Dutt p 4/III
22. *Kalhana's Rajatarangini*: Translation M A Stein VIII - SL/1357
23. Ibid - VIII SL 1377-1379
24. Ibid VIII – SL 1416
25. *Rajatarangini Jonaraja*: English Translation J C Dutt p 4/ III
26. *Kalhana's Rajatarangini*: M.A. Stein Comments SL 2264/ VIII
27. *Daughters of Vitasta*: Prem Nath Bazaz p 88
28. Ibid p 89
29. *The Saga of the Kings of Kashmir*: Translation Ranjit Sitaram Pandit Book VIII SL/3233
30. Ibid VIII SL 2376 - 2380
31. *Kalhana's Rajatarangini*: Translation M A Stein VIII SL 2376
32. Ibid VIII - SL 2386
33. Ibid VIII - SL 2395
34. *Women, Religion and Social Change*: Yuonne Yazbeck Hadad & Ellison Banks Findly p 77

Chapter- 12

1. *Rajatarangini of Jonaraja*: Translation J C Dutt p 433/III
2. Ibid p 5/III
3. Ibid p 6/III
4. Ibid p 5/III
5. *Kashmir: A Wailing Valley*: M L Gupta p 24
6. *Kalhana's Rajatarangini*: Translation M A Stein Vol-1/VIII SL/378
7. *Kashmir*: Francis Younghusband p 155
8. *Rajatarangini of Jonaraja*: Translation J C Dutt p 6/ III
9. Ibid
10. Ibid p 8/ III
11. Ibid p 8-9/ III
12. *A History of Kashmiri Pandits*: Jia Lal Kilam Chapter I p 20
13. *Rajatarangini of Jonaraja*: Translation J C Dutt p 10/ III
14. Ibid p 11/ III
15. Ibid p 12/ III
16. Ibid p 14/ III
17. Ibid

18. *History of Muslim Rule in Kashmi*r: R K Parmu p 92-93
19. *Culture and Political History of Kashm*ir: P N K Bamzai p 314
20. *Daughters of Vitasta*: Prem Nath Bazaz p 45
21. *Baharistan-i-Shahi*: A Persian Chronicle Translation Kashi Nath Pandita Chapter -II
22. *Tarikh-i-Malik Haider*: Malik Haider Chadora Translation Raja Bano p 28
23. *Rajatarangini of Jonaraja*: Translation J C Dutt p 17/ III
24. *Baharistan-i-Shahi*: A Persian Chronicle Translation Kashi Nath Pandita Chapter -II
25. Ibid
26. Ibid
27. *Daughters of Vitast*a: Prem Nath Bazaz p 45
28. *Baharistan-i-Shahi*: A Persian Chronicle Translation Kashi Nath Pandita Chapter -II
29. *A Short History of Jammu Raj*: Sukhdev Singh Charak p 62
30. *Daughters of Vitasta*: Prem Nath Bazaz p 45
31. *Baharistan-i-Shahi*: A Persian Chronicle Translation Kashi Nath Pandita Chapter -II
32. *Rajatarangini of Jonaraja*. Translation J C Dutt p 17/ III
33. *History of Kashmiri Pandits*: Jia Lal Kilam Chapter II p 31
34. *Rajatarangini of Jonaraja*: English Translation J C Dutt p 18/ III
35. Ibid p 20/ III
36. Ibid
37. *Baharistan-i-Shahi*: A Persian Chronicle Translation Kashi Nath Pandita Chapter -II
38. *Memorial of Mistakes Converted Kashmir*: Narendra Sahagala p 95
39. *A History of Kashmiri Pandits*: Jia Lal Kilam Chapter -III-p 37
40. *Kashmir's Transition to Islam*: Mohammad Ishaq Khan p 62
41. *The Spread of Islam in Kashmir*: Article G M D Sufi
42. *Rajatarangini of Jonaraja*: English Translation J C Dutt p 19/ III
43. Ibid p 20/ III
44. *Daughters of Vitasta*: Prem Nath Bazaz p 49
45. *The Valley Of Kashmir*: Walter Roper Lawrence p 258
46. Ibid p 286
47. *Memorial of Mistakes Converted Kashmir*: Narendra Sahagala p 99

48. *Daughters of Vitasta*: Prem Nath Bazaz p 52
49. *Memorial of Mistakes Converted Kashmir*: Narendra Sahagala p 97
50. *Rajatarangini of Jonaraja*: English Translation J C Dutt p 30/ III
51. *Baharistan-i-Shahi*: A Persian Chronicle Translation Kashi Nath Pandita Chapter -II
52. *Kalhana's Rajatarangini*: Translation M A Stein Vol. 1/VIII - p 480
53. *The History of the Mahometan Power in India*: Translation J Briggs Vol. IV/440
54. *Tarikh-I-Hasan*: Pir Gulam Hassan p 169
55. *Rajatarangini of Jonaraja*: English Translation J C Dutt p 31-32/ III
56. *Cultural and Political and History of Kashmi*r: P N K Bamzai P 178
57. *A History of Kashmiri Pandits*: Jia Lal Kilam Chapter -III p 347

Chapter- 13

1. *Kalhana's Rajatarangini*: Translation M A Stein Vol-1 Book-I, SL-17,18
2. *The Doctrine of Vibrations*: Mark S G Dyczkowski p 11
3. *Isvara-Pratyabhijna-Karika Of Utpaladeva*: Baljinnath Pandita
4. *The Doctrine of Vibrations*: Mark S G Dyczkowski p 11
5. *Encyclopaedia of Indian Philosophies*: Harold G Coward, Vol-V, p 32
6. *Indian Literary Criticism*: G N Devy p 61
7. *Saints and Sages of Kashmir*: Triloki Nath Dhar p 55
8. *Indian Literary Criticism*: G N Devy p 31
9. *Kashmir Shaivism*: (Article) P N K Bamzai
10. *A Concise History of Classical Sanskrit Literature*: G Shastri Bhattacharyya p 150
11. *Three Satires*: Translation Somadeva Vasudeva p 15
12. *Encyclopaedia of Indian Literature*: Amaresh Data Vol-1 p 437
13. *A Concise History of Classical Sanskrit*: G Shastri Bhattacharyya p 150
14. *Indian Poetics*: T Nanjundaiya Sreekantaiya p 56

15. *Bihalana*: Prabhakar Narayan Kawthekar p 6
16. Ibid p 59
17. *Encyclopaedia of Kashmir*: S R Bakshi p 116
18. I*ndia as Seen in the Kuttani-mata of Damodaragupta*: A M Shastri p 5
19. Ibid p 41
20. *Yuan Chwang's Travels in India*: and Translation Thomas Watters p 217
21. *A Hindu Critique of Buddhist Epistemology*: John A Taber p 120
22. *Encyclopaedia of Indian Philosophies*: Harold G Coward K Kunjunni Raja p 203
23. *Isvara-Pratyabhijna-Karika of Utpaladeva*: Baljinnath Pandita
24. *Encyclopaedia of Erotic Literature*: Gaetan Brulotte and John Phillips p 732
25. *The Doctrine of Vibrations*: Mark S G Dyczkowski p 26
26. *Desopadesa and Narmamala of Kshemendra*: Edited Pandit Madhusudhan Kaul Shastri p 29
27. *Three Satires*: Translation Somadeva Vasudeva p 17
28. *Desopadesa and Narmamala of Ksemenra*: Edited Pandit Madhusudhan Kaul Shastri p 11
29. *Indian Poetics*: T Nanjundaiya Sreekantaiya p 56
30. *Kalhana's Rajatarangini*: Translation M A Stein Vo-1 Book III/ 261
31. *History of Indian Literature*: Maurice Winternitz Vol III p 162
32. *Katha-sarit-sagara*: Somadeva Translation C H Tawney [Introduction]
33. *Medieval Indian Literature*: Ayyappapanicker p 215-216
34. *The Doctrine of Divine Recognition*: Introduction K C Panday Vol III, p-4
35. *Doctrine of Vibrations*: Mark S G Dyczkowski p 17
36. *Isvara-Pratyabhijna-Karika of Utpaladeva*: Baljinnath Pandita p-24
37. Ibid p-14
38. *Kashmiri Scholars Contribution to Knowledge* S Bhatt p 5
39. *Shiva Sutras*: *The Yoga of Supreme Identity*: Translation Jaideva Singh p 247

40. *K P An Important Component of the Indian Civilization*: [Article] Upendra Fotedar
41. *Kashmir Shaivism*: M G Chitkara p 27
42. *Kashmiri Scholars Contribution to Knowledge*: S Bhatt p 5
43. *Tantra*: Hugh B Urban p 34
44. *Trika Shastra*: [Article] Prem Nath Bazaz
45. *The Pratyabhijna Philosophy*: Ganesh Vasudeo Tagare p 5
46. *The Doctrine of Vibration*: Mark S G Dyczkowski p 84-85
47. *Isvara Pratyabhijna Karika of Utpaladeva*: Baljinnath Pandita p 35
48. *Spanda-Karikas*: Jaideva Singh p 14
49. *Svara Pratyabhijna-Vimarsini:* K A Subramania (Introductory note)
50. *The Krama Trantricism of Kashmir*: Navjivan Rastogi p 4
51. *Kashmir Shaivism*: M G Chitkara p 27
52. *Nilamatapurana*: Translation Ved Kumari Ghai, Verses 709 -710.
53. *On Yuan Chwang's Travels in India*: Translation Thomas Watters p 264
54. *Kalhana's Rajatarangini*: Translation M A Stein Vol-I, p 64
55. *On Yuan Chwang's Travels in India*: Translation Thomas Watters p 270
56. *The Wonder That Was India*: A L Basham p 276
57. *Hinduism and Buddhism*: Sir Charles Eliot Vol-I p 214
58. *Kalhana's Rajatarangini*: Kalhana Translation M A Stein Vol-1Book III/12
59. *Cultural and Political History of Kashmir*: P N K Bamzai p 72
60. *Kashmir Saivism and Its Echoes In Kashmiri Poetry*: (Article) B N Kalla
61. *Buddhism in Kashmir*: (Article) R L Aima
62. *Culture and Political History of Kashmir* P N K Bamzai p 75
63. *An Introduction to Buddhist Esoterism*: Benoytosh Bhattacharyya p 147
64. *On Yuan Chwang's Travels in India*: Translation Thomas Watters p 325
65. *Saints and Sages of Kashmi*r: Triloki Nath Dhar p 8

Chapter- 14

1. *Baharistan-i-Shahi*: A Persian Chronicle Translation Kashi Nath Pandita Chapter-II
2. Ibid Chapter II
3. *The History of India Muhammad Qasim Firishta*: Translation General J Briggs Vol-4 p 445
4. *A History of Kashmiri Pandits*: Jia Lal Kilam Chapter-III-p 35
5. *Cultural and Political History of Kashmir*: P N K Bamzai Vol-II/ 320
6. *A History of Kashmiri Pandits*: Jia Lal Kilam Chapter -III p 36
7. *Rajatarangini of Jonaraja*: English Translation J C Dutt p 33-34
8. Ibid p 34
9. Ibid p 37/ III
10. Ibid p 35/ III
11. Ibid p 36
12. *Baharistan-i-Shahi*: A Persian Chronicle Translation Kashi Nath Pandita Chapter –III
13. *Rajatarangini Of Jonaraja*: English Translation J C Dutt p 38/ III
14. Ibid p 38/ III
15. *Baharistan-i-Shahi*: A Persian Chronicle Translation Kashi Nath Pandita Chapter –III
16. *Tarikh-i-Hassan*: Pir Gulam Hassan Khuihami p 173
17. *Rajatarangini of Jonaraja*: English Translation J C Dutt p 44/ III
18. Ibid p 53 III
19. *Cultural and Political History of Kashmir*: P N K Bamzai Vol-II p 325
20. *Rajatarangini of Jonaraja*: English Translation J C Dutt p 53/ III
21. *Daughter of Vitasta*: Prem Nath Bazaz p 143
22. *Kashmir*: A Waling Valley: M L Gupta p 26
23. *The Rise of the Mahometan Power in India*: Translation General J Briggs Vol 4- p 461
24. *The History of Struggle for Freedom in Kashmir*: Prem Nath Bazaz p 53
25. *Rajatarangini of Jonaraja*: English Translation J C Dutt p57

26. *Tarikh-i-Hassan*: Pir Gulam Hassan Khuihami p 178-80.
27. *The Valley of Kashmir*: Walter Roper Lawrence-p 302
28. Ibid p 191
29. *The Rise of the Mahometan Power in India*: Translation J Briggs Vol-4 p 461
30. *Kashir*: G M D Sufi, Vol-I p 106
31. *Rajatarangini of Jonaraja*: English Translation J C Dutt p 57 III
32. Ibid
33. *Baharistan-i-Shahi*: A Persian Chronicle Translation Kashi Nath Pandita Chapter -III
34. Ibid
35. *Rajatarangini of Jonaraja*: English Translation J C Dutt Vol-III p 59-60
36. *Where Three Empires Meet*: E F Knight p 36
37. *Halat-i-Asad Beg*: Assad Beg Qazvini Translation B W Chapman p 445
38. *Memorial of Mistakes Converted Kashmir*: Narendra Sahagala p 126
39. *Baharistan-i-Shahi*: A Persian Chronicle Translation Kashi Nath Pandita Chapter -III
40. *Kashmir Wail of Valley*: Mohan Lal Kaul p 20
41. *Rajatarangini of Jonaraja*: English Translation J C Dutt p 64 III
42. Ibid p 72 III
43. *Srivara's Zaina Rajatarangini*: Translation Kashi Nath Dhar SL-19
44. *A History of Kashmiri Pandits*: Jia Lal Kilam Chapter –IV p 48-49
45. *Srivara's Zaina Rajatarangini* Translation Kashi Nath Dhar W-1/ I-SL-21
46. Ibid W-1/ I SL-22
47. *Cultural and Political History of Kashmir* P N K Bamzai II-p 336
48. *Baharistan-i-Shahi*: A Persian Chronicle Translation Kashi Nath Pandita Chapter-IV
49. *Rajatarangini of Jonaraja*: English Translation J C Dutt p 88/ III
50. Ibid p 83
51. Ibid p 86

52. *Srivara's Zaina Rajatarangini*: Translation Kashi Nath Dhar W-1/ I-SL-28
53. Ibid W-1/ V-SL-80
54. *Medieval Indian Literature*: K Ayyappancker p 229
55. *A History of Kashmiri Pandits*: Jia Lal Kilam Chapter IV p 55
56. *The History of the Rise of the Mohammedan*: Translation J Briggs Vol-IV/470
57. *Srivara's Zaina Rajatarangini*: Translation Kashi Nath Dhar 1/ VI/29
58. *Kashir, Being a History of Kashmir*: G M D Sufi Vol-I p 161
59. *Temple Architecture of the Western Himalaya*: Omacanda Handa p 107
60. *Srivara's Zaina Rajatarangini*: Translation Kashi Nath Dhar W-1/ 3-SL-42
61. Ibid W-1/ I-SL-32
62. Ibid W-1/1-SL-37
63. Ibid W-1/1-SL-74
64. Ibid W-1/1-SL-48
65. Ibid W-1/ 2-SL-19
66. Ibid W-1/ 3-SL-12
67. *Kashmir*: Francis Younghusband p 156
68. *Srivara's Zaina Rajatarangini*: Translation Kashi Nath Dhar W-1/ I-SL-18
69. Ibid W-1/ V-SL-32
70. Ibid W-1/ V-SL-34
71. *Nilamatapurana*: Translation Ved Kumari Ghai SL 238
72. *Srivara's Zaina Rajatarangini*: Translation Kashi Nath Dhar W-1/ III-SL-54
73. *Rajatarangini Of Jonaraja*: English Translation J C Dutt p 86
74. *Srivara's Zaina Rajatarangini*: Translation Kashi Nath Dhar W-1/ I-SL-56
75. *Rupa Bhavani*: S L Sadhu p 27
76. *Tarikh-i-Hassan*: Pir Gulam Hassan Khuihami - p 184
77. *Srivara's Zaina Rajatarangini*: Translation Kashi Nath Dhar W1/ III-SL-108
78. *Kashmir under the Sultans*: Mohibbul Hasan p 86

79. *Kalhana's Rajatarangini:* Comments M A Stein Vol-II/ 480
80. *Srivara's Zaina Rajatarangini*: Translation Kashi Nath Dhar W-II/ SL-11
81. Ibid W-II/ SL-23
82. *Tarikh-i-Firishta:* Muhammad Qasim Firishta P 475
83. *Srivara's Zaina Rajatarangini*: Translation Kashi Nath Dhar W-II/ SL-125
84. Ibid W-II/ SL-97
85. Ibid W-II/ SL-55
86. *Daughters of Vitasta*: Prem Nath Bazaz p 144
87. *An Historical Atlas of Islam*: William C Brice p 329
88. *Srivara's Zaina Rajatarangini*: Translation Kashi Nath Dhar W-II/ SL-40
89. Ibid W-III/III SL-11
90. *Rajatarangini of Jonaraja*: English Translation J C Dutt p 231
91. *Tarikh-i-Hassan*: Pir Gulam Hassan Khuihami p 210
92. *Srivara's Zaina Rajatarangini*: Translation Kashi Nath Dhar W-III/III/ 96
93. *Cultural and Political History of Kashmir*: P N K Bamzai II-p 350
94. *Daughters of Vitasta*: Prem Nath Bazaz p 148
95. *Srivara's Zaina Rajatarangini*: Translation Kashi Nath Dhar W-III/III/ 437
96. Ibid W-IV/SL-16
97. *Cultural and Political History of Kashm*ir: P N K Bamzai Vol-II p 355
98. *Srivara's Zaina Rajatarangini*: Translation Kashi Nath Dhar W-IV/SL-87
99. *Rajatarangini of Jonaraja*: English Translation J C Dutt p 338
100. *Kashmir under the Sultans*: Mohibbul Hasan p 118
101. *Rajatarangini of Jonaraja*: English Translation J C Dutt p 338-339
102. *A History of Muslim Rule in Kashmir*: R K Parmu p 191
103. *Tarikh-i-Rashidi*: Mirza Haydar Duglat Translation E Denison Ross p 435
104. *Kashmir under the Sultans*: Mohibbul Hasan p 11-12
105. *Rajatarangini of Jonaraja*: English Translation J C Dutt p 339
106. *A History of Muslim Rule in Kashmir*: R K Parmu p 199

107. *Cultural and Political History of Kashmir* P N K Bamzai p 365
108. *Kashmir under the Sultans*: Mohibbul Hasan p 123
109. *A History of Muslim Rule in Kashmi*r: R K Parmu p 200
110. *Kashmir under the Sultans*: Mohibbul Hasan p 124
111. *Rajatarangini of Jonaraja*: English Translation J C Dutt p 354
112. Ibid p- 364
113. Ibid p- 368-369
114. *Cultural and Political History of Kashmir*: P N K Bamzai p 370
115. *Tarikh-i-Rashidi*: Mirza Haydar Duglat Translation E Denison Ross p 441
116. *Cultural and Political History of Kashmir*: P N K Bamzai p 370
117. *The History of Struggle for Freedom in Kashmi*r: Prem Nath Bazaz p 66
118. *Kashmir under the Sultans*: Mohibbul Hasan p 140
119. *Rajatarangini of Jonaraja*: Translation J C Dutt p 369-370
120. Ibid p-373
121. Ibid p/376
122. *Kashmir under the Sultans*: Mohibbul Hasan p 141
123. *The History of Struggle for Freedom in Kashmir*: Prem Nath Bazaz p 67
124. *Kashmir under the Sultans*: Mohibbul Hasan p 147
125. *History of Muslim Rule in Kashmir*: R K Parmu p 229
126. *Tarikh-i-Rashidi*: Mirza Haydar Duglat Translation E Denison Ross p 434
127. *Kashmir under the Sultans*: Mohibbul Hasan p 146
128. *History of India*: Henry Miers Elliot & Dawson Vol-IV p 497-98
129. *History of Muslim Rule in Kashmir*: R K Parmu p 233
130. *History of India*: Henry Miers Elliot Vol-V p 127
131. *Kashmir under Sultans*: Mohibbul Hasan p 142
132. *Tarikh-i-Rashidi*: Mirza Haydar Translation Henry Miers Elliot Vol-V p 135
133. *History of Muslim Rule in Kashmir*: R K Parmu p 228
134. *Kashmir under the Sultans:* Mohibbul Hasan p 158
135. Ibid
136. Ibid p 159
137. *Cultural and Political History of Kashmir*: P N K Bamzai p 374

138. *Kashmir under the Sultans*: Mohibbul Hasan p 160
139. Ibid p 161
140. *Rajatarangini of Jonaraja*: Translation J C Dutt p 389
141. *History of Muslim Rule in India*: R K Parmu p 224

Chapter- 15

1. *History of Muslim Rule in Kashmir*: R K Parmu p 250
2. Ibid p 251
3. *Cultural and Political History of Kashmir*: P N K Bamzai p 376
4. *Rajatarangini of Sukha*: Translation J C Dutt p 390
5. *History of Muslim Rule in Kashmir*: R K Parmu p 254
6. *Rajatarangini of Jonaraja Translation*: J C Dutt p 391
7. *Culture and Political History of Kashmir*: P N K Bamzai p 377
8. *Rajatarangini of Jonaraja*: Translation J C Dutt p 392
9. Ibid p 393
10. *Culture and Political History of Kashmir*: P N K Bamzai p 378
11. *History of Muslim Rule in Kashmir*: R K Parmu p 261
12. *Tarikh-i-Haider*: Haider Malik p 62-63
13. *Rajatarangini of Jonaraja*: Translation J C Dutt p 396
14. Ibid
15. Ibid
16. *History of Muslim Rule in Kashmir*: R K Parmu p 254
17. *Culture and Political History of Kashmir*: P N K Bamzai p 379
18. *History of Muslim Rule in Kashmir*: R K. Parmu p 263
19. *Kashmir under the Sultans*: Mohibbul Hasan p 178
20. *History of Muslim Rule in Kashmir*: R K Parmu p 264
21. *Rajatarangini*: Sukha Translation J C Dutt p 397
22. Ibid p 402
23. *An Historical Atlas of Islam*: William C Brice p 366
24. *History of Muslim Rule in Kashmir*: R K Parmu p 272
25. Ibid
26. *Rajatarangini:* Sukha Translation J C Dutt p 403
27. Ibid

Chapter- 16

1. *History of Jahangir*: Beni Prasad p 2
2. *Rulers of India*: Stanley Lane-Poole p 8
3. *Kashmir under the Mughals*: Abdul Majid Mattoo p 3
4. *Rajatarangini of Jonaraja*: Translation J C Dutt p 404
5. *Baharistan-i-Shahi*: A Persian Chronicle Translation Kashi Nath Pandita Chapter III
6. *Rajatarangini of Jonaraja*: Translation J C Dutt p 412
7. Ibid
8. *The History of India, as Told Its Own Historians*: Henry Miers Elliot Vol-V p 454
9. *Baharistan-i-Shahi*: A Persian Chronicle Translation Kashi Nath Pandita Chapter III
10. *Akbarnama*: Abul Fazal Translation H Beveridge op.cit III, p 798)
11. *Kashmir under Sultans*: Mohibbul Hassan p 201
12. *Kashmir under the Mughals*: Abdul Majid Mattoo p 9
13. *History of Muslim Rule in Kashmir*: R K Parmu p 264 or 283
14. *Akbarnama*: Abul Fazal Translation H Beveridge op.cit III p 958
15. *Rajatarangini of Jonaraja*: Translation J C Dutt p 416
16. *Akbarnama*: Abu-l-Fazal Translation H Beveridge, op.cit III, p 817
17. Ibid p 817
18. Ibid p 820)
19. *History of Muslim Rule in Kashmir*: R K Parmu p 284
20. *Kashmir under the Mughals*: Abdul Majid Mattoo p 10
21. *Kashmir under the Sultans*: Mohibbul Hasan p 205
22. *Akbarnama:* Abul Fazal Translation H Beveridge op.cit III p 817
23. Ibid p 819
24. *Rajatarangini of Jonaraja*: Translation J C Dutt p 420
25. *The Valley Of Kashmir*: Walter Roper Lawrence p 194

26. *History of Muslim Rule in Kashmir*: R K Parmu p 285-286
27. *Rajatarangini of Jonaraja*: Translation J C Dutt p 418
28. *History of Muslim Rule in Kashmir* R K Parmu p 291
29. *Memoirs on the History*: Henry Miers Elliot p 190
30. *A History of Kashmiri Pandits*: Jia Lal Kilam p 97
31. *Memorial of Mistakes Converted Kashmir*: Narendra Sahagala p 144-145
32. *The Valley of Kashmir*: Walter Roper Lawrence p 243
33. *Akbarnama*: Abul Fazal Translation H Beveridge op.cit III, p 395
34. *Rajatarangini of Jonaraja*: Translation J C Dutt p 418
35. *A History of Kashmiri Pandits*: Jia Lal Kilam p 99
36. *Rajatarangini of Jonaraja*: Translation J C Dutt p 419
37. *A History of Kashmir Rule in Kashmir:* R K Parmu p 295
38. *Akbarnama:* Abul Fazal Translation H Beveridge op.cit III p 1084
39. *History of Muslim Rule in Kashmir*: R K Parmu p 297
40. *Rajatarangini of Jonaraja*: Translation J C Dutt p 426
41. Ibid p 427
42. *Ancient Monuments of Kashmir*: Ram Chandra Kak p 89
43. *Culture and Political History of Kashmir*: P N K Bamzai p 402
44. *Valley of Kashmir*: Walter Roper Lawrence p 194
45. *Culture and Political History of Kashmir*: P N K Bamzai p 404
46. *History of Muslim Rule in Kashmir*: R K Parmu p 303
47. *Cultural and Political History of Kashmir*: P N K Bamzai p 403
48. *Valley Of Kashmir*: Walter Roper Lawrence p 194
49. *An Outline of the History of Kashmir*: L N Dhar (Article)
50. *Mughal Rule in India*: Stephen Meredyth Edwardes Herbert Leonard Offley Garrett p 322
51. *The Indian Empire*: William Wilson Hunter p 302
52. *A Short History of Muslim Rule in India*: Ishwari Prasad p 475
53. *India Past and Present*: C H Linsay-Forbes p 53
54. *Tales from Rajatarangini*: S L Sadhu p 85
55. *Advanced History of Medieval India*: S R Bakshi p 74-75
56. *Kashmir*: Francis Younghusband p 80 - 157
57. *History of Muslim Rule in Kashmir*: R K Parmu p 303

58. *Memorial of Mistakes Converted Kashmir*: Narendra Sahagala p 145-146
59. *Memoirs on the History, Folk Lore of the North*: Henry Miers Elliot Vol-VII, p 62
60. *Rupa Bhawani*: S L Sadhu p 51
61. *History of Muslim Rule in Kashmir*: R K Parmu p 308
62. *Tuzuk-i-Jahangiri: Jahangir* Translation Alexander Rogers p 422
63. *History of Muslim Rule in Kashmir*: R K Parmu p 305
64. *Advanced History of Medieval India*: S R Bakshi p 15
65. *A Short History of Jammu and Kashmir*: Sukhdev Singh Charak p 87
66. *Tuzuk-i-Jahangiri: Jahangir* Translation Alexander Rogers and Henry Beveridge p 232
67. Ibid p 260
68. Ibid p 90
69. *Culture and Political History of Kashmir*: P N K Bamzai p 406
70. *Our Summer in the Vale of Kashmir*: F Ward Deny p 23
71. *The History of India as Told Its Own Historians*: Henry Miers Elliot Vol-VII p 128
72. *History of Muslim Rule in Kashmir*: R K Parmu p 311
73. Ibid p 315
74. *History of India as Told Its Historians*: Henry Miers Elliot Vol-VII p 284
75. *Cultural and Political History of Kashmi*r: P N K Bamzai p 409
76. *Rupa Bhawani:* S L Sadhu p 55
77. *History of India as Told its Historians*: Henry Miers Elliot VII p 159
78. *Cultural and Political History of Kashmir*: P N K Bamzai p 409
79. *History of Muslim Rule in Kashmir*: R K Parmu p 397
80. *Memorial of Mistakes Converted Kashmir:* Narendra Sahagala p 147
81. *A History of Kashmiri Pandits*: Jia Lal Kilam p 109
82. *History of Muslim Rule in Kashmir*: R K Parmu p 319
83. Ibid

84. *Cultural and Political History Of Kashmir*: P N K Bamzai p 410
85. *Rulers of India*: Stanley Lane-Pool p 59
86. *History of India as Told Its Historians*: Henry Miers Elliot Vol-VII, p 196
87. *Daughters of Vitasta*: Prem Nath Bazaz p 162
88. *History of India as Told Its Historians*: Henry Miers Elliot Vol-VII p 200
89. *Dewan-i-Makhfi*: Zeb-un-Nissa Translation Magan Lal and Jessie Duncan (Introduction)
90. *Daughters of Vitasta*: Prem Nath Bazaz p 162
91. *Travel in the Mugul Empire*: Francois Bernier p 352
92. *Cultural and Political History of Kashmir*: P N K Bamzai p 411
93. *Maasir-i-Alamgiri*: Muhammad Saqi Mustad Khan Translation Jadunath Sarkar p 28-29
94. *Travel in the Mugul Empire*: Francois Bernier p 352
95. *History of Muslim Rule in Kashmir*: R K Parmu p 321
96. *Travel in the Mugul Empire*: Francois Bernier p 351
97. *History of Muslim Rule in Kashmir*: R K Parmu p 322
98. *The Valley of Kashmir*: Walter Roper Lawrence p 197
99. *History of Muslim Rule in Kashmir*: R K Parmu p 322
100. *Cultural and Political History of Kashmir*: P N K Bamzai p 411
101. *A History of Kashmiri Pandits*: Jia Lal Kilam p 112
102. *Cultural and Political History of Kashmir*: P N K Bamzai p 412
103. *History of Punjab*: D N Kundra p 134
104. *History of Muslim Rule in Kashmir*: R K Parmu p 325
105. *E. J Brill's First Encyclopaedia, 1913-1936*: M Th Houtsma p 574
106. *Cultural and Political History of Kashmir*: P N K Bamzai p 414
107. Ibid p 415
108. Ibid
109. Ibid p 416
110. *History of Muslim Rule in Kashmir*: R K Parmu p 334
111. *Music of India*: Reginald Massey p 55
112. *Great Diamonds of India*: Monisha Bhardwaj p 15
113. *History of Muslim Rule in Kashmir*: R K Parmu p 336

114. *Cultural and Political History of Kashmir*: P N K Bamzai p 423
115. *History of Muslim Rule in Kashmir*: R K Parmu p 337
116. *Culture and Political History of Kashmir*: P N K Bamzai p 424
117. *History of Muslim Rule in Kashmir*: R K Parmu p 337
118. Ibid p 338
119. *Baburnama*: Translation Wheeler M Thackson p 352
120. *Kashmir under the Mughals*: Abdul Majid Mattoo p 39
121. *Tuzuk-i-Jahangiri*: Jahangir Translation Alexander Rogers and Henry Beveridge p 300
122. Ibid
123. Ibid
124. *The Indian Empire*: William Wilson Hunter Trubner's Oriental Series p 296

Chapter- 17

1. *Press and Freedom Struggle in Jammu and Kashmir*: [Article] Zahid G Muhammad
2. *History of Kashmir Rule in Kashmir*: R K Parmu p 348
3. *The Journey from Bengal to England*: George Forster p 278
4. *The History of Struggle for Freedom in Kashmir*: Prem Nath Bazaz p 111
5. *The Kashmiri Pandits*: Anand Kaul p 59
6. *History of Muslim Rule in Kashmir*: R K Parmu p 354
7. Ibid p 335
8. *Memorial of Mistakes Converted Kashmir*: Narendra Sahagala p 163
9. *Travels in Kashmir, Ladakh, Iskardo*: T G Vigne Vol- II p 29
10. *A History of Kashmiri Pandits*: Jia Lal Kilam p 148
11. *A Short History of Jammu Raj*: Sukhdev Singh Charak p 102
12. *History of Muslim Rule in Kashmir*: R K Parmu p 357
13. *A History of Kashmiri Pandits*: Jia Lal Kilam P 160-161
14. Ibid p 165
15. *History of Muslim Rule in Kashmir*: R K Parmu p 361
16. *Culture and Political History of Kashmir*: P N K Bamzai p 442-443
17. Ibid p 443

18. *History of Muslim Rule in Kashmir*: R K Parmu p 362
19. *Culture and Political History of Kashmir*: P N K Bamzai p 443
20. Ibid p 446
21. Ibid p 447
22. *A Journey from Bengal to England*: George Forster p 27
23. *A Short History of Jammu Raj*: Sukhdev Singh Charak p 121
24. *Culture and Political History of Kashmir*: P N K Bamzai p 449
25. *Memorial of Mistakes Converted Kashmir*: Narendra Sahagala p 170
26. *A Journey from Bengal to England*: George Forster p 29
27. *History of Muslim Rule in Kashmir*: R K Parmu p 365
28. Ibid p 366
29. Ibid p 366
30. *Culture and Political History of Kashmir*: P N K Bamzai p 445
31. Ibid p 447
32. *A History of Kashmiri Pandits*: Jia Lal Kilam-p 198-199
33. *The Kashmiri Pandits*: Anand Kaul p 62
34. *History of Muslim Rule in Kashmir*: R K Parmu p 368
35. *Daughters of Vitasta*: Prem Nath Bazaz p 175
36. *A History of Kashmiri Pandits*: Jia Lal Kilam p 203
37. *Tehreek-i-Hassan*: Pir Gulam Hassan p 482 - 483
38. *Culture and Political History of Kashmir*: P N K Bamzai p 457
39. *History of Muslim Rule in Kashmir*: R K Parmu p 348
40. *A History of Kashmiri Pandits*: Anand Kaul p 64
41. *History of Muslim Rule in Kashmir*: R K Parmu p 370
42. Ibid p 372
43. *Culture and Political History of Kashmir*: P N K Bamzai p 459
44. *A History of Kashmiri Pandits*: Jia Lal Kilam p 208
45. *History of Muslim Rule in Kashmir*: R K Parmu p 373
46. *The Valley of Kashmir*: Walter Roper Lawrence p 198
47. *A History of the Sikhs*: Joseph Davey Cunningham p 155
48. *Maharaja Ranjit Singh:* Kartar Singh Duggal p 78
49. *A History of Muslim Rule in Kashmir:* R K Parmu p 375
50. *Culture and Political History of Kashmir*: P N K Bamzai p 459
51. *The History of Struggle for Freedom in Kashmir*: Prem Nath Bazaz

52. *Memorial of Mistakes Converted Kashmir*: Narendra Sahagala p 178
53. *A History of the Sikhs*: Joseph Davey Cunningham p 155
54. *The Kashmiri Pandits*: Anand Kaul p 66
55. *Daughters of Vitasta*: Prem Nath Bazaz p 173
56. Ibid p 174
57. Ibid
58. *A History of Muslim Rule in Kashmir*: R K Parmu p 383
59. *A History of the Sikhs*: Joseph Davey Cunningham p 157
60. *The Kashmiri Pandits*: Anand Kaul p 69
61. *A History of the Sikhs*: Joseph Davey Cunningham p 159
62. *The Valley of Kashmir*: Walter Roper Lawrence p 198

Chapter- 18

1. *History of India*: Mediaeval India: Stanley Lane-Poole Vol-III p 162
2. *Saints and Saviours of Islam*: Hamid Naseem Rafiabadi p 252
3. *Kashir*: G M D Sufi p 106
4. *Kashmir Transition to Islam*: Mohammad Ishaq Khan p 4
5. *A History of Kashmiri Pandits*: Jia Lal Kilam p 37
6. *A History of Muslim Rule in Kashmir*: R K Parmu p 108
7. *Lal Ded and Kashmiri Chroniclers*: [Article] P N Kachru
8. *Lallvakyani*: Sir George Grierson p 4
9. *Lalleshwari*: B N Parimoo p 12
10. *Daughters of Vitasta*: Prem Nath Bazaz p 126
11. *Lall Ded: A Poet Who Gave Voice to Women:* [Article] Neerja Matoo
12. *Apostle of Tolerance*: [Article] Arjan Nath Kaul
13. *Daughters of Vitasta*: Prem Nath Bazaz p 126
14. *Aesthetics*: Yuri Borev p 70
15. *Kashmir's Transition to Islam*: Mohammad Ishaq Khan p 70
16. *Lallvakyani*: Sir George Grierson p 7-8
17. *Some Stray Thoughts on Lall Ded*: [Article] S L Sadhu
18. *Medieval Indian Literature*: K Ayyappapanicker p 221
19. *Culture and Political History of Kashmir*: P N K Bamzai p 554
20. *The Voice of the Marginalised*: [Article] Neerja Matoo
21. *World of Lalla the Prophetess*: Richard Carnac Temple p 161

22. *Lal Ded*: [Article] Shashi Shekher Toshkhani
23. *Gems of Kashmiri Literature*: [Article] P N Razdan/ Manohari
24. *Language of Belonging*: [Article] Chitralekha Zutshi p 19
25. *Culture and Political History of Kashmir*: P N K Bamzai Vol-II p 551
26. *Daughters of Vitasta*: Prem Nath Bazaz p 125
27. *Some Stray Thoughts on Lall Ded*: [Article] S L Sadhu
28. *Converted Kashmir Memorial of Mistakes*: Narendra Sahagala
29. *Buddhist Stains in Lalla's Teaching*: [Article] J N Ganhar
30. *Lallvakyani*: Sir George Grierson p 1
31. *Daughters of Vitasta*: Prem Nath Bazaz p 132
32. *Kashmir's Transition to Islam*: Mohammad Ishaq Khan p 52
33. *Language of Belonging*: [Article] Chitralekha Zutshi p 22
34. *Kashmir's Transition to Islam*: Mohammad Ishaq Khan p 97
35. Ibid p 77
36. *Lalleshwari*: B N Parimoo p 58
37. *Lall Ded: A Poet Who Gave Voice to Women*: [Article] Neerja Matoo
38. *Medieval Indian Literature*: K Ayyappapanicker p 223
39. *Kashmir's Transition to Islam*: Mohammad Ishaq Khan p 64
40. Ibid
41. Ibid p 36
42. *Language of Belonging*: [Article] Chitralekha Zutshi p 26
43. *Habba Khatoon Philomela of Medieval Kashmir*: [Article] K N Dhar
44. *An Historical Atlas of Islam*: William Charles Brice p 332-333
45. *Habba Khatoon Philomela of Medieval Kashmir*: [Article] K N Dhar
46. *An Historical Atlas of Islam*: William Charles Brice p 333
47. *Habba Khatoon Philomela of Medieval Kashmir*: [Article] K N Dhar
48. *The Clash of Fundamentalism*: Tariq Ali p 221
49. *Rupa Bhawani*: S L Sadhu p 60
50. Ibid p 61
51. *A History of Muslim Rule in Kashmir*: R K Parmu p 322

Bibliography

Kalhana's Rajatarangini, Kalhana
The Saga of the Kings of Kashmir, Kalhana
Dvitiya Rajatarangini, Jonaraja
Zaina Rajatarangini, Srivara
Vikramankadevacharita, Bilhana
History of Kashmir, Haydar Malik
Tarikh-i-Rashidi, Mirza Mohammad Haydar Duglat
A in-i-Akbari, Abu-Al-Fazl Allami Mubarak
Akbarnama, Abu-L-Afazl Allami Mubarak
Tuzuk-I-Jahangiri, Jahangir
Diwan-I Mahfi, Zib-al-Nisa
Halat-I Asad Big, Asad Big
Ancient Monuments of Kashmir, Ram Chand Kak
The Kashmiri Pandit, Pandit Anand Kaul
Desopadesa and Narmamala of Kshemendra, Kshemendra
Isvara-Pratyabhijna-Karika of Utpaladeva, Utpaladeva

Kashmiri under Mughals, Abdul Majid Matoo
India as seen in the Kuttanimatam of Damodaragupta, Ajay Mitra Shastri
Cultural and Political History of Kashmir, P N K Bamzai
The Philosophy of Sadhana, Deb Brata Sen Sharma
The History of Struggle for Freedom in Kashmir, Prem Nath Bazaz
Daughters of Vitasta, Prem Nath Bazaz
Kashmir in Crucible, Prem Nath Bazaz
Kashmir Myth of Autonomy, Mohan Kishen Teng
Essential documents and notes of Kashmir dispute, Pl Lakhenpal
Between Two Fires, Iqbal Singh
Kashmir under Sultans, Mohibbul Hassan
A History of Muslim Rule in Kashmir, R K Parmu
A Short History of Jammu Raj, Sukhdev Singh Charak
Nilamatapurana, (Author unknown)
Swacchanda-Tantra, Ksemaraja
Duggar Ka Itihas [Hindi], Shiv Dutt Nimohi
Ishvara Pratyabhijna Karika, Utpaladeva
A History of Kashmiri Pandits, Jia Lal Kilam
India Wins Freedom, Abul Kalam Azad
Memorial of Mistakes, Narendra Sahagala
Glimpses of History of Jammu and Kashmir, Jyoteeshwar Pathik
Hijacking and Terror in Sky, Giriraj Shah
Kashmir's Transition to Islam, Mohammad Ishaq Khan
History of Kashmir Saivism, Baljinnath Pandita
Vaishnava Art and Iconography of Kashmir, Bansi Lal Malla
History of Punjab, D N Kundra
Ancient India, R C Majumdar
Low Intensity Conflicts in India, Vivek Chadha
On Roads, Bhumesh Sharma
Hindu Rulers, Muslim Subjects, Mridhu Rai
Clash of Fundamentalisms, Tariq Ali
Kashmir 1947, Prem Shankar Jha
Slender Was the Thread, Lionel Protip Sen

Advance History of Ancient India, Shiri Ram Bakshi
Advance History of Medieval India, Shiri Ram Bakshi
A Text Book of Historiography, E Sreedharan
Crisis in Kashmir, Sumit Ganguly
The Aftermath of Partition, Tia Yong Tan
Remembering Partition, Gyanendra Pandey
India-Pakistan in War and Peace, J N Dixit
Bilhana, Prabhakar Narayan Kawthekar
Maharaja Ranjit Singh, Kartar Singh Duggal
History of Indian Theatre, M L Varadpande
Medieval Indian Literature, K Ayyappapanicker
Ancient Indian History and Civilization, Sailendra Nath Sen
The Splendor of Himalayan Art and Culture, Ashok Jerath
Dogra Legends of Art & Culture, Ashok Jerath
Kashmiri Scholars Contribution, S Bhat
The Evolution of The Artillery, R C Butalia
Kashmir: A Wailing Valley, M L Gupta
The Traditional Music of Kashmir, Sunita Dhar
Kashmir Shaivism under Siege, M G Chitkara
The Pratyabhijna Philosophy, Ganesh Vasudeo Tagare
Krama Trantricism of Kashmir, Navjivan Rastogi
The Other Side of Silence, Urvashi Butalia
Kashmir and United Nations Encyclopaedia of Kashmir Series, Suresh K Sharma/Shiri Ram Bakshi
An Introduction to Buddhist Esoterism, Benoytosh Bhattacharyya
Indian Literary Criticism, G N Davey
Crafting Peace in Kashmir, Verghese Koithara
Kashmir Roots of Conflict, Paths to Peace, Sumatra Bose
The Constitution of Jammu And Kashmir, Adarsh Sein Anand
Images of Indian Goddesses, Madhu Bazaz Wangu
Kashmir's Constitutional Status, Santosh Kaul
Vaishnava Art and Iconography of Kashmir, Bansilal Malla
Companion to Tantra, S C Banerji

Kashmir Myth of Autonomy, Mohan Kishen Teng
Indian Epigraphy, Dinesh Chandra Sircar
Ancient India, Dilip Kumar Ganguly
Remembering Partition, Gyanendra Pandey
Indian Muslims, Rafiq Zakaria
My Frozen Turbulence In Kashmir, Jagmohan
Rupa Bhavani, Shyam Lal Sadhu
Tales from Rajatarangini, Shyam Lal Sadhu
Indian Airports, Kishin R Wadhwaney
War and No Peace over Kashmir, Maroof Raza
Terrorism, History and Facets, NS Saksena
Saints and Saviors' of Islam, Hamid Naseem Rafiabadi
Language of Belonging, Chitralekha Zutshi
India wins freedom, Maulana Abul Kalam Azad
History of Ancient India, Ram Shankar Tripathi
Saints and Sages of Kashmir, Triloki Nath Dhar
A Concise History of Classical Sanskrit Literature, G S Bhattacharyya
The Encyclopaedia of Indian Literature, Amaresh Datta
Indian Poetics, T Nanjundaiya Sreekantaiya
Three Satires, Somadeva Vasudeva
Jammu Kashmir and Ladakh, Desh Bandu
Jammu and Kashmir War, 1947-1948, Kuldip Singh Bajwa
My Life and Times, Sayyid Mir Qasim
Low Intensity Conflicts in India, Vivek Chadha
On Yuan Chwang's travels in India, Yuan Chwang
Alberuni's India, Alberuni
The Happy Valley, W Wakefield
Travels In Kashmir and the Punjab, Baron Charles Hugel
A Journey from Bengal to England, George Forster
Tree and Serpent Worship, J Fergusson
Soldier and Traveller, Alexander Haughton Gardner
Thirty-Five Years in the East, J M Honigberger
Travels In Kashmir, Ladak, Iskardo, Godfery Thomas Vigne
Travel In the Mogul Empire, Bernier Francois

The Vishnu Purana, Horace Hayman Wilson
Ladakh, Alexander Cunningham
Al-Hind, Andre Wink
Folktales of Kashmir, J Hinton Knowles
Hinduism and Buddhism, Charles Eliot
Lallavakyani, George Abraham Grierson
Where Three Empires Meet, E F Knight
The History of India as told by its own Historians, Henry Meir Elliot
Kashmir, Francis Younghusband
Rulers of India, Stanley Lane-Poole
The Valley of Kashmir, Walter Roper Lawrence
History of Indian Literature, Moriz Winternitz
Our summer in the Vale of Kashmir, F Ward Denys
Tarikh-i-Firishta, Mohammed Qasim Firishta
A History of Sikhs, Joseph Davey Cunningham
Halat-i-Asad, Assad Big Kazvin
A Hindu Critique of Buddhist Epistemology, Kumarila Bhatta
Encyclopedia of Indian Philosophies, Harold G Coward
Encyclopedia of Erotic Literature, Gaetan Brulotte
A Historical Atlas of Islam, William Charles Brice
Kashmir in Conflict—India, Victoria Schofield
The New Cambridge History of India, Barbara N Ramusack
The Princes of India, Ian Copland
Kashmir in Comparative Perspective, Sten Widmalm
Jinnah, Pakistan and Islamic Identity, Akbar S Ahmed
The Sole Spokesman, Ayesha Jalal
Freedom at Midnight, Larry Collins/ Dominique Lapierre
The Aftermath of Partition, Tai Yong Tan
A Region in Turmoil, Rob Johnson
Pakistan, Arif Hussain
Pakistan and the Emergence of Islamic Militancy in Afghanistan, Rizwan Hussain
Peace Parks, Saleem Hassan Ali
Encyclopedia of Religion and Ethics, James Hasting

Silk and Empire, Brenda N King
India: A History, John Keay
A Dictionary of Kashmiri Proverbs and Sayings, James Hinton Knowles
The Written Languages of the World, Heinz Kloss
A grammar of the Kashmiri Language, Thomas Russel Wade
Modern India and the Indians, Monier Williams
Women, Religion and Social Change, Yvonne Yazbeck Haddad

INDEX

Arjan Nath Chaku (1917-2011) was born in the Valley of Kashmir during the reign of the Dogra rulers. In 1947, frenzy and chaos engulfed India, especially Kashmir. Arjan Nath came to Delhi with his family and young son, Inder in 1948 and become a journalist with the *Daily Hamdard.* As a journalist he met Mohammad Ali Jinnah who was on holiday in Gulmarg. He also met Acharya Jivatram Bhagwandas, JB Kripalani and Pandit Jawaharlal Nehru, on their visits to Kashmir. He regularly wrote articles on Kashmir politics for *Koshur Samachar, New Age* and *press Trust of India.*

In the 1990s, Inder K Chaku headed the Media Office I Srinagar. His dream of living in Kashmir was shattered when he had to join the exodus of Kashmiri Pandits from the Valley. He moved to Jammu and then to Deli, where he worked for the Song and Drama Division of the Ministry of Information and Broadcasting. He wrote plays and translated them into performances and also directed programmes for the armed forces. He participated in International Film Festivals and worked with Theatre Titans of India, Shambhu Mitra, Bansi Kaul and the famous dancer, Birju Maharaj. He writes regularly for *Koshur Samachar* and *Naad.*